THE LETTERS IN THE STORY

The long tradition of mixta-genera fiction, particularly favored by women novelists, which combined fully transcribed letters and third-person narrative has been largely overlooked in literary criticism. Working with recognized formal conventions and typical thematic concerns, Eve Tavor Bannet demonstrates how narrative-epistolary novels opposed the real, situated, transactional, and instrumental character of letters, with their multilateral relationships and temporally shifting readings, to merely documentary uses of letters in history and law. Analyzing issues of reading and misreading, knowledge and ignorance, and communication and credulity, this study investigates how novelists adapted familiar romance plots centered on mysteries of identity to test the viability of empiricism's new culture of fact and challenge positivism's later all-pervading regime of truth. Close reading of narrative-epistolary novels by authors ranging from Aphra Behn, Charlotte Lennox and Frances Burney, to Jane Austen, Wilkie Collins and Anthony Trollope tracks transgenerational debates, bringing to light both what Victorians took from their eighteenth-century forbears and what they changed.

EVE TAVOR BANNET is George Lynn Cross Professor Emeritus at the University of Oklahoma. Her monographs include *Empire of Letters* (Cambridge, 2005), *Transatlantic Stories and the History of Reading* (Cambridge, 2011), *Eighteenth-Century Manners of Reading* (Cambridge, 2017), and *The Domestic Revolution* (Hopkins, 2000).

THE LETTERS IN THE STORY

*Narrative-Epistolary Fiction from Aphra Behn
to the Victorians*

EVE TAVOR BANNET

University of Oklahoma

CAMBRIDGE
UNIVERSITY PRESS

Shaftesbury Road, Cambridge CB2 8EA, United Kingdom

One Liberty Plaza, 20th Floor, New York, NY 10006, USA

477 Williamstown Road, Port Melbourne, VIC 3207, Australia

314–321, 3rd Floor, Plot 3, Splendor Forum, Jasola District Centre, New Delhi – 110025, India

103 Penang Road, #05–06/07, Visioncrest Commercial, Singapore 238467

Cambridge University Press is part of Cambridge University Press & Assessment, a department of the University of Cambridge.

We share the University's mission to contribute to society through the pursuit of education, learning and research at the highest international levels of excellence.

www.cambridge.org
Information on this title: www.cambridge.org/9781009001823

DOI: 10.1017/9781009003698

© Cambridge University Press & Assessment 2022

First published 2022
First paperback edition 2024

A catalogue record for this publication is available from the British Library

Library of Congress Cataloging-in-Publication data
NAMES: Bannet, Eve Tavor, 1947– author.
TITLE: The letters in the story : narrative-epistolary fiction from Aphra Behn to the Victorians / Eve Tavor Bannet.
DESCRIPTION: Cambridge, United Kingdom ; New York , NY Cambridge University Press, 2021. | Includes bibliographical references and index.
IDENTIFIERS: LCCN 2021024754 (print) | LCCN 2021024755 (ebook) | ISBN 9781316518854 (hardback) | ISBN 9781009003698 (ebook)
SUBJECTS: LCSH: Epistolary fiction, English – History and criticism. | Narration (Rhetoric) – History. | BISAC: LITERARY CRITICISM / European / English, Irish, Scottish, Welsh
CLASSIFICATION: LCC PR830.E65 B36 2021 (print) | LCC PR830.E65 (ebook) | DDC 823.009/23–dc23
LC record available at https://lccn.loc.gov/2021024754
LC ebook record available at https://lccn.loc.gov/2021024755

ISBN   978-1-316-51885-4   Hardback
ISBN   978-1-009-00182-3   Paperback

Contents

Preface: "To the Reader"

In addition to the epistolary novel and the first- or third-person narrative "history," there was from the first a vibrant tradition of narrative-epistolary fiction that mixed the two forms. In embedding multiple letters in her narratives – most obviously in *Pride and Prejudice* (1813) – Jane Austen was working in a long-standing, but now apparently forgotten, narrative-epistolary genre, which began to flourish in England in 1685 with Part 2 of Aphra Behn's *Love Letters between a Nobleman and His Sister*. This narrative-epistolary genre was used predominantly by women writers such as Jane Barker, Mary Davys, and Eliza Haywood during the first half of the eighteenth century. It was sufficiently familiar by 1742, for Henry Fielding to be able to mock it quixotically in *Joseph Andrews*. It continued to be used throughout the eighteenth century on both sides of the Atlantic, still predominantly by women – for instance, in Eliza Haywood's *Betsy Thoughtless* (1751), Henry Fielding's *Amelia* (1752), Charlotte Lennox's *Henrietta* (1758), Fanny Burney's *Cecilia* (1782) and *Camilla* (1796), Charlotte Smith's *Emmeline* (1782) and *Celestina* (1791), Susannah Rowson's *Charlotte Temple* (1794), Robert Bage's *Hermsprong* (1796), and Maria Edgeworth's *Belinda* (1801). Adapted during the nineteenth century to new epistemologies and new ideas of the self, it was redeployed by Anne and Charlotte Bronte, Frances Trollope, Wilkie Collins, Thackeray, and Dickens among others, reaching its apotheosis during the 1860s and 1870s in Anthony Trollope's prolix corpus where this study ends. But exemplars are still to be found in twentieth-century British, American, and Anglophone postcolonial fiction where they are often viewed as radically new, postmodern departures from the mainstream realist or modernist novel.[1] Historically, then, narrative-epistolary fictions had a far longer life than the epistolary novel, which was abandoned at the end of the eighteenth century. Narrative-epistolary fiction lived on in part because it proved far more versatile and multifaceted formally, and far more "philosophical" and rewarding intellectually, than the epistolary novel (Samuel

vii

Richardson notwithstanding), and in part because it enabled writers to combine the familiarity, immediacy, instrumentality, and emotional power of letters with narrative supplementation, narrative pacing, and a narrator's often equivocal guidance on how embedded letters should be understood and used.

From Aphra Behn to the Victorians, narrative-epistolary fiction had its own, recognized, formal conventions for embedding letters in narrative and its own typical thematic concerns. These themes and conventions were put in place in England early on by Aphra Behn, popularized by Eliza Haywood, and subsequently followed, assumed, varied, and adapted by other novelists, including Jane Austen, and those like Charles Brockden Brown in *Wieland* (1798) or George Eliot in *Middlemarch* (1871–1872), who only included an embedded letter or two. Some novelists worked exclusively in this genre – Mary Davys, Eliza Haywood, and Anthony Trollope among others. Some also tried other formal vehicles: Charlotte Smith also wrote two epistolary novels; Charlotte Lennox, Susannah Rowson, and Anne Bronte also wrote first- or third-person narratives. Some, such as Aphra Behn and Frances Burney, produced prose fictions of each sort. Others, such as Jane Barker, Jane Austen, or Charlotte Bronte, reverted to narrative-epistolary writing for key sections of first- or third-person narratives. As we will see, the virtues of different novel forms were hotly debated, albeit not always in the standard critical outlets.

Questions of form are not empty technical questions as many narratologists would have us believe. Narrative-epistolary conventions and clever variations upon them permitted novelists to explore and debate contemporary epistemological, psychological, and historical questions about our reading and misreading of characters, texts, and events, and thus to make fiction a popularly accessible vehicle for Enlightenment inquiries and concerns. Varying their combinations of narrative and letters enabled eighteenth-century authors to test the viability of empiricism's new "culture of fact" and to explore cognate issues of reading and misreading, perception and misperception, ignorance and knowledge, and credulity and doubt, while demonstrating how such issues arose from people's mental processes, as well as from culturally promoted norms of concealment and from their exploitation by willful deceivers. Nineteenth-century narrative-epistolary authors working with these inherited conventions were more likely to relativize empiricism by reintroducing forms of narrative-epistolary writing, and modes of being and narrating, banished by empiricism's imperious, and now all-pervasive, regime of truth. They were more inclined to show how a determined investigator or curious reader might use letters to detect things about people's characters, lives, and conduct that they had taken some pains to conceal, and to treat misread letters psychologically as expressions of characters' involuntary self-deception. But in both periods, narrative-epistolary conventions challenged historians' merely documentary use of letters, by insisting upon what the narratives in supposedly true histories perversely elided about the true historicity of letters: their social and circumstantial embeddedness; their situated meaning(s) and performative function(s); the sliding significances deriving from their multiple temporalities and transactional character; their often unexpected long-term social and historical effects; and failure of some letters, however important in themselves, to have any effect on reality and history at all. In both periods too, narrative-epistolary writers challenged the efforts of scientists and empiricist philosophers to oppose true to fictional narratives, and the sciences of man to other poetical inventions, by insisting on what empiricism's boasted grasp on reality perversely elided: the roles played by preconceptions, spurious conjectures, and imagination in reasoning inductively from experience and in drawing inferences from acts, words, and texts; the mutability of facts; the plausibility of *false* empirical fact-based narratives; the propensity of the invisible, unnoticed, unseen, or unknown to falsify observation-based reasoning, and of contingent particulars to derail supposedly universal truths; the unsoundness of probable links in empiricist "chains" of cause and effect; and the fallacy of expecting that we can judge the future by the past.

Until recently, the multiplication of embedded letters in a story was studied primarily as the stylistic peculiarity of a single novel (Behn's *Love Letters*, Austen's *Pride and Prejudice*) or of a single novelist (Jane Austen, Anthony Trollope). Unlike embedded narratives whose aporias were extensively theorized by narratologists and exploited by deconstructive critics, embedded letters were otherwise either comprehensively ignored even in analyzing novels studded with them or treated as intrinsic elements of the narrative, which are "both psychologically revealing and also plot furthering."[2] The recent rise of scholarly interest in the letter form has directed interesting new work toward letters as drivers of "postal plots" in nineteenth-century novels.[3] Joined to current concerns with reading and material culture, this has produced some outstanding close readings of epistolary scenes and some important studies of fictional representations of letters as material objects. These include Catherine Golden's study of the role played by the post, and by such epistolary furniture as portable writing desks, in the plots of novels written after the Post Office Reform Act of 1840; William Warner's analysis of Austen's narrative about the Marianne–Willoughby correspondence in *Sense and Sensibility*; and Thomas Karshan's "Notes on the Image of the Undelivered Letter," which argues that the undelivered letter is "one of modernism's central images."[4] More traditional sociohistorical approaches have demonstrated the same tendency to subsume embedded letters under narrative. Mistakenly viewing the embedding of letters in narratives as a "generic innovation" of the 1790s, Nicola Watson, for instance, argued in an influential book that this innovation "can be linked directly to changes in political, cultural and ideological structures" in Britain during the backlash to the French Revolution, and that it can be explained as an attempt to "contain" the dangerous freedom of the epistolary novel and to "discipline" unruly and potentially subversive correspondence.[5]

By contrast, scholars wishing to rescue the letters in a story (as well as their subject) from narrative effacement and academic marginalization have equated embedded letters with the letters in epistolary novels. Like Robert Adams Day's *Told in Letters*, which traced "stories in which imaginary letters figure in various quantities" back to late Greek romances, Janet Gurkin Altman's structuralist monograph, *Epistolarity*, tried to "show that, though novels like *Mitsou* and *Herzog* would have to be classified as 'mixed forms' in terms of narrative technique, they arguably are epistolary novels in a more specifically generic sense."[6] Julia Epstein's account of Jane Austen's *Juvenalia* likewise groups Austen's early epistolary novels with those early prose fictions that contain "significant epistolary interpolations, though they are not altogether written in letters," and discusses them in the same terms. Or again: to characterize twentieth-century postcolonial novels in which unseen letters serve as "mirrors" for the protagonist and drivers for the plot, Elizabeth Campbell argues that "novels which are not composed exclusively of letters can be classified as epistolary . . . if the plot is determined, advanced and resolved in letters."[7] One might include among the scholarship that equates embedded letters with the letters in epistolary novels those studies that treat "the letter" in nineteenth-century novels metaphorically without regard to its contents, and those that analyze embedded letters as separate entities with functions that can be listed more or less independently of the narrative.[8]

There is much to be learned from these and other examinations of what catalogers call "letters-in-literature." But they also show why classing narrative-epistolary writing with epistolary novels is as unsatisfactory as tipping embedded letters seamlessly into narrative. Both classifications render invisible the wide variety of conjunctive and disjunctive relations between narrative and embedded letters, together with the many different uses to which these were put. By causing us to overlook narrative-epistolary conventions that were used, adapted, and reused by novelist after novelist, they also efface consequential writerly issues and debates, and blind us to how authors writing in, or briefly invoking, the narrative-epistolary tradition expected to be read. Like traditional periodization (Restoration, Eighteenth-Century, Romantic, and Victorian), this "purist" binary taxonomy of narrative *or* epistolary fiction has a limiting effect on our awareness of the practices that shaped literary history. As Franco Moretti has shown, modern critical categories can erase their object by turning self-referentially upon themselves.[9] Setting them aside for a while reveals the links between narrative-epistolary works in successive periods – enabling us to recognize modernism's undelivered letter, for instance, not merely as a figure for the lack of communication in modern life, but also as a comment on nineteenth-century literary realism that cites and creatively recycles a common eighteenth-century narrative-epistolary *topos*.

About this book

This study is neither a comprehensive literary history nor a work of classical narratology. It seeks to make some preliminary inroads into narrative-epistolary fiction by pursuing a few formal and thematic threads within the larger history sketched out more fully in the Introduction. It does so through close reading and in a manner more consonant with an "historical narratology" in which "literary historical research is combined with narratological conceptualization" than with the still primarily fixed, schematic, and universalizing bent of formalist, structuralist, and cognitive narratology.[10] Here, this means recovering historically changing uses and configurations of formal devices considered as "open sets" and looking to literary, historiographical, and philosophical theories that were discussed at the time for explanation and conceptualization.[11] Women writers predominate in the texts selected for close reading both because in this period this was a primarily female novelistic tradition that was first cited or mocked and later appropriated by male authors, and because I agree with Rachel Carnell that "one reason for the continued marginality of ... women writers in the canon ... is that their work has been analyzed most frequently in terms of political or cultural history rather than in terms of the development of the novel's formal structure."[12]

A preliminary overview in the Introduction of the principal formal conventions and principal empirical and historical issues to be explored in this study provides the framework for what follows. Each subsequent chapter addresses a formal feature of narrative-epistolary fiction together with a topic connected with it through close readings of several dialoguing texts. Texts within each chapter are discussed in chronological order, but new chapters begin with the earliest well-developed version of a formal feature rather than at the point in time where the previous chapter ended. Novels or narrative-epistolary episodes have been selected, which expand, alter, or adapt the same formal device and add in important ways to the substance and representation of the issue in question. Each text is therefore significantly different from the one(s) before. They are linked by repeated reprinting, by later authors' familiarity with them and/or by the practice originating in Quintilian of responding to prior texts by rewriting, altering, and correcting their characters and scenes. That suspends modern categorizations of novels and means that there are large temporal gaps in each chapter; but it makes it possible to view dialoguing texts both as part of a narrative-epistolary tradition that runs through other conventional novel groupings and as preliminary "soundings" of the state of play at different historical moments. Readers wishing to reconstruct a single ongoing literary tradition or to see, for instance, all that Jane Austen gleaned from her narrative-epistolary forbears can do so retrospectively by inserting novels discussed in later chapters into the temporal gaps in earlier ones. The chapters can also be read either singly or in combination.

One might add that moving back and forth across single works in time echoes reading practices supported historically by the widespread use of circulating libraries. The presence and continuing popularity in the circulating libraries of the 1790s and early 1800s of exemplary narrative-epistolary novels by Behn, Haywood, Davys, and Barker from the 1680s, 1710s, and 1720s is a case in point. In turn-of-the-nineteenth-century libraries like that in Leadenhall Street and in their alphabetically randomized catalogs, Behn, Barker, or Haywood were as evident and as easy of access as the later fiction of Charlotte Lennox, Frances Burney, Robert Bage, or Elizabeth Meeke to the numerous nineteenth-century authors who report having spent countless unforgotten youthful hours devouring circulating library fiction. Here novels born at different chronological moments enjoyed an interlocking simultaneity and shared currency, which invited readers to peruse them in any order. This belies literary history's conventional linear sequencing of novels by date of first publication, as well as modern period divisions, to remind us that the Ancients and *Don Quixote* were not the only texts that "lived on."[13]

Chapter 1 describes how, in establishing and popularizing narrative-epistolary fiction, Aphra Behn and the Haywood of the 1720s and 1730s used narrative frames describing the writing and reading of fully transcribed letters to situate letters in relationships and in the demands of particular occasions. It also shows how this first scaffolding convention enabled them to address contemporary concerns about the irresistible power of rhetoric by demonstrating to the credulous and unlearned that gentlemen's letters were artificial rhetorical constructions, and by showing how and why they were misread. During the 1740s, when Fielding and Richardson appeared on the novel-writing scene, concerns about the power of persuasive language to engender misplaced credulity were being directed to the effects of constant, absorptive novel-reading on manners and morals, particularly those of women.[14] Section 3 (Debating Novel Forms") revives a debate that Haywood, Richardson, and Fielding conducted at mid-century primarily through their fictions, which turned on whether epistolary, narrative, or narrative-epistolary novels were best equipped to interrupt readers' headlong, credulous, desirous, imaginative reading, and make them pause to reason skeptically about the labyrinth of true and false characters, relations, and perspectives constitutive of epistolary commerce and contemporary social life. Writing Haywood back into the now-familiar debate between Richardson and Fielding shows her impact on both men's work, while bringing to light some unique advantages of narrative-epistolary over epistolary fiction and what Fielding perceived as its principal shortcoming. Section 4 ("Letters and Secret Histories") looks forward to *Pride and Prejudice*, the *locus classicus* of narrative-epistolary fiction, to show how Austen addressed this shortcoming while appropriating and adapting her predecessors' narrative-epistolary themes, framing conventions and hermeneutics of suspicion. The chapter concludes by linking the devices discussed here to narrative strategies in the long-standing Aristotelian Romance tradition on which they were all drawing, where plots turn on secrets of identity.

Chapter 2 considers narrative-epistolary novelists' uses of their second scaffolding convention – comparison of letters to narrative realities – to investigate whether empirical methods made it possible to detect a person's true identity; determine the truth about letters and past events; and resolve the difficulties that shifting, empirical, and occasional selves posed for cognition. The focus is on novellae and narrative-epistolary episodes in which protagonists use empirical evidence to try to discover the truth of anonymous letters that make damaging claims about another protagonist's true character and past actions. The fictions examined here expanded the narrative context beyond writing and reading "to the moment" to portray letters' empirical relation to reality as an ongoing dynamic interaction in which letters occasioned by social relations also reshaped them, often unexpectedly and sometimes more than once, and in which the truth about letters and about characters' real identities could be discovered empirically – if at all – only over time. But where at the beginning of the eighteenth century, Delarivier Manley and Mary Davys exhibited the utility of empirical tests in detecting the secret of another's identity and past conduct, albeit with certain reservations, Haywood, Smith, and Braddon attacked empiricist pretensions by highlighting flaws in forms of empirical evidence and modes of reasoning that were accepted in history and law, and by demonstrating the dangerous plausibility of the fictional, fact-based narratives that empiricists now presented as truth. This chapter concludes by relating changes in their treatment of empiricism to changes in the laws of evidence.

Chapter 3 addresses uses of this second scaffolding device to address questions of futurity. Like laws in the natural sciences or universal truths about "human nature" in history, expectations in everyday life that were based on cultural archetypes or conduct book rules assumed that the future would probably resemble the past. While demonstrating the primacy of expectations over sense perceptions, and of received ideas over "facts," the novels and narrative-epistolary scenes included here re-examined the claim of men of learning that the predictive, manipulative, and controlling power of scientific knowledge in the natural and human sciences proved its superiority to other forms of knowledge. This chapter introduces what I call encapsulating letters – letters that expand their temporal reach to epitomize a situation grounded in the past, exercise agency in the present, and delineate expectations for the future – as these were deployed from the middle of the eighteenth century at the beginning of a novel or narrative movement. In this position, encapsulating letters were used to provide novel-readers with a concise but elliptical forecast of things to come, and a yardstick for narratives that went on to empirically test the validity of characters' culturally sanctioned expectations of situations and of other characters against the unexpected, surprising, and unforeseen contingencies of ordinary life. Since the shortcomings of expectations of the future could only be identified in retrospect once these had demonstrated themselves empirically, Lennox in *Henrietta* and Burney in *Cecilia* introduced retrospective narratives that corrected or revised past narratives with the wisdom of "hindsight." Subsequent sections describe how Edgeworth, Collins, and Trollope adapted their use of expectations and of encapsulating letters either to reassert the value and dependability of culturally sanctioned expectations or to even more radically destabilize them. This chapter concludes by inverting its earlier analyses, to focus on questions of contingency.

Chapter 4 turns back to a long-standing Romance feature. It examines peripatetic or pivotal letters that were used to engender or make conspicuous a sudden *peripeteia* or reversal in the course of events and a surprising *anagnorisis* or discovery associated with it, which retrospectively alters characters' and/or novel-readers' previous understanding of characters and events. We will have encountered in passing in previous chapters' letters in eighteenth-century novels, which also performed this function. This chapter takes a closer look at some of its more innovative forms. Beginning with Jane Barker's brilliant, unexpected epistolary *peripeteia* in *Love Intrigues*, it goes on to consider nineteenth-century exemplars where formal innovations are used to re-examine or discredit sudden *peripeteiae* and surprising *anagnorises* themselves. The thematic focus is on novels addressing a critically neglected issue that I call the "dilatory lover" – the problem presented for women by the beloved man who has shown serious interest but somehow fails to propose, and instead courts and sometimes marries another woman. The concluding section ("Retrospective: On Chimeras in Literary Realism") considers a curious and paradoxical shift from eighteenth-century writers' confidence that distinctions between true and false *anagnorises* could ultimately be made to nineteenth-century narrative-epistolary writers' increasingly insistent efforts to discredit literary realism's naturalization of the idea that a single, all-encompassing, retrospective narrative told from "the vantage point of the end" can reflect reality and truth.

Letter-narratives were already deployed in Charlotte Smith and Jane Austen to explore the distance both of letters and of narratives from the reality inhabited by their character-readers and to juxtapose different realities that provide perspectives on one another. Chapter 5 turns to fictions by Walter Scott and Wilkie Collins, which took the further step of eliminating the omniscient narrator to fragment the narration into a patchwork of letter-narratives and other narrative-epistolary forms authored by character-narrators with different perspectives on events. Superimposing personal and generic perspectives enabled them to present the limitations both of perception and of genre in a manner consistent with contemporary "dioptrics," which described how perspectives are created by refracting objects through different media. The last section ("Retrospective: *Mixta Genera* and the Hermeneutics of Perspective"*)* uses Scott's observation in *Redgauntlet* that narrative-epistolary writers can be compared to "dragoons who were trained to serve either on foot or on horseback as the emergencies of service required," to conclude this study by re-envisioning *mixta genera* and the formal narrative-epistolary devices discussed in previous chapters retrospectively in perspectival terms.

The principal goals of this study are to demonstrate that, unexpected as it seems and artificial as such classifications inevitably are, the tradition of narrative-epistolary writing was what my students would call "a thing"; and that writers in this tradition combined narrative and letters in an amazing variety of interesting ways for significant, historically shifting, literary, and cultural purposes. I therefore take my examples from a range of fictions without attempting to fix boundaries for the genre. I say more about this in the Introduction, but hope that others with different goals will be intrigued enough by this mode of writing to consider borderline cases and decide on the utility of sub-genres, as well as to explore combinations and thematic concerns that are missing here. This initial foray into a subject that seems to expand the more one looks is also incomplete in other ways. Its focus is on fiction, on a couple of centuries, and on Britain, but narrative-epistolary writing was confined to none of these. Originating among the Ancients, it reappeared in Shakespeare, in seventeenth-century French and English history-writing, in seventeenth-century French romances, and in early American fictions.[15] And though abandoned by British historians in the course of the eighteenth-century, thanks to the gradual ascendancy of the footnote, it continued to figure in other nonfictional genres —in pamphlets, essays, antiquarian works, reports, stand-alone biographies, and the "Lives" preceding treatises or collections of letters. Like transnational relations among British, French, and North American narrative-epistolary fictions, or their boundaries and/or sub-species, nonfictional uses of narrative-epistolary forms are beyond the scope of this study and invite further work.

The chapters here return in different ways to issues of identity, genre, and reading; to relations between cultural conventions, social archetypes, representations, and empirical facts; and to questions of gender, law, and contingency, as treated by authors skeptical of Enlightenment or Positivist methods of arriving at truth or anxious to defend them. Their issues and positions are sometimes uncannily echoed by postmodern theorists. Whether this means that we have never been modern; that some writers in earlier periods were always already postmodern; that postmodern theorists re-presented "subjugated knowledges" for their own time; or that, like the plural and decentered occasional subject, the same figurations recur in endless iterations, I will not venture to say. But it is important to notice a key difference: the authors whom we are about to meet had not given up on reality and truth. After demolishing our pretensions to knowledge of reality in his *Treatise of Human Nature*, and confining us to the prison house of signs and mental representations, even Hume pointed out with a grin that we demonstrate the ludicrousness of his arguments whenever we stand up and walk across a room.

Acknowledgments

Since this topic has accompanied me for some time, I am profoundly indebted to numerous colleagues who generously invited me to write or talk about it and/or who provided notable feedback and support. They include Zoe Beenstock, Claire Brant, Nicholas Cronk, Elizabeth Eger, Ann Gardner, Theresa Strouth Gaul, Sharon Harris, Rob Hume, Andrew Kahn, Susan Manning, Carla Mulford, Menushag Powell, and Gary Schneider. The manuscript was immensely improved by three brilliant and absolutely model readers: Roxanne Wheeler, Rebecca Barr, and Tom Keymer. I can't thank them enough for the time, care, and thought they put into their invaluably critical and constructive comments. I am grateful to Brenda Mackey, the staff at Bizzell Library and the Ohio Link for making it possible to do this work remotely; to Alan Bannet for IT support; and to Bethany Thomas for her unfailing efficiency, good humor and good sense.

In this deadly year of 2020, this volume is dedicated to the memory of the departed, among them my very dear, longtime friends Zephira Porat, Arlyn Imberman, and Jo Herzog.

The Letters in the Story

William Jones observed in 1780 that "compositions are like machines, where one part depends upon another: the art is to use method as builders do a *scaffold*, which is to be taken away when the work is finished; or as good workmen, who conceal the *joints* in their work, so it may look smooth and pleasant to the eye, as if it were all made of one piece."[1] As he noted, relations between parts of a composition are not necessarily obvious because, in good writing, the method of construction is artfully concealed. The same may be said of the contemporary thinking on which a method of construction draws and upon which it rests. This chapter therefore offers an overview of the scaffolding. It addresses the formal conventions and the ideas that good narrative-epistolary builders used their joints to connect during the period book-ended by Trollope and Behn, and concludes by discussing some key continuities and changes during this extended period in writers' treatment of history, narrative, and letters.

Some Characteristics of Narrative-Epistolary Fictions

Writers constructed their formal narrative-epistolary scaffolding from two basic, and unexpectedly versatile, conventions: narrative framing of embedded letters and juxtaposition of narrative and epistolary accounts of the same characters and events.

The first convention consisted of framing each inset and fully transcribed letter with a narrative describing its writing and reception.[2] The prefatory narrative to each letter described the occasion its author-character had for writing it. In its fullest form, this included the circumstances requiring the letter, the circumstances in which it was written, the writer's reason(s) or motives for writing, the writer's designs in crafting the letter as s/he did, any process of drafting, rereading, reflecting and rewriting involved, and how the letter was sent, transmitted, or delivered. The reception narrative following each transcribed letter addressed the occasion or occasions upon which it was read. In its fullest form, this included the circumstances of the letter's reception, the effect(s) of its material appearance, the way or ways in which it was understood by one or more reader-characters, their immediate intellectual and emotional reactions, any reflections, conversations or debates the letter produced, what was done with the letter subsequent to its first reading, any actions taken as a result of reading it, and how the letter was reinterpreted as characters discussed, or reread and reflected upon it, at different times. This might be characterized as the Enlightenment's more intricate and pragmatic version of Jakobson's idealized communications model.[3]

This convention's basic tri-partite structure – prefatory narrative, transcribed letter, reception narrative – presented letters as an "occasional genre," a genre which, like the Elizabethan sonnet or the occasional poem, arose from and was produced for a particular occasion, usually with a specific person or audience in view. Letters too are commonly written in response to a particular situation, in accordance with generic and social conventions, on a particular date, by a particular person in particular circumstances, who is purposefully addressing a particular person or particular people in particular circumstances of their own. As the instantiation of an occasional genre that was shaped by the factors actually or potentially included in the framing narrative, a letter's real meaning(s) and actual effects depended less on *what* it said or how it said it, than on its occasion, reception and circulation, on transitory circumstances and unforeseen accidents, and on how a complex series of temporal and local, social and psychological transactions between letter-writer and letter-reader(s) happened to play out.[4]

Framing fully transcribed letters with a narrative of their writing and reading presented letters as a relational and dialogical, as well as a pragmatic, occasional, genre. It reflected the early modern view that correspondence was only "written conversation" – the "silent speech" of each letter addressed others, at once anticipating and inviting a reply.[5] Like polite speech whose rules had devolved from the conventions of Jacobean courtiers, the silent speech of eighteenth-century letters obeyed conventions descending from their courtly, scribal and mercantile past. Along with injunctions to "write as you would speak," the Enlightenment inherited a formal taxonomy of letter "kinds" corresponding to different speech acts, each with its own commonplaces and proper forms. There were, for instance, letters of thanks, of condolence, of congratulation and of invitation; letters of compliment, of exhortation, of petition, of business and of reproach; letters of news or intelligence, and "mixed" letters combining two or more of the other kinds.[6] As polite speech became more informal and supposedly more "sincere" in the nineteenth century, there was a shift in balance or proportion: letter-writers were more apt to follow the injunction to "write as you would speak" in their private correspondence, while the number of distinct letter-kinds in active use contracted but did not disappear. Even now, there are proper forms for certain kinds of letter: we don't write a business letter, a letter of condolence, a letter of application and a wedding invitation in the same way; and we know, or take the trouble to find out, the sorts of things each should say and how they should be phrased.

Like speech acts too, each letter's content, style, language, and use of extant conventions had to be shaped by the character, interests, and concerns of its addressee(s); by the relationship in which the writer stood to them; by the level of familiarity or intimacy between them as set against power, status, and gender differentials in what was still a hierarchical society; and especially during the eighteenth century, by the inhibiting likelihood that, even when not intercepted at the post office, a letter sent to one person would be shared with or read aloud to others in domestic and/ or social situations and become a subject of conversation in its turn. As a relational, dialogical, and transactional genre, then, letters bore witness to the character, quality, and state of *relationships*, as well as to efforts to establish, preserve, manage, understand, alter, or terminate them.

Letters bore witness to relationships; but for participants to a correspondence, the immediate problem was to correctly gauge their correspondent's character, purpose(s), and meaning, in order to know how to answer or act upon the letter they received. Like modern critics who view letters as a means of characterization, contemporaries agreed with Locke that "the Writing of Letters has so much to do in all the occurrences of Humane Life that no Gentleman can avoid shewing himself in this kind of writing." But Locke expected a gentleman's letters to show his "Breeding, Sense and Abilities," not his true character or essential nature.[7] And eighteenth-century narrative-epistolary fictions demonstrated why discovering who a man truly is from his letters was less straightforward than we now assume. Early novelists, such as Aphra Behn and Eliza Haywood, often used their narrative frames to inculcate an Enlightenment hermeneutics of suspicion – for instance, by describing a letter-writer's conflicted or dishonest motives in the prefatory frame, for writing what appeared from its transcription to be a perfectly innocent letter and demonstrating how and why a too credulous reader-character foolishly took it at face value. Contrary to what we used to think, neither real nor fictional letters in this period were designed or expected to be transparent "windows into the bosom." As Aphra Behn told a lover: "You bid me not dissemble . . . Nor doe I follow all my Inclination neither, nor tell all the little Secrets of my Soul."[8] Johnson observed that "There is, indeed, no transaction which offers stronger temptations to fallacy and sophistication than epistolary discourse."[9] Or as Hugh Blair put it in 1783: in letters, we "please ourselves with beholding the writer in a situation which allows him to be at his ease, and to give vent occasionally to the overflowings of his heart;" but "it is childish indeed, to expect that in Letters we are to find the whole heart of the Author unveiled. Concealment and disguise take place, more or less, in all human intercourse."[10]

To add to the difficulty, readers were themselves thought to be subject to impediments that might conceal the meaning or import of a letter from their understanding. Indicating in the reception narrative that a reader-character lacked information provided to us, the novel's readers, by the prefatory frame enabled eighteenth-century novelists to show how mis-readings arose from reader-characters' misprision of key facts about the writer, occasion, or relationship, from their ignorance of epistolary or rhetorical conventions, from their own passions, desires, prejudices, or illusions, or from any of the other bars to understanding that Enlightenment philosophers such as John Locke or Isaac Watts listed and described.[11] In Victorian novels, conscious "concealment and disguise" became signifiers of villainy – only wicked or criminal characters now weaponized their letters by consciously concealing their malice, greed, self-interest, or ambition behind manipulative, affable, and altruistic-sounding prose. And reader-characters' bar to seeing such letters for what they are, was more likely to derive from unsuspecting innocence, from lack of self-knowledge or from the assumption that, like language in Victorian linguistic theory, letters are normally expressive, transparent, and sincere.

Ideally, polite conversation and its written double, correspondence, both resembled a graceful and harmonious minuet, where the successive movements of partners to the dance mirror one another perfectly and without apparent effort. The meanings encoded by the speaker or writer and the meanings decoded by reader(s) or hearers correspond with well-bred ease; and the readers' or hearers' written or verbal responses effortlessly "answer" the writer's meaning, expectations, and concerns. But as novelistic pairing of written and oral conversation showed, mirroring correspondences between the parties were far harder to achieve in written than in oral exchanges. Janet Altman observed that "in epistolary works, acts of communication (confession, silence, persuasion, and so on) constitute important events" that are "enacted rather than reported in discourse."[12] By contrast, narrative-epistolary fictions used "reports in discourse" to subject "enactments" of epistolary communication to critical re-examination. As we will see in Chapter 1, they used "enactments" to display and narrative to comment upon causes of disjunctions and misunderstandings in a writing where communication depended on rhetorical proficiency and on successfully penetrating cultural norms of politeness, while negotiating writers' and readers' different assumptions, expectations, or emotions under conditions of imperfect knowledge. Their "reports in discourse" highlighted the folly of taking letters at face value as true, obvious, or complete expressions of what their writers had really thought, felt, wished, or done.

The second basic scaffolding convention consisted of juxtaposing narrative and epistolary representations of the same characters or events, and of measuring the truth of one against the other. The default mode used the narrative's representation of characters and events to establish what counts as empirical reality in the novel's fictional world as well as the chronology pertaining within it, and explicitly compared this to a letter's account of the same characters and events. This enabled novelists to present narrative-epistolary fiction as a self-conscious, fact- and document-based, historical genre, and to address epistemological questions bearing on letters' relations to reality, which were relevant to a reading public that was increasingly relying on letters in their everyday personal, social, commercial, and bureaucratic interactions, and central to other fact- and document-based genres. These genres included "true histories," whose information about the past often depended on surviving letters, epistolary dispatches, and epistolary reports; biographies, whose narrative representations of their subjects' lives were based on surviving "papers;" trials in which judges and juries weighed the credibility of epistolary evidence and narrative accounts; and investigations employing letters to discover a secret, resolve a mystery, or detect a crime. Narrative-epistolary novels explored issues that these others often preferred to ignore. As we will see in Chapter 2, testing the truth of letters against evidence from the narrative's empirical world, or the narrative's empirical world against the evidence of letters enabled narrative-epistolary fictions to portray mental processes of induction and inference by which characters reached true or false conclusions about the evidentiary character of missives and/or actions. It also enabled them to problematize empirical evidence by demonstrating where there were obstacles in reality itself to timely discovery of necessary or relevant facts. Narrative-epistolary writers showed that, in practice, the relevant empirical evidence was sometimes obscure, sometimes misinterpreted, sometimes overlooked, sometimes absent, sometimes understood only in retrospect, and sometimes something that presented itself, by chance, only at a much a later date. Some even put in question the proposition that the empirical reality people need to verify epistolary or narrative constructions, is a reality that plainly exists.

Novels, as opposed to romances, are still widely associated by modern critics with "the culture of fact" and thus with the more or less naively "formal," "circumstantial," or documentary realism that Virginia Woolf characterized as the realism of the earthenware pot.[13] Assuming like Ian Watt that "the credo of an empiricist age is that knowledge of the world starts with [sensuous] particulars" and "concrete facts," has led to the assumption that novels were realistic to the extent that they reflected the lives of particular individuals in a particular time and place with all the factual specificity and concrete detail of common life.[14] But for Enlightenment scientists and empiricist philosophers, empiricism did not start from sensuous particulars or concrete facts. It started from questions about what particulars our senses are capable of perceiving, how our minds apprehend and process what we perceive, and how we ought to "conduct our understanding" to obtain true empirical knowledge of whatever our minds are looking at. Bacon had insisted that "before we can reach the remote and more hidden parts of Nature, it is necessary that a more perfect use and application of the human mind and intellect be introduced."[15] Newton had prefaced the second edition of his *Principia* with thirteen Rules for Reasoning. Enlightenment and Victorian empiricist philosophers likewise began with essays on human understanding, treatises on human nature, or analyses of the human mind, which inquired into the impact of language, memory, imagination, and the passions on our perceptions and reasoning; argued the influence on our thinking of education and extant cultural archetypes; and debated whether operations of the mind they described or devised enable us to think as coldly, rationally, and impartially as the human and natural sciences now required.[16]

Empiricists assumed, in other words, that empiricism is a *relationship* between the mind and its objects – that what one sees depends on how one looks, and what one understands or discovers about real phenomena, on how one thinks. Narrative-epistolary novelists were empiricists in this sense. They participated in a series of empiricist debates about relations between the mind and its objects; and from the 1680s on made "realist fiction ... a narrative mode premised on questions of knowledge and the representation of truth."[17] Narrative-epistolary fictions described how characters reached true or false conclusions by applying or misapplying rules of evidence common to law, history, and science, while critically examining changing convictions in these fields about the credibility of personal testimony, the reliability of circumstantial evidence, the validity of probability-based expectations in predicting the future, and the role of conjecture in constructing a chain of evidence and reconstructing the course of past events. One might say that, with regard to relations between empirical facts and fictions, narrative-epistolary novels made the prose texts of completely transcribed letters stand in for all writing and all text. The word "letters" meant missives or epistles; but it did not escape contemporaries that "letters" also meant written texts in general and the learning acquired through them (as in "man of letters"), and the arbitrary written or printed alphabetical signs or "letters" on which "letters" (epistles) and "letters" (texts) depend.

Juxtaposing letters and narratives enabled narrative-epistolary writers to impugn self-serving historicist treatments of letters as fixed repositories of facts, by highlighting letters' dynamic and often unanticipated impact on the real. At a time when letters were the only means of distance communication at home and abroad, narrative-epistolary novelists emphasized the agency of letters in everyday life, from their most trivial instrumentality (for instance, in arranging a meeting) to their transmission of information, expectations, and implicit or explicit narratives that reshaped or distorted empirical phenomena, and thus altered how their addressees would think and act. Like modern narratologists who regard letters as instruments of the plot, they understood that letters could affect, drive, or alter the course of events. But they gave letters a more multifaceted and pluri-temporal relation to the action than we generally notice or expect. Expanding the narrative frame to relate a letter to events earlier or much later on the chronological line, or reintroducing the same letter several times at later points in the chronological sequence, belied historians' assumption that a letter enters time and (hi)story only once – at the moment of its initial writing and transmission. Expanding or doubling the prefatory frame to include prior temporal moments showed how earlier events or encounters shaped the writing or reading of a letter; or how a letter might induce reader-characters to re-view and change their earlier understanding of the past. And complicating the temporalities within what I will call "encapsulating letters" to encompass futurity as well as the present and the past made it possible to consider how cultural, economic, and/or personal expectations shaped the elements of reality that characters noticed and conveyed in their letters, and to compare the often unexpected way things turn out in the future to plans or assumptions based on experience in the past. As we will see in Chapter 3, use of such devices enabled narrative-epistolary novelists to question how – and indeed, whether – it was reasonable for people to use cultural norms and injunctions as guides to future action, wise for the young to rely on guardians or mentors for direction, and possible for readers then or later to correctly reconstruct interactions and chains of events in which letters did not so much attest to what had or would occur, as directly intervene in the action by playing their own dynamic, formative, and unpredictable parts.

Dropping fully transcribed and narratively framed letters irregularly into a narrative's temporal sequence highlighted another, complementary facet of letters as an instrumental, occasional genre: that letters are *read* as well as written *in medias res*, while lives, events, and conversations are moving on. For narrative-epistolary novelists, letters were not only "written to the moment" while the meaning and outcome of events were still uncertain and hidden in the womb of time, as Samuel Richardson would later claim; they were also *read to the moment*, and by character-readers and novel-readers for whom the same conditions of ignorance and uncertainty prevailed. While underlining the durability of writing in contradistinction to speech, reintroduction of the same letter at several points in the narrative's chronological sequence showed how its unperceived meanings and intended or unintended empirical consequences emerged or unfolded over time as circumstances changed; how a letter might be belied or overtaken by events; or more disturbingly, how even false, willfully deceptive or unconsciously self-deceptive letters could impact and radically alter the course of events. When the circumstances of their writing and the history of their reading were fully understood, letters supplied evidence of the peculiar mixes of blindness and insight, hope and fear, knowledge and ignorance, confident interpretation and unintended misinterpretation, demonstrated by writer and readers at different past and present times. Rather than treating letters as fixed repositories from which historians, biographers, judges and later, detectives could confidently extract whatever information they needed to construct narratives of their own devising, narrative-epistolary novelists displayed letters' dubious time-bound knowledge of unfolding events, as well as the likelihood that they would be read and acted upon in questionable time-bound ways.

Some novelists in each period liked to bring this home to novel-readers by exposing our reading of embedded letters to some of the same ignorance and uncertainty that cause reader-characters to blunder. A narrative that was silent on key facts or omitted essential information about the letter-writer's character, purposes or motives from a letter's narrative frame or that neglected to alert novel-readers to a letter's false, manipulative or lying character, placed novel-readers in the same situation as reader-characters, and made them liable to the same mistakes. Novel-readers who failed to notice omissions in the frame or to suspend judgment until missing information emerges later on the narrative timeline, could experience on their own pulses how readily we too mistakenly assume that we know enough about characters and a story to interpret letters correctly and see how they fit in. The same effect could be achieved by quietly omitting explicit comparisons between the narrative reality and its epistolary representation(s) and leaving novel-readers to compare epistolary to narrative accounts for themselves. Here, novel-readers who overlook discrepancies between narrative realities and epistolary representations may discover at story's end or upon a more careful review of the text, that they have completely misread the story or mistaken its tendency and moral. In Victorian novels, the hermeneutics of suspicion and the imperative earlier incumbent on all letter-readers to detect falsehoods and willful epistolary deceptions often passed to a new, specialized class of characters –amateur and professional detectives who scanned letters for "clues" to what had "really" transpired in the past. This device made it possible to demonstrate the difficulties of historical reconstruction and the shortcomings of empirical methods of detection, while reassuring the public that, in the end, truth would come out, so that present evils rooted in the past could be suppressed and disempowered, or corrected and reversed. As we will see in Chapters 3 and 5, nineteenth-century novelists such as Walter Scott, Wilkie Collins, and Anthony Trollope continued to put novel-readers in play to confront them with the inconvenient possibility that the whole truth about "reality," personal identity, and past events might never be known. But by asking readers to piece together a patchwork of subjective and discontinuous letter-narratives and narrative-epistolary reports that leave some curious aspect of the story mysteriously inexplicable and unexplained, they also explored the limitations both of empirical knowledge and of narrative-epistolary forms. This could either undermine or augment the authority of the narrator as indisputable story-teller and prime raiser of questions about lives and texts.

Combining letters and narrative not only enabled novelists to inquire into the documentary truth of letters and into the credibility of their self-representations, but also to control the pace of the story better than epistolary novelists generally could. Novelists soon found that all the letters in a story did not have to be fully transcribed and set off on the page. Some could be rapidly summarized by the narrator. Others could be partly summarized and partly transcribed, to highlight the section that mattered most to the story and ensure that novel-readers did not get distracted by something else. The language and contents of some letters could be partly or wholly rendered in free indirect discourse and focalized through a character's mind, as s/he wrote, read, or subsequently reflected upon it. The substance of a letter could also be allowed to emerge from a character's reflections or from conversations with other characters. Alternatively, the narrative could treat the letter as a material object to portray a character's agonies when an awaited letter failed to appear or, passing over its contents in silence, describe a letter's observable but now unaccountable effects on its addressee. The narrative could present a character's telling speculations about what an unseen letter might contain; show a character exercised by whether other characters were corresponding; or highlight the significance of epistolary silences, refusals to correspond, or efforts to prevent letters from being written or read. There were endless possibilities for variation.

Letters themselves were an exceptionally capacious, versatile, and flexible form.[18] They could not only emulate and reproduce a wide variety of everyday speech acts, but also accommodate a wide variety of other literary forms. Letters could contain stories, narratives about characters and events, descriptions and observations, anecdotes, reported dialogue, commentary, introspective analyses, passionate sentimental effusions, and arguments or reflections. Letters were also used in Enlightenment print and manuscript cultures as the preferred platform for a range of other genres. Letters delivered political, philosophical or theological argument, thematic essays, commercial or administrative reports, military or diplomatic dispatches, autobiographical memoirs, legal documents, scientific reports, historical narratives, conduct-book chapters, public addresses and petitions, and travel writing that complied with contemporary scientific, historical, or ethnographic investigative and discursive norms.[19] Eighteenth-century narrative-epistolary novelists were able to capitalize on this range of options to deploy a far wider variety of kinds of letter and to do so in a far wider variety of ways than epistolary novelists could, burdened as the latter were by the requirement that letters between intimates who enjoy each other's confidence perform the whole work of narration and characterization.

The framing narrative proved equally versatile. Bald statements of the relevant facts about a letter's production, transmission, and reception could be replaced by narrated scenes that conveyed the requisite information through conversations among characters, focalized reflections, character analyses, narrator commentary, or all of the above. Prefatory frames could be doubled or expanded, positioned in varying proximity to the letter, or fragmented to both precede and follow it. Prefatory and reception narratives could be inverted, so that readers encountered the latter first. Prefatory frames could also be eliminated altogether, and whole chapters devoted to reception narratives instead. Reception narratives could be filled with conversations that multiplied the possible interpretations of a letter and put its meaning in doubt. The relation between narrative and letters could also be quietly inverted, to make letters contain the key to the truth about characters and events in the fictional world and belie the narrative's account of reality. When this was done consistently, it created an ambiguous, double-voiced text, with (at least) two possible readings, as in Mary Davys's *The Reform'd Coquet* (1724), Jane Barker's *Love Intrigues*, and much of Jane Austen.

Narrative-epistolary novelists also played with the relations between narrative and epistolary forms. They might, for instance, insert a narrative-epistolary story into a letter, thus capturing the narrative between the letter that contained it and the letters it contained, as in Delarivier Manley's *Bath Intrigues* (1725), Anne Bronte's *The Tenant of Wildfell Hall* (1848), or less obviously, Charlotte Bronte's *Villette* (1853). Alternatively, they might insert a narrative-epistolary story into a narrated scene describing the give-and-take of a conversation, as Jane Barker did in *Love Intrigues* (1713) or Charlotte Smith in *The Wanderings of Warwick* (1794), in order to precede, follow, or interrupt the narration with meta-critical discourse issuing from a character-auditor or from conversations among characters. Narrative-epistolary novelists could also experiment with different ways of parceling out the narration between narrative and embedded letters, or of juxtaposing first-person letter-narratives with third-person narration and/or with other first-person forms such as the journal or the diary, as Charlotte Smith did in *The Banished Man* (1794), Anne Bronte did in *The Tenant of Wildfell Hall* (1848), Scott did in *Redgauntlet* (1824), or Charlotte Bronte did in *The Professor* (1857). Alternatively, they might insert the tripartite structure of a narratively framed letter (prefatory narrative, transcribed letter, reception narrative) into a third-person narrative or into a first-person letter, journal or memoir, as what might be called a citation of the genre, as Henry Fielding did in *Joseph Andrews* (1742), and George Eliot in *Middlemarch* (1871–1872). They could also use this tripartite structure more locally for what I will call their narrative's epistolary *peripeteia*, to highlight a major turning point in a predominantly narrative text and the discovery it generated, as Jane Austen did in *Sense and Sensibility* (1811), *Mansfield Park* (1814) and *Persuasion* (1817), or Charlotte Bronte did in *Villette*.

This plurality of uses to which these scaffolding conventions could be put, together with the flexibility of the component genres and of their combinations, make it as difficult to define narrative-epistolary fiction as to circumscribe its boundaries. Though most narrative-epistolary fictions contain multiple letters, the number of letters embedded in a story is not necessarily the conclusive factor. Cases like *Love Intrigues*, where the only two letters in the text radically alter the meaning(s) of the whole narrative seem to me to be narrative-epistolary in genre; but I would argue that narrative-epistolary conventions are only "cited" in cases like the letter that Dorothea receives from Casaubon before their wedding in *Middlemarch*; for here narrative-epistolary conventions are invoked rapidly and in passing only to highlight a local point in an otherwise narrative text – Dorothea's blindness to what Casaubon's letter presents to her view before her marriage, together with its terrible self-evidence to more acute and less desirous novel-readers. Like that letter, this distinction is a matter of interpretation and a judgment call. On the other hand, I think we can usefully draw a line between epistolary novels that occasionally resort to editorial narrative to connect letters or clarify events and narrative-epistolary fiction proper. For in one case, a story is told "in a series of letters" and narrative interpolations are borrowed from the conventions of third-person omniscient narration; and in the other, the story is largely or wholly narrated and letters are embedded in the story by means of the recognized scaffolding conventions. But the boundaries here too may prove to be porous; and further research is required to determine whether inserting narrative interpolations in epistolary fiction is the mark of authorial failure we have thought it, or indicative of experimentation with an "epistolary-narrative" form of fiction.

Because the scaffolding conventions described here are employed in all the exemplars I have examined, I include under narrative-epistolary fiction different combinations and narratives delivered in diverse ways: by first- or third-person narrators; as part of a conversation or of a journal entry; in an open letter (where all features of letters but their superscription and subscription are preserved); in a letter-narrative (where a narrative with its embedded letter(s) is itself embedded in a letter); and where narrative and embedded letters tell partially complementary or rival stories. Further scholarly work may reveal that these or other combinations of narrative and letters are recurrent enough and different enough from one another in other ways to constitute distinct narrative-epistolary subgenres. Further work is also needed on nonfictional *mixta genera* such as the newly popular *Life and Letters* genre of biography or pamphlets like Richard Steele's technically brilliant *The Crisis* (1713), and perhaps especially on forms where narrative and letters are juxtaposed rather than intertwined.

But for this initial foray into narrative-epistolary fiction, the important thing to notice is that while figuring as distinct genres that retain their separateness, letters and narratives are designed to be read together and against one another throughout the narrative-epistolary work. Narrative-epistolary fiction's scaffolding conventions repeatedly connect them in ways which, as Scott will say, "instruct the reader for his full comprehension of the story."[20]

Mystery Plots and Romance Conventions

While drawing on shifting empiricist views of probability in history, law, and natural philosophy for their representations of common experience and everyday life, narrative-epistolary fictions often looked, for the structure of their plots, to the long-standing interpretative and writerly tradition that had extended Aristotle's account of epic in the *Poetics* to romance and to prose fictions dealing with love. Individual fictions drew on these diverse currents selectively and gave what they appropriated contemporary relevance and modern "dress." But combining elements from these two currents added to fiction's flexibility by permitting it to be weighted to different degrees in either direction – toward the marvelous, fantastic, supernatural, and uncanny; or toward the empirical, ordinary, probable, and mundane. Despite eighteenth-century efforts to oppose "romance" to "novel" in these terms, this ensured that even fact-based "realistic" novels retained traces of romance.[21]

Terence Cave's work is particularly useful for understanding why narrative-epistolary novelists, who made the difficulty of determining the true identity of others central to courtship and to women's domestic lives, often used the Aristotelian romance tradition to structure their plots. As Cave explains, Aristotle's favored examples of tragedy and epic in *The Poetics* – *Oedipus Rex* and *The Odyssey* – both turned on secrets of identity. The chief structural components of their exemplary plots – *hamartia, anagnorisis,* and *peripeteia* – were thought to be common to tragedy and epic, with this difference that epic could contain several discoveries or recognitions (*anagnorisis*), and several revolutions in the course of relationships and events (*peripeteia*). In *Oedipus,* the *peripeteia* and discovery of the protagonist-investigator's true identity from the testimony he hears, involves detection

and revelation of his earlier scandalous crimes of parricide and incest. In
The Odyssey, Odysseus's own occluded identity, impenetrable disguises,
lapses of memory and deceptive narratives, together with the dangerous
snares and fantastic adventures to which he is exposed and the more minor
anagnorises and *peripeteiae* these entail, precede and delay the conjoined
peripeteia and *anagnorisis* on his return home, which bring his identity to
light and restore him to his proper social and domestic place. Though not
unique in this regard, women's narrative-epistolary fiction often favored
plots that turned on a scandalous secret about a lover's or guardian's true
character or social identity and/or on the mystery of their vicious or
criminal past, described the process by which these secrets were detected,
and ended "happily" by restoring all the characters to their proper social
and interpersonal place.[22] As we will see in Chapter 4, they also often
highlighted their Aristotelian romance structure by using a fateful letter or
correspondence to occasion and underline the *peripeteia* and explore,
extend, or subvert the *anagnorisis* that reveals the secret of the plot.

Though ignoring eighteenth-century British fiction, Terence Cave has
shown that plots in the Aristotelian romance tradition which were built
"systematically" around a secret of identity had "a dual structure, combining an apparent determination [of characters and events] with an at least
partly hidden (but effective) determination. At the *peripeteia*, the hidden
level shifts to the surface . . . and discloses the true sense of the action." He
observes that this dual structure presents in one of two ways. Readers or
spectators who are brought into the secret by the narrator see it in operation among characters, as when we watch Odysseus deceiving Penelope
with a false and misleading story to conceal his true identity. In *Love
Letters*, part 2, in many ways a seminal text for narrative-epistolary novelists, Aphra Behn emplotted her secret history as this kind of Aristotelian
romance: readers are brought into the secret of Philander's defection and
pursuit of Callista, which all the male characters carefully hide from the
heroine, to permit us to watch Silvia's painful discovery from his letters
that Philander was not the true lover she had thought him. Even when they
averted catastrophe, the passage from ignorance to knowledge, turns from
good fortune to misery and/or from misery to good fortune, pity for the
heroine's sufferings and perhaps fear for oneself, remained crucial to stories
constructed around the harm done to a young lady by an intriguing
philanderer who was discovered too late not to be what he seemed.

However, as Cave explains, narrators did not have to bring readers
into the secret; they could also demonstrate that "mastery of the art of
telling lies" that was attributed to Homer, by practicing the same kind

of deception on novel-readers or spectators that was practiced on protagonists. Narrators who withhold key information and induce us to take the manifest story and apparent determinations of character and events for the true story, only to produce the hidden or partially hidden story at the end, make novel-readers experience a *peripeteia* and *anagnorisis* as well as the characters. In the hands of narrative-epistolary novelists, this created what Cave calls a "recursive structure" where the manifest story reads differently upon a second reading or retrospective view, after the hidden story has been revealed.[23] Interestingly, Todorov and Barthes respectively attributed this same dual structure to the classical detective story and to nineteenth-century realism, characterizing the two narratives stemming from what Barthes called the "enigma" as the story of the investigation and the story of the crime.[24]

Aristotle's demand that incidents in the plot or "Argument" be presented and related "according to probability or necessity" opened the door to empiricism which had been preoccupied with questions of probability since the seventeenth century. Empiricists argued that probabilistic reasoning afforded the highest degree of certainty in fields such as law, history, and the natural sciences which, like the novel, addressed real and therefore contingent and aleatory phenomena, where absolute demonstrative certainty was considered unattainable. In these fields, probabilistic reasoning underpinned the evaluation of evidence, the formation of hypotheses and generalizations, interpretations of the past, and predictions of the future conduct of persons or phenomena. "Moral belief" or "moral certainty" was considered the highest degree of certitude attainable by probabilistic reasoning about empirical evidence in history and law. This meant that where the probability of conjectures or hypotheses based on contingent evidence seemed "violent" rather than "light" or "moderate," one could now "morally believe" them and be "morally certain" they were true. Using empirical evidence to uncover secrets of character and identity, in conjunction with narrative-epistolary fiction's second scaffolding convention, enabled narrative-epistolary writers to explore and expose the danger of mistaking even "violent" probabilities for truth, given the contingency of ordinary life.

Another aspect of this issue derives from the fact that, in addressing the contingent experiences of life, history, secret history, and novels were themselves expected to be probable in the above sense. As Delarivier Manley put it, "Secret Histories" were "Historical Novels" that take "great Care to observe the Probability of Truth, which consists of saying nothing but what may Morally be believed."[25] However, as a character observes in *The Moonstone,* "nothing in this world is probable, unless it appeals to our own trumpery experience; and we only believe in a romance when we see it in the newspapers."[26] Or as we might say post-Foucault, what passes as probable depends on the current regime of truth. Between Manley and Collins, there were significant shifts both in the kinds of evidence and in the kinds of reasoning that were held to yield moral certainty. As we will see in Chapter 3, the most problematical of these for narrative-epistolary novelists were introduction in the second half of the eighteenth century of circumstantial evidence and the concurrent practice of treating conjectures based on circumstantial evidence in history and law, and hypotheses in the sciences, at least *pro tem,* as evident and universal truth.

In what concerned the structure, narrative presentation and empirical investigation of plots centered on secrets of character or of social identity, there was therefore more community between woman-authored, eighteenth-century narrative-epistolary fiction, Victorian proto-detective "sensation" novels, Victorian blackmail plots and detective novels proper, than is generally acknowledged. In this, as in other respects, Victorian narrative-epistolary novelists altered, adapted, extended, or revived issues and techniques that their eighteenth-century predecessors had examined and devised, or sometimes abandoned, long before.[27] Victorian narrative-epistolary novelists were working in an inherited tradition. Instead of treating the Victorians as originals and reading eighteenth-century novels for the ways in which they (ineptly) prefigured the great tradition of nineteenth-century realism, the Victorian writers considered here will be viewed as heirs of their seventeenth- and eighteenth-century forbears, who used their considerable individual talents to innovate by adapting a popular genre of Enlightenment fiction to Victorian mores, values, epistemologies, and sociohistorical concerns.

Letters, Mystery Plots, and Occasional Selves

Mystery plots descending from *The Odyssey* and *Oedipus Rex* and from the Romance tradition that turned on secrets of identity and on hidden crimes were considered cliché by Henry Fielding and others, who nevertheless continued to use them. To understand their persistence and renewed relevance during the eighteenth and nineteenth centuries, as well as how letter-writers were thought to "show" themselves in their letters, it is helpful to go back to Locke's account of how the empirical subject presents himself to observation in everyday life, and to the fluid, indeterminate being he described who left selves behind as he went. The self who presented himself to Locke's observation as the personage manifest in his diverse interactions with others and in his shifting consciousness of himself, was heir to the protean subject associated both with Pico della Mirandola's human microcosm and with the Devil during the Renaissance. This plural, decentered and occasional self gained yet another lease of life during the last quarter of the eighteenth century with the publication of Chesterfield's *Letters to his Son* (1774), to continue to haunt narrative-epistolary fiction into the Victorian era as the personage whose true identity and past crimes present the enigma that a detector's empirical investigation is tasked to resolve. Nineteenth-century writers associated characters still demonstrating plural, eighteenth-century "occasional selves" with criminals, pathologized them as "multiple personalities" and classed them among what Thackeray called "the barbarians of civilized life." Occasional selves with shifting social identities flouted the fixed identity and consistent character that normal individuals were now ideally supposed to have. But Victorians also continued to struggle with the problems of cognition they posed.

Recent work on Locke's chapter on personal identity in *Essay Concerning Human Understanding* Book 2, by philosopher-historians such as Udo Thiel, Gideon Yaffe, and Galen Strawson has finally given us a Lockean self more closely resembling that which contemporaries such as Hume, Diderot and Condillac embraced, and orthodox Christians feared would skeptically undermine all religion and morality.[28] They have begun to show that for Locke, personal identity (or our sense of self) was as fluid, as discontinuous, as situated, as various, and as subject to revision and alteration as consciousness itself. As Strawson put it, in Locke, personal identity "may be said to be a very gappy thing."[29] This section builds on their work to show how this "very gappy thing" expressed itself in the equally "gappy" form of letters as well as in the conduct of eighteenth-century people. As we will see, the diverse ideas of selfhood that modern scholars have identified in the period easily attached to this fluid, gappy and always situated self, which then, as now, presented difficulties for cognition beyond those delimited by the binary between appearance and reality. Locke was ubiquitous in Britain, France, and America throughout the eighteenth century, and continued to be foundational during the nineteenth century, which marked fluid, plural, occasional selves as deviant and transgressive.

In Locke, a human is *"a conscious, thinking being"* that *"has Reason and Reflection, and can consider it self as it self, the same thinking thing in different times and place."* But there is no "someone" there – no virtual agent or subject of experience to figure as the permanent substratum of thoughts and reflections or unify them over time as the thoughts and reflections of one, perhaps conflicted, but nevertheless consistent underlying self.[30] Locke's *Essay Concerning Human Understanding* described only what can be observed empirically. As he explains in his Introduction, *"the Understanding [is] like the Eye, [which], whilst it makes us see, and perceive all other Things, takes no Notice of itself."* The *Essay* "sets *[the understanding] at a distance"* and *"makes it its own Object"* (I, i. 1) in order to describe what the mind's eye sees when it does take notice of itself and reflect empirically upon its own workings.

Our sense of self, or of personal identity, derives from an instantaneous version of this same reflexive act. Awareness accompanies all our perceptions of outward phenomena and inward feelings, all our thoughts and mental operations; but our sense of self appears to consciousness only when we think of these with "concern," "concernment," or "care," "when we appropriate" or "own" them *as* our own. I "consider my self as my self" when I appropriate or own particular perceptions, passions, or thoughts *as* my own, as "affecting" or concerning me for good or ill. Because a sense of self or personal identity is an identity over time, this always involves a relation of present consciousness to past consciousness: *"As far as any intelligent Being can repeat the Idea of any past Action with the same Consciousness it had of it at first, and with the same Consciousness it has of any present Action; so far it is the same* personal Self. *For it is by Consciousness it has of its present Thoughts and Actions, that it is a* Self *to it Self now, and so will be the same* Self, *as far as the same Consciousness can extend to Actions past or to come."* (II. xxvii.10) I am conscious that I am the same self I was a minute ago, an hour ago, last year, or in my youth, because, my consciousness now can *repeat* in the present the same consciousness I had of my perceptions, feelings, thoughts, or actions *then*, together with the consciousness I had then that these concern me. When we do not have the same consciousness we had at some earlier point in time, we are not the same self we were then. A Nestor who no longer remembers his past thoughts, feelings, and actions, is not the same Nestor.

The key point, however, is that the self is fluid and radically discontinuous because what presents itself to consciousness, is fluid and radically discontinuous – like time itself, which Locke characterizes as a transient succession of discrete and separate instants. *"Reflecting on what passes in itself, [the mind] observes a constant change in its ideas, sometimes by the impression of outward objects of the senses, and sometimes by the determination*

of its own choice." (II. xxi. 1) The consciousness that accompanies the ideas
that literally *pass through* our minds is also constantly being "interrupted:"
we sleep, we get drunk, we forget. Because consciousness is repeatedly
interrupted and memories fade and disappear, Locke stresses that *"we
constantly lose the Sight of our past Selves."* (II.xxvii. 10) We leave selves
behind all the time as we go. We also lose sight of past selves when we are
engrossed in present business or not thinking about our self at all; and we
lose sight of one part of our self when we are thinking about another. We
also lose past selves because we are never our whole self, *"there being no
Moment of our Lives wherein we have the whole Train of all our past Actions
before our Eyes in one View; But even the best Memories losing the Sight of one
part whilst they are viewing another; and we sometimes, and that the greatest
part of our lives, not reflecting on our past selves, being intent on our present
Thoughts . . . "* (II.xxvii.10) At any given point on the fleeting succession of
discrete moments in time, then, we are conscious only of that part of our
"self" and of its past actions, passions, and thoughts that we are able and
willing to summon up to present consciousness because it is of concernment to us now.

  Considered in these terms, the self that a letter puts on view is the self as
it considers itself and its own concernments at a single discrete point in
time, the time of writing. A letter directly or indirectly documents the
writer's consciousness and concernments, what he or she cares about, at
that moment. Contrary to the way we often distinguish the letter from the
memoir, this always involves a relation of the present to the past; it is always
also a present act of retrospection. At one extreme, the past may be almost
entirely mediated by present consciousness, as in Lady Mary Pierpont's
letter to Anne Wortley in 1708:

> I am convince't, however dear you are to me, Mrs Anne Wortley, I am no
> longer of anny concern to you; therefore I shall only trouble you with an
> insignificant Story, when I tell you, I have bin very near leaveing this
> changeable World, but now by the Doctor's assistance and heaven's bless-
> ing, am in a condition of being impertinently troublesome to you as
> formerly. A sore throat, which plague'd me for a long while, brought me
> at last to such weakness, you had a fair chance for being released from me,
> but God has not yet decreed you so much happiness, tho I must say this, you
> have omitted nothing to make your self so easy, having strove to kill me by
> Neglect, but Destiny triumphs over all your efforts; I am yet in the land of
> the living, and still Your M.P.[31]

Here Lady Mary's account of her past illness is entirely shaped by her
present concern to inform a friend that she is recovered from an illness that

may not have given her friends excessive concern. At the other extreme, as in travel letters or the letters in Richardson's *Clarissa*, past events or encounters may be rendered with the consciousness the writer had of them as they transpired – here detailing past events and experiences with the consciousness the writer had of them when they occurred, "proves" that the self who underwent them is the same self who is relating them now. But in either case, a letter shows only part of the writer's present and past actions, passions and thoughts, the part with which he or she is concerned at the time of writing. Like a portrait or a photograph, a letter is a still that documents the self's consciousness and concernments at a particular, and quite possibly fleeting, moment in time. Lady Mary was not always or forever the lively, cheeky, witty, hopeful, self that shows its self in this letter to Anne Wortley. This may be one reason why eighteenth-century readers delighted in reading the single letters that filled miscellanies and periodicals: for understood in this way, a single letter gave them access to the experiences, passions, and/or thoughts of a self that considered and delineated itself in the relation, as that self had existed at the time of writing and would never, perhaps, exist in quite the same way again. There was no need for more.

Letters written by a writer at different dates and times in a series or sustained correspondence documented a succession of such moments. In their own punctual and gappy fashion, letters could therefore register changes in or of the self over time. Whether the same, or a different self appeared at different times in different letters was established by comparing them. In Behn's *Love Letters*, as we will see, comparison between letters shows Silvia that Philander is no longer the same passionate desiring lover now that he was in letters earlier written to her in her father's house.

Locke equated identity over time with repetition: the same or a similar self reappears at different times or in multiple letters by repeating the same characteristic features. For instance, in the letters that Locke wrote to William Molyneux between 1692 and 1695 that were published in *Familiar Letters between Mr. John Locke and several of his Friends* in 1708, Locke repeatedly showed a serious, dispassionate, demanding self whose principal concern was to obtain from Molyneux, criticisms of *Essay Concerning Human Understanding* that Locke could use to correct the *Essay* for a prospective second edition. This was a self who in successive letters repeatedly described exactly what it wanted in exchange for its proffered "friendship," and ruthlessly flattered, cajoled, invited, reassured, and demanded this from Molyneux. But this was not Locke's "whole self." If, as diverse contemporaries claimed, Locke also had a facetious self with a good sense of humor who figured as an easy and entertaining companion, and a reserved, taciturn, secretive and conspiratorial self, there is no evidence of either here.

The same self did not have to repeat at different times; indeed, at the extreme, people could inhabit multiple identities "losing the Sight" of past selves as they went. In her recent study of Mary Carleton, Mary Jo Kietzman calls this "self-serialization." Carleton inhabited serial identities both orally and in her writings: she was successively Mary Carleton, wife; Maria von Wolway, the German Princess; Maria Darnton, horse thief; Mary Blacke, shoplifter, Maria Lyon, member of a gang that robbed clothes-shops; Darnton or Lyon, indentured servant transported to Barbados, and Maria von Wolway again. Kietzman found herself confronted with "a series of lives" or with "a life composed of lives," each with "different narrative styles," different "cultural icons or social types:" and different accoutrements (clothes, accent, facial expression, demeanor). Kietzman could find no "principle of coherence" to unite these identities; like Fantomina, Carleton "herself" remained *Incognita*. Kietzman argues that serialization of identities was not yet limited to people in the criminal classes like Carleton, Jack Shephard, or Bamfylde-Moore Carew[32] – this "was in fact a widely practiced behavioral style," for instance, at court, for social climbers, or on the stage.[33] One might add that Locke himself inhabited serial names and identities during the ten years he spent in Holland evading the government of James II, which wanted his head. Like Locke, Carleton or Fantomina, nineteenth-century characters such as Lady Audley, Redgauntlet, or the heroine of *No Name* exhibited and distinguished their diverse occasional selves by inhabiting serial names and social identities.

Scholars have found the same phenomenon of serial or alternating identities in seventeenth- and eighteenth-century letters. In her study of *Lady Mary Wortley Montagu and the Familiar Letter*, for instance, Cynthia Lowenthal found no "controlled or sustaining thread of coherent narrative weaving the events of [Lady Mary's] life together"– only "a series of performative selves ... identities configured through varying styles and embodying varying emotions."[34] There were the variously passionate or sentimental selves of Lady Mary's letters to Edward Wortley, to Algarotti, and to her daughter; the romanticizing self of the Embassy letters; the satirical spectatorial self of the letters to her sister and other aristocratic women. A careful and astute reader of letters, Lowenthal argued that Lady Mary's diverse "self-performances" were responses to "the complications of the [epistolary] transaction," and to the "interdependence of the writer and recipient." (24, 27)

This is an important point that Locke addresses too. For in Locke, the relation of consciousness to itself that constitutes "self-consciousness" is only one of multiple relations of which consciousness is aware at any given time. Just before discussing personal identity, Locke devoted two chapters to all those other social and cultural relations "which are productive of obligations and duties to others" for which we have "Occasion" in our "Communication with one another." (II.xxviii.2) Socially, as he points out, "one single Man may at once be concerned in, and sustain, all these following Relations, and many more: viz. Father, Brother, Son, Grandfather, Grandson, Father in Law, Son in Law, Husband, friend, enemy, Subject, General, Judge, Patron, Client, Professor, European, Englishman, Islander, Servant, Master ... Superior, Inferior, Older, Younger, Contemporary, Like, Unlike etc in an almost infinite Number." (ii.xxv.7) The empirical self was imbricated in a nexus of relationships to others, one or more of which could be activated at any time. The empirical self was therefore also what can be called a "relative self," a self that was shaped, and in many ways determined, by relationships and by the diverse roles, expectations, obligations, and duties they involved. Lady Mary was not the same self in all her letters, because she did not stand in the same relations to her daughter as to her sister, to her husband as to Algarotti, or to the public of strangers for whom she revised the Embassy letters, as to their original recipients.

The empirical Lockean self was likewise imbricated in a web of cultural relations, since consciousness considers its thoughts, words, and actions not only in relation to its self, and to its multiple diverse relations to others, but also in relation to divine law, civil law, and what Locke called laws of fashion, reputation, or opinion. Laws of fashion, reputation, or opinion that Locke claimed most people privileged over the others, were different in different "societies, tribes and clubs of men in the world" at different times; but they were always established by "a secret and tacit Consent" among people, to reward some opinions, forms of expression and conduct with praise and reputation and punish others with discredit and contempt. Other ideas of the self that modern scholars have found in the period attach here. It was by considering the self in relation to divine law, that eighteenth-century clergy and philosophizing Christians, described a person's true self as consisting of the immortal substance of the soul, or more naturalistically, of some invisible rational substance that persists through all changes including death into the afterlife. It was by considering the self in relation to the law of fashion that people conceived of themselves and others as well-bred, sociable beings who politely masked boredom, displeasure, hatred, ambitions, selfish interests, and natural physical functions under polished and amiable manners – convinced by the law of opinion that this conduct of the polite was at once the summum of civilization and the source of deception, masks, and disguise. This was the self that we now call "performative," "masquerading" or "divided." It was also by considering themselves in relation to the law of opinion that, from the seventeenth century through Romanticism, people conceived of themselves as porous "sensible" selves, buffeted by "boisterous passions" or moved to pity despite themselves by the suffering of others, who were by nature open and passively subject to sway and declension from the outside, by the language, rhetoric, emotions, watching eyes, or social disapproval of others.[35] As Locke stressed, the cultural "archetypes" contained in these "laws" were different in different historical periods and in different "societies, tribes and clubs of men in the world."

Considered in these terms, letters documented the ways in which the self situated its self in a complex network of contemporary social and cultural relations. Each letter showed a self as it considered and represented its self on a particular occasion in relation to a specific, but necessarily transient, nexus of relationships – relations of the self to its self and of its present to its past, social relations to others, and cultural relations to social archetypes and the approved models of opinion, conduct, and style. These were relations that narrative-epistolary novelists were careful to indicate in the narratives framing embedded letters. And it was why to read a letter in full or partial ignorance of the occasion on which it was written and of the social relations and cultural archetypes it assumed was to misinterpret the letter, to misread the relationships that had shaped it, and to mistake the self that had authored it.

When we discover serial, alternative, relative, or fashionable selves in letters or fiction now, after poststructuralism and Judith Butler, we speak of these selves as artificial and essentially fictional constructs. We say that writers were "writing the self into existence" or people theatrically performing a role. For Locke, however, serial, alternating, relative, and fashionable selves were not fictions. They were perfectly real: they existed in consciousness and manifested in word and deed in the society around him. Occasional selves could be observed; and they could be lost sight of. The same did not hold for the terms or narratives that others produce to connect our transitory and discontinuous selves, acts, utterances, or letters to each other across time. Locke made a famous distinction between the "Man" and the "Person" to indicate that the continuity in time of the real physical organism we call "man" does not extend to the "person," except as an analogical fiction. Person is what "another" calls our self. (ii.xxvii.20) It is unlike our own sense of our self, in that others "presume" that we are the same person, drunk and sober, sleeping and waking, whether we are able to remember what we said and did or not. Person is an *ascribed* identity. It is also what Locke calls a "Forensick Term" – person was the term used in law to "appropriate Actions and their Merit" to men for purposes of judgment, so that men could be held responsible, and rewarded or punished, for "their" acts and opinions. We treat selves as persons whenever we judge whether their words, conduct, or opinions agree with divine law, civil law, or the laws of opinion or reputation currently in fashion. We perform a similar forensic act in Theophrastic descriptions of a person's character that emphasize a dominant trait, in attributing a "moral character" to others, or in narrating their *Lives*. For Locke, whether or not such constructions of the "Person" correspond to anything that exists or ever existed has to be investigated empirically each time, in a separate and subsequent act of comparison that measures the ascription of identity in someone's mind, letter, or narrative against what plainly exists. Consider the legal proposition: "By Marriage the Husband and Wife become one Person in Law; which Unity is the Principal Foundation of their respective Rights, Duties and Disabilities."[36] This is a person who plainly does not exist; it is a legal fiction.

This meant that for Locke and his eighteenth-century followers another person's true character or identity was not only difficult to know, but in a sense intrinsically secret. Like things, another person could only be known empirically from their secondary qualities – their written or spoken words, their demeanors, any acts that appeared on the occasion or occasions when they could be observed – or from reports and hearsay based on the same kinds of data. As Jonathan Kramnick put it, other people's "mental states are never observable;" "the self is accessible only through the world of social forms."[37] But considered empirically in these terms, people possessed multiple shifting selves in a culture where they normatively assumed a variety of social forms according to their rank and "relative duties" and according to the occasion and relationship to others in which they stood in the moment – as Locke indicated, a single man could be master, servant, lord, farmer, magistrate, father, son, brother, cousin, acquaintance, friend, husband, lover, and more. Considered empirically, then, a person not only possessed as many "occasional" selves as they had relationships and occasion for them; they were also "constantly losing sight of past selves" as their immediate "concernments" changed. Since the fixed identities people ascribed to others as "persons" failed to correspond to their shifting sense of their own selves, and since "characters" that were legitimately assumed could also be illegitimately aped, determining the "true" character of others empirically was not a straightforward matter. In an era, when different alphabets or scripts were reserved for men and women at different ranks and for different domains of culture, and when an accomplished writer mastered multiple scripts, a letter-writer too assumed different characters (in both senses) for different letters, and could use his characters (in both senses) to deceive.

The spread of polite manners from the court to the town at the turn of the eighteenth century aggravated these difficulties by spreading courtly practices of dissimulation down the social hierarchy. The bland, indistinguishable "viziers" that Shaftesbury and Fielding complained descended on everyone who politely masked dis-agreeable sentiments, immoral habits, ambition, self-interest or hatred under an agreeable, well-bred manner, as polished gentlemen, vicious libertines and would-be gentlemen did, certainly facilitated sociability; but such viziers also complicated with socially sanctioned hypocrisies the difficulty of discerning a person's true character on the basis of what presented to one's view.[38] Social identities were fluid too, given the increasingly ubiquitous social and geographical mobility in Britain and the empire, the growing rivalry between wealth and birth in the determination of rank, and the impact on social standing of stellar financial gains and losses, or of fateful deaths, marriages and remarriages. Social identities now seemed as easily gained, changed, forgotten, or lost as characters or reputations, and they too could be aped. Indeed, in some circumstances, it was legitimate to ape them: when someone's social situation changed – when an apprentice became a journeyman or a journeyman a master – they were expected to adopt the "character" incumbent upon them in their new station. Nor was it necessarily easy to compare ascribed identities to what plainly exists. For while natural and social reality plainly existed "out there," independently of consciousness, we only know it as it impinges on our consciousness – as it comes within the range of our observation or not, as we take notice of it or not, as we reflect on it or not, as we remember, forget or bring it back to consciousness. We know reality empirically only as retained and processed by our minds; and as narrative-epistolary novelists demonstrated against those who puffed the virtues of empiricism in history, jurisprudence and science, this left a lot of room for error. Empirical verification was, after all, just another fallible operation of the mind.

While remaining the object of investigation and secret of the plot, this enigmatic, protean occasional self traveled over time, in the novels we are about to encounter, from the mainstream of social life to its margins, and from conscious performance to the inner life.

For a century after Behn's *Love Letters*, secrets of identity in female-authored narrative-epistolary fiction generally attached to the occasional selves of other characters – to lovers and gallants, parents and guardians, female friends and older female mentors – rather than to the mistaking heroine. The question that ricochets through them is Amoranda's question of Formator/Alanthus in *The Reform'd Coquet*: "Who are you—in reality?" Contrary to what has been argued, late seventeenth- and eighteenth-century protagonists did have complex interiorities marked by consciousness, reasoning, passions, desires, and ambitions.[39] Indeed, in women-authored novels, protagonists were often overwhelmed by lust and ambition, passion and desire; they had faults and made egregious and exemplary errors. But they were rarely mysteries to themselves. The "business of inner meaning" that mattered most was the inner meaning of others, because the mental states of others were not observable, and because the key difficulty in a society where people depended on a network of familial and personal relationships for all the necessaries of life, was to detect who *others* really were and discover what *they* were concealing, in order to know whom one could safely believe and trust. A key goal for early narrative-epistolary women novelists was therefore "to open the Understanding of young Readers, to distinguish between real Worth and superficial Appearances" and to "make them discern" the passions and "intrigues in practice" underlying courtships and domestic and social interactions, because ignorance or errors here caused young people "to make shipwreck of their Fortune."[40] Narrative-epistolary novelists deployed Theophrastian typologies that indicated "what values to attach to different classes or types of person" or "moral character" conceived as a predominantly virtuous or vicious disposition that runs through all the selves, roles, social and cultural relations, cultural archetypes, and disguises that empirical subjects might assume, to show readers how to determine a priori who could and could not be trusted. But they also deployed them to question underlying suppositions: that typologies correspond to inner meaning, and that moral character is sufficiently obvious to be serviceable.[41] A related issue that concerned women writers later, after the legitimization of circumstantial evidence, was the danger that the heroine's own words, actions, and performance of social roles would be misread, by a suitor, husband or family member, or by friends and acquaintances, on whom ladies depended for their economic maintenance, social identity, sociality, reputation, and/or home. Whether married or unmarried, virtuous women paid a heavy price for being thought something they were not.

The protean occasional self gained new but more ambivalent life with the posthumous publication in 1774 of Chesterfield's *Letters to His Son*. Recommending secrecy, impassivity, dissimulation, and disguise, Chesterfield showed his son how to use occasional selves to his advantage in the polite social and political circles in which he wished him to move – "We must like the chameleon put on the hue of the persons we wish to be well with." Though his advice was met with outrage in some quarters, others said that "Lord Chesterfield did but speak out what the greatest part of mankind, and all of polite society, ...practice in silence." His maxims were, accordingly, disseminated in conduct books for gentlemen and would-be gentlemen, such as Trusler's *Principles of Politeness and Knowledge of the World* (1778), which promised to supply the morality missing in Chesterfield's "system" while using that system to make their readers, like Chesterfield, "the complete man of the world."[42] This provoked further outrage. Occasional selves began to characterize wicked men of the world in novels such as Samuel Jackson Pratt's *The Pupil of Pleasure* (1776), Henry Mackenzie's *The Man of the World* (1773), or Maria Edgeworth's *Belinda* (1801), which sought to domesticate gentlemen as well as ladies. Before Edgeworth reformed him, Clarence Hervey's "chameleon character seemed to vary in different lights according to the different situations in which he happened to be placed," enabling him to "be all things to all men and all women." The occasional self had begun to be marginalized.

Victorian novels that used occasional selves to characterize scandalously recalcitrant individuals or groups, such as criminals and ethnic or class outsiders, positioned them squarely at the margins of decent, orderly Victorian society. Like Oedipus and Odysseus, these outsiders were frequently characters without apparent antecedents like Becky Sharpe or Lady Audley, or orphans and foundlings whose parentage was unknown, like those in Dickens who took on any character that environment, education, or self-advancement dictated. These upstarts and intruders not only obscured their evil, ambitious, self-advancing plots behind charming facades, as philanderers, gallants, and false lovers had once done; they carried eighteenth-century occasional selves into an era when those who dared to "lose sight of [their] past selves" as they moved on, were criminalized or pathologized under the new, mid-nineteenth-century term, "multiple personalities." Mystery attached to occasional selves who successively inhabited multiple names and identities by exploiting social and geographical mobility to "move away from old situations," to live a series of "disconnected lives" and to "conceal their past from view."[43] Mystery was also localized in a protagonist's inwardness, where it hid behind what Elizabeth Mary Braddon dubbed "the iron mask" of self-control that social norms imposed. Repressed by what Carlyle called "the Clothes of a Man (the woolen, the fleshly, the official Bank-paper and State-Paper Clothes)," the "inscrutable venerable Mystery" that was "the Man himself" often made protagonists a mystery to themselves.[44] Victorian novelists used protean characters such as these to scrutinize the mystery of what drove those who passed for ladies and gentlemen to adultery, bigamy, madness, or crime. They turned their detective powers on those who culpably deceived respectable Victorians by seeming to fit in, and who kept their deceptions going by adopting serial identities while keeping their true origins, histories, motives, identities, and/or criminal actions, secret.[45] Where eighteenth-century narrative-epistolary fictions plunged their protagonists into the contemporary "culture of secrecy" in interpersonal, domestic and social life, then, their nineteenth-century successors centered "mystery" and what Thackeray called "riddles of character" on what was being banished from consciousness and from respectable middle-class British life.[46]

Continuities and Historical Shifts

There were, of course, significant differences between eighteenth- and nineteenth-century British cultures, and for purposes of academic topography and mental mapping, this section briefly outlines two that significantly impacted narrative-epistolary fiction. But it is important to remember also that changes did not come about all at once – they appear unevenly, in bits and pieces, emerging and disappearing sometimes several times, before taking root – and that there are also persistent, underlying continuities that should not be overlooked.

One reason for such continuities is that, until the advent of the telegraph in 1859, letters remained the only available technology for distance communication even in the same district or town. Once their use began spread down the social hierarchy in the late 1600s, letters became increasingly central not only to the business of nation and empire but also to the management and intercourse of everyday life at most ranks. Since the speed, cost, and publicity of telegrams (which were charged by the word) promoted urgent, minimalist and cryptic messaging, the primacy of letters, notes and cards in interpersonal, commercial, and official communications between people who were not physically present to each other, began to wane only with the twentieth-century spread of the telephone. It was therefore odder to ignore letters – as novelists did in many first- and third-person narratives that claimed to be realistic – than it was to employ the narrative-epistolary novel's characteristic scaffolding to represent epistolary communications as intrinsic to ordinary life and to examine letters critically – like manners, dress or conversation – for what they did and did not "show."

Another reason for continuities in narrative-epistolary fiction is that many Victorian authors were hauntingly familiar with seventeenth- and eighteenth-century writing, and treated it as the tradition against which they defined their individual talent. Some, like Thomas Babington Macaulay, had little good to say in public about the characters and writerly performances of the previous century, while remaining addicted in private to its circulating library fiction. But others expressed their admiration for eighteenth-century writers and writings; and some not only acknowledged their debts, but explained their adaptations. Charles Lamb made a strong case for preferring the "Utopia of gallantry" and the "imaginary freedom" provided by Congreve, Farquhar, Wycherley, and Sheridan in "the Artificial Comedies of the Last Century," to the nineteenth-century's "all-consuming drama of common life, where the moral point is everything."[47] Walter Scott wrote critical prefaces to works by many of the major eighteenth-century novelists and mentioned all the period's principal women writers at least in passing. Jane Austen admired Charlotte Lennox, Francis Burney, Charlotte Smith, and Maria Edgeworth, as well as Richardson and Fielding, and demonstrated her debts to her female narrative-epistolary precursors in technical as well as thematic ways.[48] Thackeray showed his admiration for Henry Fielding and extensive knowledge of seventeenth- and eighteenth-century history in the first pages of his first novel, *Catherine* (1839–1834). He set two further novels in the eighteenth century, including *Henry Esmond* (1852), which Anthony Trollope came to consider "the greatest novel in the English language," perhaps because it resembled his own youthful "castles in the air."[49] At the beginning of his own writing career, Trollope concluded, on the basis a course of reading which traced the development of prose fiction from Aphra Behn to his own time, that *Pride and Prejudice* – an obviously narrative-epistolary novel – was the greatest novel yet written in English. Trollope, who repeatedly alluded to eighteenth-century writers in his novels, also explained how changes in epistolary practices during the Victorian era impacted the realism of narrative-epistolary novels in his own time:

> Who is there can write letters to all his friends, or would not find it dreary work to do so even in regard to those whom he really loves? When there is

something palpable to be said, what a blessing is the penny post! To one's
wife, to one's child, one's mistress, one's steward if there be a steward; one's
gamekeeper, if there be shooting forward; one's groom, if there be hunting;
one's publisher if there be a volume ready or money needed; or one's tailor
occasionally, if a coat is required, a man is able to write. But what has a man
to say to his friend,–for that matter what has a woman? A Horace Walpole
may write to a Mr. Mann about all the things under the sun, London gossip
or transcendental philosophy, and if the Horace Walpole of the occasion
can write well, and will labour diligently in that vocation, his letters may be
worth reading by his Mr. Mann and by others; but for the maintenance of
love and friendship, continued correspondence between distant friends is
nought. . . . If your friend leave you, and seek a residence in Patagonia, make
a niche for him in your memory, and keep him there as warm as you may.
Perchance he may return from Patagonia and the old joys may be repeated.
But never think that the old joys can be maintained by the assistance of
ocean postage, let it be at never so cheap a rate.[50]

By the second half of the nineteenth century, then, short utilitarian letters
to suppliers of goods and services and to members of one's household that
were sent through the Penny Post, had supplanted the eighteenth-century
practice of writing long, informative, and entertaining letters to maintain
relationships at a distance with one's "friends." Indeed, if Trollope's
narrator is to be believed, it was no longer certain that letters *could*
successfully maintain love or friendship between people separated by
time and distance. The long letters of news to family and friends containing accounts of places, people, and events and reflections or arguments
based upon them, which had been prevalent in eighteenth-century life and
had proved so serviceable to epistolary novelists, were prevalent no more.
This suggests that Trollope was relying on his readers' familiarity with the
ubiquity of such letters in earlier narrative-epistolary fiction to naturalize
the many long letters containing such material that he embedded in his
own novels and enable them to pass as "real."

There were other differences between Enlightenment and Victorian uses
of letters too. In eighteenth-century face-to-face societies, where the "household-family" was the basic economic, social, and administrative unit of the
polity and the "little society" of the family was considered analogical to the
"great society" of the state, people in all walks of life worked with and
depended upon their "friends" – meaning their families, relatives, patrons,
and intimates – for jobs, advancement, services, sociality, welfare, and
support.[51] In the letters as well as in the relationships of people who
depended on a network of familial and personal relationships for all the
necessaries of life, the personal, the social, the commercial, the domestic, the

political, and the public often intermixed. People's identities were likewise
understood to be a function of their relationships. As we saw in the previous
section, eighteenth-century selves were conceived and represented as fluid,
contingent, occasional and in some ways intrinsically deceptive, precisely
because the empirical self was defined by, and created in the course of, the
successive, ever-changing occasions and relationships in which it concealed
and revealed itself. For these reasons, and because most letters were read
aloud and shared in family, social, and institutional settings, the primary
meaning of "private" was still clandestine or "secret" – not "published to the
world" but actively and purposefully withheld from the eyes and ears of
others. In this period, then, most letters were not "private" either in this or in
the later sense. As Clare Brant observes, eighteenth-century familiar letters
were "personal" rather than "private."[52] One wrote to a correspondent about
matters of personal or mutual concern in the knowledge that one's letter
would be read aloud and discussed with their family and/or friends, some of
whom one also knew, and that it might also be read by strangers in the Secret
Office at the Post.

But sometime during the nineteenth century (opinions vary as to date),
the household-family ceased to be the primary locus of production.[53] The
workplace separated from the household; the wage-earning or entrepre-
neurial "individual" replaced the household-family as the basic unit of the
polity; and the "public-private divide" set in. The "home" came to be
viewed as a more or less stable, private or personal space, separate from
work and marginal to the greater society, an "inside" as opposed to the
"outside" of labor, commerce, government, public objects, and public
events. People too were conceived as having an "inside," as well as
a coherent and more or less consistent "outside" that they presented to
the world. They were now supposed to have a self in the sense of a single
core identity, as well as an inner life that was largely indiscernible from the
"outside" through the self they presented to the world. Ideally, self-
command repressed any fluid, tumultuous or anti-social contents of their
inner life and kept individuals consistently and recognizably themselves
even when they "developed" as a result of their experiences. As individuals
acquired public and private selves, the personal letters they wrote to family
members or friends (now only meaning intimates) became "private" in the
sense of normatively restricted and withheld from public view. Private
letters were clearly distinguished from the more impersonal, formal, public
epistolary communications belonging to business, trade, and officialdom.
And as a genre in which an individual's own ideas, opinions, subjective
impressions, arguments, and life-experiences could be expressed, "private"

letters lost many of the letter's erstwhile instrumental functions, and came to encapsulate private or subjective experience instead. Scott and Anne Bronte aligned the letter with the diary as a private, subjective, confessional form; while Anthony Trollope contrasted private letters with official letters, formal cards, and the "public print" of newspapers and telegraphs. However, the privacy of letters was also qualified by the post-office scandal of 1840, which revealed to the unsuspecting that the eighteenth-century post-office's "secret office" was still in operation, opening, reading and copying letters, and thus that the postal system was not yet as safely private, anonymous, and depersonalized as it later became.

A second significant difference between the Enlightenment and the Victorians concerns fiction's relation to history. Though some effort was made to distinguish what we now call "history" from what we now call "literature," the eighteenth century still acknowledged profound resemblances between the two, resemblances that had been obvious to the learned since classical times and that were still inscribed in the language. In eighteenth-century English, a "History" was a story (as *histoire* still is in modern French). There were "true histories," "secret histories," "familiar histories," and "marvelous histories." What we call novels were often entitled Histories – *The History of Miss Betsy Thoughtless* (1751), *The History of the Life and Adventures of Mr. Anderson* (1754), *Clarissa or the History of a Young Lady* (1747–1748). Newspapers provided the public with a "history of the times," while people recounting their own lives gave auditors their "history" or readers, the "history of their own time." These kinds of texts, which we now distinguish, were all histories to the Enlightenment because they were all stories, connected narratives of people and events. At the same time, with the rise of empiricism, "true" history came to occupy a second position on the Enlightenment "Circle of the Sciences:" history was a science, a fact-based form of knowledge, whose two "eyes" were chronology and geography, as well as what it had been since antiquity, one of the rhetorical, philological or belletristic subjects alongside other narrative genres.[54]

In practice, both true and fictional histories moved within these parameters, often as rivals chasing each other's tails. Like their classical predecessors, eighteenth-century neoclassical and conjectural historians used common literary devices: they "emplotted" their narratives, attributed motives to historical actors, put invented speeches into their mouths and strove, in Bolingbroke's words to "transport the attentive reader back to the very time" and enable him to "live with the men who lived before [him] and inhabit countries [he] never saw." History was "philosophy teaching by example:" like Sidney's poet or eighteenth-century didactic novels, history taught practical moral philosophy by embodying the precept in the example and distributing "historical justice" at the end – unmasking the villain whom "experience could not unmask for a time," and justifying "the honest man who has been misunderstood and defamed."[55] From the middle of the eighteenth century, true history added to its remit to memorialize monarchs and public, political events, accounts of cultural phenomena, and of social relations in society at large – matters relevant to ordinary life that had until then largely been the province of fiction.[56] "True history," or History proper, was thus constituted by narratives that partook of prose fiction: their subject-matter increasingly overlapped with that of novels; they employed the same literary devices as prose fictions and had the same didactic, moralizing, and exemplifying goals; and they too were at once true and invented.

On the other hand, the prose fictions that descended from Secret Histories, like those of Aphra Behn or Eliza Haywood, were, like true histories, frequently "founded in fact," as their subtitles and prefaces often stressed. "Secret" or "Procopian" history was a classical genre that revealed the scandalous character, conduct, and intrigues of emperors, kings, and courts which official historians dared not make public. Early in the eighteenth century, secret historians turned from this Procopian practice of revealing what monarchs and courts concealed from the public to that of revealing the hidden and often scandalous, amatory and domestic conduct in genteel or aristocratic families, to produce the familiar "histories of private life" that we now call amatory, courtship, and domestic novels.[57] As modern critics have observed, novels made readers peeping Toms, *voyeurs* into the private business and secret affairs of others. But contrary to what we used to think, these others were not necessarily entirely invented or imaginary. Fictional secret histories of the court like those of Aphra Behn, Delarivier Manley, or Eliza Haywood disguised real events and the clandestine intrigues of real, historical actors in fictional names and/or locations.[58] Other eighteenth-century fictions that we once thought entirely invented did the same. This practice continued into the nineteenth century – for instance, in Leonora Sansay's *Secret History; Or the Horrors of San Domingo* (1808); in Anthony Trollope's *Palliser novels* (1864–1879) or in the sensational nineteenth-century novels whose plots were borrowed from the newspapers. The "familiar histories" or "histories of private life" that we categorize as amatory, courtship, seduction, or domestic fiction were, of course, also founded in fact in a second, broader sense, inasmuch as they addressed issues arising from contemporary cultural practices, and described places and kinds of character and relationship that were recognizable to contemporary readers from experience and hearsay.

As Isaac Watts' widely used *Logick* affirmed and David Hume still acknowledged in his *Treatise*, this meant that all histories mixed truth and invention, fact and fiction, whether they were marketed as true or as fictional.[59] During the eighteenth century, this confluence also conformed to the condition of all knowledge. When human organs perceived only the superficial or "secondary qualities" of things that those organs were capable of registering, and the-thing-itself could not be known, humans walked in what Addison called "an enchanted world" – a solidly existing world but one in which "we are everywhere entertained with pleasing shows and apparitions."[60] Only once reality was thought to be fully knowable from its immediately apparent surfaces to its underlying causes and inner laws, did it become both possible and necessary to assert that reality could be fully and accurately captured in and through language too. To appropriate for History all authoritative truth about past reality on a newly established sequential timeline that distanced the past from the present and the future, nineteenth-century historians insisted that history was as different from novels as facts from fictions and documents from inventions. In other words, they used binary oppositions to erase family resemblances between true and fictional histories and conceal their hybrid middle ground.

The riposte of some novelists to claims made for "true history" at the turn of the nineteenth century was to write "historical novels," which, as Thomas Babington Macaulay observed (echoing Bolingbroke's description of true history) "make the past present, bring the distant near, place us in the society of great men" or on the "eminence that overlooks the field of mighty battles" and thus "appropriate a duty" that "properly belongs to the historian." Macaulay complained that historical novelists had left to historians only the less "poetic" but more rational and mundane task of extracting "philosophy" from history by "direct[ing] our judgment of events and men, trac[ing] the connection of cause and effect, and draw[ing] from the occurrences of former times general lessons of moral and political wisdom."[61] Realist novelists, in turn, responded to claims that History alone dealt in facts by proclaiming that they too were "documenting" the real and by emphasizing their novels' historicity. As Barry Waller has shown, they also historicized their stories by setting them thirty or forty years before the publication date; by "intermix[ing] past and present times;" by introducing "references to the past which emphasize the historicity of the present;" and/or by showing how "the thrust of historical meaning is encapsulated in places and spaces."[62] Embedded letters were particularly serviceable here. As Charles Lamb explained, there was an inevitable "confusion of tenses" between letter-writer and reader(s) because "the grand solecism of *two presents*," which "is in a degree common to all postage" ensures that "news from me must become history to you." This solecism made letter-readers historians.[63] To put it differently: to frame a transcribed letter with narrative describing its writing and reading was to juxtapose (at least) two vivid presents, as well as to insert a historical past into the present of reading, and thus to turn character-readers and novel-readers into historians, whether they profess to be reading histories or not. This "confusion of tenses" in epistolary exchanges was only complicated in novels like *Villette* where, in addition, the first-person narrator herself inhabits (at least) two presents as (re)reader of her own erstwhile correspondences and historian of her own past.

At the same time, Victorian narrative-epistolary novelists remained faithful to a generic form that had once cemented the union of history, secret history, and romance. During the 1680s, when she wrote part 2 of *Love Letters*, her fictional secret history of Ford Lord Grey's elopement with Lady Henrietta Berkeley, Behn's use of narrative-epistolary form contained a three-fold allusion: to seventeenth-century French Romances, which embedded letters in their narratives of star-crossed lovers; to seventeenth-century histories, which routinely inserted transcribed letters in the body of their narratives to present "the original Instruments and authentick Evidence" as "Vouchers for what they set down;"[64] and to non-fictionalized secret histories, which likewise often inserted transcribed letters in their narratives to authenticate their revelations of what had transpired behind closed doors. As Anthony Grafton has shown, this practice of including transcriptions of whole letters in the body of historical narratives fell into desuetude during the eighteenth century with the rise of the footnote.[65] Elimination of embedded letters from the text and their replacement by footnoted references shifted the significance of retaining the older narrative-epistolary form. Catherine Macaulay complained during the 1760s that eliminating "prolax quotation" of letters from a historian's narrative silenced the voice of historical actors and changed the balance of power between narrator and readers. She argued that conjectural historians such as Hume, who willfully "conversed in generals" and replaced transcriptions of letters and speeches with their own narrative representations of characters and events, sought "not truth but victory" over their readers, and taught "passive obedience" and "necessary servitude" in the act of reading. Elimination or selective citation of snippets of actors' letters gave the narratives of historians "tyrannical, unbridled power" over past actors and events and subordinated readers to the narrator-historian's representations and didactic designs without recourse. By contrast, Macaulay's continued inclusion of full transcriptions of letters and speeches in the pages of her *History of England from the Accession of James I* (1763), allowed readers to use them to "investigate" and judge for themselves her narrative's "labour to attain truth."[66] Embedding letters and speeches was democratic, for this enabled each reader to decide whether or how far letters confirmed the narrator-historian's claims, and to catch any misreadings, biases, or blind-spots in the historian's narrative of events. There was a further shift during the nineteenth century, when a new class of professionals and statisticians was extending empirical investigation into all areas of life, since the omniscient narrator could now be taken or mistaken for the embodiment of positivism's ideal of total, all-encompassing, objective knowledge of reality and truth. Like their reintroduction of supposedly subjective, epistemologically discredited genres such as the first-person testimony or confession and the diary or journal, and their interest in marginalized or criminalized characters, Victorian writers' redeployment of narrative-epistolary form often became a vehicle for interrogating, relativizing or countering positivism's objective, depersonalizing, quantifying and generalizing regime of truth. These shifting functions of narrative-epistolary form support Franco Moretti's argument that in "the novel ... the pre-modern imaginary continues to pervade the capitalist world" because premodern features "are not archaic residues, but functional articulations of ideological needs."[67] They also remind us that to study narrative-epistolary scaffolding is to work with open sets.[68]

CHAPTER I

Framing Narratives and the Hermeneutics of Suspicion

Introduction: The Great Tradition from Aphra Behn to Jane Austen

When Henry Fielding embedded two satirical letters in *Joseph Andrews* in 1742, he and Samuel Richardson were still aspiring newcomers on the novel-writing scene. Eliza Haywood's enormous popularity as a narrative-epistolary novelist dated from 1719, when her first novel *Love in Excess* outsold *Robinson Crusoe*; and Aphra Behn's *Love Letters between a Nobleman and his Sister* (1684–1687) had recently been reprinted for the ninth time.[1] Modeling an Enlightenment hermeneutics of suspicion, both women authors had used their narrative frames to warn readers against taking letters at face value as honest brokers of their authors' thoughts and feelings. In *Joseph Andrews*, Fielding was alluding to their narrative-epistolary fiction as well as to Richardson's recent, wildly successful epistolary novel, *Pamela*, when he embedded a letter from Joseph to his sister, Pamela, at the outset of his third-person narrative. Critics who only recognized the allusion to *Pamela* argued that this letter continued Fielding's attack on Richardson's novel by showing that Joseph was as hypocritical and manipulative behind his "pretended innocence" as Pamela was in *Shamela*.[2] This critical reading assumed that a private letter *must* reveal the truth about a character – especially if it tells us something that other characters do not know. But a closer look shows that Fielding was conjoining the narrative and the letter to put this assumption in question, as Behn and Haywood had done.

Joseph's letter follows a comic scene in which Lady Booby repeatedly hints at her desire for a sexual relationship with her servant, while Joseph naively fails to understand her hints and takes her words at face value. What the narrator calls "the great purity of Joseph Andrews" is partly falsified by the letter, which reveals that Joseph has only pretended to be too innocent to understand what Lady Booby was about. The embedded letter thus reveals what is secretly going on behind what appears to the spectator-narrator who describes the seduction scene. Here the truth of the letter belies the truth of the narrative, by indicating that the narrative has not told us all we need to know about the characters or the scene. But the narrative then belies the truth of the letter. In the analogical seduction scene that follows the letter, Joseph fails to see Mrs. Slipslop's "violent amorous" assault upon him coming – he is literally saved by the bell; and there is no further instance of Joseph's supposed hypocrisy or manipulation in the novel. If anything, the narrative presents Joseph as possessing all the virtues that, in Fielding's view, Pamela lacked. We discover, at the end, that this is due to the secret of his birth and to the dramatic convention that made well-born children who were "lost," naturally virtuous and well-bred as a mark of their genteel origins. But revelation of the secret of Joseph's birth again belies the truth of the narrative, which has led us to believe that Joseph is a lower-class servant and Pamela's brother. This also reveals that the novel's whole narrative has been staged – staged as the narrative of Lady Booby's seduction scene was staged at the beginning, to deceive readers by not letting them into the secret of Joseph's character until the narrative was over and the letter produced.

Breaking the narrative plane with the embedded letter at the beginning therefore offers readers a holograph for how narrative will function in the novel. The reader who only laughs at Joseph's obtuseness about Lady Booby's hints and shakes his head at the revelation in the letter that Joseph understood them all along, is himself missing the strong hint that Fielding is giving his "sagacious reader" that the narrative will not tell him all he needs to know. But the letter is as deceptive as the narrative: for Joseph's boast in the letter about realizing that Lady Booby has designs on his chastity when she is lying naked in her bed is rendered ridiculous by his failure to realize immediately afterward, that Mrs. Slipslop has the same design when she invites him to drink a glass of ratafia with her, fully clothed. Joseph's letter is partly belied again several chapters later by his second letter to Pamela, after Lady Booby has dismissed him from her employ. Prefaced by the narrator's counterfactual observation that Joseph had until that moment "misunderstood the [sexual] drift of his mistress," this second letter contains a revised version of Joseph's thoughts during the Lady Booby seduction scene: "I am glad she turned me out of the chamber as she did: for I had once almost forgotten every word Parson Adams had ever said to me" about chastity being "a great virtue in a man." (38, 37) Narrative and letters are thus *both* unreliable; indeed, they are all the more deceptive because each is also partly true. As Hume would say, echoing Isaac Watts: all narratives are mixtures of truth and fiction, and here the letters are too.

Joseph Andrews thus demonstrated the folly of swallowing stories whole with abandon and willing suspension of disbelief, and the greater sagacity of reading them with skepticism and suspicion. The narrative-epistolary segments made the same point about letters by at once ridiculing and redeploying devices that Behn and Haywood characteristically used – discrepancies between framing narrative and letter; and comparison between disjunctive letters – to demonstrate the folly of reading letters as if they were straightforward expressions of thoughts and feelings and true accounts of events. Fielding subjected both narrative and letters to treatment that Michael McKeon regards as paradigmatic of "realism" –"the technique of combining the representation of the real with a more or less explicit reflection on its status as representation."[3] But he also indicated that he was more interested in directing suspicion at narrative representations than at epistolary ones. This distinguished him from Eliza Haywood, aka "Mrs. Novel," who at mid-century was Behn's most familiar, widely read, and prolific heir.

Fielding alluded to Haywood directly by parodying her *Philidore and Placentia* (1727) in the narrative-epistolary olio composed of Lady Booby's seduction scene and Joseph's letter.[4] In Haywood's novella, Placentia, a wealthy and high-born lady, who finds herself unaccountably drawn to her servant, Philidore, makes increasingly pressing and obvious advances to him. She does not know that Philidore is in reality an impoverished gentleman, who is passionately in love with her, and has disguised himself as a servant in order to be able to enter her household and see her every day. Thinking himself beneath her, Philidore resolutely repels each of his mistress's advances with one excuse after another, until the deadlock between them is resolved by an exchange of letters in which each confesses their love. Fielding's comic rewrite of these scenes from *Philidore and Placentia* teases his readers with the secret of Joseph's genteel birth, while foreshadowing the general course of his plot. For having broken his self-imposed silence about his love for Placentia, Philidore dismisses himself from Placentia's service and departs for a journey full of adventures, as Joseph does after Lady Booby dismisses him from his post. Fielding's ironical reference to his "sagacious readers" suggests that he expected few novel-readers to be "sagacious" enough to understand this "hint" of the secret of his plot on a first reading. Readers who believed whatever stories they were told were being set up for a fall.

In quarters of the academy where critics argue that we should return to aesthetics of "enchantment" and to a golden age when readers were pleasurably transported by fiction thanks to their uncritical surface reading of engaging texts, the "hermeneutics of suspicion" has been receiving the same bad press as "skepticism" and "freethinking" did during the eighteenth century.[5] I use the modern term here to remind us that the problem for mainstream Enlightenment educators, philosophers, and moralists was the inverse of current fears that suspicious academic hermeneutics are destroying students' reading pleasure. Enlightenment educators and moralists worried that "unlearned" readers, especially the young, the unsophisticated, and the unworldly, were too easily and unthinkingly enchanted – transported by heady fictions that left them ill-prepared to identify, much less defend themselves against, specious arguments, deceptive narratives, and persuasive lies. Rebecca Tierney-Hynes has described contemporary concerns about the seduction of figurative language and the affective impact of absorptive romance reading; but as Cathy Caruth showed, empiricist philosophers and critics were equally concerned about rhetoric's inculcation and deployment of persuasive forms of eloquence that were designed to mislead, and that swayed readers or auditors by circumventing their reason and their will.[6] As we will see in the next two sections, Behn and Haywood addressed these issues by using their narrative frames to demonstrate not only that credulous surface reading of letters was misleading, but also that women's particular susceptibility to "the Rhetoric of Love" and willingness to allow letters to rouse their imaginations and "sensibly affect" their passions put them "on the Path to Ruin." While contemporary letter manuals called letters "the Life of Love, the Loadstones that by rare/Attractions make Souls meet, and melt, and mix,"[7] they used their narrative-epistolary olios to warn those who lacked a gentleman's rhetorical education, that gentlemen's letters were artful rhetorical constructs, and love letters, only a kind of letter with its own rhetorical conventions.

The narrative-epistolary segments from *Joseph Andrews* described here formed part of an extended debate between Haywood, Fielding, and Richardson during the 1740s and early 1750s about their rival novel forms, which are addressed in section three ('Debating Novel Forms'). Writing Haywood back into literary history, which has focused exclusively on relations between Richardson and Fielding, this section retraces the concurrent debate between Haywood and Fielding that began in *Joseph Andrews* and culminated in *Betsy Thoughtless* and *Amelia*, and shows how the popularity and pressure of Haywood's narrative-epistolary fictions shaped the development of both men's novels. This triangular debate is important to any study of narrative-epistolary fiction for what it reveals about the strengths and weaknesses of their rival novel forms: narrative, narrative-epistolary, and epistolary. The last two sections ("Letters and Secret Histories' and 'Retrospective') look forward to the *locus classicus* of narrative-epistolary fiction, *Pride and Prejudice*, to show what Jane Austen appropriated and adapted from this debate, and how the novels, devices, and emplotments in this chapter inserted themselves in the Aristotelian Romance tradition to which we owe the mystery plot.

Establishing the Framing Convention: Behn's *Love Letters*, Part 2

As we know, Behn's *Love Letters between a Nobleman and his Sister* (1684) recounted, in disguised fictional form, the secret history of Ford Lord Grey's adultery with his sister-in-law, Lady Henrietta Berkeley, against the backdrop of Grey's much publicized adultery trial.[8] *Love Letters*, Part 1, inserted itself in Grey's trial as a discretely disguised print copy of the clandestine correspondence that Henrietta's sister claimed in court that Grey and Lady Henrietta had exchanged prior to their elopement, but could not produce. Consequently, the text was in an important sense "about letters, both present and absent."[9] The prefatory "Argument" to this first, entirely epistolary part stated that "the letters were found in their Cabinets at their house at St. Denice" and "are as exact as possible plac'd in the order they were sent."[10] As Janet Todd observes, Behn's letters between "Philander" and "Silvia" therefore passed in many quarters as the genuine secret correspondence of Lord Grey and Lady Henrietta.[11]

Part 2 of *Love Letters*, published a year later in 1685, describes the gradual breakup of the lovers' relationship after their flight to the continent, in a text that embeds thirty-eight letters in its 200 plus pages, many of them quite long; Warren Chernaik reckons that the proportion of letter to narrative is "roughly half and half."[12] What has not been noticed is that Part 2 also addressed the trial, but in a different way. It related to the trial's principal woman-centered portion, where a letter from Grey to Lady Berkeley was embedded in the latter's extended narrative about conspiring with Grey and her daughter to conceal their illicit passion and clandestine correspondence from her husband, the Earl. Lady Berkeley's framing narrative depicted her love for Henrietta and for Grey "as a son" and the "penitence" both repeatedly showed her through their words and tears. She explained that she had read Grey's cool letter of assurance that he would in future "avoid all places where I may possibly see the lady" as confirmation of his obedience to her commands and, in the context of the trial, as evidence that she had had no reason to suspect his honesty and good faith.[13] But the discrepancy between the pathetic, weeping, pleading, unmanned Grey she described in her narrative and his poised, sophisticated, and controlled letter to her – which was read aloud in court and reprinted in volumes of State Trials – showed how thoroughly she had misread both the letter and the man. A literal and naively credulous reader of letters and persons, Lady Berkeley had been deceived by her love for her children and by Grey's guile. The principal woman-centered portion of the trial thus turned on Lady Berkeley's misreading of a letter and a man. This was a primary issue that Behn used her narrative-epistolary olio to address in Part 2.

By embedding letters in her narrative in Part 2, Behn was not only re-presenting the form taken by this part of the trial. As we saw in the Introduction, she was redeploying a format that was also familiar from contemporary historical writing and from seventeenth-century French romances. There whole letters inserted in the text verbatim to authenticate the narrative were generally given perfunctory introductions and allowed to speak for themselves. Behn innovated by using her framing narratives to help naive readers avoid Lady Berkeley's and Henrietta/Silvia's dangerous credulity, by demonstrating that letters were rhetorical artifices – "a tissue of . . . conventions, codes and hidden signs, all needing careful handling" and "dangerous if misunderstood" – and by showing how and why they were misread.[14] Framing embedded letters with narrative about when and why they were written and how they were read enabled Behn to situate each letter in the immediate circumstances of its production and reception, as a response to the demands of a specific occasion; but introducing disjunctions between prefatory and reception narratives, and between these and fully transcribed letters enabled her to demonstrate, at the same time, how artfully letters were constructed and why they were misunderstood. My first two examples show Behn using her tripartite scaffolding structure – prefatory narrative, transcribed letter, reception narrative – to unmask epistolary snares by working with discrepancies between the character-writer's motives or goals, the letter written to attain them, and the way it was understood by a character-reader. These examples also foreground Behn's inclusion of letters that were not passionate expos-ures of the mind and heart after the manner of *The Portuguese Letters* (tr. 1678). Her insistence that instrumental, pedestrian letters, ordinary parts of the business of ordinary life, could be complex and easily misunderstood, was highly influential too.

At the beginning of part 2, Octavio, the charming and well-connected Dutchman who has befriended Philander and Silvia, writes a short note to Philander to inform him that the Council has decreed that he must leave the United Provinces within 24 hours or be delivered to the King of France. The backdrop has begun to shift from the secret history of Grey's adultery trial to the secret history of the Monmouth Rebellion (1785) and Grey's part in the conspiracy to mount an army to overthrow James II, Roman Catholic and pawn of France, and place his illegitimate but Protestant son, Monmouth, on the throne. The prefatory narrative to his note informs us that Octavio, who has fallen in love with Silvia and knows that Philander will have to leave Holland without her, "felt a secret Joy at the Thought of his Departure,"[15] which conflicts with his affection for his friend.

My Lord,

I had rather die than be the ungrateful Messenger of News, which I am sensible will prove so fatal to you, and which will be best expressed in fewest Words. 'Tis decreed, that you must retire from the United Provinces in four and twenty Hours, if you will save a Life that is dear to me and *Silvia,* there being no Security against your being render'd up to the King of France. Support it well and hope all things from the Assistance of your

Octavio
From the Council, Wednesday. (2: 139)

The narrative following this note turns to Philander's reception of it: "Philander, having finish'd the reading of this, remain'd a while wholly without Life or Motion, when coming to himself he sigh'd and cry'd . . . *rather than I'll abandon Silvia, I'll stay and be deliver'd up a Victim* . . . " (2:139) Philander grasps only part of the content of Octavio's letter – the decree that he must leave – and reacts to it with a storm of emotion. Consequently, he replies with a letter begging Octavio to use his influence with the Council to allow him to stay in a way which, as the narrative drily observes, "trusts much to the Friendship of Octavio, whose Power, join'd with that of his Uncle (. . . whom he had an Ascendant over, as his Nephew and his Heir) might serve him." (2: 140) By indicating the discrepancy between Octavio's thoughts and emotions when writing the letter and Philander's thoughts and emotions when reading it, the narrative shows novel-readers that Philander has brought to his reading of the letter a false assumption about its writer: the assumption that Octavio is unquestionably his friend. Philander has misread both the letter and the situation by "trusting much"– too much – to Octavio's friendship, which the prefatory narrative characterized as ambivalent. When

Philander acts on his misreading by crafting a letter to Octavio that the narrative tells us is intended to "move him to Compassion," (2:140) his letter is therefore misjudged. Philander's long letter, transcribed verbatim, vividly describes his passionate relationship to Silvia and the suffering their separation would cause him. This is misjudged because, rather than move Octavio to compassion, it provokes Octavio's jealousy and joy at his departure. Unsurprisingly, therefore, Philander's letter fails to achieve its object, and Octavio gracefully declines to help him stay.

The narrative framing thus provides novel-readers with a view of characters and events that the character-reader lacks, and shows us how and why even a short, basically factual, epistolary communication can be misread. Using the framing narrative to indicate disjunctions between the letter's writing and reading, shows that Octavio's letter is both factually true and less than honest – it conceals desires and calculations inimical to friendship and contains sentences such as "I would rather die" than tell you this, which are manifestly untrue. This complicates homosociality with self-interest, and masculine friendship with rivalry, even as it demonstrates that a letter can be at once true and false. But the letter also silently indicates lacunae in the narrative: this does not mention that Philander has ignored the political significance of the Council's decision, or that he has neglected to ask himself why a "friend" who promises his assistance and has such "ascendancy" over his uncle and the Council, makes no attempt to use it.

Behn developed a different version of her framing device for a letter in Philander's correspondence with Brilliard, his servant and Silvia's putative husband: here the prefatory narrative is focused on the writing process and expanded to include Brilliard's re-reading of his own letter. Philander had written to Brilliard after his departure from the United Provinces, requesting that Brilliard act as his "spy on [Silvia's] virtue" and that he "feign all dilatory excuses to prevent Silvia from coming to him" because Philander was embarking on "a new Affair of Gallantry." (2:163) Brilliard responds with a letter expressing loyalty and service, which tells Philander that Silvia has been grieving at his departure, that Octavio has been trying to comfort her, and that though he has not yet succeeded with her, Octavio has become Silvia's suitor – all of which is, strictly speaking, true. However, the truth, language and tone of Brilliard's letter and Philander's unsuspecting reading of it are belied by the prefatory narrative that tells us that "to act the Hypocrite with his Lord was [Brilliard's] business," and describes Brilliard's calculations, prior to writing, about "how to manage [Philander] to his best Advantage." Brilliard does not want the "malice" he feels toward Silvia after her rejection of his sexual advances to become evident in his letter and decides that "to be the greatest Enemy you ought to seem the greatest Friend." (2:165) Focalizing through his mind, the narrative describes Brilliard's subsequent critical re-reading of his own letter "to see whether he had cast it to his Purposes" (2:169) – he is concerned, for instance, that his portrayal of Silvia's sorrow at their parting was too moving and might reawaken Philander's love. The framing narrative thus demonstrated to novel-readers that letters were artful compositions which men designed with care to move their addressee in calculated ways. Epistolography was an art of rhetoric. Novel-readers who reread Brilliard's transcribed letter with this guidance in mind will notice how his presentation of the truth maliciously insinuates that Silvia may already have succumbed to Octavio, and see how this letter serves a self-interested Brilliard, who wants Silvia for himself, by intimating that Philander need feel no remorse for abandoning her for another woman.

Taken together, these letters show Philander to be a credulous and unsuspicious reader who accepts without question both the expressions of loyalty and service in Brilliard's letter and the professions of friendship and assistance in Octavio's. He does so most obviously because he is blinded by passion and desire – desire to remain with Silvia in one case, desire to pursue a new gallantry in the other. But this is not the only cause of his blindness, as the letters show. Philander does not "doubt" his servant's "Faith and Friendship" or Octavio's friendship and "assistance," because he expects each man to conduct himself according to the quasi-feudal norms of hierarchical ancient regime societies, where "friends" were patrons who assisted and protected their clients, and it was a servant's duty to obey his master and put the latter's interests above his own.[16] Brilliard plays on such expectations in his letter – "'Tis not my business, my Lord, to advise or counsel but to obey" (2:166) – as does Octavio with his "Hope all things from the Assistance of your Octavio." There is irony in Philander's unthinking dependence on others to act in accordance with norms of masculine "Faith and Friendship" in the patriarchal family and patriarchal state, which he himself has disregarded by seducing Silvia in her father's house and by conspiring with Monmouth against the king. Philander expects men's letters and actions to sustain what contemporaries called their "character" by conforming to the "established functions and roles" of their rank and position relative to him.[17] His erroneous reading of their polite and accomplished letters derives from taking both men and their letters at face value, and failing to look beyond the characters they assumed to the personal interests of the beings who assumed them, which their missives conceal and more darkly, reveal.

As Ros Ballaster observes, "the introduction of an omniscient narrative voice [in part 2] provides more interpretative guidance for the reader" than was provided by the purely epistolary form in Part 1.[18] One might add that Behn's introduction of this narrative voice while aping historical narratives that included "supporting documents quoted verbatim in the text proper" also marked a shift in focus between the two parts[19]: from the re-ordered archive to the worked-up historical text, and from the documentary-authenticating function of letters supposedly found in a cabinet at St. Denis, to the larger question of what a historian needs to know to correctly decipher the historical meaning(s) and import of epistolary communications. Here the interpretative guidance supplied by the narrator's framing narrative demonstrates the superiority of the secret historian, who reveals what others have concealed and what letters do not or cannot say, to the historian who merely inserts letters as authenticating documentary evidence and reads them, as Philander does, for what they seem to say. For the secret historian knows that the meaning(s) of epistolary documents and their role in a history cannot be rightly understood separately from what the narrator-historian's knowledge supplies in her framing narratives: the occasion for each letter; its author's unstated motives and designs; the rhetorical strategies he employed in writing it; his reasons for them; and the way(s) it was actually understood by its recipient(s) and acted upon (or not). Behn's disjunctions between prefatory narratives, letters, and reception narratives highlighted the difference between what a letter said and what its reader understood, to emphasize the importance to a history of discovering how a letter had actually been interpreted at the time. For characters acted on whatever they had taken from a letter rather than on all that it said. If Philander had read Octavio's note differently while he still passionately loved Silvia – if it had made him question Octavio's friendship or suspect that Octavio was his rival – would he have departed leaving Silvia behind under Octavio's care?

The secret historian knew that correct interpretation in the present of the historical significance of a letter written in the past required each letter to be situated in its own, possibly mercurial or erratic, history with a view to its actual historical effects. But Behn also inscribed the secret historian's awareness that a letter's meaning and function(s), its said and unsaid, cannot be fully discerned by viewing it solely as a bilateral exchange between writer and addressee. By delineating the forces, relationships and circumstances shaping what the letter said or left unsaid, as well as by supplying the crisscrossing correspondences of the principal actors, she showed that letters inhabit a multilateral web of historical relationships, knowledge of which is also required to interpret them correctly. The letter Brilliard writes to Philander as his "spy" is informed as much by Brilliard's fraught relationship with Silvia, by his knowledge of Philander's friendship with Octavio, by his perception of both men as his rivals, and by his awareness of Silvia's actual relationship to each man, as by Brilliard's own relationship to Philander as his servant or by his *penchant* for intrigue. Since Brilliard's letter is shaped by events and relationships that it does not mention, Philander's lack of some relevant information – notably, about Brillard's quarrel with Silvia over his marital rights and resentment at being a husband only in name – creates a blind spot that contributes to his misreading of Brilliard's letter, as much as his passions or his expectations of its author's character do.

The multilateral web of relationships in which letters are inserted serve additional functions during Silvia's *peripeteia* in Part 2 from a "controlled woman" into a "controlling woman" who is "an accomplished hypocrite . . . and dissembler."[20] Silvia's *peripeteia* results from her discovery that Philander is an inconstant lover. But this discovery is achieved not only *as* she learns that men's letters are calculated and manipulative rhetorical constructs, but *by* learning to read letters, and the men who write them, in these terms. Silvia has no information about Philander after his departure except what reaches her in his letters, since Octavio and Brilliard conspire with Philander to keep his "new Affair of Gallantry" secret from her. Consequently, it is from Philander's letters alone that Silvia has to determine how their relationship stands. This involves working her way through a palimpsest of other character-readers' interpretations: Philander sends his letters to Silvia enclosed in letters to Octavio, who forwards them to her enclosed in cover letters of his own, which are designed to direct and control her reading of them; Silvia discusses both men's letters with her maid, Antonet, and sometimes with Brilliard; and the narrator makes it clear that all these reader-characters are driven by conflicting personal interests, and trying to manipulate Silvia's reading of letter and lover accordingly. Exposing letters Silvia receives to the interpretations of several character-readers reproduced the challenges of everyday letter-reading situations where personal letters were normatively shared with family and/or friends, and the primary addressee had to negotiate other people's comments and opinions of it to arrive at or defend their own. Behn addressed the difficulty here by repeatedly offering comparison between letters as Silvia's effective method of cutting through rival interpretations to determine what a missive really meant.

Silvia's *peripeteia* and *anagnorisis* occur in the course of what is in effect a two-part reception narrative, while she is attempting to understand and answer Philander's "Blame-the-Victim" letter. Octavio has enclosed this in a cover letter in which he describes himself as "a Messenger of Love" and asks Silvia to "pity" him should Philander ever turn to some new "Conqueress." (2: 204) Philander's enclosed letter addresses Silvia's "Doubts and Fears" about his love for her, by shifting the blame to her: "'Tis you begin to unfasten the Vows that hold you . . . 'Tis you, whose Pride and Beauty, scorning to be confin'd, give way to the admiring Croud, that sigh for you," while he, Philander, is "thy faithful Lover still." Philander dismisses Silvia's complaint that his letters are cold and short by telling her that "time has made us more familiar now, and we begin to leave off Ceremony," and that he fears she "loves the Flatterer not the Man" (2: 200). Silvia's problem is that she is too attached to "the Rhetoric of Love." (2: 201)

By ensuring that novel-readers know from the correspondence between them what Octavio knows – that Philander is pursuing his sister Callista – Behn gives us a perspective that Silvia and Antonet lack. This enables us to draw conclusions of our own from these two letters – to notice, for instance, that Philander designed his letter for a double audience: to quieten Silvia and convey to Octavio that he need no longer regard their friendship as a bar to his pursuit of her (a message Octavio's cover letter indicates he got). But to make sense of Silvia's torment, Behn reminds novel-readers of how open to contrary interpretations letters appear without such knowledge by opening the reception narrative with a debate between Silvia and Antonet about what Phlander's letter and Octavio's cover-letter mean. Antonet argues that Octavio's missive can be discounted: since Philander is his rival, "'Tis Octavio's Interest, and his Business, to render Philander false." Silvia is inclined to think that Octavio's suggestion that Philander may one day replace her with another Conqueress is "no Prophesie . . . the fatal time 's already come." (2:205) Antonet argues that Silvia's fears are unfounded – Philander is only angered by her efforts to make him jealous. But Silvia founds her fears on her comparison of Philander's present letter with the letters he wrote her in *Love Letters*, Part 1: "O Antonet, said she, didst thou but see this Letter compar'd to those of heretofore, when Love was gay and young." Since every letter documents the self's concernments and relations to others at the time of writing, comparison between letters written at different times makes manifest any changes in these that have occurred. Silvia's comparison of the language, style, and tone of his past and present letters reveals in Philander's latest missive "that never-failing Mark of a declining Love, the Coldness and Alteration of the Stile of Letters." (2: 203, 202) In the absence of external information, the difference in Philander's epistolary style constitutes *prima facie* evidence that his passion for Silvia is defunct. And descending into rage and phrenzy, Silvia tries to stab herself with a penknife and curses herself for being "mad, deceiv'd, believing" and "undone." (2: 203)

Like Philander's misreadings, Silvia's difficulties in interpreting Philander's letter derive in part from inadequate knowledge about the occasion and web of relations informing it. Using narrative to ensure that novel-readers share the secret historian's knowledge of what their letters conceal enables us to see which correspondences and relationships Silvia does know something about when she reads Philander's Blame-the-Victim letter (Octavio's courtship of her, Octavio's friendship with Philander, the existence but not the content of their correspondence) and which she knows nothing about (Philander's affair with Callista, Antonet's affair with Brillard who is using her as *his* "spy"). The differences between Antonet's and Silvia's interpretations of Philander's and Octavio's letters, as well as Silvia's tormenting uncertainty about what Philander's letter really means, result directly from the different lacunae in their knowledge. Providing readers both with the personal and the bird's-eye view of their epistolary interactions that individual characters lack, enabled Behn to explore issues of ignorance, knowledge and partial knowledge, and of secrecy, partial concealment and discovery, which went to the heart of Procopian Secret History and profiled official History's cover up.

The second part of the reception narrative, which contains Silvia's answer to Philander's Blame-the-Victim letter, repeats and reinforces Behn's point about comparing letters. Silvia sits down to write to Philander "to ease her Soul of its heavy weight of Grief . . . for when a Lover is insupportably afflicted, there is no Ease like that of writing to the Person lov'd." (2: 208) But Silvia displays the opposite of "Ease." Her letter consists of a broken series of letter fragments interrupted by narratives that show Silvia repeatedly rereading and responding to Philander's letter – now rereading it and weeping; now scribbling alternative drafts of her answer, rereading them critically and tearing them up; now rereading Philander's letter to find "new Torments" (2: 212), which generate postscripts and additions in the covert of her letter even after it is sealed. The fragmentation of Silvia's letter emblematizes the "phrenzy" or "lunacy" to which fear, uncertainty, and despair have driven her. But except for mentioning that she is carrying "the Pledge of our softer Hours," (2: 214) and repeatedly demanding that Philander "let me know my Doom," these letter-fragments all address the epistolary style of Philander's latest letter:

Alas, I've read thy Letter o'er and o'er, and turn'd the Sense a thousand several ways and all to make it speak and look like Love—O I have flatter'd it with all my art. Sometimes I fancy'd my ill reading spoil'd it, and then I tun'd my Voice to softer Notes, and read it o'er again; but still the Words appear'd too rough and harsh for any moving Air, which way soe'er I chang'd, which way soe'er I questioned it of Love. ... I who've heard the very God himself speak from thy wondrous Lips, and known him guide thy Pen ... what Reflections must I make on this Decay, this ... sudden Alteration in thee? (2: 209)

Comparison between what Philander penned then and now allows Silvia to answer Philander's attribution of his coldness to their "familiarity" by telling him that in reality, it demonstrates what familiarity breeds, namely, "Contempt," and that his letter ends not on a note not of love, but of "Indifference." Her answer to Philander's accusation that she is too attached to "the Rhetoric of Love" marks Silvia's realization that she was wrong in believing that "the Rhetoric of Love is all ... flattering Speeches" (1: 41) and "unthinking, artless Speaking ... without Method" (2: 208) As she now bitterly observes, "Repetition is Love's Rhetorick" – the same "old Words" of love trotted out in due form. (2: 209) As Mertilla warned her in Part 1, the same "Ravings and Dyings," the same "dear Eloquence," and the same "Lovers Accents," repeated without thought or feeling, could be transferred from lover to lover and from letter to letter. Dictated by Rhetoric rather than by "the very God himself," repetition made "half-breathed interrupted Words," "flattering Speeches," and "broken Sighs" rhetorical conventions *comme tout autre* – "the true and secret Arts of moving" women whom men wished to seduce. (2: 151) As *The New Academy of Complements* put it in 1698: "Thou that studiest to become a Lover,/ ... must study to dissemble right:/Swear by her Beauty, seemly be loth/To break the bond of such a sacred Oath;/Sigh when she sighs, ... Gaze on her Eyes; and when thou seest her sip, Kiss thou the Glass where she shall place her Lip."[21] Dissembling was an arrow in the Lover's arsenal.

If, as the narrator claims, "Love, like Poetry, cannot be taught, but uninstructed flows without painful Study ... born in the Soul, a noble Inspiration, not a Science" (2: 216), then Silvia's error in reading Philander's letters has been a generic one. She mistook the "Love Letter" genre of epistle, with its rhetorical conventions and clichés, for the thing itself. She took Science for uninstructed Nature, studied Eloquence for Truth, and the Rhetoric of Love for what Wordsworth would (equally misleadingly) call the "spontaneous overflow of powerful feeling." Silvia's recognition now that "the Rhetoric of Love" is an artifice which cannot express "the Sense of her Soul" enables her to use that rhetoric calculatingly and sophistically herself. The next letter she receives is from Octavio, telling her that he will depart rather than betray his Honor and his Friend by "unravel[ing] all the Secrets of Philander's Letter" to her. (2: 220) Nothing daunted, Silvia arms herself with Beauty and Assurance by looking in her mirror and writes her first manipulative and dissembling letter, feigning a "kindness" for Octavio that she does not feel "from no other Inclination of her Heart than that of getting Secrets out of his." (2: 228) The best defense she has against dissemblers is to dissemble herself.

Emplotting her secret history as a romance, around the heroine's discovery of Philander's true identity as a false and inconstant lover, enables the narrator to direct her interpretative guidance to showing naïvely credulous readers like Lady Berkeley and the Silvia of Part 1 – who lacked a gentleman's rhetorical education and were inclined to take letters at face value – how to read gentlemen's letters as rhetorical instruments, which are capable of deploying even truth in content, loyalty in subscriptions and compliments, and sincerity in style, calculatingly and hypocritically, for purposes of persuasion, manipulation, or guile. In unmasking the "Rhetoric of Love," Behn was addressing concerns about rhetoric that were shared by mainstream moralists and educationists, who feared that we are so susceptible to fine words and vivid imagery that when a "Man of Eloquence" writes or speaks on any subject, "we are too ready to run into all his Sentiments."[22] Together with Silvia's shattering discovery of Philander's perfidy, the discrepancies that Behn introduced between prefatory frames and transcribed letters hammered at the naïve assumption that letters were simply expressions of "the Sense of [a writer's] Soul" that could be believed without question and permitted, unhindered, to work their powerful effects on an addressee's passions, desires, and hopes. Behn's framing narratives showed romance-readers that even letters that contained some true facts could prove what Janet Todd says all Restoration letters were: "ambiguous, manipulative and opportunistic."[23] Discrepancies between letters and reception narratives exposed common causes of misreading, such as blinding excesses of passion, mistaken assumptions about the writer or the genre, and ignorance of some circumstances, which deformed what one registered and comprehended of the missive. Soliloquies or conversations about letters in the framing narrative demonstrated that missives lent themselves to diverse interpretations, making them even harder to parse correctly in conditions of restricted or inadequate knowledge. But in Silvia's comparisons between Philander's earlier and present letters for language, style and tone, Behn offered readers the means of counterbalancing absent or limited knowledge of relevant facts by evaluating their rhetoric and cultivating a readerly "ear" for the dissonant and the unsaid. Letters were calculated, deceptive, and powerfully persuasive rhetorical constructs; but they might nevertheless give up their secrets if approached with suspicion and mistrust.

Popularizing the Framing Conventions: Eliza Haywood

Behn feared that, lacking the education and rhetorical training that gentlemen automatically received, the generality of late seventeenth-century women were, like Lady Berkeley and her daughter, naïve and credulous readers of letters, especially from men they loved, who needed to be taught the rhetorical artifices, subtleties, and complexities of the epistolary game. This, at least, is how Haywood seems to have read Behn, whose *Love Letters* were reprinted several times during the first decades of the eighteenth century, and whose plots, scenes, and themes Haywood often varied and rewrote. Haywood too made the reading and interpretation of letters a central issue in her fiction, embedding letters in almost all the secret histories of amatory adventures she wrote between 1719 and Fielding's satire of her works in *Joseph Andrews* (1742). Because Behn also wrote in purely narrative or purely epistolary forms, this mix of narrative and letters became an obvious hallmark of Haywood's fiction. We should not forget how popular her narrative-epistolary novels and novellas were. According to Paula Backscheider, Haywood's first novel, *Love in Excess*, which contained more than thirty embedded letters, sold more copies than any novel before Richardson's *Pamela*.[24] Kathryn King describes Haywood as a highly "fashionable" writer who "reigned supreme as an amatory novelist" during the 1720s and 1730s and was widely imitated.[25] Haywood made her narrative-epistolary fictions as popular and widely accessible as they were by radically simplifying Behn's baroque *copia*, and almost invariably explaining what she was about.

An essay called "A Discourse Concerning Writings of this Nature" in *The Works of Mrs Eliza Haywood* (1724), explained why Haywood thought that warning women about the many ways in which letters could prove false, treacherous, or misleading "may be of so general Service to my Sex": being naïve and credulous correspondents was, she claimed, drawing women "into the Path of Ruin."[26] Like Behn, Haywood wanted women to know that, with few exceptions, men were deceitful, manipulative, inconstant, and ungrateful for sexual favors and that their letters were too. Haywood went beyond Behn by arguing that love letters from an attractive lover were far more dangerous to a woman's peace and virtue than "all the Tongue can utter" because letters were more durable, and because in reading and rereading them, women permitted men's "artful, tender and passionate Way of Writing" to "sensibly affect" their passions:

> Though we know each Line is an Arrow aimed at our Virtue or our Peace; our Curiosity or our Inclination, seldom fails engaging us to peruse them: from that we fall to examining the happy Turn of Thought – ... discover unnumbered Beauties in every Sentence—and admire the Author's Love, or Wit, or both, which have inspir'd him with so uncommon a Delicacy: thence we reflect on his Behaviour while he was writing—think in what Manner he looked—how he sigh'd—what he wish'd—imagine we dive into his Soul—find out Meanings there, to which perhaps he was a stranger— and prepossess'd by this time, construe everything to the advantage of his Passion, and our own Desires. In this pleasing, but destructive Amusement, we lose ourselves so long, that the return of Reason is too weak to drive it from our Minds."[27]

Haywood also observed that, because reading love letters fed their imagination, aroused their passions, and sensibly affected their soul, women wrongly assumed that their own passionate letters of love or reproach would have the same powerful effect on their lovers. Haywood's narrative-epistolary novellae often dramatized points made in this Discourse about women's mistaken expectations of letters, as the two following examples will show.

The first comes from *Fantomina* (1725), a story about a young woman, Lady X, who keeps an inconstant lover faithful by "self-serializing" in a variety of guises to lead him to believe that he is seducing a different woman each time. Haywood's "Discourse" argued that a philanderer will read a letter differently if it comes from a woman he desires or from a mistress of whom he is tiring; *Fantomina* showed that he will write letters differently to each woman too. The two embedded letters in *Fantomina* are not, as one might expect, letters demonstrating how Lady X disguises her language and epistolary style as she disguises her voice, manners, and dress to assume the characters of different women. Instead, her two letters to Beauplaisir are merely summarized in the prefatory narrative to Beauplaisir's answers: we are told that Lady X has written him a letter of invitation in her identity as Widow Bloomer, the woman whom Beauplaisir is currently pursuing, and "a long letter of Complaint" subscribing herself "his unalterably affectionate Fantomina," in her identity as the mistress he is in the process of discarding.[28] Beauplaisir's two answers are what we are given to read, fully transcribed and neatly juxtaposed on

the page. This enables novella-readers to compare the letter a man writes to
a woman he desires ("My Angel." "the Infinity of Transport the Sight of
your dear Letter gave me." "I will be with you this Evening about Five,"
"sweet lovely Mistress of the Soul") with the letter he writes to the woman
of whom he is tiring, and thus to see how his protestations of love subtly
take on the character of excuses once his desire has faded ("you were not
persecuted every Post with a Declaration of my unchanging Passion"
because . . . ; "PS: I fear I cannot see you till To-morrow; Some Business
has unluckily fallen out . . . "). The reception narrative's account of Lady
X's reaction to these letters makes the lesson explicit: "Traytor! (cry'd she)
as soon as she had read them, 'tis thus our silly, fond, believing Sex are
serv'd when they put their Faith in Man: So had I been deceiv'd and
cheated, had I like the rest believ'd, and sat down mourning in Absence,
and vainly waiting recover'd Tendernesses." (59) We do not need to read
Beauplaisir's letters verbatim to know that he is inconstant. We do need to
read them to see that it is foolish ("silly" and "fond") for women to believe
what men's love letters say. Haywood's narrative-epistolary olio showed
credulous women readers that a lover's letters should be read only as
signifiers of his waxing or waning desire. Reading men's letters as gauges
of their inconstant desire, with an eye to betraying stylistic distinctions in
the expression of their "unchanging Passion," would, as the narrative puts
it, save women from "burning in fruitless Expectations," and "wak[ing] at
last to all the Horrors of Dispair." (59)

Analogies between this segment of *Fantomina* and Silvia's *peripeteia*
make visible what Haywood has done. She has made Lady X from the
moment of her fall, what Silvia became after her *peripeteia*: a character who
deceives and manipulates others by assuming occasional selves. Haywood
has also stripped Silvia's discovery that Philander no longer loves her as he
once did of its obscuring web of interlocking relationships and conflicting
interpretations, to zoom in on the core triangular relationship between
Beauplaisir, Fantomina, and Widow Bloomer (Philander, Silvia, Callista)
and on the technique that permitted Silvia to make her discovery: comparison of the style of love letter written by a Philanderer in hot pursuit,
with that written by a Philanderer who is moving on. Haywood concretizes
Silvia's comparison and discovery and makes it easier for readers to "see,"
by juxtaposing a short, fully transcribed example of each on the page and
by articulating in her reception narrative what she wants novel-readers to
take from the comparison. Moving in and out of Lady X's thoughts, the
reception narrative develops and explicitly contrast two ways of reading
a lover's letters, the credulous and the suspicious, to indicate that the

choice lies in a woman's hands. Women can allow themselves to be deceived by their lovers' letters and (like Silvia) "make their Life a Hell, burning in fruitless ..., Hopes and Fears, then wake up at last to all the Horrors of Dispair." Or, facing up to men's "Inconstancy and Levity of Heart," they can, like Lady X, guard their hearts from "real Tenderness," take the game into her own hands, and "outwit even the most subtle of the deceiving Kind" by ensuring that "while he thinks to fool me, is himself the only beguiled Person." (59) Haywood's heroine is already the calculating dissembler that Silvia becomes. But she is a dissembler in the comic rather than tragic mode because her reaction to finding herself unexpectedly "undone" was to recognize that "Complaints, Tears and Swoonings ... have little Prevalence over a Heart inclined to rove" (51), and to use her "discernment" and "imagination" to "avoid all those Ills which might attend the Loss of her Reputation" as well as those attending loss of a lover whose "sighs", "languishing" and "Transports" she is unwilling to forgo. (51) Setting questions of virtue aside and reversing the genders of deceptive seducer and unsuspecting seduced, *Fantomina* shows that a woman who knows it for what it is and properly guards her heart, can enjoy the Rhetoric of Love as much as she wants – unless she is found out.

Haywood developed her contrast between these two ways of reading a lover's letters in a novella that was referenced and rewritten by later authors into the nineteenth century. *The City Jilt* (1726) tells the story of Glicera, a woman of fortune who is seduced and abandoned by Melladore, the man she is engaged to marry, when they discover that her father has died a bankrupt. Three of the embedded letters illustrate Haywood's argument in the "Discourse" that when a woman has been deceived by an inconstant lover, she should reflect on "the small probability there is of having those Grievances redressed by him who has inflicted them" and "never stoop to a Humiliation at once so mean and vain" as to write begging him to return. Glicera writes two letters "To the Ungrateful and Perfidious Melladore" when she discovers, after he has abandoned her, that she is with child (like Silvia), and he responds to one of them. The prefatory narrative to the first letter tells us that Glicera wrote it reluctantly: "sooner would she have sent a Dagger to his Heart ... had not the Condition she was in compell'd her to it, and forced her trembling Hand, in spite of Pride, to write ... "[29] Using what Kirsten Saxon describes as "strategies of immediacy, direct testimony, emotional appeal and lavish language,"[30] Glicera's first letter appeals to "Nature, Religion, Pity and Love" and pleads their parental duty to "the guiltless Consequence of our mutual Raptures." (90) Glicera writes her second letter when she receives no answer to the first, to ascertain "the Certainty of her Fate." This letter is a letter of complaint or reproach, which castigates Melladore for his cruelty and describes "the Agonies of my distracted Soul, divided between Love and Rage" and the "tumultuous Passions," which "o'erwhelm my Reason." Here the narrative tells us outright that this is misjudged: "Whoever has the least knowledge of the Temper of Mankind will believe a letter of this sort would have but little Effect on the Person to whom it was sent." (93) Haywood highlights Melladore's cruel indifference through the contrast between the impassioned length of Glicera's letters and the narrative's single sentence summary of Melladore's reception of it: "being now wholly taken up with making himself appear as agreeable as he could in the Eyes of a fine Lady, who was represented to him as a great Fortune, he either forgot, or had not the leisure to compassionate the Complaints of the undone Glicera." (91) As the "Discourse" observed, "when once Desire is fled," reminding a man of his duty, of his past promises, or of love's erstwhile delights, is just a waste of time. Glicera's reproaches only give Melladore the "Opportunity" to "come to a downright Quarrel" in order to rid himself of her importunities. (93) The framing narrative to his fully transcribed letter tells us that Melladore "takes a little time for Consideration" before writing, to calculate how best to craft a letter that will insult her enough to ensure that she "sends no more [Letters] on any score." (94) The reception narrative then describes Glicera's response to Melladore's insulting missive as a "Hurricane" of emotion – "in the first Gust of her Passion," she tries to kill herself, her unborn child aborts, and she is close to death for some time. While echoing Silvia's doubts and desperation in *Love Letters*, part 2, Glicera's letters and Melladore's response dramatize Haywood's insistence in the "Discourse" that women who "think they have the right to upraid a man" who fails to live up to his promises, will find that upraiding him only "provokes the Insults of the disdainful Repellor" and show her "how little a Man who gives Occasion of Complaint, is worth complaining to."[31] Like Silvia, Glicera has no knowledge of her lover's pursuit of another woman; but Haywood suggests that she had no need to, to know that repeatedly appealing to a man she already had reason to address as "Ungrateful and Perfidious" would be as fruitless as it was humiliating.

Glicera is transformed from passive victim to active manipulator by this experience, which constitutes the novella's *peripeteia* and *anagnorisis*. In the sequence of the plot, she takes her revenge on mankind as Silvia does, by treating men as deceitfully, as inconstantly and as ungratefully as Melladore has treated her. But in the sequence of letters, the transformation occurs in the way she reads letters. Glicera now reads men's letters as Haywood advised women to read them in the "Discourse:" coldly, distrustfully, and with "a more than manly Resolution" – "manly" because "that Sex makes no difficulty to resolve to throw off their Passion, on the least Appearance of any Inconvenience attending it."[32] When Melladore writes to Glicera again many years later, he has been bankrupted by Helena, the woman he foolishly married in her place, and Glicera holds the mortgage to all his estates. This time his letter is a letter of petition – long, pleading, apologetic, charming, and respectful. "To the most deserving, yet most injur'd of her Sex, the lovely Glicera . . . my Business now is to implore your Mercy . . . I intreat the favour of a speedy Answer." (117–118) As the reception narrative informs us, Melladore's utter "Humiliation" satisfies Glicera's desire for revenge. But Glicera no longer allows herself to succumb to this or any other passion. Instead, she shows "manly Resolution." Despite "his most earnest Entreaties" in this and subsequent letters, Glicera "persever[es] in her Resolution" not to "again receive the Traitor into Favour and relapse into the former Fondness by which [she] had been undone." (118) By agreeing to allow Melladore a sum to buy a commission in the army, she rids herself of *his* continued importunities. And she so far succeeds in "throwing off her Passion," that she hears of his death in battle with manly indifference. (118) Glicera has learned not to read men's letters, as Haywood's credulous women do, who permit every sentence to act as "an Arrow aimed at [their] Virtue or [their] Peace" and to "sensibly affect [their] Soul." If, as Margaret Case Croskery has argued, Haywood encouraged "sympathetic identifica- tion" and "absorptive reading" of her narratives in order to use readers' "affective experiences" to educate them through their passions, then Haywood was arousing readers' sympathy and indignation on her heroine's behalf to teach them that the proper approach to letters was *dis*-passionate.[33]

Like Behn, then, the Haywood of the 1720s and 1730s used disjunctions between prefatory narrative, transcribed letter, and reception narrative, and comparisons between contrasting letters, to show her credulous sex that it was foolish, and ruinous to them, to take men's letters and protest- ations of "unchanging Passion" at face value, and allow themselves to be deceived by the Rhetoric of Love. But while leaving her readers some interpretative work to do, she simplified the web of relationships inhabited by Behn's letters, eliminated conflict among rival interpretations from her reception narratives, explicitly articulated what she wanted readers to notice and/or learn from the disjunctions or comparisons she displayed, and often repeated the point she wanted to make in the narrative or in both narrative and letter. Haywood also corrected Silvia's errors by modeling empowering ways for women to read letters from their lovers, as well as ways for them to deploy occasional selves to manage philandering men. In these regards, Haywood was more overtly didactic, even during the 1720s, than Behn had ever been.

Debating Novel Forms: Haywood, Richardson, and Henry Fielding

Haywood had been warning women and the unlearned for two decades about the dangers of allowing letters to transport their imaginations and sway their passions, when Richardson burst onto the marketplace with *Pamela* in 1741. *Pamela* was a story told in letters that Richardson described in his Preface as "draw[ing] characters *justly*" and "giv[ing] *practical* examples, worthy to be followed … in so probable, so natural, so lively a manner, as shall engage the passions of every sensible reader and strongly interest them in the edifying story."[34] Richardson was presenting Pamela's letters as a faithful record of characters and events, and inviting novel-readers to let loose their passions while they read her letters absorptively for the supposedly edifying story they told. In other words, he was encouraging novel-readers to read letters like the credulous women readers Haywood criticized in her 1724 "Discourse," who naively believed what letters said and lost themselves in imaginative and desirous readings that permitted letters to "sensibly affect the[ir] Soul." No wonder Haywood was outraged.[35] Fielding took her part. One way of characterizing his response in *Shamela* is to say that he complicated Richardson's novel with other correspondence to reaffirm that letters should be read with the hermeneutics of suspicion that Behn and Haywood taught.[36]

When Fielding took up his critique of Richardson in *Joseph Andrews*, however, he opened a three-way debate about their rival novel forms, to which we now turn. For here, as we saw in the Lady Booby segments at the beginning of this chapter, Fielding was not only reiterating his critique in *Shamela* of Pamela's "pretended innocence;" he was couching his dig at *Pamela* in Haywood's narrative-epistolary form.[37]

Ridiculing *Pamela* in a segment replete with allusions to the female tradition of secret amatory histories in which Haywood wrote enabled Fielding to ridicule Richardson as an interloper in a writerly tradition he did not understand. When Lady Booby imputes Joseph's silence to his "secrecy," asks if Joseph can keep her "familiarities" secret, asks again if she can trust to his secrecy to ensure that "the world will never know anything of the matter," Fielding was invoking secret amatory history to imply (correctly, I think) that the content of *Pamela* was squarely in the tradition of Behn, Manley, and Haywood's scandalous revelations about the "family secrets" of the genteel and about the dangers that libertines presented to innocent young girls. Fielding ridicules Richardson's use of epistolary form to insert himself in this longstanding female tradition when Joseph affirms his unwillingness to "betray the secrets of the family to the world" to Lady Booby three times, only to betray them in his first letter to Pamela. The absurdity of this act is heightened in the letter itself, which "folks" are in the process of reading even as Joseph writes "Dear Pamela . . . Don't tell anybody what I write, because I should not care to have folks say I discover what passes in our family." (24) To publish the purloined clandestine letters of people who had been corresponding secretly on matters of concern to themselves, as the whistleblowing authors of true Secret Histories did or as Behn pretended to do in *Love Letters*, was different from pretending to secrecy while busily confiding all "the secrets of [one's] master's family" to correspondents outside it, as Pamela did. Fielding was also making a larger generic point that Janet Gurkin would later rediscover: letter-writers in epistolary novels had to tell their own secrets to the world by pretending to be writing truthfully and in the strictest confidence to a single trusted confidant. In epistolary novels, even liars have to tell us truthfully that they are liars, and deceivers have to describe their deceptions without deception, as Pamela does in Fielding's reading, as Lovelace will in *Clarissa*, and as Joseph's letter so absurdly does here. In narrative-epistolary fiction, by contrast, framing narratives did the revelatory work: narrative framing enabled Haywood to reveal Beauplaisir's epistolary deceptions and Behn to use letters to complicate homosociality and masculine friendship by showing Brilliard and Octavio at once writing honestly as Philander's "friends," patrons, surrogates or agents, and concealing from him plans, intrigues, desires, and feelings of their own.

The "double, yet separate correspondence" in *Clarissa* (1747–1748) represented a retreat on Richardson's part from his technique in *Pamela*. It also signaled his attempt to assert his superiority to the narrative-epistolary writers of secret amatory histories by rewriting one of their most seminal texts in his preferred epistolary form. *Clarissa* follows the outline of Behn's *Love Letters*: the long seduction in her father's house; the elopement; the fall; the innocent young girl matched against the sort of deceiving and manipulative philandering libertine who populated the pages of Behn and Haywood; discovery of her error too late; the fragments of letter marking her phrenzy, madness and passionate regret; the transformation occasioned by her madness and fall. In *Love Letters*, part 2, Behn had already deployed a baroque version of the "double, yet separate correspondence" that Richardson supposedly invented for *Clarissa* seventy years later. Like Lovelace and Belford, Philander, Octavio, and Brilliard correspond with one another separately from their dealings with Silvia and conspire to keep key information from her. In both novels too, separate correspondences give novel-readers a bird's-eye view of the action that the heroine and her confidante lack. Fielding was among the first to hail *Clarissa* as a masterpiece; and the novel established Richardson's superiority to Behn and Haywood for generations of critics. But as Richardson was the first to realize, departing from what they had done by eliminating letters' narrative framing to produce an entirely epistolary novel altered the character of his letters in ways that exposed further shortcomings of novels written "in a series of letters." Richardson could neither moderate novel-readers' desirous absorptive reading nor guide their judgments, and these shortcomings proved more intractably generic than Richardson initially supposed.

One fundamental generic difference between Richardson's epistolary and Behn or Haywood's narrative-epistolary form is indicated by his famous announcement in the Preface to *Clarissa* that his characters' letters were "written to the moment." Behn's or Haywood's narrative framing described how letters were not only *written* to the moment but *read* to the moment too. Narrative framing enabled them to address the difficulties facing characters who had to read and interpret each letter, not only while "the mind [is] tortured by the pangs of uncertainty (the Events then hidden in the womb of Fate)," but also with imperfect knowledge of the letter-writer, of all the relevant circumstances, and of their correspondent's motive(s) for writing when and as they did. Abolishing narrative framing, as Richardson did, also abolished the advantages that Behn and Haywood drew from this: the ability to guide novel-readers' reading of letters and to reinforce this guidance by distancing them from their immediate emotional reactions. Mediating novel-readers' responses to embedded letters with cold analyses of character-readers' reception of them, helped novel-readers to bring reason and reflection to bear on epistolary texts themselves. After reading Behn's narrative frames, novel-readers might sympathetically identify with Silvia; but they would also be looking to see whether and how she would manage to discern from Philander's letters that he was no longer devoted to her. Haywood's more overtly didactic approach regularized and intensified this effect. Narrative framing placed novel-readers at one remove from the immediacy of epistolary expression in order to turn sympathetic identification with a character-writer or character-reader into observation of a letter-writer's design and discernment of its success and/or of a character-reader's faulty, over-emotional, partial, or over-hasty understanding of the letter they read.

Richardson recognized that his purely epistolary form could do none of this. In the first part of *Clarissa*, Richardson tried to emulate the reasoning and reflection in narrative frames by attaching letters from the Harlowes to Clarissa's letters and framing them with reception narratives in Clarissa's and/or Anna Howe's correspondence. But analyses and judgments of letters from the Harlowes in Clarissa's letters were necessarily filtered through her memory and opinions. They could be contested by Anna; but contested is not corrected. The epistolary framing of letter-attachments only added to the dizzying plurality of competing subjective, character-generated interpretations in and of letters, without reproducing the interpretative guidance that narrative-epistolary fiction supplied. Confronted with their fully transcribed letters as attachments, novel-readers could take the Harlowes' part despite all that Clarissa and Anna could say against them; and many did. Moreover, readers of *Clarissa* continued to lose themselves in imaginative and desirous readings that permitted the letters to "sensibly affect the[ir] Soul." Richardson's contemporaries record how they identified with Clarissa, wept as they read or paced the room to calm their nerves, found themselves pleasurably aroused by the "warm" scenes, or got so absorbed in the novel that they read by candlelight throughout the night. The letters in *Clarissa* "engaged the passions of every sensible reader" not only thanks to the vividness, detail, and genius of Richardson's prose, but due to the conjunction of this prose with his epistolary form. Readers were engaged and their passions aroused by their direct, unmediated, and unchecked exposure to the language and rhetoric of letters that the "editor" had merely placed "as exact as possible . . . in the order they were sent."

Richardson tried to solve these generic problems by substituting a series of editorial and paratextual devices for the narrative-epistolary novel's narrative frames: he introduced meta-critical discourse in the form of repeatedly rewritten prefaces, repeatedly revised summative tables of contents, pointed notes, and collections of maxims drawn from the letters. But novel-readers directly exposed to Lovelace's epistolary wit and rakish bravura continued to like him so well, despite his open exposure of his lies and deceptions, that many defended him passionately, and declared Clarissa dull and prudish for refusing to marry him at the end. As Thomas Keymer showed, Richardson proved more successful in centering *Clarissa* on moral "cruxes," which provoked contemporary debate than in regulating readers' responses to the letters or the position they took in those debates.[38] From a technical per-spective, *Sir Charles Grandison* (1753), which eliminated attractive villains and fell back on evaluative summaries of some letters, can be described as a further retreat.

Fielding's invocation of Haywood in *Joseph Andrews* was certainly more flattering. He and Haywood were aligned in their agreement on the importance of restraining novel-readers' tendency to plunge headlong into absorbed and desirous reading, and in their commitment to teaching the public to approach words, texts, and characters with skepticism and hermeneutics of suspicion. In *Joseph Andrews*, and later in *Tom Jones*, Fielding not only repeatedly demonstrated characters' folly in swallowing stories whole; he also paused novel-readers' headlong forward flight on the wings of the story and broke in on their absorption in the characters and plot, by introducing meta-critical discourse. Inserting chapters of cold criticism and reasoned analysis on such passion-numbing topics as chapter divisions distanced novel-readers from the narrative, and created interludes for reflection. But admiring as he was, Fielding did criticize what he viewed as major failings in Haywood's form.

One criticism bore on Haywood's transition from secret histories to "modern novels."[39] Having described the authors of official histories of England, France, or Spain as "romance-writers" (157), Fielding reproached "the authors of immense romances, or the modern novel and Atalantis writers" for abandoning the terrain of history and fact in order to record "without any assistance from nature or history," the exploits of "heroes . . . of their own creation" and "facts which never did, nor possibly can, happen." (158) Atalantis writers were secret historians such as Behn, Manley, and Haywood in her youth, who had unmasked the falsity of official histories and shown them up as "romances" by penetrating the false facades that the great presented to the world and revealing how badly people's "betters" behaved behind closed doors. Secret history, as practiced before Atlantis writers "abandoned the terrain of history and fact" for "the modern novel," had been "true history;" and Fielding blamed Haywood and the modern novel for abandoning it.

Haywood responded in *The Female Spectator* (1744–1745) and again in *The Invisible Spy* (1751) by contrasting "outsider narrators" like Mr. Spectator or Fielding's narrators – "Lookers-On" who created univer-sal types by observing and describing the "public shews" of characters and events from the outside – with Female Spectators and Invisible Spies who, like the secret historian, "plucked off the mask of hypocrisy," and revealed "the secrets of families and characters of persons." She argued that there was no difference between writing a secret history and a history of private life; – indeed, the two expressions were synonymous since the primary meaning of private was still "secret." Modern novels were secret histories of domestic life rather than of the court. But both spied into peoples' private lives to "see into the real Springs which gave rise to Actions" and "bring real Facts upon the Stage." Both unmasked hypocrisy and deceit "by acquainting [readers] with other People's Affairs" to "teach everyone at the same Time, to better regulate their own."[40] The "modern novel" exposed genteel and mercantile society's scandalous personal, social, and familial secrets, as secret history had once done those of kings and courtiers, and as official historiography would later begin to do.[41]

Fielding's second criticism of Haywood bore on her uncritical treatment of narrative. By using the narrative to belie Joseph's letters, and Joseph's letters to belie the narrative, Fielding showed that narratives could prove as partial, deceitful, and incomplete as letters. This Haywood neglected to do; she typically kept her narrative framing reliable and "true" in order to use narrative to explain where the letters embedded in it were false, unreliable, deceptive, or untrue. By putting the narrative in play as well, Fielding's corrective suggested that Haywood allowed novel-readers to trust to narrative too much. She failed to alert them to the dangers of believing the stories that people told about themselves, about events, or about others, and to the folly of accepting without question "the authority of those romance-writers who entitle their books 'The History of England, the History of France, of Spain etc'." (157). Fielding was more interested in the ways in which *narratives* distort truth and deceive or mislead the credulous. In *Joseph Andrews* and later in *Tom Jones*, he often used embedded narratives to show how easily characters were misled by the stories they were told about other characters, or by the narratives they themselves concocted to explain the words or acts of others. Fielding also ensured in both novels that novel-readers discover on their own pulses that narrative histories might wholly or partly mislead them by ensuring that his narrators mislead us themselves. William Warner has argued that, in his "concern with the education of the reader," Fielding was countering uncritical "absorptive novel reading" by "weaving an open matrix of variable reading practices" in which "there is one sender text, but many diverse sites and modalities of reception" in order to show readers that narratives were unreliable, deceptive, or misleading, and that they must take responsibility for their own reading practices.[42] If so, we might say that Fielding was transposing to narrative, devices and concerns that Haywood and Behn had long since applied to letters, and doing for narrative histories what Behn and

Haywood had already done for letters: warn readers not to accept what they read at face value and demonstrate how else they might read.

Haywood responded to Fielding's criticism of her trustworthy narrative frames in *The History of Betsy Thoughtless*, (1751) her narrative-epistolary *tour de force*. It contains well over a hundred embedded letters, seventy-seven of them fully transcribed, the others summarized or partly summarized and partly cited. Alternating between trustworthy framing narratives and unanimous reader-character judgments, Haywood displayed her mastery of the epistolary form through her panoramic range of character-appropriate letter-kinds and letter styles. After overtly criticizing Fielding's "low humour" and inability to "distinguish satire from scurrility," she answered his critique of her too reliable framing narratives in scenes centered on Hysom, a low sea captain who had made his fortune in the East-India trade.[43] To demonstrate why her clearly articulated narrative guidance was preferable to Fielding's obscure and easily overlooked "hints," she reproduced Fielding's favorite device – use of "lowly" characters like Joseph or the maid in the puppet-master chapters in *Tom Jones* to supply "sagacious" readers with a hint to the secret of the plot.[44] Hysom erupts onto the scene of courtship with a blunt and vulgar letter:

Fair Creature,

I am no courtier, –no beau, –and have hitherto had but little communication with your sex; but I am honest and sincere, and you may depend on the truth of what I say. I have, heaven be praised, acquired a very large fortune, and for some time have had thoughts of marrying, to the end I might have reason to enjoy the fruit of my labours, after I am food either for the fishes, or the worms: –it is no great matter which of them. Now I have been wished to several fine women, but my fancy gives the preference to you; and if you can like me as well, we shall be very happy together . . . .I am turned of eight and forty, 'tis true, which maybe you may think too old; but I must tell you, dear pretty one, that I have a constitution that will wear out twenty of your washy pampered landmen of not half my age. Whatever your fortune is I will settle accordingly . . . .let me know your mind this evening at five o'clock when I shall come to Mr. Goodman's . . . (129)

Prefaced by a warning from Betsy's guardian against having "romantic notions" about marriage, this letter is followed by a reception narrative describing "the immoderate fits of laughter" into which "some passages" of this letter throw Betsy and Flora, who has to keep stopping to "hold her sides" with mirth as she reads it aloud to Betsy's guardian, Mr. Goodman and his wife, Lady Mellasin. As Lady Mellasin observes, though Mr. Hysom is an "honest man" and a rich one, "much politeness cannot be expected from" a man who has "lived at sea" for "twenty-five years in the service of the East-India Company." (130) Analogical chapters follow detailing how Betsy's two other serious "lovers," Mr. Staple and Mr. Truelove, conduct their polite courtships. This permits Betsy to contrast Hysom's "blunt addresses" to Mr. Staple's "assiduities" and Mr. Truelove's "respectful passion," and their delightful "presents" to Hysom's determination to settle his "business" with her without delay. To punish Hysom for his rudeness and presumption (138), Betsy decides to make a "sport" of him when he comes for his answer. And though unaccustomed to polite "raillery," Hysom soon realizes that he is being made "the jest of all the company" and departs in a huff, telling Staple and Truelove that Betsy "will find you employment enough, as long as you shall think it worth your while to dance attendance;" and Lady Mellasin that Betsy "was no better than a young flirt, and did not know how to use a gentleman handsomely." (147–148)

The characters' laughter and derision of Hysom's lack of politeness and lack of *savoir faire*, the narrator's reminder that Hysom was "altogether unacquainted with the manners and behavior of the polite world" (140) and the incongruity between his blunt businesslike epistolary proposal and Staple's or Truelove's polite epistolary courtships, all conspire to make Hysom a ridiculous figure who is easily dismissed as an outsider and a clod. But the satire cuts both ways. Hysom's blunt missive shows up the artificiality and intrinsic dishonesty of polite courtships such as Staple's and Truelove's, where the financial "business" is settled a priori among men, and gentlemen who are in reality like Hysom just seeking a suitable and conformable wifeand must "dance attendance" on a girl and promote "romantic notions" of marriage by expressing sentiments of admiration and love in the prescribed manner. As Mr. Goodman observed, marriage was not, in reality, a romantic thing; it was, as Hysom's letter bluntly stated, about money and mutual convenience. Hysom's parting shots also reveal "the secret springs which set the fair machine [Betsy] in motion" and keep her plot going (32). More interested in flirting than in marriage, Betsy will always keep lovers hanging until they no longer think it worth their while to pursue her; she will continue to treat them "unhandsomely" until forced by her brothers to marry the one who still happens to be around. Hysom's rough unromantic courtship also foreshadows the rough unromantic marriage to Munden that Betsy will then be forced to make.

The joke against Hysom also turns back on novel-readers who laugh at him and dismiss him derisively when he departs. For in their anxiety to read on to discover whether Staple or Truelove will succeed with Betsy, such readers prove themselves as thoughtless, and as easily seduced by the pleasures and artifices of prolonged and ever-renewed polite courtships, as Betsy Thoughtless herself. This demonstrates why Fielding-like hints, which are easily missed even by sagacious readers, would not do. Readers who overlook the narrative's subtle hints will miss the points made by Hysom and his letter and learn nothing from them. Haywood's Hysom episodes showed that she could use narrative-epistolary form to do a Fielding if she chose – and why she preferred a narrator whose didactic reasoning a reader could follow to one who made a jest of readers with a sagacity that was easy to overlook.

Fielding countered Haywood's critique with fury in his last and, critics agree, most uncharacteristic novel, by showing that he too could do a Haywood.[45] "Romance-writing" was, after all, the most profitable, least meritorious, and "easiest work in the world."[46] Sentimental and woman-centered, *Amelia* (1752) reproduced Haywood's characters and reworked Haywood's characteristic plots and themes (seduction, reputation, prostitution, inconstancy, betrayal of two or more women by the same man, to say nothing of secrecy, passion, and deceit).[47] Miss Matthews' history was a rewrite of *The City Jilt* in which the heroine does to the lover who abandons her what Haywood's heroine only dreamed of doing: "send a dagger to his heart." Together with his usual embedded histories, Fielding inserted sixty-two letters in *Amelia*, fifteen of them fully transcribed – an astonishingly large number for him. He took issue with Haywood's Hysom scenes by arguing that "bluntness or rather rudeness ... is not always so much a mark of honesty as it is taken to be." (1, 127). And he gently parodied what he borrowed. In the last chapter of Book V, for instance, Miss Matthews sends Colonel James a passionately distraught letter which indicates that Booth is still the man she loves. In its reception narrative, James shows her letter to Booth, who is his friend. The two men establish in short order that their interests are compatible: since Booth is anxious to prevent Amelia from finding out about his earlier affair with Matthews, and James "likes her beyond all other women," they amicably agree to pass her on between them. (1: 251) Settling such matters between gentlemen did not require Octavio and Philander's protracted round-aboutation – just a short walk and half a conversation. Presenting the situation from the gentlemen's pragmatic point of view defamiliarized

Miss Mathews' typical Romance hysterics, and made them faintly comical. Seduced women disappointed in love, like Silvia or Glicera – who wrote passionate letters of complaint, plunged histrionically into despair and thought themselves forever destroyed by one inconstant lover – invariably found another lover waiting conveniently in the wings.

Letters and Secret Histories in *Pride and Prejudice*

Rejecting its putative original epistolary form, Jane Austen rewrote "First Impressions" as *Pride and Prejudice* (1813), a narrative-epistolary novel that recycled some of her predecessors' characteristic *topoi* and subjected the reading both of letters and of narratives to hermeneutics of suspicion. Wickham proves to be the attentive, manipulative, and deceptively attractive philanderer by whom Elizabeth, the credulous heroine, is beguiled; but her usual fate is parceled out between Elizabeth's sister Lydia, who elopes with Wickham, and her sister Jane, who faces abandonment by the man she loves. This enabled Austen to focus on Elizabeth's deception not by sex or passion – "had I been in love, I could not have been more wretchedly blind" (361) – but by prejudices that predispose her to believe Wickham's duplicitous (hi)story of his past relations with Darcy together with its false representations of the characters of the two men. The text could thus both enchant readers with the familiar pleasures of romance and recycle these for the enjoyment of a more skeptical readership. As recent critics have argued, Elizabeth's seduction is primarily mental and emotional because this was a novel "about the difficulty of determining the truth—about the character of another or the nature of an event—and about the mistakes and injuries that are possible when persons attempt to form such conclusions." Austen extended the hermeneutics of suspicion to the point where it "destabilizes the concept of truth" and "sifts, queries and explores issues rather than solving them."[48] Aided by what Thomas Keymer calls Austen's "reticence which extends to withholding information, even to active misdirection,"[49] the novel invited skeptical readings as well as traditional ones.

To this end, Austen used the same conventions of narrative framing for her embedded letters in *Pride and Prejudice* as Haywood and Behn, with two important differences: her narrator rarely explained why letters were written or what they meant; and she liked to invert the default mode by using letters as a measure of the narrative's truth. In the two examples that follow, novel-readers have to interpret embedded letters for themselves and judge the narrative against them to understand more than the characters do and discover what the misdirecting narrator has withheld.

In the familiar scene where Mr. Collins' letter is read aloud to the Bennets, Austen avoids the usual prefatory narrative explanation of the motives and circumstances prompting the letter-writer to write, by replacing this with what is already a reception narrative. Before reading the letter aloud to his wife and daughters, Mr. Bennet, who has already read it, informs them that his cousin, Mr. Collins, has written to announce his impending visit to make himself known to the family; and Mrs. Bennet comments on the entail of the Longbourne estate to Mr. Collins, which will leave the Bennet daughters penniless after Mr. Bennet's death. After Mr. Collins' fully-transcribed letter has been heard, everyone in the family comments on it in ways which, as critics have observed, do more to characterize the speakers than the letter. Prejudiced by Mr. Bennet's derisory view of Mr. Collins "manner of expressing himself," Elizabeth judges he must be "an oddity." Only an oddity or a pompous and pretentious fool would introduce himself to virtual strangers by entertaining them with so much more than they could possibly wish to know about his situation in life. Assuming like her father that Mr. Collins' letter is a letter of introduction, Elizabeth concludes from his "extraordinary deference for Lady de Burgh," that Mr. Collins cannot be "a sensible man." The scene concludes with Mr. Bennet looking forward to finding Collins "the reverse" of a sensible man" – a judgment confirmed again by Mr. Bennet after Collins' arrival (275) and by the narrator, who agrees that Mr. Collins "was not a sensible man" and that he demonstrated that "mixture of servility and self-importance" that Mr. Bennet had discovered "in his letter." (276, 273) Austen deploys repetition, narratorial authority, and the sanction of the cleverer characters, to encourage novel-readers to view Mr. Collins as an absurd and comic character, to be enjoyed and derisively dismissed. This conveniently distracts us from the import of Mrs. Bennet's question about what Mr. Collins "can mean" by writing that he "is disposed to make them . . . amends" for the cruelty of the entail.

However, the letter belies the framing narrative. The novel-reader who reads the letter for herself independently of Elizabeth and her father, and applies that hint about "amends" and/or her familiarity with contemporary marriage practices, can discern what has been left unsaid: that Mr. Collins was punctiliously doing what was expected of a young man who intended to propose to a gentleman's daughter. He was writing to his potential future father-in-law to explain his situation and prospects in life. His letter assured Mr. Bennet that he could support a wife by stressing the key point for a clergyman in the Church of England – that he had a powerful patron in Lady de Burgh, whom he was worldly enough to keep happy, and thus an assured income and promising future even without the Longbourne estate. Mr. Collins' style is certainly wrong – pompous, self-important, and inept. He proceeds by hints rather than candor, whether from delicacy or because, though "com[ing] prepared to admire" one of the Bennet girls, he was not sure that he would. But his principles are right, and so is his sensibility – he was "very sensible of the hardship" in store for the Bennet daughters (273) and sought to prevent the entail from injuring them by marrying one of them. The novel-reader who reads his missive independently of Elizabeth and her father, as the letter of a "sensible" and principled man awkwardly proposing himself as a husband, will view both Mr. Collins marriage proposal to Elizabeth and Charlotte's decision to marry him with less surprise than Elizabeth does, and settle back to enjoy a story that might be called (with a mischievous glance at Hannah More) Collins' in Search of a Wife.

Like Haywood in the Hysom scenes, then, Austen was using narrative-epistolary form to do a Fielding: she misdirected novel-readers through her narrator and the weight of characters' opinions while placing her "hint" in the mouth of the most vulgar character and lowliest intelligence present. She left novel-readers to discern for themselves that the satire directed at Mr. Collins turns back on Elizabeth and her father: the wittiest and most intelligent characters in the room make an elementary generic error in reading Collins' letter as a Letter of Introduction, and prove even less "sensible" in practical matters like the entail than obvious oddities, silly mothers and romantic fools. The embedded letter from Mr. Collins thus shows novel-readers, long before the narrative does, that Elizabeth's confidence in her unerring ability to judge persons and situations is misplaced, and that her pride in her intellectual superiority to those around her may be heading for a fall.

Elizabeth proves a poor reader of narratives as well as of men and of letters. Austen made Fielding's point about the unreliability of narrative as he did – by omitting to tell novel-readers all they need to know about the characters and the plot. By appearing to endorse Elizabeth's often mistaken views of characters and situations, the narrator leaves us to discover the truth about Wickham and Darcy and the reason for Bingham's abandonment of Jane when Elizabeth does and by the same means – the letter Darcy writes her after she has rejected him. The first-time reader of *Pride and Prejudice* who trusts entirely to the narrator therefore finds herself in the same situation as the reader of *Joseph Andrews* or *Tom Jones* – caught off-guard by narrative omissions and surprised by the secret of the plot when it is finally revealed. What Jenny Davidson says of *Emma* is also true of *Pride and Prejudice*: "it reads completely differently the second time around. Clues to the secret underlying story—the one we learn about at the novel's end and that will inform our subsequent re-readings—are so subtly placed that they are genuinely invisible the first time through and will remain indeterminate thereafter ... "[50] Upon a second reading, it is also possible to notice, as Felicia Bonaparte does, that warning hints scattered throughout the narrative include the frequency with which the narrator employs the language of conjecture – words such as "suppose" (ninety times), "suspect," "presume," "surmise," "guess," and "believe;" the many times characters are "deceived" or "imposed upon;" and the regularity with which those who claim to "know" or have a "conviction" are wrong.[51]

Darcy's letter reveals the true secret histories of Wickham's past and Bingley's defection; but the focus in the framing narrative is on how letters and people are read, and here again the letter belies the framing narrative.

The prefatory narrative to Darcy's letter is confined to telling us how he delivered it to Elizabeth, who opened it "with no expectation of pleasure, but with the strongest curiosity." (353) Darcy's motive for writing is conveyed, instead, in his first paragraph: he is writing not to renew his offer of marriage, but because "my character required [the letter] to be written and read." (354) The two narratives the letter contains about his past interactions with Bingley and Wickham are designed to change Elizabeth's opinion of Darcy's character by changing her perception of the characters of all three men.

The reception narrative, to which an entire chapter is devoted, is initially all about *re*reading. Though aided this time by coming to the letter without any misleading expectations – "Elizabeth ... had formed no expectation at all of its contents" (358) – she has nevertheless to "read and reread [it] with the closest attention," "examine the meaning of every sentence," "put down the letter and weigh every circumstance," and "pause" on key points "a considerable while" before "she once more continued to read" (359, 360) in order to achieve the "clearer attention" and "impartiality" required to understand the letter's import and judge the veracity of what it says. The first time she reads the letter, Elizabeth reads it as Haywood's headlong desirous readers read love-letters and novels: "with an eagerness which hardly left her power of comprehension" so that "from impatience of knowing what the next sentence might bring, [she] was incapable of attending to the sense of the one before her eyes." (358) To understand it properly, Elizabeth must combat her "contrariety of emotions" as well as her prejudices and preconceptions – all she "wished to discredit" (358, 359) – and reread the letter coldly, analytically, and piecemeal. One might say that Austen was demonstrating that the distance created by narrative framing on which her predecessors had relied to promote thought and reflection was insufficient by itself to produce the desired effect. This had to be supplemented by novel-readers' willingness to pause in their headlong forward flight and reread embedded letters attentively, subjecting each sentence to close examination and reflecting impartially on its truth and import, as Elizabeth did. Like the novel as a whole, the embedded letters "read completely differently the second time around."

Austen's second important corrective of Haywood and Behn consists of Elizabeth's subjection of each part of Darcy's narrative to empirical verification. Comparison of letters, on which these predecessors had largely relied to determine the truth, was insufficient because it only showed that Darcy's and Wickham's opposite stories contained the same basic facts: "each recital confirmed the other," but "there must be gross duplicity on one side or the other." (359) Which was the true and which the duplicitous secret history of their common past could not be discovered just by rereading the letter or comparing the two men's narratives; it must be decided by resorting to empirical evidence outside their verbal texts. Realizing now that neither she nor anyone else "had ever heard of [Wickham] before his entrance" on the scene, and that "his countenance, voice and manner" alone had "established him at once in the possession of every virtue" –that she had judged by surface appearances – Elizabeth searches her memory for "some instance of goodness, some distinguished trait of integrity or benevolence" that would "rescue" his character from Darcy's attacks – and finds none. Indeed, Wickham fails both evidential tests: the test of others' testimony to his character and the test of testimony by his actions. In retrospect, Elizabeth sees Wickham's impropriety in telling his (hi)story to a stranger like herself and the "inconsistency of his professions with his conduct." Darcy, by contrast, has not failed either test – Elizabeth realizes that she had not "seen anything that betrayed him to be unprincipled or unjust" (360–1); that "among his own connections he was esteemed and valued" (361); and that if his narrative were untrue, he would not have told her that he could "summon more than one witness of undoubted veracity" for "the truth of every particular." (356, 360) Elizabeth thus demonstrates that a letter's truth, or mixture of truth and untruth, must be decided empirically, piece by piece, on the basis of external empirical evidence. However, Elizabeth relies here on a retrospective view fashioned from memories and reinterpretation; she obtains real evidence of Darcy's character and of Wickham's villainy only later.

The disjunction between Darcy's design in writing and Elizabeth's reception of his letter shows that Elizabeth's epiphany did not consist, as Darcy intended, in her recognition of *his* true character; it consisted of a discovery about *her* own character instead: "Till this moment, I never knew myself." This trumpeted and uncharacteristically unsubtle statement of *anagnorisis*, which twentieth-century critics regarded with admiration as a moment of achieved self-knowledge, appears to separate Austen from her narrative-epistolary predecessors. For Elizabeth takes all shame and all blame for her misreading of human and written characters upon herself. "Till this moment" she announces – the moment in which she realizes that "she has been blind, partial, prejudiced, absurd," that she has "courted prepossession and ignorance" and that "vanity, not love, has been her folly" – "till this moment, I never knew myself." (361) *Mea culpa maxima.* Austen's narrative-epistolary predecessors, who were equally cognizant of the prepossessions, partiality, prejudices, and ignorance that could blind women readers to men's true characters and to the true meaning of their words and letters, showed male characters (Bellamour, Philander) being deceived in the same ways. Too innocent, too honest, too persuadable, too passionate, or too unsuspicious, those who fell victim to a deceiver's manipulations, and to the power of language to enchant or beguile them, demonstrated first and foremost that they were no match for those wickeder than themselves.

Elizabeth assumes, by contrast, that – despite all the gaps in her knowledge about the two men – she could and should have known without Darcy's counter-narrative that Wickham's (hi)story was suspect. She assumes that, had she looked for empirical evidence of the truth or untruth of Wickham's narrative without prejudice, she must have found it. Blaming herself for blindness, she accuses herself of "driving reason away" and of deceiving herself. However, as Peter Knox-Shaw and John Wiltshire remind us, it is important to remember the dictum in *Emma* that "seldom, very seldom does complete truth belong to any human disclosure" and to "read against the pull of complicity with Elizabeth."[52] Rereading Darcy's letter independently of Elizabeth, and without complicity with her reaction, counters the overt narrative and her own perspective with a very different view.

Darcy's letter explains that in separating Bingley from Jane, he acted on empirical evidence:

> "From that moment I observed my friend's behavior attentively; and I could then perceive that his partiality for Miss Bennet was beyond what I had ever

witnessed in him. Your sister I also watched.—Her look and manners were open, cheerful and engaging as ever, but without any symptom of peculiar regard, and I remained convinced from the evening's scrutiny, that though she received his attentions with pleasure, she did not invite them by any participation of sentiment. –If *you* have not been mistaken here, *I* must have been in an error ... But I shall not scruple to assert, that the serenity of your sister's countenance and air was such, as might have given the most acute observer, a conviction that, however amiable her temper, her heart was not likely to be easily touched. .... I did not believe her to be indifferent because I wished it; – I believed it on impartial conviction, as truly as I wished it in reason. (354–355)

After this, he writes, the task of "convincing" Bingley "that he had deceived himself" about Jane's feelings for him "was scarcely the work of a moment." (355) Elizabeth accepts Darcy's explanation without reservation:

He had declared himself to have been totally unsuspicious of her sister's attachment; –and she could not help remembering what Charlotte's opinion had always been. –Neither could she deny the justice of his description of Jane. –She felt that Jane's feelings, though fervent, were little displayed, and that there was a constant complacency in her air and manner, not often united with great sensibility. (361)

In other words, the evidence provided by empirical observation of a person's conduct and demeanor could be objectively misleading, regardless of how impartial the observer might be. Darcy had judged Jane from what presented to his view, regardless of gaps in his knowledge of her, as Elizabeth had judged Wickham. No less proud or prejudiced than Elizabeth, Darcy's conclusion conformed to his wishes, just as Elizabeth's had; and like her, he got his conclusion wrong. But Darcy does not blame himself for being mistaken or attribute his misjudgment to his moral shortcomings. Elizabeth does not blame him either – even for being "unsuspicious." As they both agree, Darcy has been deceived, as anyone might have been deceived, by a person whose real thoughts and feelings were too "little displayed." Is it less reasonable for Elizabeth to have been deceived by Wickham, whose real thoughts and feelings were likewise "too little displayed?" Bingley's reaction to Darcy's observations adds another twist, for it demonstrates that one can be deceived in believing that one has deceived oneself. This raises the further question of whether Elizabeth too was deceiving herself at this moment when she condemned herself for being entirely self-deceived and yet claimed to know herself.

Traditional readings of this scene assume a familiar, positivist nineteenth- and twentieth-century epistemology in which, like nature's underlying laws, the hidden springs of character and of social relations are capable of becoming known to an impartial observer, and failure to discern or discover them only reflects the moral failings and/or epistemological limitations of the individual knower. Here the only mind that can really betray or deceive one is one's own. In this episteme, the past too can be redeemed, its errors corrected, once its secrets are discovered and told. After Elizabeth "develops" by discovering and correcting her hitherto unperceived moral and epistemo-logical failings, and after the truth about hidden elopements (Georgiana's, Lydia's) and concealed affections (Jane's, Elizabeth's) has been brought to light, a happy ending is possible for all concerned. On this reading, then, there is a "substantial shift" in "the last third of the novel," from exploration of the many partial and mistaken conclusions possible when "evidence-gathering and judgment-making are dependent upon the subject or per-ceiver," to "the assurance of certainty in Jane Austen's world" that "heals the split between the subjective and the objective."[53]

But the more skeptical reading is reinforced when Darcy's epistolary narrative about Bingley's self-deception is verified, and the question of erroneous judgment is raised again, during Elizabeth's conversation with her sister after Jane's engagement to Bingley. Jane repeats what Bingley told her: that "nothing but a persuasion of *my* being indifferent, would have prevented his coming down [to Longbourne] again." (447) Elizabeth's response is a variation on her response to Darcy's error about Jane's true feelings: Bingley "made a little mistake to be sure; but it is to the credit of his modesty." (447) This is "a little mistake" for Bingley despite its fatal consequences for Jane, which have now, very fortuitously, been averted. Ecstatically happy herself, Jane tells Elizabeth: "If I could but see *you* as happy! If there *were* but such another man for you!" Elizabeth's response is striking: " . . . perhaps, if I have very good luck, I may meet with another Mr. Collins in time." (447) Understated as this is, it conveys the magnitude of the catastrophe. What was a "small mistake" for a gentleman who had many opportunities to meet other possible brides, was a fatal mistake for a gentleman's daughter without fortune, living in a small, undistinguished village, who was unlikely to meet many eligible men in her lifetime, much less eligible men who proposed. Darcy's letter had made it clear that his offer of marriage would not be repeated; there would be no second chance. In reality, Elizabeth was saying, a woman who mistook her man and refused the only Mr. Right she was ever likely to meet, had missed the only chance at marital happiness she was likely to get. In reality, then, Elizabeth's mistake was irredeemable – as were Lydia's mistake in eloping with Wickham and Jane's mistake in allowing Bingley to mistake her feelings. Elizabeth's one-sided, self-blaming monologue in the wake of

Darcy's letter had not been a cool, impartial judgment, but a violent emotional outburst of regret and bitter self-reproach for her terrible, irreparable mistake.

To bring about a happy ending, what follows "little mistakes" that were in reality fatal to a girl's marital chances, belongs to wish-fulfillment, to the marvelous and to romance. In this last third of the novel, forms of evidence that Rosanna Cavellero shows were discredited earlier (the testimony of witnesses, of actions and of narratives) become reliable and true representations of characters and events, to permit a rapid series of improbably fortuitous encounters and the incredibly convenient communication of key information to bring Darcy back and marry him to Elizabeth.[54] This is where the letter's narrative about Darcy's relations to Wickham is verified by Elizabeth unexpectedly obtaining testimony to Darcy's character from his housekeeper and Lady de Burgh, and proof of the benevolence his actions from Pemberley and his rescue of Lydia. Elizabeth bleak and understated assessment of her real prospects indicates why the narrative has to take what critics agree is a different, romantic turn after Cinderella has turned her back on her Prince: to enable him to find her again, however improbably with a slipper, and ensure that he marries her despite her awful family in the end. On this reading, the wonders of impartial analysis, timely testimony, reliable evidence, empirical certainty, and accurate self-knowledge belong where Fielding had placed histories of England and Haywood, newspapers – in the bin labeled "Romance."[55]

Retrospective: On Omissions, Misdirection, and the Practice of Romance

As a reviewer observed in 1809, "the scene of the familiar *epopee* [had] shifted from the tilt-yard to the drawing-room."[56] The plots of all the novels and novellas considered in this chapter belonged to the Aristotelian romance tradition descending from *The Odyssey* insofar as they turned on discoveries of secrets of identity – a lover's true character, or in Fielding, a protagonist's true birth.[57] The story could be varied and made to seem quite novel – as in *Fantomina*, where Haywood reversed the gender of the character keeping their true identity secret, or *Pride and Prejudice*, where Austen parceled out the romantic heroine's typical fate among different characters and reversed the trajectory of the desirable lover who proves to be false by making Darcy begin as a false and undesirable lover and end by captivating the heroine. But what differentiates these stories for our present purposes is whether they took narrative, narrative-epistolary or epistolary form, and which of the two traditional methods of managing their "dual structure" they chose.[58] Pursuing these questions offers another perspective both on what Austen appropriated from each, and on where misdirections and omissions typically occurred.

In *Pride and Prejudice*, Austen reworked and modernized Behn and Haywood's typical romances about credulous young girls who were deceived and seduced by charming philanderers and discovered their lover's true character too late, as Richardson too had done. But she followed Fielding rather than Behn, Haywood, or Richardson in the construction of her plot. Behn and Richardson had used the first method of managing the story's "dual structure" that Terence Cave described: they withheld the secret history of their philanderer's intrigues from their heroine, but not from novel-readers. Fielding favored the second technique, where the narrator demonstrates his "mastery of the art of telling lies" by withholding key information from novel-readers and inducing us to take the manifest story and apparent determinations of character and events for the true story, in order to make us experience an *anagnorisis* and *peripeteia* along with the characters.[59] Austen's narrator too acted as master of lies by concealing the secret histories of Wickham's villainy and Bingley's manipulation, as Fielding's narrator had concealed those of his foundlings in *Joseph Andrews* and *Tom Jones*, until protagonists and novel-readers were enlightened together. Theorists in the Aristotelian romance tradition considered this second manner of managing the story's dual structure superior to the first because it had the virtue of surprise as well as that of arousing readers' interest all over again by giving them a whole new perspective on the story they had previously encountered. But it left novel-readers smugly satisfied at the end, after discovery of the heretofore hidden story, that they now finally had the truth and knew all they needed to know. In *Tom Jones*, Fielding avoided this outcome, which ultimately left the credibility of narrative or at least of the *right* narrative intact, by giving this novel two contradictory endings. Austen did something similar through the marvelous and improbably fortuitous turn she gave the last third of her novel, to cast her happy ending as wish-fulfillment and fairy tale.[60]

But when it came to the embedded letters, Austen followed her narrative-epistolary predecessors. Like them, she used everyday instrumental letters and discrepancies between the letter and reception narratives to demonstrate that, in conditions of incomplete knowledge, it was all too easy for character-readers to mistake the genre of letter they were reading or the character its author was assuming for the occasion, to overlook a key point the letter was making or to be deluded by its style. These errors that the Bennetts made in their reading of Mr. Collins's letter were errors that Philander and Silvia had made before, and that Haywood had warned readers against. Austen also took to extremes a device that Behn and Haywood had deployed more sparingly: that of leaving novel-readers to notice for themselves, from their own reading of a letter, whatever character-readers had overlooked and the narrator had omitted to say. Haywood, I have argued, withheld narrative guidance in favor of narratorial misdirection in the Hysom episodes primarily to defend her otherwise consistently instructive and reliable narrative frames by turning Fielding's critique back on him. But Austen's reuse of this ploy here showed that it cut two ways. What was a disadvantage to a novelist writing didactically to prevent letters from drawing women "into the path of ruin," was of the greatest benefit to a satirical novelist taking aim at characters' and novel-readers' absurd misreadings of letters, of narratives and of others, and ludicrous blindness to truth. By withholding reliable narrative guidance and focalizing letters' reading and writing through character-readers and character-writers; by minimizing prefatory narratives or replacing them with partly or wholly misleading reception narratives; and/or by presenting characters' debates or conjectures about a letter and using her narrator to misdirect novel-readers; Austen left embedded letters to do the work of monitoring both the characters' and the narrative's "labour to attain truth." Together with her use of irony, this heightened the possibility that unsuspecting novel-readers would be misled by taking letters at a character's valuation or by their own too rapid and inattentive reading, and be surprised by discovery later on or upon a second novel-reading of something inscribed, unnoticed, in a letter before.

This brings to the fore key differences between the kind of withholding employed by narrative-epistolary novelists and that favored by Fielding and Aristotelian theorists of romance. The master-of-lies method left novel-readers at the mercy of the narrative, albeit in expected ways. If Fielding's "sagacious readers" recognized that the narrator had assumed the traditional role of master of lies, they would be primed to expect to be surprised by the eventual emergence of a hidden story, and to admire the author's skill in managing the manifest story to retard and effect that surprise. But they had no means of guessing what the manifest story had suppressed. Fielding highlighted the absurdity here by twice resorting for his hidden story to the formulaic old tale of lost or abandoned children that he had himself condemned as *cliché*, while presenting his manifest narratives as doing something else. The joke here was that the story discovered hidden beneath the author's brio and skill was always the same old story; the expected surprise was really no surprise at all. One might say that Austen too achieved this effect by hiding the familiar features of a Behn or Haywood romance beneath the scintillating satirical surfaces of a manifest story about gentlemen universally known to be seeking a wife.

But as Austen emphasized by making letters the measure of the narrative's truth, narrative-epistolary novelists who withheld information while presenting fully transcribed letters on the page, went about withholding quite differently: they gave "sagacious readers" an opportunity to discover what their narratives had omitted. Sagacious readers could see from the letters transcribed on the page before them what was unnoticed by character-readers, omitted from the narrative frame, or subject to narratorial misdirection, just as they could see from discrepancies between prefatory and reception narratives where communication among characters had gone awry. By reading embedded letters as Elizabeth read Darcy's – more than once, with close attention, piecemeal, while comparing each fragment to empirical realities in the storyworld – a novel-reader could launch her own investigation into the truth of characters' observations and into the reliability of the narrator's interpretations of characters, letters, and events.

Appropriating elements both from her narrative-epistolary predecessors and from the romance tradition that Fielding had both mocked and re-invoked, Austen combined their contrasting methods of withholding key information. This exponentially increased the skeptical indeterminacy of her novel, while enabling her to take aim at the self-evidence both of narratives and of letters. However, this was not all she gleaned from her narrative-epistolary predecessors. Like her adoption of piecemeal reading from Frances Burney and of letter-narratives and the language of conjecture from Charlotte Smith, Austen's treatment of empirical verification in the Darcy scene comments on a line of argument about empiricism that her predecessors had developed by comparing epistolary representations to narrative realities. This will be the subject of the Chapter 2

Letters and Empirical Evidence

Introduction: Identity, Secret Histories, and Detection

It was not easy to pin down the true identity of an occasional self that normatively acted and presented itself differently on different occasions according to the ever-changing and recombining relations in which it stood to other people – a self moreover, whose occasional character was tirelessly promoted by conduct books prescribing the proper conduct of the same person in different social and interpersonal relations (as master and servant, husband and wife, parents and child, mistress, companion, daughter, sibling or friend, etc.). Considered empirically, such a self was almost inevitably deceptive – as deceptive as only viewing the side of Plato's table that presented itself to one's gaze and assuming or imagining the rest. As we saw in the Introduction, Locke described ascriptions of identity to this empirical self as forensic fictions – constructions of some part(s) of the subject that shifted according to the interlocutor, the observer and the occasion on which a self was invoked, and left the subject's true being as indeterminate and mysterious as "the thing in itself" to an observing eye. As Locke stressed, no one could observe what was really going on inside someone else's head or heart; and what was going on inside one's own was changing all the time. The problem was compounded by a culture of politeness, which required the well-bred to conceal their thoughts and passions behind agreeable sentiments, complaisant conduct, and an amiable demeanor. Since polite letter-writers too assumed any character required by the occasion and the relation in which they stood to their addressee(s), letters were paradigmatic instantiations of the deployment of shifting occasional selves, and of the problems of identity they posed, especially since, like people posing on the internet, letter-writers could assume characters that did not exist. Yet for those dependent on others in a hierarchical face-to-face society, especially women, it was essential to determine who others really were, in order to know how far they could be trusted or if they were safe to marry.

Locke had posited that the truth or falsity of ascriptions of character could be discovered by empirical verification. The novelists in this chapter used narrative-epistolary fiction's second scaffolding device – juxtaposition of epistolary and narrative accounts of the same characters and events – to put this claim to the test. Thus where the narrative-epistolary texts considered in Chapter 1 concentrated primarily on issues of writing and reading, those in this chapter give greater weight to letters as speech acts whose illocutionary and perlocutionary force made things happen in what their narratives mark as the real world, by requiring their character-recipients to act.

The formal and thematic differences this entailed are usefully exemplified in the following passage, which is taken from one of four letters composing *Bath Intrigues* (1725), a work attributed to secret historian Delarivier Manley, where it figures as one of several scandals that an unnamed gentleman in Bath is recounting to his friend, Will, in London. Here the letter-writer's narrative about how "my Lord *Wordy*" was "made the Jest of all the Company" is sandwiched between the letter that contains it and the letter it contains:

> You know he was ever addicted to boast of Ladies Favours—some waggish gentlemen here contriv'd to send him a Letter as from a Woman of Quality, but left him to guess at the Name, signing no other than *Incognita*; this was an Assignation to meet in a Field about a Mile distant from the *Bath* – the day they chose, happen'd to be the most rainy we have had this year; the meeting was to be so private that he was charged to leave his Coach a good Distance from the Place, and while he went, Knight-Errant like, defying Wind and Weather, walking for a good space of time expecting his *Dulcinea*, those who had sent him on the Adventure, order'd their Servants to go disguis'd, and cut all the Harnesses of the Horses; and at his Return, he found himself oblig'd to walk to his Lodgings in the most miry and piteous Condition that ever disappointed Lover was in. But I should have inform'd you, that having communicated the Invitation he receiv'd from this imaginary Lady, to those very Gentlemen who had laid the Plot, and promis'd to acquaint them with his Success; in spite of the Fatigue he had endur'd, he now dress'd him, and went to the Tavern where they had appointed to meet; and on their asking him if he had been happy. O! Beyond Imagination, (*cryd he*) the loveliest, most enchanting of her Sex —one you little think on; – the kind Creature was there before me, and after she had discover'd to me who she was, consented to go with me to a place I always make use of when my Amour is with Women of Condition . . .[1]

The passage continues in much the same vein, as the company's increasingly searching questions prompt Lord Wordy to increasingly improbable inventions.

In this passage, the waggish gentlemen use their letter to move Lord Wordy to action in order to unmask his real character by comparing his words to his actions. The narrative works throughout with the disjunction between the realities of the situation and the letter's effects on Wordy. Recurrent Quixotic imagery underlines this disjunction by highlighting the distance between Lord Wordy's conventional romantic inventions and the true facts of the case, and between the libertine virility he seeks to project and the physical beating he takes. The effect of the jest is to make Lord Wordy as ridiculous as Don Quixote, thanks to that vanity about his sexual prowess, which makes him act on the letter without doubting its authenticity and then enact his absurdly protracted cover-up of a nonevent. The jest thus empirically tests and narratively "proves" the company's suspicion that Lord Wordy is not what he pretends to be, and mocks the folly of men, like Lord Wordy, who are "all talk."

Making the narrating letter-writer a party to the joke enabled Manley to use his framing narrative to inform intra- and extra-diegetic readers at the outset that the letter Lord Wordy receives is fake. Manley has retained the usual tripartite framing structure, but transcription of the letter in its entirety has been eschewed to direct readerly attention to the letter's agency by summarizing its principal illocutionary and perlocutionary features – function, signature, instructions – and by linking each to its effects. This is a Letter of Assignation, whose function is to arrange a clandestine meeting. Its pseudonymous signature, borrowed from drama and romance ("Incognita"), persuades Wordy to come by arousing his curiosity and persuading him that the writer is a desirable sexual partner – a lady who, though willing to engage in an "Amour," is obliged to be careful of her reputation. The letter's agency is highlighted by detailing its instructions, apparently designed to further protect the lady's reputation by ensuring the secrecy of the tryst and by describing their effects as these unfold in a series of scenes which transpire at a later date. On the date the letter has appointed for the tryst, its instructions have the expected effect of causing Wordy to walk some distance from his coach, and the unexpected effect of getting him soaked. Worthy's interview with the company occurs at a tavern that evening. The narrative frame is thus expanded to follow the empirical consequences of the letter as these unfold at different dates and times from scene to scene. As we will see, the quest for empirical verification always expanded the narrative frame beyond writing and reading "to the moment" to relate the initial moment of writing or reception to subsequent empirical discoveries, to remembered earlier interactions, and/or to intended and unintended consequences occurring later on the narrative timeline, which verify the truth of epistolary affirmations, reveal their deceptive character, or demonstrate that even false and lying letters can have real long-term effects.

Manley used her letter-writing narrator and the agency of an anonymous fictional letter to make a point about the inscrutability of letters judged by their words alone and to reveal larger empirical truths about the duplicity of characters – Lord Wordy's certainly, but also that of the waggish gentlemen in their dealings with him. Wordy's error lay in assuming he could ascertain Incognita's identity and the truth about the letter from what it said. When words stood for ideas in the mind of the speaker or writer, not for real things, a letter could as easily convey the false or fictitious ideas of an "imaginary lady," as the honest sentiments of a real person. Wordy's error lay in not seeking empirical verification, for if he had put Incognita's written words to some empirical test, as the company did Wordy's oral ones, he too would have discovered the deception practiced upon him and who the writer really was. But what the "jest" reveals empirically is that no one in this company showed their true self either in their oral or written conversations. Like Wordy, the gentlemen embrace a range of different duplicities: as Wordy prepares to assume a different character when meeting the lady from that which he assumed in his boasts or in his desperate walk to his lodgings, so the gentlemen act different parts when planning the jest with the narrator, when composing the letter as a Lady, and when interviewing Wordy after the nonevent. The jest thus unmasks both Wordy and the company by showing that gentlemen were not any of the selves they assumed, without indicating who or what they were beyond a series of assumed characters or "masks."

The narrative-epistolary novels and episodes examined in this chapter assess and debate what Manley here accepts unquestioningly: that empirical verification could, and necessarily would, enable a person to discover whether a letter was factually true and whether others truly were the self-ascribed to them and/or the self they presented to one's view. Mary Davys, Eliza Haywood, and Charlotte Smith all treat anonymous letters which made damaging claims about the character and past history of others as limit-cases that raised questions about empirical evidence, written testimony, and satisfactory verification in particularly acute and obvious ways.[2] They followed Locke's advice by showing characters looking to reality to determine the validity of the charges in these letters, usually by trying to detect the truth and past history of characters hiding their secrets behind the occasional self they displayed. Treating empiricism as a relation between the mind and reality, they countered knowledge-claims in law, history, and natural philosophy by identifying impediments in reality to empirical discovery of the truth, and by demonstrating the shortcomings of mental acts upon which empiricism increasingly relied – inference, conjecture, judgments of probability, and construction of plausible fact-based narratives. In *Lady Audley's Secret*, Braddon adapted this model for the nineteenth century by having her investigating character use pseudonymous letters and an unsigned telegram as clues to the identity of a woman with a secret history of inhabiting shifting occasional selves under different names, and by representing her detective's empiricist use of conjecture and probability to construct a chain of evidence against her, as the obsessive working of a diseased mind.

Davys, Haywood, Smith, and Braddon's texts belong to different historical moments and to different phases in empiricist arguments about empirical evidence. Beginning from the 1720s, they show how Manley's faith in empirical verification gave way to increasing skepticism about the accuracy of the inferences we make from putative facts. After the introduction of circumstantial evidence during the 1740s, they began to demonstrate that induction is a far more dynamic and time-related process than empiricists pretended, and one in which the fluidity of social relations and/ or an investigator's changing knowledge were disconcertingly capable of turning facts into fictions, and fictions into facts. Their critiques of successive empirical laws of evidence are discussed in the concluding "Retrospective" section .

Detecting Occasional Selves: Mary Davys's *The Reform'd Coquet*

Read as a linear, causal narrative, *The Reform'd Coquet* (1724) is still viewed as "the first in a long line of coquettish heroines and lover-mentors [who] reform them."[3] On this view, her uncle, Traffick, sends orphaned, fifteen-year-old Amoranda a guardian, Formator, to transform her from a coquette into a docile and conformable wife by subjecting her to Formator's patriarchal domestic government. Formator takes charge upon his arrival, rids Amoranda of her unsuitable suitors, manipulates her, reeducates her, and – after she and we discover at the end that he is a handsome young Marquis in disguise – marries the creature he has thus "formed . . . to his own liking." (96) To read the novella in this way is to accept without question Uncle Traffick's ascription of Amoranda's identity and Formator's version of events. But, as recent critics have argued, the novel is "more complex than this," not least because it "stresses questions of agency in domestic structures" and "raises the question of who reforms whom."[4] Davys did, after all, call it *The Reform'd Coquet*, not *The Reform'd Coquette*.

As in *Pride and Prejudice* almost a century later, a different story emerges from reading Davys's novella through its fourteen embedded letters. This reveals a subtext that counters Traffick and Formator's manifest plot, together with an Amoranda who uses a versatile combination of occasional selves to address "every tinker in his own language" and manage the variously deceptive relationships that dominate her world. Warning novel-readers with the novella's first letters that letters and verbal professions must be tested empirically against documents, actions, and facts, Davys often left novel-readers to determine empirically for themselves – as Amoranda must – what is verified by narrative realities and what is not. Davys constructed a double-voiced text, capable of diametrically opposite interpretations, by leaving readers to compare Amoranda's words and conduct to other characters' ascriptions of identity to her. To demonstrate the parallel impossibilities of reading a letter accurately "to the moment" and of judging a character accurately on first impressions, Davys omitted key information from letters' immediate narrative frames; used reception narratives for conversations offering competing views of a letter's meaning and truth; and deferred revelation of empirical information on which the correct interpretation of some letters depends, to much later on the story's timeline. While expanding her narrative frames to follow the meaning(s) and consequences of some letters as they unfold in changing circumstances over time, Davys segmented her text thematically to create a number of coherent letter-series with a beginning, middle, and end.

Letters 1–3 introduce questions, both formal and thematic, that will reverberate through the novella and be settled only at the end. The warning that letters may prove wholly or partially deceptive unless their author is identified and their contents verified empirically is given with the first embedded letter. This is a short, anonymous note cautioning Amoranda against one of her suitors: "Take care of Lord Lofty, who carries nothing but Ruin to our whole Sex: believe me who have too fatally experienced him ... If you fall into his Snare after so fair a Warning, nobody but yourself deserves the Blame."[5] The framing narrative informs us that this note is found in Amoranda's garden by Lord Lofty who dishonorably reads it and confirms its characterization of him. Aware that she too must have read it, Lofty now "fears his hopes of Amoranda are at an end," and is surprised to find that "her Behaviour is as free and open as ever." (16) A second reception narrative containing a conversation between Amoranda and her maid, Jenny, is prompted by Amoranda's discovery, sometime later, that she has lost the note. Amoranda explains to Jenny that she refused to "take notice on't" (17) because she will not accept the note's "believe me who have too fatally experienced him" without knowing who that "me" is and what her motives and circumstances are. The identity and social authority of a speaker or writer was still the principal criterion for the truth of their utterances, especially in courts of law. Amoranda's objection, accordingly, is that the note could as easily have been written for "Spite" by "one of [Lofty's] Tenants' Daughters" (and therefore carry no weight) as be what Jenny thinks it – the genuine letter of a "poor Lady" that conveniently confirms Jenny's own suspicions about Lord Lofty's character and intent. Lofty had been honest with Amoranda about his disinclination to marry, a point on which they agree; and she is willing to "take notice" and act on the note only with certain knowledge of its author and its empirical truth. The reader who accepts Jenny's view of the letter and of Lofty's character will see Amoranda as a thoughtless coquette, agree with Jenny that she ought to dismiss Lofty immediately, and understand why her uncle thinks she needs Formator's guidance to keep her safe. But Davys was still only making the same point as Manley: no action should be taken on a letter without knowing exactly who and what occasioned it and obtaining empirical evidence of its truth.

This note recurs at later points on the narrative timeline until these questions are settled. Amoranda finds evidence confirming the note's account of Lofty's character several scenes later, when Jenny brings her a letter-document he dropped in the garden, dated a month earlier, in which Lofty promised to marry an unspecified lady or forfeit L.10,000. As the reception narrative tells us, Amoranda discovers from this evidence that Lofty has been lying to her about his disinclination to marry, and "impudently" feigning his "Devotions" to her in order to use her as a "Play-Thing," a mere "Diversion," for his idle hours. With material proof of his baseness and duplicity now before her, Amoranda vows revenge: "I have so just a resentment against his Behaviour to me, that if the Lady this Paper was design'd for, will accept it, I will certainly make her a present of it tomorrow." (40) Amoranda meets Altamira, the author of the anonymous note, several scenes after this, and hears her account of how Lofty deceived her by his "devotions" and used the promissory note Jenny found to ruin her, before abandoning her to poverty, sickness, and despair. Amoranda now has enough information about the letter-writer's identity and circumstances, and enough evidence of the truth of the anonymous note's testimony to Lofty's character and past history, to believe that "me who have too fatally experienced him," and to act. She gives the promissory note to the lady it was designed for, devises a plot to force Lofty to marry his ruined mistress, and reforms a male coquet.

The first letter, then, confronts Amoranda with true written testimony in potentially deceptive guise. By revealing key information about the author, motives, and circumstances that engendered the anonymous note, not in its prefatory frame, but subsequently, piecemeal, and over extended story-time, the narrative shows that Amoranda chose the wisest course. Prudently waiting until enough reliable information has been discovered about the letter's author and content to know what past events engendered it and determine whether it is truth or "spite," enables Amoranda to act effectively to serve the letter-writer and right her wrongs. Amoranda's reading of this first note – which extends over a long, discontinuous series of scenes and involves comparing letters and professions to acts and facts to decide if they should be believed – also models the kind of reading that this novella demands of its readers.

The second embedded letter is analogical to the first: it too is anonymous and contains an accusation and a warning. But this time the accusation is against Amoranda and novella-readers are left to do the work of empirical verification for themselves. The prefatory narrative explains that this letter is delivered in a glove thrown through a window by a male stranger who immediately rides off. His fully transcribed Letter of Reproach tells Amoranda what "none have Courage or Honesty enough to tell you" though "many have the same opinion of your Behaviour." The writer admonishes her to: "Consider how unhappy that woman is, who finds herself daily hedg'd with self-ended Flatterers who make it their business to keep up a Vanity in you, which may one day prove your Ruin." And he instructs her to immediately "discard three Froths of your daily Attendants who, like so many Locusts, are striving to devour you." (28–29) Again raising questions about its author's identity, the letter's reception narrative records a conversation in which Jenny and Amoranda offer conflicting views of it. Amoranda considers it "impudent" and argues that he can have no "good meaning . . . who persuades me to banish the Bees and live by my self." Jenny, who "believe[s] he means well," thinks Amoranda "mistakes him, 'tis the Wasps he would have you discard." (29)

This letter raises the question of Amoranda's identity by producing the "opinion" of the "many" who observe her conduct from the outside. Novella-readers who believe the "many" and treat this letter as true testimony to her identity are likely to dismiss Amoranda as a coquette and to interpret the rest of the story as the account of how she is reformed by the lover-mentor who is about to appear. But this letter does not explicitly accuse her of coquetry. It warns her that she is putting herself in danger by surrounding herself with self-interested men who seek to ruin her sexually and/or financially. And the framing narrative enables us to compare the "opinion" of the "many" to what Amoranda herself thinks, says, and does by supplying Amoranda's "inward private inclinations" (40) through focalization and candid conversation with the maid she trusts, and by confirming her words by her actions as they unfold over time. Examining what Amoranda herself actually thinks, says, and does shows that she stands in no need of the note's warning. She considers flirting with men who "all love Variety [so] well" that their "Affections, like [their] money, circulate all the Nation over" (35) is only "pay[ing] them in their own coin" (38) and treating them as they deserve. She has been entertaining such men in order not to "live by my self," and using her "sprightly wit" (5) to keep them at bay. This has pleased her vanity and kept her (and us) entertained. But she has prudently taken practical precautions too. Amoranda has surrounded herself with faithful and protective servants – her maid, Jenny; the housekeeper who reports overhearing two suitors plotting to abduct her; the stout footmen she uses in the "counter-plot" she designs to punish them for it. Amoranda acts as the prudent mistress of a household, who organizes her family of servants to supply her with information and protection that she lacks in her solitary and orphaned state. The identities ascribed to her by others – thoughtless coquette or foolish young girl whose vanity leaves her helpless before predatory men – are belied by the shrewd, prudent, and proactive young woman who actually thinks and acts. For Amoranda, the empirical question to be settled by experiment is not whether she can be "reformed," but "who comes best off" when she pits her wits against "the whole contrary Sex." (32) This is the question that *her* story will address.

The third letter illustrates cases where even a reader aware of the need for empirical verification is unlikely to do due diligence, for here anonymity does not raise its red flag. Written by one of the "many" who think her a coquette, this is the Letter of Introduction that Amoranda's uncle, Traffick, sends with the seeming old gentleman, Formator. His letter appears honest and straightforward but proves in retrospect to be the considered instrument of a complicated deception, which is launched at the moment of its reception. Information essential to its correct interpretation, which is missing here, is supplied to Amoranda and to novella-readers only with Traffick's second letter at the novella's end. Traffick's first letter here only informs Amoranda that Formator is "one for whom I have the greatest value" and "my friend," and that he is "putting [her] into his hands." (32–33) The reception narrative makes it clear that Amoranda takes this letter at face value. Because she knows its author, it does not occur to her to question Formator's identity or the character in which Traffick writes. The "questions of agency in domestic structures" and of who will govern and mentor whom, which are raised by this letter, are addressed in its reception narrative. Amoranda is not best pleased that she is "no longer my own Mistress," but "is now to live under [Formator's] Restrictions." (34) Upon reflection, however, she consents to "use him as directed in that Letter" because her uncle stands her "Friend" in loco parentis and she owes him "Proof of [her] Duty." (36) Amoranda now adopts the character expected of dutiful young women in hierarchical, patriarchal eighteenth-century families. But she also proactively strikes a "Bargain" with Formator about what her "Duty" and his "Restrictions" will entail. She agrees to take Formator into her "Confidence," to "always listen to [his] Advice, and take it as often as [she] can"; while he promises to be "very cautious how I presume to advise; and if I ever do so, it shall be when your own Reason must side with me." (34) This is not your typical patriarchal situation, all masculine strength, will, and power on one side, and all feminine softness, obedience, and dependency on the other. Nor is it *The Taming of the Shrew*. The relationship Amoranda establishes with her new guardian in the wake of Traffick's letter assumes that she has reason, sense, and a will of her own. Empirically, Formator's first act as her guardian is to participate in the counterplot that Amoranda has already put in place against the two fortune-hunting suitors who plan to abduct her, and thus to follow *her* directions; while Amoranda's first act of "duty" – refusing admittance to Lofty at Formator's behest – comes after her discovery of the promissory letter has revealed Lofty's baseness and duplicity.

Amoranda refuses to take Formator's advice later when he advises her against going on a boat trip with her cousin and her cousin's female friend because Formator can offer no rational grounds for his "strange uneasiness" about it, much less for his "suspicion" that her cousin's female friend is really a man in disguise. (101) She reasons that she must be safe with her male servants rowing the boat. The misadventure that follows, in which she has to be rescued from violence, abduction, and rape by a gallant stranger, Alanthus, shows Amoranda not only that her female cousin has been in league with a fortune hunter (disguised as the female friend) but also that her servants were bribed to betray her into the hands of the abductor. Servants could be bought. Here "see[ing] who comes best off" in her encounters with the "contrary Sex" teaches

Amoranda that empirical evidence of deception and danger does not necessarily present itself in time, and that she cannot invariably rely on servants to provide the physical protection from male violence she seeks.

Letters 5–10 concern Amoranda's plot to trick Lofty into marrying Altamira, the author of the first anonymous note, again disproving the characterization of Amoranda by the "many" in the anonymous Letter of Reproach. The first in this series is a Letter of Assignation that Lofty sends Amoranda, to persuade her to meet him secretly. This provides Amoranda with the opening she needs to launch her plot. Letters 6–9 are, like Traffick's letter, the deceptive instruments of a plot, this time with Amoranda as its author. Amoranda instructs Altamira to write informing Lofty that she is now in possession of his promissory letter and means to hold him to its terms at law. The two Letters of Assignation that Amoranda writes Lofty are deceptive in all but their instructions: Amoranda pretends that she is willing to meet and marry him, to get him and his chaplain where she needs them to pull off her trick of secretly exchanging Altamira for herself. Readers observing the actions and facts presented by the narrative will notice that this is the second time Amorinda uses deceit against those who would deceive her, and the second plot she has devised. That Amoranda differs markedly from Lofty's previous victims is under-lined when this letter sequence is interrupted by Altamira's narrative about how Lofty ruined her when she acceded to just such a secret meeting upon receipt of just such a letter of assignation, and by her account of how Lofty bribed her maid to steal the promissory letter from her room. While supplying further empirical evidence that servants could be bought, this shows the path that Amoranda's story might have taken had she been the credulous prey of designing men that the "many" thought her. That she is not this Altamira (other view) is underlined by Amoranda's "resolve" not to explain her plot to Formator and Altamira in order "to have the Merit of it wholly to herself." (82) By emphasizing that Amoranda designs this plot alone and that Formator and Altamira follow her directions, the narrative shows her governing them, and demonstrates that another girl, who is willing to pit her wits against the contrary sex, is the best friend a ruined girl can have.[6] There is a notable alternation too between the self Amoranda shows her fellow-plotters and the foolish Altamira-like self she assumes for Lofty to gain her ends.

The concluding letter-series, 11–14, deals with Alanthus's courtship of Amoranda. Alanthus's two missives invite comparison with Lofty's earlier epistolary communications. Alanthus writes to beg Amoranda's permission to visit her and – in contrast to Lofty's letter of assignation – to state that his intentions are honorable: "If I can but make my-self acceptable to you, Formator and I will talk about the Estate." (127) Unlike Lofty, Alanthus means marriage. A reception narrative prompted by Amoranda's later re-reading of his letter while her maid is undressing her, contains Jenny's discovery that the same hand that now signs itself Alanthus also wrote Amoranda the very unloverlike anonymous Letter of Reproach that arrived in a glove. Alanthus has accidentally betrayed himself by forgetting to alter his handwriting, as Lofty accidentally betrayed himself by losing his promissory note to Altamira in Amoranda's garden.

The possibility of being deceived by falsified evidence is presented when Alanthus writes Amoranda a Letter of Apology for failing to visit her as he promised, claiming to be too ill to come – a lie he perpetuates in his character of Formator. Unaware as yet that these are alternating, occasional selves assumed by the same man, Amoranda believes Alanthus to be sick because Formator brings her "news" of his fever. She had discovered the truth about Lofty from a written document and the testimony of a witness; but though she has the same forms of evidence before her again, she cannot discover from them "what new Mystery has introduced itself into the Behaviour of Alanthus now." (150) For now the complicity of a lying witness with a factitious letter conspire to conceal Alanthus-Formator's secret and prevent the mystery of his conduct from being solved. Like her demonstration earlier that empirical evidence of deception and danger does not necessarily present itself in time, Davys's demonstration here that evidence can be rigged and that key facts may emerge only by chance, shows where empiricist methods of verification can prove defective, and how elusive a person's true identity can remain as a result.

After Formator has been unmasked as Alanthus by Jenny thanks to an accidental fire, he tells Amoranda unrepentantly that he "value[s] [him] self . . . on carrying on so clean a Cheat so long a time." (156) Outraged, Amoranda articulates the problem with such "cheats" and with the occa-sional selves who perform them: "What am I to believe? Not my Eyes, for they have deceived me already, not Alanthus, for he has deceived me too."(156) Until she "knows who in reality you are," she says, she is finished both with Alanthus as a lover and with Formator as a guardian. To prove that he has not deceived her uncle and that the latter's instructions still hold, Formator presents Amoranda with the novella's last embedded letter. Written in her uncle's hand and designed for "whenever [Formator] thinks fit to discover himself," this informs Amoranda that Formator has "pro-mis'd to make you the Partner of his Bed, if he liked you when he saw you, and could find a means to win your Affections." (159) Uncle Traffick has been party to Alanthus-Formator's deception all along. But as Amoranda's questions indicate, Traffick's epistolary confession raises troubling questions: how can a guardian justify exposing her to the danger of living unchaperoned with a virile young man for eight months and plot with him to deceive her, never mind rest satisfied with the latter's promise to "make her the Partner of his Bed?" This was, after all, precisely the danger presented by predators like Lofty, which Traffick thought Amoranda incapable of escaping on her own. Amoranda challenges the self-justifying answers that Alanthus-Formator supplies in Traffick's place, during conversations between them that frame Traffick's letter.

Formator offers one justification for the "Cheat" prior to Amoranda's discovery of it, when Amoranda informs him that she has discovered that Alanthus is a Marquis, with a sister and a sizeable estate (and thus that he would be a highly eligible husband). Formator tells her that her uncle has already provided a husband for her, "a Man of Worth, of Wealth and of Quality," and sent Formator to "take care you married nobody else." (145) He dismisses her objection to being "forc'd into the arms of a Man I never saw" by telling her that Alanthus is the very man her uncle chose. Backed by his view that girls "are the worst Guardians we can possibly have," this supports the lover-mentor reading and justifies Traffick-Formator's plot, by insisting that Amoranda needs Formator and her uncle to ensure she marry the right man. For the patriarchally minded, it also heralds a happy ending that fulfils every eighteenth-century girl's marital dream of being permitted by her family to "spend her days" with the man who "pleases" her best. (150) But Amoranda chose the same man as her uncle after independently checking his background and circumstances and independently determining that he would make an eligible as well as a pleasing husband. There was no need for their Cheat. Amoranda's actions have proved that she can "contrive a Companion" for herself (as she puts it) who is suitable in every way, without interference from a guardian. Indeed, the girl seems more responsible in "contriving a companion" for herself who honorably offers marriage than her trafficking merchant-uncle who conspires to make her "a partner for a marquis' bed."

Formator's second justification for the "Cheat" forms part of the reception narrative to Traffick's letter. Explaining that he thought "the sage Advice [Amoranda] needed would be better received from an old man," Formator uses the "vast difference between her behavior then and now" (159) to justify the deception, arguing that everything he did as Formator or Alanthus – including what Amoranda characterizes as "cruelties" – was perfectly fine because it reformed her or "made Tryal" of her. The end justifies the means. Convinced that "foolish girls are not to be trusted ourselves," (97) Formator has failed to notice that Amoranda was never the "giddy, thoughtless, inconsiderate Mortal fit only for the Company of those Coxcombs she conversed with" that he and the "many" thought her and boasts of his success in reforming her to his liking. Describing herself as his "willing Proselyte," Amoranda meekly agrees to his version of her character and of the course of events. (160) This too provides support for the reforming lover-mentor reading of the story, which here rests on the authority we grant the speaker as a man, lord, and guardian. But for novella-readers who have paid attention to the letters and to Amoranda's actions, and do not find "giddy, thoughtless and inconsiderate" convincing descriptors of her conduct, the "vast difference" between then and now lies in Amoranda's willingness to marry and in the character of modest and docile young girl that she now assumes.

Maria, an old spinster, appears at the end of the novella to question the "vast difference" between the Amoranda willing to marry Alanthus now and the Amoranda at the outset of the novella, who compared herself to a goldfinch who loved its freedom so much that it used "cunning" to evade all "the Trap-Cages" set for it, and who argued that women "must live single in our own defence." (26) Maria attributes the difference to Cupid and Amoranda agrees, (143) again supporting a reforming-lover reading of the story. But Amoranda offers a different explanation for changing her mind about marriage in her concluding assessment of Formator-Alanthus's alternating occasional selves. Amoranda has found Formator "a very agreeable Companion" – he has provided "a choice Collection of Books" for her, offered her "sprightly conversation" as well as sage advice, and prevented her from having to "live by my self" with no one but servants to talk to. Amoranda has "only one acknowledgement to make to Alanthus ... and that is the great Deliverance he brought me in the Wood." (161) She repeatedly characterizes Alanthus as "the Man who has snatched me from the Jaws of Death and Ruin" (134) because *his* principal advantage lies in being young enough and strong enough to protect her physically from the violence of other men. Again addressing the question of "who comes best off" when a woman pits her wits against "the whole contrary Sex," Amoranda states what she has discovered empirically from multiple attempts to abduct and/or violate her body: that there is reason to "fear" that gentlemen will resort to force to get what they want, and that servants cannot be relied upon to protect her, as a strong, young husband can. Ideally, the companion of her mind and protector of her body would be the same man, as Formator-Alanthus is. But failing that, a woman's physical vulnerability and need for physical protection, remains one (the only?) rational empirical reason for a woman of quality, wit, and fortune, like Amoranda, to marry.

The alternating and serializing selves of Formator-Alanthus and of cross-dressing characters like Altamira or the cousin's friend, highlight the plural and fluid character of the duplicitous occasional selves that everyone in this world assumes – including Amoranda. Amoranda models ways in which women can use their "sprightly wits" to deceive and govern gentlemen who seek to deceive and govern them by cleverly deploying serial and alternating occasional selves herself. She uses lively Restoration wit on Lofty and the fortune hunters, while concealing from them that she is apprised of their "base Designs." (36) This allows her predatory suitors to deceive themselves into thinking that she can be won, or easily seduced, by flattery and the rhetoric of love. To Formator, she speaks seriously and respectfully, accepting his guardianship as a "duty," making a parade of following his advice when she thinks he is right, and meekly agreeing that she was a thoughtless giddy creature before she met him. But she conceals from him with a "Smile" her displeasure at no longer being entirely her own mistress. And by sagely neglecting to mention to him that he has followed her directions in each of her plots, she allows him to deceive himself into thinking that he has taken charge and (re)formed her. To Alanthus, she speaks with modesty and gratitude, shyly showing her love in ways that both flatter him and mark her as a properly meek and conformable wife. Amoranda is invariably candid only to her maid. One moral of *her* story is that concealment of her true thoughts, and the deceptive complaisance of adopting whatever occasional self a gentleman expects, are the price a girl has to pay to manage her domestic governors and enthrall a marquis. Like Fantomina, Amoranda is a phantom clothed in the characters ascribed to her by others and masked by the faces she assumes to meet the faces that she meets.

In this social world where men are deceivers all, the difference between Lofty, the fortune-hunting suitors or the cross-dressing abductor and Traffick or Formator-Alanthus – who have tricked and "cheated" Amoranda more thoroughly than Lofty and his ilk ever could – lies in what the period called "moral character." What distinguishes the good from the bad is that, through all the occasional selves they assume, the good men act as Amoranda's "Friend" – they are "good" characters because a thread of benevolence toward her runs through their deceptive occasional selves. The Lofties and fortune-hunters are "bad" men because self-interested villainy generates the characters they assume. Moral character – whether a person was fundamentally virtuous or vicious – assumed the importance it did in eighteenth-century texts in part because moral character subsumed the various fluid, situated, changeable and gappy occasional selves that presented themselves empirically, under a single encompassing characterization that answered the crucial question of whether a person could be trusted or not.

Davys demonstrated that the truth about moral character could be determined over time by testing letters and professions empirically against acts and facts. Like Manley, she warned readers against trusting to letters' words alone, and demonstrated the importance of verifying them by collecting empirical evidence in the form of reliable firsthand oral testimony, written documentation, overheard conversations, and agreement or disagreement between professions and deeds. Letters in which evident truth conceals falsehood and apparent falsehood masks honest truth underscore the importance of constantly asking Amoranda's question – "Who are you—in reality?" – and of looking to empirical evidence to prove or disprove the truth of epistolary communications, determine the identity of their authors, and verify their written testimony to the character and past history of others.

But Davys also included some darker warnings. Amoranda's "cheat" by Formator and Traffick, and by the cross-dressing abductor, shows that Amoranda mistakes characters in both senses when she falsely believes that she already knows who and what they are, and suspects no deception. Here like Philander, she ascribes to men the character they assume in relation to her, as uncle, guardian, or female friend, and confuses an occasional self with the truth about a person. Lofty, Traffick, and Formator-Alanthus do the same in ascribing to Amoranda, forensically, the character of coquette or of foolish young girl, whom they can manage, seduce, or reform. Their conventional, conduct-book expectations blind these male protagonists to conduct and sentiments inconsistent with ascribed character and conduct-book roles, and can blind us to empirical evidence that Amoranda, like everyone in this world above the servant class, inhabits a series of partly or wholly deceptive occasional selves in their interactions with others. Interestingly, Amoranda also mistakes the character of others when her maid or her housekeeper are not nearby to tell her what their sharp-eyed empirical observations have detected. Like the gentlemen of the Royal Society who left the menial work of observation and experiment to lowly "mechanics," Amoranda leaves her servants to make empirical observations and discover the material evidence she needs to determine the truth about characters and letters. Together, Amoranda's vulnerability when menials are not by to supply empirical facts and the gentlemen's obliviousness to empirical conduct that escapes their stereotyped taxonomies, suggest that this division of labor was a foolish error: the genteel needed to observe and detect empirical facts for themselves. The problem is that detection is not a matter of holding a mirror up to nature. Amoranda's discovery of evidence about the truth of letters and their authors piecemeal over extended story-time belies assumptions, like those promoted by theories of reflection, that letters and reality are seamlessly aligned on the same vertical axis. What time and reality offer piecemeal are only bits of oral and written testimony that come to light at different times, moments of inadvertent self-betrayal, and/or sudden fortuitous disclosures of a relevant fact, to be noticed, collected over time, and assembled in the mind, in circumstances where essential empirical information is not necessarily encountered until its use-date has passed.

That Davys's double-voiced text operated on multiple levels helped to ensure its continued popularity. At once a conventional moral tale about a reformed coquet, a conduct book for women's survival by deception and detection, an exercise in deception and detection for its readers to crack, and a lesson about empirical evidence, *The Reform'd Coquet* saw its seventh edition in 1760.

Debating Empirical Evidence: Haywood and the Historians

When rewriting the story about reforming a coquette at mid-century in *The History of Miss Betsy Thoughtless* (1751), Eliza Haywood was less sanguine about the efficacy of empirical verification, about our ability to plumb moral character and about the certainty that the truth about letters and their authors must be detected in due course. Through Flora, Lady Mellasin, Munden, and Betsy herself, she showed that the moral character of persons competently performing their occasional selves could not be discovered *without* some inadvertent, self-betraying accident. Betsy's moral character is no more obvious to Truelove than the moral character of Lady Mellasin is to her husband, Munden's is to Betsy's brothers, or Miss Flora's is even to her mother. Betsy practices no deceptions – she repeatedly declares that she does not wish to marry, much less promise to obey. But thanks to her dominant trait of thoughtlessness about how her words and acts appear to others, she is variously (mis)taken for a whore, an innocent maiden, a potential bride, a potential mistress, a coquette, and a cunning deceiver. The fact that opposite moral characters can be ascribed to her, and that her Truelove has to rely entirely on empirical evidence to determine who and what she is, is central to the agency of the anonymous letter that Mr. Trueworth receives from a "well-wisher" warning him that Betsy, his "intended bride, has been a mother without the pleasure of owning herself as such," and that she has put out her baby to nurse at Denham.

This anonymous letter is transcribed in full; but it is given both a double and an expanded narrative frame. Like Behn's narrative framing of Brilliard's deceptive letter to Philander, Haywood's inner narrative frame displays Miss Flora's motives for writing it (her desire to separate Mr. Trueworth from Betsy) and her efforts to devise a stratagem for the letter "such as Mr. Trueworth, on the most strict examination, could not discover the deception of."[7] The narrative following the writing of the letter reinforces this point by showing that, like Brilliard, Flora reexamines every sentence she has written to ensure that "it would work the desired effect," and uses a copyist and the penny post to conceal her authorship. This inner frame about the composition of the letter as a deceptive but persuasive rhetorical act is preceded by another, equally essential to the novel-reader's understanding of it. By narrating the events that led Betsy and her friend, Miss Mabel, to financially support the orphaned baby of a common soldier's widow and send it out to nurse, this outer prefatory frame ensures that novel-readers know the truth about Betsy and the child before encountering the letter. The narrator highlights the distance between the real events detailed in this outer framing narrative and their representation in Flora's letter: "Who would imagine that such a glorious act of benevolence should ever be made a handle to traduce and vilify its author? – yet what cannot malice, accompanied with cunning do?" (249) Together with Flora's confidence that Trueworth will be unable to discover the letter's deception, this rhetorical question invites novel-readers not only to marvel at how "cunning . . . can give the fairest virtue the appearance of the foulest vice," (249) but also to reexamine the letter, as Flora does, to notice how credible a letter can seem when malice is couched in a sincere and perspicuous epistolary style, and a lie is disguised in a plausibly fact-based narrative.

All the elements here in Volume 2, chapter 12 – the frames and the letter – expand the relevant context by explicitly pointing backward and forward on the novel's diachronic sequence of chapters and events. The outer frame describing Betsy's adoption of the soldier's babe presents itself as a flashback to "an incident in Miss Betsy's life not hitherto mentioned," (248) which occurred before Betsy went to Oxford with her brother early in Volume 1, while the inner frame refers Miss Flora's motives to her "disappointments as related in the sixth chapter of this volume." (249) The letter itself points forward to its illocutionary and perlocutionary effects by inviting Mr. Trueworth to "make what enquiry you shall think proper into fact" (251) and by observing that his "friends" will not expect him to marry Betsy if he does find the fact "real." The narrative looks ahead too, by promising to "relate . . . how far the event answered [Miss Flora's] expectations" that she could "trust the success of the mischief she intended by the letter." (251) The focus, then, is squarely on the letter's agency and effects.

After portraying at length the analogical situation of Mr. Goodman's discovery of Lady Mellasin's adultery and decision to divorce her, Haywood devotes the whole of chapter 17 to Trueworth's reaction to Flora's anonymous letter. This reception narrative describes him as torn between reason and passion, so that "at some times did he believe her [Betsy] no less guilty than the letter said, but at others, sentiments of a different nature prevailed." (280–281) His passions tell him she is virtuous, his reason fears she is not. Reason wins out. Reflection convinces him that the anonymous letter has "too much the face of truth" to be "the work of meer invention." It is too "circumstantial" to be made up – it specifies the village and the nurse's name, it gives him "a particular direction how I may convince myself of the shameful truth." Trueworth cannot believe that anyone "would forge a lie, and at the same time present the means of detecting it to be so." (280) Betsy's moral character is not as evident. As he canvases her conduct from his first acquaintance with her at Oxford in Volume I when there was that unfortunate "adventure with the gentleman-commoner" to her late insistence on going to a play with Miss Forward against his advice, he finds that his knowledge of her character does not make the letter's accusation impossible. As the narrator stresses, "Miss Betsy had, by her own mismanagement, prepared his heart to receive any impressions to her prejudice." (280–281) Determined to be just nevertheless, Trueworth decides to "follow the directions given him in the letter" by traveling to Denham to interview the baby's wet-nurse in order to discover for himself if "the letter-writer has told the truth." (281)

The wet-nurse, who has not been entrusted with any information about the baby's parentage and has only met Betsy once, confirms the fact that Betsy gave her the baby and is supporting it. By adding the further apparently damning facts that "the lady has given it her own name, Betsy" (283) and means to pay for its schooling, she conveys what she conjectures: that Miss Betsy is probably baby Betsy's mother. Trueworth has made the enquiry and has the empirical evidence he sought: "He had seen the child, –had heard by whom, and in what manner it was delivered: – the

charge given with it, and the promises made for its future protection." He
has forms of evidence that would have been acceptable in a law court:
evidence of the "fact" of the crime from a letter and the testimony of a firsthand witness to the circumstances of Betsy's involvement. The reality
seemed plainly to exist, which proved the anonymous letter true: "the fact
as related in the letter, appeared to him so plain, from every circumstance as
to admit no possibility of doubt." (284) Marrying Betsy now is therefore out
of the question, as the anonymous letter pointed out. Trueworth goes on to
break with Betsy in an embedded letter that reproaches her for her frivolous
lifestyle and hints at her "imaginary crime." As Miss Flora foresaw,
Trueworth is unable to detect the deception; and her letter has the intended
effect of separating him from Betsy. However, its effects do not end there.
For Trueworth's defection leads Betsy's brothers to get her off their hands by
making her marry Munden, who proves a mean and cruel husband; and,
after being drawn into an affair by Flora, Trueworth goes off to court and
marry someone else.

     The question hovering over the deceptive letter and its several, momen-
tous long-term effects is that raised by the narrator as Trueworth confronts
the evidence against Betsy at Denham: "What now could this enquiring
lover think? – Where was the least room for any conjecture in favour of
Miss Betsy's innocence, to gain entrance into his breast?" (284) The answer is
not encouraging. For the sequel suggests that there was no way for
Trueworth to challenge facts that seemed to speak for themselves, short of
asking Betsy, whose word he no longer trusts. Betsy cannot volunteer an
answer to the charge against her in his last letter to her because, being
innocent of the "crime," she does not understand his hints. When much
later (in volume 3), Trueworth discovers the truth about the baby, he does so
by chance. He happens to be visiting Betsy's friend, Miss Mabel, when the
babe's soldier father appears to claim his child. When questioned about this
and told about the anonymous letter, Mabel informs him that she and Betsy
have been "half-mothers" to the child since its mother's death and characterizes the anonymous letter as an "impudent . . . .[and] unparalleled slan-
der." (404) Trueworth learns that the letter's content is a malicious lie exactly
as novel-readers do – not through independent rational investigation but
because he happens to be informed by a narrator he trusts. Trueworth also
discovers the anonymous letter's author by chance later still, when he runs
into Flora in the street and she happens to drop an anonymous letter to
Miss Harriot, his future bride, in which she has tried the same trick. Flora's
use of the same copyist's hand for the anonymous letter to Miss Harriot that
she used as Trueworth's anonymous "well-wisher" before is what gives her

away. Like Alanthus, she is detected by her failure to attend to a technicality, rather than by any betraying flaw in her epistolary "invention."

As Trueworth demonstrates, therefore, a worthy and rational person can check the facts in a letter to see if they correspond to a reality that plainly exists, and even seek legally valid forms of evidence; but containing facts that can be verified does not make a letter true. The constructions that writers' "stratagems" and "inventions" place on facts to achieve their ends, distort them in ways that cannot necessarily be discerned or discovered, despite a recipient's best empirical efforts. The same holds of a witness's conjectures. Even letters and firsthand testimony that have the "face of truth" may not re-present a past reality truly. Letters mixing fact and fiction, truth and invention, as Flora's does, are particularly readily believed because, as Hume observed and Trueworth illustrates, when we discover part of a narrative to be true, we believe the whole, just as, when we find a part false, we assume the whole to be false. The problem is compounded when judgments of culpability are arrived at by fleshing out circumstantial facts with probable cause and conjecture. There is therefore no guarantee that empirical enquiries will detect the truth. The danger, rather, is that empirical enquiries generate mixtures of fact and conjecture that are mistaken for truth because the investigator cannot conjecture how the same circumstances might be capable of a different, more innocent explanation.

Haywood's anonymous letter also indicates another troubling empirical truth about the agency of letters: letters can have real effects and far-reaching consequences whether they are true or not. Once a letter is believed and its information and directions are acted upon, even a false and deceptive letter can create new realities and become the cause of real long-term consequences and effects. Conversely, discovery of the falsity of a letter is of no consequence if it cannot be acted upon. When Trueworth discovers the truth about Flora's letter, he and Betsy are both either married or about to be married to other people, and there is no way of turning back the clock. For the biographer or narrator-historian of *Miss Betsy Thoughtless*'s life, then, like for Behn, the recipient's response and the missive's specific empirical effects are what must be discovered and recorded for posterity because its agency, rather than its account of events, is what gives a letter its reality, empirical relevance and historical truth.

Haywood's treatment of Miss Flora's anonymous letter can be viewed as a defense of narrative-epistolary histories against the kind of narrative history that Hume favored during the 1740s and Fielding aped. Hume had promoted neoclassical history and its conjectural descendant by arguing that when, in narrating a "series of Actions in their natural Order," an historian "remounts to their secret Springs and Principles and delineates their most remote Consequences," he must "sometimes suppl[y] by Conjecture what is wanting in Knowledge" in order to construct the "chains of events" that "perfect . . . his Production."[8] The unity of action and impression requisite in this "Production" precluded gaps in the chain of cause and effect despite lacunae in the historical records; it invited historians to fill in what was missing by conjecture. At the same time, extracting what one wished from letters and eliminating transcriptions of them from the body of the text, shifted agency from historical actors and their letters to the conjecturing historian as the author and narrator who made sense of the past. Hume's *History of England* (1759) was a "production" in this sense. It offered its readers the companionship of an engagingly urbane and worldly wise narrator whose conjectures often contradicted extant sources to quite deliciously reveal what he thought had *really* been going on in the past. Anglo-Saxon Edgar was not *in reality* the pious, saintly figure that monkish documents made him; circumstances like his removal of a girl from a convent suggested "amours" that confirmed Hume's conjecture, based on his knowledge of human nature, that Edgar was *in fact* a libertine (like Charles II).[9]

Catharine Macaulay who, like Haywood, promoted narrative-epistolary writing, criticized histories such as this, which eliminated letters from the text, for augmenting the authority of the narrator-historian at the expense of historical actors and contemporary readers in order to pass off their own false or partisan views as historical truth.[10] The force of such objections is rapidly and usefully illustrated by Oliver Goldsmith's biography of Beau Nash. Goldsmith's Preface to his *Life of Richard Nash, of Bath, Esq.; extracted principally from his original Papers* (1762) describes it as "a genuine and candid recital compiled from the papers he left behind, and others equally authentic; a recital written with . . . scarce any other art, than that of arranging the materials in their natural order." Goldsmith embedded full transcriptions of some of Nash's letters in his portrait of Nash's character and narrative of Nash's life. But adducing only "Specimens" of those letters in case "the reader may be curious to see one of these memorials written by himself," he framed them fore and aft with his own, derogatory observations. Goldsmith prefaced one Nash "memorial," for instance, by describing it as "a specimen of the stile and manner of a man, whose whole life was past in a round of gaiety" and followed its transcription with his own readerly reaction: "this carries little the air of bagatelle, it seems a sermon in miniature, so different are some men in the closet, and in conversation." Goldsmith treated letters from Nash's noble correspondents in the same manner, pronouncing "anecdotes and letters of the great ... dull and insipid," and transcribing letters from them "collected at a venture from several others" only to show "what a parcel of stupid trifles the world is ready to admire."[11]

The advantage of literally "*extracting*" Nash letters from the correspondences in "*his original Papers,*" from their reception, and from the network of relationships in which they had once played an active and instrumental role, and of denigrating their style, dismissing their content, and denuding them of agency, is that this enabled Goldsmith to subordinate "Nash" to his own purposes as historian and narrator: "None can properly be said to write history, but he who understands the human heart, and its whole train of affections and follies," and who uses this knowledge to "instruct.. the generality of mankind." Goldsmith's narrative "delineate[d] [Nash's] mind without disguise" to demonstrate his own profound understanding of human nature and the human heart. This told him that Nash was not, after all, the ruler and trend-setter for the polite that "imagination" made him, but only "a weak man, governing weaker subjects."[12] The Fielding of the 1740s, who equated neoclassical "Histories of England" with the productions of "Romance-writers," took pleasure in demonstrating the folly of mistaking anyone's narrative, including his own, for the whole truth and nothing but the truth. But during the 1760s, Goldsmith echoed Fielding's description of himself as the narrator-historian of fictional biographical histories to contrast truth-telling historians like himself with mere novelists:

> "Were I upon the present occasion to hold the pen as a novelist, I could recount some amours, in which he [Nash] was successful. I could fill a volume with little anecdotes, which contain neither pleasure nor instruction; with histories of professing lovers and poor believing girls deceived by such professions. But such adventures are ... easily written ... truth, which I have followed here ... presents in the affair of love scarce any variety. The manner in which one reputation is lost, exactly resembles that by which another is taken a way ... such is the substance of every modern novel."[13]

The historian's superiority to novelists is displayed by a narrative demonstrating *Goldsmith's* understanding of society and the human heart, not the understanding of society and the human heart that had enabled Nash to reign for three decades in Bath as the successful leader, reformer, and refiner of polite society. The embedded letters provide no evidence that Goldsmith's understanding of society or the human heart was correctly applied in any particular case, or indeed, that he has done anything more than supply the place of historical documentation with his own conjectures to produce a biography of Nash that was, in its own way, as fictional as any novel. Indeed, whether writing as the historian of Richard Nash or of the Vicar of Wakefield (1766), Goldsmith as historian-narrator introduced letters only to show that the curiosity of those who wanted a sight of them was misdirected and better replaced by perceptive and instructive historical-biographical narratives like his own, which exhibited the narrator-historian's profound knowledge of human nature and of the probable course of events. As Catherine Macaulay complained, historians of this ilk who "converse in generals" (universal truths about human nature) and subject readers to their narratives without recourse, were engrossing to themselves all power over historical actors, over the past, and over present interpretations of both.[14] Though the historian had been neither an actor nor an eyewitness of events himself, he was presenting himself as the subject-supposed-to-know, and making the value of history depend, not on the experience of historical actors, or on the judgments of readers measuring epistolary documents against the narrative's "labour to attain truth," but on the unchallenged experience and judgment of the storytelling historian himself who arrogantly presented his own partial version of the past as historical truth.[15]

Fielding had both assumed and mocked the primary role of Hume's narrator-historian as master of ceremonies and host of the feast in *Joseph Andrews* and *Tom Jones*; but he dismissed Haywood's concerns about false narratives and impediments to empirical verification in *Betsy Thoughtless* with insultingly facile responses. In the masquerade scene in *Amelia*, an anonymous letter found lying in the ballroom is read aloud to "a crowd of the polite," before being handed to Booth. Booth "immediately concludes" upon reading it that Doctor Harrison is its author, for "this letter contained all the particularities of the doctor's character." (2: 181) A man's character is so evident in his letter that discovering the author of an anonymous letter presents absolutely no difficulty. This letter also fails to impact the course of the history: its content, a sermon on fidelity, is ridiculed by the "crowd of the polite," and the false suspicion about his wife's fidelity it initially generates in Booth is rapidly dissipated.[16] It was a simple matter for a narrator-historian, or anyone else, to see how a letter reflected its author and the facts of the case and to write their history accordingly; there were no impediments here. But Haywood and Macaulay were not wrong, and the problems they raised were not so rapidly or readily dismissed.

Circumstantial Evidence and Conjectural Histories: Charlotte Smith's *Emmeline*

Hume defended reliance on conjecture by rearticulating Hobbes' argument that the causal reasoning we apply empirically is derived from experience and therefore necessarily only "conjectural:" Clouds are signs of rain, and rain a sign that there have been clouds, but we cannot conclude from this that every time there are clouds, there is rain, for "Experience concludeth nothing universally." Experience, being contingent, only yields a degree of probability: "according as [relations of cause and effect] have often or seldom failed, so their Assurance is more or less; but never full and evident." Hume argued similarly that the connections we make between cause and effect to construct "chains of events" are only "customary Conjunctions" imported from prior experience that can tell nothing certain "concerning the real Existence and Matter of Fact" or about invariable relations among facts. Reality is always contingent: circumstances differ somewhat from case to case, and "there is no known Connexion between the sensible Qualities [we observe] and the secret Powers and Principles" that cause them.[17] This validated the "Productions" of historians like himself who supplied lacunae in the historical record with conjectures derived from experience in the past, used customary conjunctions to connect circumstantial facts into causal chains of events, and related the sensible words and actions of historical actors to the secret powers and principles that supposedly informed them. For conjectures based on what experience has shown to be the most probable, because the most usual, motives, causes and connections between facts are as close to truth as empirical reasoning about contingent circumstances can attain.

By the time Charlotte Smith wrote *Emmeline* (1788), probable conjectures and circumstantial facts had been admitted as evidence in law courts, and conjectural historians were "fill[ing] lacunae in the historical record" with "Conjectures or Speculations" that were presented and remembered as historical truth.[18] Issues of *auctores* and *auctoritas* that engaged Fielding, Haywood, and Goldsmith had become secondary to debate about where the resulting intermixture of facts with conjectures left the accused in law and the "labour to attain truth" in history and natural philosophy. Thomas Reid, for instance, complained that his contemporaries were no longer following the practice of "the great Newton" who "distinguished his conjectures from his conclusions, and put the former by themselves;" instead, they were "trafficking in conjecture" in "contraband and illicit" ways.[19] Earlier, when conjecture had been viewed as mere speculation, historians, antiquarians, philosophers and courts of law had marked their conjectures as such: "There seems enough therein ... to countenance our conjecture ... ;" This "which I propose but as Conjecture ... hath some Countenance from the Practice of Earlier Ages;" "This I mention only as my Conjecture."[20] Courts of law had distinguished between "matters of deed" and "matters of record" by leaving juries to determine the former, and lawyers and judges to make judgments about the latter. But with the introduction of circumstantial evidence into courtrooms during the second half of the eighteenth century, prosecutors were permitted to present *as* empirical proofs, conjectural narratives of the crime composed of merely probable inferences from merely circumstantial facts; and these increasingly outweighed the testimony of any witness.[21] By the 1760s and 1770s, natural philosophers too were arguing that conjecture was "the principal instrument of Investigation in what is now called experimental philosophy" and that though its "conclusions can only amount to a probability or to a conjecture," they are to be taken for truth unless overturned by an instance to the contrary. "Conjectures or Hypotheses" now passed as violently probable truth until their truth was discredited.[22]

For Charlotte Smith, therefore, the empirical problem was not primarily, as it was for Haywood, that the truth about characters and letters might never come to light – hidden in two caskets for over twenty years, the letters and legal documents containing the truth about Emmeline's birth and family history are in her possession from the novel's opening pages, waiting to be found and read. The empirical problem that concerned Smith was the credence now given to narratives constructed by conjecture from circumstantial facts. In volumes 3 and 4 of *Emmeline* (which contains ninety-six letters, twenty-three of them fully transcribed[23]), Smith reworked the anonymous letter episodes in *Betsy Thoughtless* to explore problems with conjectures based on circumstantial evidence that Haywood had barely touched. In these volumes, where she also demonstrated the ubiquity of conjecture in everyday social interactions, she used "conjecture" in several senses: for surmises as to what is likely or probable, inferences drawn from signs or appearances, and unverified suppositions and opinions formed on grounds insufficient to furnish proof (OED). But the definitions in Johnson's *Dictionary* (1755) went to the heart of the problem that Smith was addressing: to conjecture is "to entertain an opinion upon bare probability;" a conjecture is "preponderation of opinion without proof;" put baldly, a conjecture is just "a guess."[24] Thus where Haywood's narrator presented Miss Flora's anonymous letter as a malicious compound of fact and invention, Smith's narrator presents Crofts' anonymous letter as a malicious compound of circumstantial facts with what Emmeline foolishly discounts as conjecture: "I care not what they think—leave them to their conjectures." (247)) Like Austen in *Pride and Prejudice* later, Smith deployed the vocabulary of conjecture – suspicion, surmise, imputation, supposition, and the rest – to show how conjectures produce "ideas" and narratives about others on insufficient empirical grounds, and to explore the nefarious consequences of mistaking them for reality and truth.

Emmeline is usually rightly read as a rewrite of Burney's *Cecilia*. But in volumes 3 and 4, Smith indicated that she also had *Betsy Thoughtless* in view by creating analogous situations and scenes. Like Betsy and her friend Miss Mabel, Emmeline Mowbray and her friend Mrs. Stafford perform a charitable act in secret: they hide and nurse a run-away wife, Adelina, and her adulterously conceived newborn child. Like Trueworth, Emmeline's almost-fiancé, Delamere, is sent an anonymous letter by jealous and self-interested intriguers to "undeceive [him] in regard to Miss Mowbray" by intimating that she has eloped with his friend, Colonel Fitz-Edward, and borne his child.[25] Like Trueworth too, Delamere verifies the anonymous letter's truth empirically. He returns from France to see for himself and discovers Emmeline in a cottage in the woods holding the baby. Here the empirical proof is ocular and seems incontrovertible: "Till I *saw* this, all the evidence they brought me was insufficient to cure my blind attachment. But now—oh! Infamy—madness—damnation! . . . .It *is* then true." (287) Because "the child which she held in her arms . . . made in his opinion all vindication impossible" (287), Delamere does not stay for an explanation. In his mind, Emmeline stands convicted of what is in reality Adelina's crime – an affair with Fitz-Edward that produced a child. The anonymous letter therefore acts on Delamere as it did on Trueworth: it causes him to break with Emmeline and plan to marry someone else.

Smith corrected Haywood in part by using the different phases of the anonymous letter's reception narrative to mark Delamere as the wrong potential husband for Emmeline. Initially speechless with shock at Delamere's reaction to his incontrovertible proof of her guilt, Emmeline later concludes that "she would be fortunate in escaping from an engage-ment with a man who had . . . so little reliance on her principles as to be driven on a mere suspicion into rudeness and insult." (288) A man who knew and trusted her so little, and was so apt to fly into a jealous rage, had no True Worth as a husband – marriage to such a man was no happy ending. Smith also dismissed the possibility that the truth about the baby could emerge only by chance. Emmeline "leave[s] it wholly to Delamere to discover and recant his error." But searching for his sister, Godolphin discovers Adelina's hiding-place from the address on a letter a housemaid wrote her old mother; and once he appears in their midst and witnesses Emmeline's "angelic" kindness to his distraught sister, he has to be told what Adelina has done. Later still, to explain Delamere's break with Emmeline and prevent her reputation from being tarnished with Adelina's crime, Lady Westhaven, Delamere's sister and Emmeline's friend, also has to be told. The truth about the baby and about Emmeline's conduct therefore soon reaches Delamere through their common friends. By calling Adelina's child his son and giving him his name, Godolphin could "throw an obscurity over the truth which would hardly ever be removed when none were particularly interested to remove it" (278) and thus shield his sister's public reputation. But such things could not be kept secret for long in families or in small societies where everyone knew and was related to everyone else. In such circles, there must always be some secret sharing of the secret among the interested few.

Smith also corrected Haywood's treatment of conjecture by setting her world in motion both to represent the conjectural *process* of narrative construction and to describe the effects of contingency on mental acts. In the prefatory narrative to the anonymous letter that Crofts' and Mrs. Ashwood send Delamere, she showed how its authors use conjectures to fill lacunae in the available circumstantial facts. To this end, the outer prefatory narrative juxtaposes what occurs in reality with what the letter's authors conjecture from the few, merely circumstantial facts they obtain. The real facts described by the narrative are these: Emmeline meets Fitz-Edward in a copse to persuade him to talk to Mrs. Stafford before confessing his affair with Adelina to Godolphin (Adelina's brother and his old friend) to prevent a duel between them; she later sets off to join Adelina by sneaking out of Woodfield at night, to ensure that she does not lead James Crofts, who has been watching and following her, to Adelina's hiding-place. The two events are not connected. But in their conversation about her, Crofts' report about seeing Emmeline with Fitz-Edward in the copse is connected to the "mystery" of Emmeline's "clandestine" departure from Woodfield by Mrs. Ashwood's "suspicion" that Emmeline prefers Fitz-Edward to Delamere and by her "surmise" that Emmeline left Woodfield because their "entanglement" was now "at a period when it could no longer be concealed"– the implication being that her pregnancy now showed. (251) The absurdity of using conjectures to patch unconnected circumstances into a narrative of what had probably occurred is satirized when James Crofts proceeds to eavesdrop on Fitz-Edward's conversation with Mrs. Stafford. From Mrs. Stafford's part in the conversation he "could distinguish only broken sentences:" "Could no longer be concealed – in all probability may now remain unknown – the child, I will myself attend to." From Fitz-Edward's words, Crofts "could only catch indistinct sounds." (253). But "he thought he had heard enough" – this "broken and disjointed discourse ... left not a doubt remaining of the cause of Emmeline's precipitate departure from Woodfield." (253) In both cases, broken bits of information and unrelated circumstantial facts are turned into a plausible story by conjecturing motives for the actors and imagining probable connections between unconnected circumstances; but in the second case, the empirical facts are assumed to fit the preexisting, purely conjectural narrative about Emmeline's pregnancy. Even more absurdly, speculation is given the weight of fact to enable the history thus constructed to pass for the undoubted truth. As a modern scholar observes of conjectural history, "mere facts can too easily fall victim to how things, to quote Dougald Stewart, *may have been* produced by natural causes," or worse still, *must have been* produced."[26] The possible easily slides into the probable, and the probable into the undoubtedly true.

The anonymous letter that Crofts and Mrs. Ashwood "manufacture" to "alarm the jealous and irascible spirit of Delamere" and separate him from Emmeline (254) exhibits the disjunctions and conjectural connections that produced it, but in such a way as to make Delamere use conjecture himself to connect the dots and understand what the letter is telling him:

Sir,

A friend to your worthy and noble family writes this; which is meant to serve you, and to undeceive you in regard to Miss Mowbray—who, without any gratitude for the high honour you intend her, is certainly too partial to another person. She is now gone from Woodfield to escape observation; and none but Mrs. Stafford is let into the secret of where she is. You will judge what end it is to answer; but certainly none that bodes you good. One would have supposed that the Colonel [Fitz-Edward] being very often her attendant at Woodfield might have made her stay there agreeable enough; but perhaps (for I do not aver it) the young lady has some particular reasons for wishing to have private lodgings. No doubt the Colonel is a man of gallantry; but his friendship to you is rather more questionable . . . . (254)

This letter does not state what its authors imagine they know: that Emmeline has eloped with Fitz-Edward and gone into hiding to conceal her pregnancy. Instead, it forces Delamere to make conjectures himself about why Emmeline left Woodfield to escape observation and how this relates to her partiality for a man of gallantry like Fitz-Edward. The letter "throws an obscurity" over the derogatory conjectures it invites by calling them "judging for himself."

As its initial reception narrative is careful to show, Delamere's reaction to the anonymous letter is not impetuous or irrational for once. Suppressing his initial fury and anguish, he reflects that the letter may be "an artifice" of his mother's or the Crofts' to "separate him from Emmeline" and waits for a letter from Emmeline, thinking "it was possible" that this "might dissipate his doubts." (256) But the post seems to confirm the anonymous letter: a factitious missive to Crofts from Lord Montreville confirms that Emmeline has left Woodfield; and the awaited letter from Emmeline, which he "fancied unusually cold," presents Delamere with a "mystery:" it tells him that she is going to Bath with a nameless friend unseasonably in March and keeps her address there secret without explaining why. This "mystery," the anonymous letter "served too evidently to explain." (257) The ability of conjectures to explain the available facts does not make them true, however probable or self-evident the explanation seems; but like Delamere, we often assume it does. This was not just a technical point: constructing, believing, and repeating plausible but unfounded tales of their misconduct could destroy the marital prospects of young women like Emmeline. It was equally damaging to ladies who depended on their reputations for social acceptability, and to servants who needed a "character" to obtain and retain employment.

Prefiguring Lady Delacour and Elizabeth Bennet, Delamere uses the "fatal letter" to reinterpret and rewrite the past. Searching his "recollections" in light of it, he supplies its intimations of Emmeline's and Fitz-Edward's "attachment" with empirical proof by highlighting and exaggerating conduct to which he had given no weight before: "forgetting all the symptoms which he had before fondly believed he had discovered of [Emmeline's] returning affection, he exaggerated every circumstance that indicated indifference, and magnified them into signs of absolute aversion . . . .He tortured his imagination almost to madness, by remembering numberless incidents, which, tho' almost unattended to at the time, now seemed to bring the cruelest conviction of their intelligence . . . " (257) In the wake of Hume, all the characters' reasoning is driven by their passions – Delamere's to excess. But it is empirical reasoning nevertheless. As Delamere correctly recalls, Emmeline *has* resolutely adhered to a promise not to marry him that she need not have given his father, Lord Montreville; Fitz-Edward *does* have a history of "dishonorable" relations with his friends' wives and mistresses, which heightens "the probability of his present attachment." That Fitz-Edward's attachment is to Emmeline, that Emmeline adhered to her promise from partiality for Fitz-Edward – these are conjectures on Delamere's part. They satisfy him that he has arrived at the truth because they plausibly connect observed but merely circumstantial and unconnected facts into a coherent narrative of what has probably occurred. These "imaginary proofs" (318) and the narrative they support then act on Delamere's imagination to heighten his passions until he "gave himself up to all the dreadful torments of jealousy—jealousy even to madness." (258) By the time Delamere bursts in on Emmeline to find her holding a baby, he is wild with "rage, fierceness and despair" and armed with a story stemming from the anonymous letter that immediately explains what he sees: "It *is* then true! . . . What? For Fitz-Edward for the infamous plunderer of his friend's happiness!" Interpreting the sight of Emmeline holding a baby as proof of Fitz-Edward's infamy and her defection, and "convinced" that "vindication [was] impossible," Delamere "looked in a frantic manner around the room, as if entirely bereft of reason," and ran out into the woods "like any mad." (287)

Like Betsy Thoughtless, Emmeline cannot answer the anonymous letter's false charge against her because she knows nothing about it. But Smith complicates this situation by demonstrating that differences in the information Delamere and Emmeline each has, together with the different lacunae in their knowledge, mean that they are in effect living in different realities. Because she has forgotten all about James Croft's malice and Mrs. Ashwood's envy and "dreamed not that she had an enemy on earth" (284), these characters form no part of Emmeline's present reality. Conduct emanating from their enmity and real intrigues therefore seems as unreal and unaccountable as a dream. When she receives no letters from Delamere, Emmeline "imputes his silence" to his frequent changes of place;'" and when Lord Montreville too ceases writing, Emmeline is so "far from supposing that her uncle was estranged from her" by the Crofts' "artful misrepresentations," (325) that she considers his omitted letters "merely accidental." (283) Emmeline's does not connect these connected events and, though probable, her conjecture about each is erroneous, because in her reality, there were no malicious Crofts and no changes to her relationships with Delamere and his father. (284) Having failed to recognize the absence of letters from both Delamere and his father as "signs" of their "estrangement," she is surprised when a letter from Lord Montreville arrives to inform her that her engagement to Delamere is at an end.

Delamere's reality, by contrast, is shaped by "the imaginary proofs with which the invidious artifices of the Crofts had furnished him" in the anonymous letter. (381) Acting in a reality where Fitz-Edward has seduced Emmeline and betrayed him, Delamere goes to London to challenge him to a duel, only to find that Fitz-Edward no longer intends to return to London from Ireland. With "Emmeline and Fitz-Edward haunt[ing] his dreams" and "ever present to his imagination" (294), Delamere "supposes that Emmeline, aware of the danger which threatened her lover from the vengeance of his injured friend, had written to him to prevent his return." (294) Later, piecing together what he has learned from separate letters – that Emmeline has accompanied Mrs. Stafford to France, that Fitz-Edward has gone to France – he is "convinced beyond doubt that Fitz-Edward had met Emmeline in France by her own appointment." (313) Delamere's history of past events governs his understanding of more recent ones; and, "imaginary" though this history is, it is repeatedly confirmed empirically by ever new interweavings of conjectures with facts. Where Emmeline is deceived about the danger of others' conjectures about her, Delamere deceives himself into believing that he has been deceived.

Eighteenth-century physicians held that excesses of passion like Delamere's in the wake of the "fatal letter," led to madness and to disordered imaginations possessed by fantastic visions and dreams. But Smith makes it clear that "mad" visions may be correct; and that if sanity consists of accurate perceptions of reality, these are as nebulous and impermanent as visions because reality itself is fluid and contingent. Driven to "phrenzy" by guilt and fear and into delirium by a fever, Adelina's dreams are haunted by a vision of Godolphin and Fitz-Edward murdering each other in a bloody duel. This vision is delusional when she knows Godolphin to be in the West Indies; but, unbeknownst to her, Godolphin is now in England, planning exactly what she envisioned. Her "mad" vision is therefore true and prophetic – until the duel is averted by Emmeline's success in convincing Godolphin *not* to fight. (269). When Godolphin appears unexpectedly on a Swiss beach, eminently sane and rational Lord Westhaven also has to "stop a moment to consider whether the figure of Godolphin which rose before him was not an illusion." Godolphin's peregrinations re-mark the uncertain status of visions and the impermanence of supposedly certain, empirical facts. Dream and reality, sanity and madness, are not binary opposites because the line between real empirical facts and what is dreamed, conjectured, suspected, or imagined is unstable, impermanent, and easily crossed. The fact that Godolphin is in the West Indies becomes an illusory fiction when he is in England; his presence in Switzerland is an illusory fiction until it is an established fact. Godolphin's agreement not to fight Fitz-Edward turns Adelina's vision of their duel back into a mad delusion. Likewise, once the letters in the casket are read, the certain facts with which the novel opened become fictions: that Emmeline is the illegitimate daughter of Lord Montreville's deceased brother and as such, a "being belonging to nobody" and "having no right to claim the protection of anyone," (49) who was "suffered to remain" at Mowbray Castle (46) as a charity case. The facts to which the casket letters and documents attest not only alter Emmeline's history; they give her a different reality and a different social identity as a woman of family, wealth and rank, and Mowbray Castle's legitimate heir.

Difficulties presented by the fluidity and contingency of reality are compounded in society by the necessity the polite are under to habitually conceal their thoughts and feelings from others for reasons of propriety, prudence or tact. Smith demonstrates that polite habits of concealment made conjectures like Delamere's intrinsic to the everyday interactions of the well-bred, even among friends. In Switzerland, Emmeline conceals her true feelings about Delamere from Godolphin and Lady Westhaven; Lord Westhaven conceals discovery of the casket letters from Lady Westhaven; Godolphin conceals Adelina's pregnancy from Lord Westhaven and his love for Emmeline from everyone. Because (as Godolphin points out) one character has "no means of knowing" what is passing in another's mind, and has to conjecture what that might be to know how to conduct themselves, the interactions among these polite and virtuous friends are governed by the sentiments and feelings they "impute" to each other. Since their imputations are mostly mistaken, their conjectures produce "restraint" or "mistrust" (374) and keep them speaking and acting at cross-purposes. The twenty-some letters in volumes 3 and 4 that fail to be written or to arrive at their destinations symbolize and extend such failures of communication. Bursts of candor can break through these impasses and lead to what Smith calls *eclaircissements*; but they are rare, impermanent, and incomplete. Godolphin, Emmeline, and other characters continue to conceal things from each other. Norms of politeness, prudence, and restraint and habits of concealment ensured that imagining what others were thinking and feeling, and conjectures about why they were speaking and acting as they did, preponderated in polite conversation and well-bred social life. Smith showed that the sympathetic imagination operative here was as liable as the Crofts' malicious imagination to "throw an obscurity over the truth" by inducing people to interpret the words and actions of others as empirical proof of conjectures which, however probable or "natural" they might seem, were chimerical and untrue.

Crofts' anonymous letter could not therefore be dismissed merely as the work of malicious intriguers and deceivers. It encapsulated a fundamental problem with observation, induction and empirical reasoning that plagued polite society as well as conjectural history and the law: resort to conjectures to fill gaps in the available facts and explain the words and actions of others in a world where facts themselves were not necessarily fixed, and those with different facts and different lacunae might be inhabiting a reality different from one's own. The conjectural imagination – with its imputations, surmises, and interpretations as well as its visions and dreams – was everywhere intermixed in what we take for reality; and even at its most sympathetic, the conjectural imagination was often wrong.

Smith fell back on an older, legal standard of proof to give Emmeline her happy ending. Analogies between the letters in the casket and the anonymous "fatal letter" indicate why one conjunction of evidence is more reliable than the other. Like the Crofts' anonymous letter, the casket letters invite their readers to rewrite the past, and contain an implicit charge of criminal misconduct – this time against Lord Montreville for robbing Emmeline of her father's title and estate. Here too the Crofts have intervened unbeknownst to the principals – this time by suppressing the caskets' contents and silencing those who knew of them. But the almost forty letters in the casket, which were written by Emmeline's grandmother and by her parents, are supported by legal documents – a marriage certificate, a will – which provide ocular legal evidence of the facts that the letters affirm. The history of Emmeline's ancestry outlined in the letters and documents is also confirmed by an eyewitness encountered in Switzerland by chance – a servant who accompanied Emmeline's parents during the crucial years when (echoing Burney's *Evalina*) the heroine's mother eloped with her father and married him secretly in France, unintentionally leaving their newborn daughter a nameless "nobody." Limousine's eyewitness narrative fills lacunae left by the letters and documents: it describes why her father married her mother formally twice, how each parent died, how the caskets containing the all-important letters and documents had reached England, and who they had been delivered to there. The history narrated by her parents' old servant thus not only tells Emmeline and Lord Westhaven what the letters and documents do not and, in many cases cannot say; it also vouches for their provenance and authenticity and thus for their evidential truth.

Together, letters, legal documents, and eyewitness narrative constitute a legal standard of proof that even Lord Montreville's lawyers cannot dispute. This interlocking system of oral and written evidence contrasts on every point both with Delamere's method of reaching his conclusions about Emmeline's guilt and with what he had to go on there: a single anonymous letter whose provenance was unknown; his own conjectures about what must have happened in light of merely circumstantial facts; ocular "proofs" that were capable of different interpretations; and a rush to judgement before witnesses could be found to confirm, correct, or add to the limited information he had. These were false and misleading bases for reconstructing what had happened in the past, and for serious, life-changing charges against another for committing a villainous or criminal act. By contrast, the casket combination of letters, legal documents, and eyewitness testimony constituted certain proof of Emmeline's true identity, making it possible to do her justice by restoring her to her rightful inheritance and social position.

The fact that Emmeline possessed the casket from the beginning suggests that requisite evidence is always there, just waiting to be found. But how probable was it that one would encounter the eyewitness one needed, by chance, somewhere in the Swiss mountains? Or find all necessary legal documents neatly attached to letters authenticating them already in one's possession? Or that such papers would have passed through the hands of scheming lawyers like the Crofts without being destroyed? Perhaps Smith's answer also lay in the casket; for resolving the plot by finding evidence of a protagonist's true identity in a casket was a hoary old cliché of Romance. Perhaps it was also in acknowledgement of this hint in a novel she admired, that Austen concluded *Pride and Prejudice* by tossing Smith's combination of reliable evidence to a character's true identity into the bin marked "Romance." The idea that all necessary evidence would suddenly appear to change the course of a history and give a powerless heroine her happy ending, belonged to the marvelous and improbable, to fairy tale, wish-fulfillment, and romance.

Circumstantial Evidence and the Letter-Clue: Braddon's *Lady Audley's Secret*

Circumstantial evidence remained a major issue for women writers. In bitter comment on the flood of crim con (adultery) cases at the turn of the nineteenth century, a wave of third-person narratives by women novelists at the Minerva Press showed how dangerous circumstantial evidence could prove to married women when used by jealous husbands or gossiping servants to convict them of adultery they had not committed in fact.[27] *Lady Audley's Secret* (1862), which contains thirty-eight letters (eleven fully transcribed) and is replete with allusions to eighteenth-century figures, is now read principally in relation to Wilkie Collins' *The Woman in White* (1860). But it is also usefully seen as another link in this transgenerational dialogue among women writers about the damage done to women by false narratives constructed by conjecture on the basis of circumstantial evidence. Exposing the fallibility and madness of that dogged pursuit of circumstantial evidence that now underpinned the "science" of the new detective police and was, by the 1860s, subject to renewed debate, Mary Elizabeth Braddon too presented a married woman as its victim, and concluded, with only formal deference to happy endings, on a highly ambiguous note.

Robert Audley, the barrister-detective in Braddon's best-seller, affirms the "common saying . . . gathered from experience," that "there are some things that cannot be hidden" – sooner or later, perhaps "by the remotest accident," the "mystery" of George Talboys's fate would be resolved, and "secrets" concealed by characters in the small interconnected society of Audleys and Maldons, discovered.[28] The truth must in time be detected, as long as an investigator had the patience to persist. Characterizing "circumstantial evidence" as a "wonderful fabric which is built out of straws collected at every point of the compass;" Audley claims that the "inductive evidence" he draws from such straws – the fragment of a letter, an incautious word, and "a thousand slight circumstances, so slight as to be forgotten by the criminal" – form valid and unbreakable "links of iron in the wonderful chain forged by the science of the detective officer" that is "strong enough to hang a man." (1: 174–175) Audley was echoing Sir James Graham, founder of the detective police, who had explained to the public that a detective's "success" depends on "a bloodhound tenacity in pursuit," "the knack . . . of making a *cast* in the right direction in search of a clue," and "sagacity in drawing inferences from slight things."[29] Audley was also endorsing the now widespread judicial view that "a concurrence of well-authenticated circumstances composes a stronger ground of assurance than positive testimony, unconfirmed by circumstances" for "circumstances cannot lie."[30]

Letters and a telegram figure prominently as "the clew to the mystery" (1: 147) and as "links in that terrible chain of evidence" that Audley "slowly forge[s]" for his "criminal case" against Lady Audley for the murder of George Talboys. (1:74) These metaphors are analogical. Braddon was using "clew" (clue) in the contemporary sense of "thread" leading through a maze, puzzle, or labyrinth – as in: "Let me prevail on them to furnish the people with a clue to extricate them from the labyrinth;" or "the physician requires a theory for a clue, a thread on which to string his ideas and systematic practice, and a line to direct him at the sick bed."[31] Letters and an anonymous telegram supply Audley with a thread through the maze of related and unrelated circumstances that confront him when conducting his "retrograde investigation" into Lady Audley's previous life. Indeed, he is the only character to obtain and read all the missives embedded in the text.

An early correspondence with his cousin, Alicia, demonstrates what Audley has to do to letters to convert them into clues. The prefatory narrative describes Audley writing to Alicia on August 31, the anniversary of Helen Talboys death, to tell her that he will bring Talboys with him to Audley Court when he comes to meet Lady Audley, his new aunt. Return of post brings a partly transcribed letter from Alicia "in an indignant running hand:" Audley and his friend cannot come because "my lady has taken it into her silly head that she is too ill to receive visitors (there is no more the matter with her than there is with me) and she cannot have gentlemen (great rough men, she says) in her house." (1:73) During the reception narrative, Audley twists Alicia's letter to light his pipe, thinks better of it, and thrusts it into a pigeonhole in his desk marked "*Important.*" A first-person interjection from the narrator, informing us that there was nothing of "judicial importance" in that pigeonhole yet, and that his cousin's brief Letter would one day become "a link in that terrible chain of evidence" forming Audley's "criminal case," (1: 74), invites us to notice that in this scene, every necessary step has been taken to prepare a very pedestrian letter for forgery into just such a judicial link. It has been extracted from its original correspondence and abstracted from the relationships described in its framing narrative. It has been kept and, however accidentally, pigeonholed as "*important.*" The ways in which it is *judicially* important may not be immediately apparent, but they are supposedly capable of discovering themselves in other connections, with other information, at some later date. Finally, the few "portions" of a letter that, singly or in combination, give it judicial importance are singled out: handwriting, date, the sender's name and address; the writing-paper; a choice sentence or two of content. Audley's criminal case will be built primarily on epistolary "evidence of time and place," "evidence of handwriting," and decontextualized fragments of letter-text used in ways unintended by their authors. (2: 62)[32]

Braddon's narrative initially confronts novel-readers with a variety of circumstances that may or may not be related to Talboys disappearance or to each other, and may or may not constitute evidence of a crime. Indeed, her narrator narrates "the story" from George Talboys' voyage to England to his disappearance and Audley's vain search for him, much as Audley does to Talboys's father when he gives him "a minutely detailed account of all that had happened to George ... in any way touching upon that subject" and carefully "avoid[s] making any deductions from the circumstances he ... submit[s]," (1:274, 285) in order to leave his auditors to decide if his suspicions of foul play are warranted. Like the "Journal of Facts connected with the Disappearance of George Talboys" that Audley compiles after Talboys goes missing, the novel's narrative is "inclusive of Facts which have no apparent Relation to that Circumstance." (1:145) Audley compiles this "official" *Journal of Facts* by searching his memory for "straws" that he had not deemed significant before, and puts it alongside Alicia's letter into the pigeonhole marked "*important.*" The shortcomings of an investigative "science" that "narrows the circle" by arbitrary selection, extraction, and decontextualization are illustrated and parodied here.

The "record" in Audley's *Journal of Facts* is composed of "short, detached," and numbered sentences, such as: "1. I write to Alicia, proposing to take George down to the court; 2. Alicia writes, objecting to the visit on the part of Lady Audley." (1:145) Missives figure large on this list, which Audley draws up after much reflection with frequent "alternatives and erasures." (1:147). The first half consists of "facts" connected to Lady Audley: her refusal to be introduced to Talboys, a telegram summoning her to London, the letter she wrote Alicia from London asking when Audley and Talboys mean to leave Essex, the men's clandestine entrance into her locked apartments and discovery of her portrait. The second half bears on George Talboys: his "exceeding strange" conduct the evening her portrait is discovered, his departure from their fishing expedition while Audley slept; his last sighting by a servant who thinks Talboys told him he was going to look for Lady Audley in the grounds of Audley Court; information that he had taken a train "which may, or may not, be correct;" the affirmation of Colonel Maldon, his father in law, that Talboys had briefly visited him at Southampton; and "the telegraphic message" to which I will return. Though recognizing that this list of disconnected "facts" leaves Talboys' disappearance "as dark as midnight from first to last," Audley conjectures from them that "the clue to the mystery must be found either at Southampton or in Essex." (147)

Selection, isolation, and abstraction of these "detached" circumstances make them the official "facts" of the case; but they also darken the "mystery" of Talboys's disappearance – and not merely because this list makes no obvious sense. To turn them into objective "facts," Audley has excised from the "record," along with the situations in which they originated, his motives for selecting these, and erasing other "alternative" facts that could easily have been substituted for them. As becomes apparent from "a retrograde investigation" or second reading, Audley has discounted or excised from the "record" the circumstantial evidence required to reconstruct what he and we later learn about Talboys's movements from Luke Marks deathbed confession and Talboys's account of himself. This evidence hides in plain sight among the many circumstances that Audley and we have already encountered in the narrative: Talboys has repeatedly stated his determination to return to Australia in consequence of his wife's death; he had already left his family with his father-in-law Colonel Maldon once and has now, in addition, made Audley his son's legal guardian; Audley has found indications that Talboys boarded a train in Essex, that he briefly visited Maldon in Southampton, and that in Liverpool, a young man with his arm in a sling had boarded an emigrant ship to Melbourne. Omission of these on Audley's list of facts shows that a detective can easily miss or dismiss the facts most relevant to his case – a point underlined by indicating that, just before starting his list, Audley remembered Talboys "as he had often seen him spelling over the shipping adverts in the *Times*, looking for a vessel to take him back to Australia." (1:125) Why then does Audley reject the circumstantial evidence that suggests that Talboys has done so, and insist instead that Talboys has been murdered?

In his influential *Essay on the Principles of Circumstantial Evidence* (1860), William Willis warned those who insisted that "a fact is a fact" and that "circumstances cannot lie," that it was far easier to be "misled" by circumstantial evidence than they assumed. For "facts may be true, and the inference mistaken;" or "facts may be indisputable and yet their relation to the principle fact may be only apparent and not real." And though circumstances do not lie, "the narrators of them may;" or our judgement of them may be "biased or mistaken." For "the mind is apt to take pleasure in adapting circumstances to one another, and even in straining them a little, if need be, to force them to form parts of one connected whole." The mind may also "mislead itself, by supplying some little link that is wanting, to take for granted a fact consistent with its previous theories, and necessary to render them complete." Motive is one such link. Willis warned against "imputing guilt" by "ascribing motives" or any of the "common inducements to crime" to "facts of conduct," since "a crime may be advantageous to many who do not commit it," observing at the same time, that finding "no discoverable motive" does not mean there was none.[33]

That Audley makes these errors can be demonstrated by restoring the last item on his list of facts, "the telegraphic message," to the situations from which Audley abstracts it. Audley finds this message on his visit to

Colonel Maldon after Talboys's disappearance, on "a twisted piece of paper [which] lay half burned upon the hearth rug." The telegram is anonymous, because the date, address, and sender's name have been burned off; but the surviving portion contains what Audley judges to be "the most important part, the greater part of the message:" (1: 66)

> . . ..alboys came to . . . last night, and left by the mail for London, on his way to Liverpool, whence he was to sail for Sydney." (1: 67)

That Audley "blanches" upon reading these straightforward words suggests that he has read something into the gaps on the page and supplied with "alarming" conjectures the lacunae of a sentence missing its crucial principle clause. Maldon had just informed him that Talboys came to Southampton by the mail-train the previous night on his way to Liverpool, and that he was determined to return to Australia. But though agreeing that return to Australia "was always in his mind more or less," Audley can find no "motive for [Talboys] leaving England in this manner, without a word to me, his most intimate friend—without even a change of clothes." (1:65) As Willis says, that he cannot discover the motive, does not mean there was none. And while it is factually true that "it isn't like him" to leave without a word to Audley – we later learn that Talboys had in fact written to his friend – Audley demonstrates the wonderful "sagacity" of his "science" in "drawing inferences from slight things" by inferring, mistakenly, that not writing indicates "some treachery . . . towards George." Audley had misliked slovenly, drunken Colonel Maldon, the half-pay officer who isn't quite a gentleman, when he first visited him with Talboys, suspecting him immediately and without evidence of mistreating his daughter and grandson. Now, already biased against him, he imputes to Maldon one of the "common inducements to crime:" "What if [Talboys'] greedy old father in law had made away with him, after decoying him to Southampton," in order to get his hands on Talboys' money? (1: 65) Having pursued the hint in the telegram and found no George Talboys on the passenger list of the Australia-bound ship, Audley is certain that "George Talboys never sailed for Australia" and may be dead. (1: 65) By the time he visits Maldon again, Audley has twisted the "indisputable fact" of the telegram to connect it to what he considers "the principle fact" – Talboys' death – and has ingeniously adapted the telegram to fit his theory that Talboys was murdered by Lady Audley at Audley Court. Audley tells Maldon that he "knows" Talboys was not seen after going to the Court and therefore never came to Southampton; he makes the telegram fit what he "knows" by construing its message as "the lie dictated" to Maldon by Lady Audley and "repeated" by him. (1: 240)

Once he begins to "fit the pieces of the terrible puzzle, and gather together the stray fragments which, when collected, may make a hideous whole," Audley construes almost any circumstance his investigation uncovers as confirmation of his conjecture that Talboys was murdered by Lady Audley. Audley's failure to entertain possibilities that do not fit his theory and contribute to the criminal case he is determined to build against her, is dramatized by his repeated rejection of any other explanation of the facts than murder. There are several of these, some more credible than others: Harcourt Talboys's insistence that his son has "only pretended to disappear;" (1: 226) Maldon's "Hiding away, perhaps—bribed to keep out of the way perhaps; but not dead" (1: 241); Mr. Dawson's observation that Audley's suspicions exist only in his mind (1:313); Dr. Mosgrove's judgment that Audley has "no evidence of [Talboys's] death," and that "if [he] could produce evidence of his death, [he] could produce no evidence against this lady, beyond the one fact that she had a powerful motive for getting rid of him." (2:216) The surprises of the plot are engineered by producing reasonable explanations that Audley has ignored or failed to imagine; while Audley's rejection of these characters' observations helps to substantiate Lady Audley's later charge that Audley is monomaniacal – he "looks at common events" with a "mental vision" distorted by his "one idea." (2: 87).

With wicked wit, Bradford presents what Sir James Graham called the detective's "bloodhound tenacity in pursuit" as a textbook case of monomania. Monomania was considered "partial insanity" because "the individual affected is rendered incapable of thinking correctly [only] on subjects connected with a particular illusion; while in other respects he betrays no palpable disorder of the mind." Its first symptoms were "changes in disposition and habits;" but later, when the monomaniac's mind became "possessed" by a "fixed idea," he became "destitute of the power to withdraw his attention from [it] . . . and as irresistibly impelled to act in accordance with this, as the lower animals are to act in accordance with their instincts."[34] Irrationally driven to aberrations of judgment by what he experiences as "a hand that is stronger than [his] own," Audley abandons his erstwhile indolent, sybaritic habits to energetically pursue his erroneous conviction that Talboys was murdered by Lady Audley and "build up some absurd theory" that "has no existence except in [his] own overheated brain." (2:45, 62). As Lady Audley observes, Audley's monomania is accompanied by hypochondriasis. Brought on by "real grief . . . and even love," in a mind "long stagnant" because "continually employed upon one point," the primary symptoms of this disease were "a vague alarm of impending evil" or "fear of death."[35] Audley's "hypocondriachal" madness is manifest in his constant alarm about evil befalling Talboys, and in his projection onto his friend and alter ego of his fear of his own disappearance and death as a superfluous man.

Braddon also treated with wicked wit Audley's exhibition of another trait that Sir James Graham considered essential to the detective: "the knack ... of making a *cast* in the right direction in search of clue[s]," by demonstrating that Audley's "clews" lead him through a different labyrinth to a different crime. "The chain of circumstantial evidence which unites the mystery of [Talboys's] fate with the person whom [Audley] suspects" (2:47) leads him not to Talboys's murderer, but to a bigamist and protean, occasional self. Like Mary Carleton, Alanthus-Formator, Fantomina, or Locke, Lady Audley has serial occasional selves – she is Helen Maldon, Helen Talboys, Lucy Graham, and Lady Audley. She also has multiple contradictory ascribed identities – conscientious governess, innocent child bride, sexual fascinator, angel, devil, embodiment of vanity, selfishness and ambition, kind mistress, wax doll, empty-headed coquette, indifferent aristocrat, trickster, and arch-deceiver. In one occasional self, she has been Talboys's impoverished, embittered, and demanding wife; in another, the loving and devoted wife emblematically seated by Sir Michael Audley's sickbed stroking his hand. Audley could have proved "the identity of two individuals who have no apparent connection" to make the case that Lady Audley was Helen Talboys and still Talboys's wife. But he ignores what his evidence does and does not prove, and charges her monomaniacally with murder anyway: "I have sworn to bring the murder of George Talboys to justice ... I say that it was by your agency that my friend met with his death." (2:60). Audley pronounces bigamy "wicked" – an attitude that may not have been widely shared in the 1860s, even by the courts;[36] but it is for Talboys murder that Audley sentences Lady Audley to a "living death." Neither man believes her mad, but Audley makes an informal gentleman's agreement with Mosgrove to incarcerate her in a Belgian madhouse even though, or perhaps because, "no jury in the United Kingdom would condemn her upon such evidence." (2:216)[37]

As Ann-Marie Dunbar observes, Lady Audley's confession of her bigamy "point[s] the reader to a substantially different narrative."[38] This narrative, which counters the story of Audley's investigation with "the story of the crime," emerges from conjoining this first confession to three others in which she and two other characters reveal their secrets. Braddon used now largely discredited forms of evidence – confessions and the whole contents of letters – to present a discontinuous counter-narrative that can be pieced together by novel-readers who "begin at the other end" and conduct their own "retrograde investigation" by working "backwards" from two fully transcribed letters to their "antecedents" earlier in the novel. Presented to Audley during Marks's deathbed confession, these are the letters that Marks had neglected to deliver, which Talboys wrote to Audley and Lady Audley while engineering his own disappearance. Coming on top of Audley's joyful discovery that Talboys is still very much alive, and after he learns of Lady Audley's violent altercation with Talboys at Audley Court, these elliptical letters only "bewilder" Audley. For Talboys's letter to him asks him to forget Talboys – Talboys cannot tell him what has happened, only that it will drive him from England and that Audley's "counsel" cannot help him. Talboys's letter to "Helen," his wife, forgives her for what she has done, and tells her that she may now "Rest in Peace. You shall never hear of me again . . . You need fear no molestation from me; I leave England never to return." (2:277). The mystery here, at least for modern readers, is why Talboys was suddenly bowing out, and without explanation to his friend.

One answer is that there was a long tradition of unofficial self-divorce among the common people, accomplished by a husband's desertion of his spouse and departure for the new world or some distant part of Britain, to permit each partner to remarry and start another life.[39] Lady Audley's confession tells us that she thought this was her situation as Helen Talboys after three years passed without any "token of my husband's existence." She "looked upon this as a desertion" and resenting it bitterly, thought she "had a right to think that he is dead, or that he wishes me to believe him dead." (2:178, 179, 180) There is evidence in the novel's previous narrative to confirm these statements: the first chapter told us that Talboys had not written to his wife while seeking his fortune in Australia; and Audley's visit to Yorkshire turned up witnesses to the scandal created there by Talboys's "desertion" and to Helen Talboys's departure to seek "another life and fortune" after a quarrel with her father over what he spent on drink. After Helen's "death," there was also Talboys's "bitter self-reproach at his recognition of that desertion which must have seemed so cruel to her who waited and watched at home." (2:20) Lady Audley believed that Talboys had deserted her to free them from their marriage so each could marry someone else.

During the nineteenth century, cases of bigamy were reported to the courts only when informal accommodations among the parties had failed. As Dr. Mosgrove tells Audley, there were informal methods for settling awkward bigamous marriages without scandalous court cases, just as there were informal gentlemen's agreements to put a troublesome wife in a madhouse – Audley had only to send the lady back to her first husband if he agreed to take her. But as we learn from Lady Audley's second confession in Belgium and as Talboys confirms, the violent altercation between them resulted from Talboys's discovery that she was determined not to return to him or to her "old life;" and chose to stay with her second husband. Talboys's undelivered letter to her indicates that, upon reflection, he had opted for the other way of settling the matter informally – to disappear himself and leave her Sir Michael Audley's wife. The counsel of his barrister-friend was of no use to Talboys here. Audley's failure to recognize the handwriting on Talboys's letters, which Talboys wrote with his left hand, symbolizes how far Talboys's solution lay outside Audley's domain. As barrister and detective, Audley belonged to a prosperous class of professionals closely allied to the gentry, which had not known poverty themselves and did not understand "how far poverty can affect a life" (2:179). Braddon demonstrated that the mutually supportive members of this class – detectives, lawyers, physicians, and keepers of madhouses – equated their "duty" with making the law work for those who governed. Gail Turley Houston has argued that the novel "proves the self-interestedness of the law and male lawmakers" by showing that individuals and classes "do constantly support laws or institutions which they deem beneficial to themselves, but which certainly are in fact injurious to the rest of the world."[40] But it also showed, through their backroom deals, that well-connected gentlemen in the upper classes were unwilling to let even these laws stand in their way; and that in usurping the functions of police and courts by their informal accommodations, they were also usurping the power of other citizens, like Talboys and his Helen, to reach private informal accommodations of their own.

Braddon presented the "duel to the death" between the two modes of being, acting, thinking, and decoding letters that Audley's manifest narrative and Lady Audley's counter-narrative re-present, as "a duel to the death" to determine which of their two forms of madness will "conquer" the other. Lady Audley's "madness" was the madness of serial identities – shifting occasional selves that enabled her to pass as different characters from different social classes – in a society that now demanded the consistent, controlled display of a single, orderly personal identity and required people to know and keep to their station. This inherited, shifting and protean manner of being-in-the world was being feminized, criminalized as "deviant" or "transgressive" and abnormalized by a medical discourse that conveniently blurred the lines between insanity, vice, and crime.[41] Arguing that "unless through every change of circumstance the thread of personality is continuous, personality is an illusion," medical men now characterized what Locke had presented as ordinary and empirically observable – that *"we constantly lose the Sight of our past Selves."* (II.xxvii. 10) – as "a certain sign of disease." They argued that "an essential note of mental health is a strong personal identity," and that "a certain sign of disease is that hysterical multiplicity of states ... " which they now dubbed "multiple personality."[42] Braddon understood, by contrast, that fluid, protean selves with their transitory and inconsistent passions and driving social ambition had not disappeared from society. They had only been forced into hiding, incarcerated behind the "iron mask" that society imposed: "surely it is strange that [madhouses] are not larger, when we think how many helpless wretches must beat their brains against this hopeless persistency of the orderly outward world, as compared with the storm and tempest, the riot and confusion within." (1:202). Where contemporaries claimed that "insanity and the varieties of the disease, [had] increased in modern times as a consequence of the highly-wrought and somewhat artificial condition of modern society,"[43] Braddon argued that beating their brains against the bars of the single invariable identity that society now demanded was what ensured that "many minds must tremble upon the narrow boundary between reason and unreason." If sufficiently "goaded" and frightened, anyone was therefore capable of sudden bursts of madness – of being "mad today, sane tomorrow"– because "this invisible balance upon which the mind is always trembling" is "so fragile." (2:251) Brought on by "mental excitement, slight bodily injury or fear," the symptoms of "acute hysteria" that Lady Audley displayed in her violent attacks, came on suddenly and as suddenly disappeared.[44] Audley's monomaniacal madness, by contrast, was the monomaniacal madness of the bloodhound, in carica-ture of the dogged excess of the centered self's single, strong, and continu-ous "thread of personality."

Audley's final letter to Lady Audley in her Belgian madhouse offers a particularly shocking perspective on these dueling madnesses. It is prefaced by Audley's "humble" recognition of the faultiness of his detective "science" and by his pious admission that God's wondrous ways have shown him the "folly" of "trust[ing] to the pitiful light of his own reason." But this does make Audley retract or repent of the sentence he passed on Lady Audley for murdering Talboys. Instead, he "comforts himself" for his errors and follies as detective, barrister, and self-appointed judge by telling himself that he had only tried to "do his duty." (2:292) Without perceiving the irony, he then writes to "Madame Taylor" (aka Lady Audley) in her Belgian madhouse to tell her that Talboys is alive, thinking "it may be some comfort to her to hear that her husband did not perish in his youth by her wicked hand, if her selfish soul can hold any sentiment of pity or sorrow for others." (2:293) Piety and recognition of his own "pitiful light" notwithstanding, Audley sees no need to forgive her "wickedness" as he has his own, or as Talboys forgave it, much less to reopen the case. Piety and pity do not prompt him to ask himself if the sentence he considered fit punishment for Talboys's murder (being buried alive for the rest of her life) is just, pitiful or even appropriate, when there has been no such crime.[45] But as critics note, Audley has successfully repelled the lower-class intruder, and is now poised to rise into Sir Michael's governing place. Audley's madness thus appears to "conquer" Lady Audley's, by its superior, gendered, social, and institutional power, and by remaining complacently monomaniacal to the end.

The case is, of course, complicated by Lady Audley's bigamy, and by the fact that, while under the "acute hysteria" brought on by "bodily injury or fear," she attempted murder twice. This makes it possible for novel-readers to agree with Audley that she ought to be punished, or to meditate on the difficulty of judging fairly between the contending parties in this case. Consequently, what the narrator sardonically calls the "happy ending" points two ways, to allow both Audley's madness and Lady Audley's madness to "conquer" at the death. The ending shows the Audleys reorganizing themselves around Robert Audley's professional middle-class family, "happy" and "at peace" in the knowledge that, with Lady Audley's death, they have securely buried their aberrations of judgment, abuses of power, abdications of responsibility, secret injustices, violence, cruelty, and unremitting vengefulness, together with her crimes and the scandal of her occasional selves, in "Mrs. Taylor's" distant, unremembered, Belgian grave. But burying her in this way has made Lady Audley's secret the Audley family's scandalous secret. To build the peace, respectability, self-righteous virtue, professional success, and sociopolitical aspirations of a middle-class Victorian family on such a secret was to build on shaky ground – as evidenced by the reemergence and publication of the very secret they imagined so securely buried, under Lady Audley's name.

Retrospective: On Laws of Evidence, Personal Testimony, and Particular Facts

Perhaps from a sense that novelists had little of theoretical interest to say in their own defense, our scholarly focus has largely been on the objections to fiction made by empiricist philosophers and historians who sought to exclude novelists from empiricist debates by arguing that "feigned events and the causes contrived for them, as they did not exist, cannot inform us what happened in former times, nor by consequence assist us in a plan of future conduct."[46] Fiction supposedly has no relevance to facts. But as we saw, narrative-epistolary novelists made their arguments in their fictions by using their second scaffolding convention, comparison of letters to narrative realities, to interrogate empiricist historians, lawyers, philosophers, and scientists on their own terrain, and show where fiction and imagination intervened in "scientific" methods of processing facts.[47] This section articulates ways in which the novels discussed here addressed successive shifts in the treatment of empirical evidence in history, natural philosophy and law, and identifies a position they all maintained throughout.[48]

At the end of the seventeenth century, law, history, and the natural sciences held that direct eyewitness testimony was the kind of evidence with the highest probability of being true. In law, the "probability of truth" assigned to oral and written testimony was judged by the rank, gender, age, integrity, and access of the witness. The Royal Society deployed considerations of character to determine the validity of epistolary reports about unfamiliar and seemingly improbable natural phenomena observed in the New World. In history, the accounts of great men like Clarendon or Burnet who had participated in the events they described were particularly prized, and historians embedded transcriptions of whole letters from men of stature in their narratives as direct evidence of the truths they were affirming. But the impact of empiricism, of antiquarians' discovery of forged ancient documents, and of warnings by skeptics like Bayle about the biases of witnesses and the partiality of earlier memorials and histories on which later historians had relied, led to increasing suspicion of oral and written testimony. By the 1720s when Manley and Davys were writing, this had created the demand that oral and written testimony be validated by empirical verification and available facts. It seems odd now to think there might have been a time when most people did not automatically check oral and written assertions against facts (or that we may be in that situation again); but Manley and Davys clearly thought it necessary to warn readers of the danger of accepting letters, and other people's representations of themselves or of others, *without* seeking empirical evidence of their truth. Lord Wordy, Amoranda and Lordy Lofty all make ludicrous errors when they assume that the testimony of a letter alone will tell them all they need to know. Indeed, Manley's "jest" jokingly suggested that people inhabiting a society of occasional selves should resort to empirical experiment, as the sciences did, to discover the truth about a person.

Publication of the first treatise on rules of evidence during the 1740s and introduction in trials of the criterion "beyond a reasonable doubt" for juries charged with judging "matters of fact," can be used to benchmark a period when recognitions about facts that had long been familiar to rhetoricians and learned casuists, began to move to center stage in history and law. One recognition was that the facts available were often indirect (i.e. "artificial" or "circumstantial"), especially for crimes that could not be observed directly and for past events. Another was that, whether direct or indirect, "naked facts, without the causes that produced them and the circumstances that accompany them are not sufficient to characterize actions."[49] "Facts" were turned into evidence by the addition of circumstances and probable inferences about their causes or about "the secret Springs of Actions," which went beyond what was available for observation. Particular facts were thus signs pointing beyond themselves to conjectured meanings and probable connections that the lawyer, scientist, or historian superadded to insert them into "chains of events" and into "the sort of narrative that, by gaining consent to a series of events, can make circumstantial evidence entirely convincing."[50] This meant that what juries and empirical inquirers were weighing was the probability, and thus the credibility, of evidence in which "a thing certainly known to be a real occurrence or to represent a truth known by actual observation or authentic testimony" was already thoroughly imbricated with "inference, conjecture or fiction."[51] Their judgments, moreover, involved making inferences of their own. As Giles Jacob explained in 1749, judgments of evidence worked with what was called "presumption" in law – "an opinion or belief so strong as to amount to Proof and Evidence thereof" – about the signification of facts and the probable connection between them. His example presents three bare facts, which function as signs that derive their significance from inferences that he does not state and that we have to supply: when a person is found dead in a house, a man is seen coming out of it with a bloody sword, and there is no one else in the house, there is "a violent Presumption to be admitted as evidence that he is the murderer." Jacob recognized that this falls short of certainty – "presumption is what may be doubted" (hence "beyond a reasonable doubt"); but he insisted nevertheless that "it shall be accounted true, if the contrary be not proved."[52]

Haywood's treatment of Trueworth's response to Flora's anonymous letter displayed the fallacies in this line of argument. Baby Betsy is a "fact," as is Betsy's financial support. Trueworth and the wet-nurse draw false inferences from them to produce a narrative about Betsy's maternity that is "accounted true" because it seems probable and because nothing "contrary" presents itself. Miss Mabel's much later narrative gives the same facts a different significance by supplying different causes and connections. This demonstrates not only that "the contrary" might be proved too late to change the sentence passed on the accused, but that presumption was an unreliable gauge, because the same facts could support entirely different inferences and connections, and an entirely different narrative of events. Trueworth's presumption that Betsy was the mother of an illegitimate child amounted to his failure to conceive of any explanation for the facts he had ascertained other than the obvious one that came to mind. The same holds for Giles Jacob's example. The man he accounted a "murderer" beyond a reasonable doubt could have found the already dead man in the empty house and rushed out, frantically brandishing the bloody sword to show neighbors at a distance, who might see but could not hear him, that a violent murder had been committed.[53] Haywood's description of the human cost to innocent victims like Betsy of men's conviction that their violent presumptions could, and should for all practical purposes, be accounted true, addressed a serious lacuna in mainstream arguments.

Blurring distinctions between propositions squarely derived from observed phenomena and conjectures they "accounted true," lawyers, historians, and natural philosophes began to make conjecture "the principal instrument of investigation," and probable conjunctions the means of constructing "chains of evidence," which they argued had all the force of truth, given the contingency of experience that a priori precluded absolute certainty and invariable truths. Charlotte Smith re-marked the now blurred distinction between conjecture and truth by ridiculing the ways in which characters' like Croft and Delamere used conjectures and fictional connections between unconnected facts to construct erroneous but plausible narratives about what had happened that they mistook for truth and re-applied to new facts. She showed that, far from being the province of experts in the human or natural sciences, conjecture was intrinsic to social intercourse in polite society and everyday life. Everyone "trafficked in conjecture" to make sense of other people's words and actions, of the letters they read, and of the little they saw or were told of events. But experience showed that the ability of any set of conjectures to explain the available facts did not make them true. Conjectures turn facts into fictions; and facts change their ontological status with changes in empirical circumstances, information or cognition, creating mutable and ever-changing understandings of the present and the past in which what is conjectured, imagined and not imagined shape our perceptions of the real. Smith thus turned the fluid contingency of experience back against methods of reasoning and narrating which empiricists claimed could explain experience and master contingency itself.

Braddon was writing after the rise of positivism, which held that "facts" are the only scientifically valid objects of knowledge and that correct use of rational scientific methods ensured that laws and universally true propositions could be inferred from them in the human and social as well as in the natural sciences. Positivism's rise in Britain has been dated from John-Stuart Mill's highly influential *System of Logic, Rationative and Inductive, being a Connected View of the Principles of Evidence and Methods of Scientific Investigation* (1843). This mixed elements of empiricism, rationalism, and utilitarianism to provide "a system of rules" for "operations of the human understanding in the pursuit of truth" that were designed to ensure that we "judge rightly" of whatever evidence presents itself in investigations.[54] Mill is interesting not only for his influence, but because he established rules for thought that solved the problems identified above by simply excluding them from consideration. Mill eliminated difficulties proceeding from the "original data" – including faulty perceptions, the irregular, biased, or erroneous workings of consciousness and any distortions of judgment produced by an investigator's or judge's desires, interests, or goals – by beginning from the (counterfactual) proposition that "Whatever is known to us by consciousness is known beyond possibility of question" (4) and by assuming a perfectly rational and dispassionate investigating mind. Ignoring, along with reasonable doubt, the impact on investigations or judgements of anything that had not appeared to consciousness ("from nothing . . . no consequences can proceed") kept the focus on "positive facts" – on those "positive conditions of a phenomenon" that exercise agency – and on the investigator's task of determining which, in the "chaos" of positive facts and conditions, was generally or always the cause or "active antecedent" of another positive fact. (200, 201) Mill acknowledged that "nearly all our knowledge is a matter of inference," much of it probabilistic; but he circumvented this difficulty by attaching the knowledge with which positivist logic was concerned to "inferences from truths previously known" whether from general propositions or from observation, and by providing rules for inference. What Mill did not acknowledge was how his own utilitarian interest in mental operations only "as they conduce to our own knowledge and to our command over that knowledge for our own uses" skewed his logic by limiting logic's purview to investigation of the uniform succession and causation of facts that give us "whatever power we possess of influencing those facts to our advantage." This made his argument circular: universal truths that had supposedly been inferred from previous unscientific investigations – that there are "uniformities in the course of nature" and of human actions; that "every phenomenon has a cause which it invariably follows" – "warranted" operations of the mind that he designed to prove these propositions "scientifically," and guarantee the "rigorous universality of which we are in quest." (184, 191, 195, 343)

As we saw, Braddon attacked the widespread legal doctrine that "circumstances cannot lie" by illustrating William Willis's arguments about how they could. But her novel can also be seen in the context of complaints, like that of Richard Simpson in 1858, that "the realm of positive definite forms" ignores "the obscure movements of our will, our knowing faculties and the other mysterious forces which make up our soul" and that positivism's "immense simplification of thought ... reduces all knowledge to an ignorance at the level of the meanest capacity."[55] Braddon showed how Audley's investigation and judgments were distorted by his utilitarian goal – to prove that Talboys had been murdered by Lady Audley. She showed through her treatment of Audley's "Journal of Facts," that what Mill had called the "chaos" of facts would not be tamed by methods of selection and elimination as he claimed. Audley's stubborn adherence to his judgment of Lady Audley also suggests that "inferences from truths previously known" retain their power even against countervailing positive facts (Talboys's living presence), to keep thought tied to general ideas that had once been thought true long after they had been disproved. Braddon was also among the Victorian novelists who reintroduced mysterious and uncontrollable psychic forces that complicated, derailed, or invalidated supposedly rational, methodical analyses of positive facts.

Perhaps the most remarkable feature in this shifting trajectory is the resistance of *all* these novelists to the increasing depreciation of eyewitness testimony that accompanied empiricist valorization of "facts." The novels here all gave credence to eyewitness testimony and first-person confessions. They did not deny the importance of empirical verification; indeed, first-person testimonies are always validated somewhere in the narrative by what figure there as true facts. But they all insisted on the importance of admitting personal testimony and, if possible, of combining it with other kinds of evidence – letters, legal documents, observable actions, inadvertent "self-discovery," physical or scriptoral marks, direct and circumstantial facts, even hearsay. They also argued the importance of considering all the *circumstances*: not only the empirical circumstances in which a piece of evidence initially figured, but also the empirical circumstances in which evidence was collected, facts were selected, gaps were missed, narrative chains of events were constructed, judgments were made, and actions were taken.

CHAPTER 3

Cultural Expectations and Encapsulating Letters

Introduction: Judging the Future by the Past

From the middle of the eighteenth century, narrative-epistolary novelists tended to distinguish investigation of the past from investigation of expectations of the future. Expectations are convictions about the probability of future conduct or events based on the likelihood that what mostly happened in the past and mostly happens in the present will also happen in the future.[1] Given the supposition of Romanticists that concern with "futurity" was new in their period, it is important to notice that efforts to foresee or predict the future were intrinsic to probabilistic reasoning in science, commerce, and law from the seventeenth century, especially in areas where prudent practical action depended on a person's ability to make rational "prognostications" or to proportion risk to gain.[2] The financial instruments introduced during the 1690s, for instance, caused merchants, insurers, sellers of annuities, and speculators in joint-stock companies to bet on the future based on "reasonable," because probable, expectations about what was likely to happen to a ship, company, stock, or human body in future time.[3] "Expectations" also came to refer euphemistically to a person's "prospects of inheriting wealth or property" (OED) as uncertainty about such prospects grew, thanks to the unprecedented rapidity with which wealth and estates were changing hands. Probabilistic expectations supplied a credible means of offsetting and endeavoring to control their contrary – contingency and the un-expected, accident, chance, the unintended, and the un-designed.[4]

Expectations, then, were imbricated with probabilistic thinking from the first. But as Lorraine Dalston has shown, they came increasingly to the fore during the eighteenth century when philosopher-mathematicians sought to construct a "calculus of expectations" by quantifying probabilities and translating "prudence" into mathematical terms, and when science increasingly based its knowledge-claims on its ability to predict and control the future conduct of natural, social, or medical phenomena. Chance, which threatened to "overturn the predictability of life in society as well as mechanic trajectories," was now dismissed with the claim that "what the vulgar call chance is nothing but a secret and concealed cause." And in calculations assuming a "strictly determined natural order that displayed God's providence through regularity and foresight," there was "systematic conflation of possibility and probability" as well as a shift to reliance on the truth-value of predictive a priori rules and laws. Probabilistic thinking now took "expectations founded on past experiences" to be "the unique rule of our opinions and our actions;"[5] and made expectations "a yardstick against which all human beliefs were to be gauged."[6] As the doctor put it in *The Female Quixote*, "we can judge of the future only by the past." (372)

Charlotte Lennox ridiculed characters using expectations derived from the past to rule their opinions and actions in all three of *The Female Quixote*'s (1752) epistolary courtship episodes. In the first, she used a double prefatory narrative to present Arabella's and Mr. Hervey's incompatible expectations of the letter that Hervey writes to declare his love. The outer prefatory narrative addresses Arabella's conviction that Hervey, a stranger who stared at her in church, "was excessively in Love with her," and that she might "soon expect to have some very extraordinary Proofs of his Passion."[7] That she expects this proof to take the form of a letter is clear from her instruction to her woman, Lucy, not to "be accessary [sic] to Conveying his presumptuous Thought to me either by Letter or Messages" and not to "suffer him to corrupt your Fidelity with the Presents he will very probably offer you." (11) Lucy takes this as "a Hint of what she ought to expect from her Lady's Lovers." (11) The inner prefatory narrative describes Hervey's very different expectation, based on "advice" from his cousin that "was continually in his mind and flattered his Vanity with the most agreeable Hopes [of] Success." (11) His cousin assured him that Arabella, who "has been kept in confinement" and has "never had a lover in her life," would easily succumb to "the first Person who addresses her." (9) Hervey therefore "conceives that there was no great Occasion for much Ceremony in declaring himself to one who had been educated in the Country;" and that to win this wealthy and aristocratic prize, his letter need only tell Arabella "in plain Terms ... how *deeply* he was enamour'd of her." (13)

Double reception narratives demonstrate that, though each notices the discrepancy between what they expect of the other and what the other empirically says or does, and each is surprised and annoyed by the other's unexpected reactions, neither Arabella nor Hervey recognize such discrepancies as empirical evidence that they have mistaken the reality of the situation, much less as cause to inquire more closely into who the other really is. Each has empirical evidence that the other is not what they expected them to be; but each tries to account for this evidence in ways that support and confirm their expectations. Hervey is "astonished" when Lucy tells him that Arabella is convinced that he is "*distractedly* in love" with her (12) and that Arabella has instructed her not to allow herself to be bribed into carrying letters or messages from him. But rather than recognizing that this is not the conduct of a simple, unceremonious country girl, Hervey takes Lucy's words as a "hint" that she *is* willing to be bribed to carry a letter to her mistress, and proceeds to write one for her to take. Interpreting Arabella's words to mean the opposite of what they say confirms the expectation, so flattering to his vanity, that it "will not be difficult" for a smart London gentleman like himself "to persuade" a simple country girl like Arabella "to free herself by marriage" from "confinement" in her father's castle. Consequently, when Lucy returns from her mistress with a letter, he "supposes it to be the answer he expected," and is "surprised" and "disappointed" to find that Arabella has returned his letter unopened. (14) But this discovery touches his vanity, not his expectations: fearing that Arabella has made him look ridiculous in Lucy's eyes, he pretends to treat this as a jest – and resolves to make another, similar, attempt on Arabella before departing for London. And having learned nothing from the reality of his "bad success" on either occasion, he makes a third attempt.

Arabella's conduct is similar. She is "disappointed" and "mortified" that her charms have not had more effect when a week passes after noticing Hervey in Church "without the Importunities she expected." (11) And having "expected to hear that the Return of his Letter would make her Lover commit some very extravagant Actions," she is again "surprised" to learn from Lucy that he "laughed heartily at discovering his mistake." (15) But she too continues to interpret Hervey's words and actions in accordance with her expectations. Hearing later that Hervey is in bed indisposed, she assumes that he must be dying for love of her, and attributes his recovery to the letter she wrote him commanding him to live. Arabella is made to appear as ridiculous as Hervey fears he will be – especially when, like Amoranda in *The Reform'd Coquet*, she commands her manservants to protect her from abduction when encountering Hervey during a ride. Arabella does not know that Hervey never received her letter commanding him to live or that his illness was only a migraine; Hervey does not know about Arabella's "foible" of adhering to the conventions of Romance. But here missing information, like unseen letters, are adduced by the narrator for the same purpose as the empirical evidence that the characters explain away: to ridicule the imperviousness of people's expectations to reality and their willingness to fill in with preconceived ideas inherited from the past anything they do not know. Arabella and Hervey are each satisfied with whatever explanations of the other's unexpected conduct their false expectations suggest, because where expectations supply the place of facts, the presence or absence of epistolary evidence or empirical facts can have no weight. This courtship is dissolved by the failure of each to meet the other's expectations.

The other epistolary courtship episodes are analogical to the first. The expectation set against Arabella's Romance expectations in the second episode is common to her father who "expects her to conform to his Will in the Choice of a Husband I have made for you," (41) and to Glanville, the husband he has chosen. But this time, Glanville eventually "understands the Examples she thought it her duty to follow" and realizes that he must "endeavor to gain her heart by a Behaviour most agreeable to her." (48) The third epistolary courtship episode, in which Sir George writes her a letter in "the Heroic Style" as "Bellmour," addresses the danger of deception presented by lovers who cynically set out to meet a girl's expectations. This danger is fortuitously averted here by Arabella's too literal reading of his letter. But allusions to Haywood's romances – through Sir George's "Heroic Style," which is that of Haywood's novellas of the 1720s and 1730s; and through the intervening scene where Arabella mistakes a gardener with superior manners for a Philidore – invite comparisons that indicate Lennox's corrections: Haywood had overlooked the extent to which expectations based on familiar cultural archetypes enter into our perceptions of "reality" and the role they play in determining what any individual does and does not see as evidence.

Novel-readers who follow the characters' example by assuming that, because Arabella is the Quixote figure, they can expect her to be absurdly mistaken and ridiculously wrong, will read these episodes as quixotic satires on the conventions of Romance. But these episodes "surprise" by comically portraying the clash of *two* received cultural "archetypes," to use Locke's term, both of which had been promoted by literature and would continue to be.[8] The men's expectations are based on familiar literary stereotypes (the naïve country girl impressed and taken in by the seductive fine town gentleman) or on conduct-book precepts and socially promoted norms (the already slightly dated expectation in conduct books describing the relative duties of parents and children, that a daughter must obey a father's will and accept his choice of husband). The empirical inefficacy and inapplicability to particular cases of such conventional masculine expectations cooperate with the errors proceeding from Arabella's Romance expectations, to discredit the doctor's confident assertions that "the Power of Prognostication may, by Reading and Conversation, be extended beyond our own Knowledge; and the great Use of Books is that of participating without Labour or Hazard in the Experience of others," (372) and that we must judge of the future by the past. As Mrs. Barbauld observed, the doctor's "grave moralizing" only produced an ending that was "not very well wound up."[9]

The narrative-epistolary texts in this chapter follow Lennox by testing expectations consisting of preconceived ideas drawn from conduct books, social norms, or cultural stereotypes against empirical reality as it subsequently unfolds in the narrative sequence of empirical events. This enabled novels to confront received ideas and supposedly universal a priori truths with particular cases, and expectations with the contingency and unpredictability of everyday life, in order to show, among other things, that rules and expectations derived "by authority" from the past were poor guides to future action; and that the inadequacy of their expectations often became evident to people only on a retrospective view. Some retrospective rewriting of past perceptions and events was involved, as we saw, whenever one character discovered another's true or falsified secret history from a letter, and whenever the emergence of a heretofore hidden story created a new perspective on the manifest story initially presented by the narrator. But narrative-epistolary novelists now highlighted this narrative feature to show, contrary to the doctor, that we can judge the past only by the future. Hindsight judges expectations based on preconceived ideas by their empirical outcomes and effects, and reinterprets earlier understandings of characters and events that have involved such expectations from an empirically informed retrospective view that knows how things turned out.

The expectations in play were highlighted by what I call "encapsulating letters." Introduced by Charlotte Lennox in *Henrietta* and refined by Frances Burney in *Cecilia*, encapsulating letters are letters that escape their immediate occasion: while performing an instrumental function in the present, they epitomize relationships or summarize situations rooted in the past that the narrative is about to develop, and indicate expectations of the immediate or more distant future, which more or less obscurely foreshadow the narrative course of events. In this regard, they can prove quite deceptive, since readers on a first reading may not recognize which (if any) of an encapsulating letter's statements constitute "prognostications" of the story's future, much less predict how they will play out. As narrative-epistolary novelists expanded their notion of expectations to include associated forms of perception ("prospects"), mental processes (fore-thought, foresight, retrospection), emotions (surprise, disappointment), and moral traits (prudence), encapsulating letters began to be used at the beginning of a novel or narrative thread, as a yardstick – at once summative thematic signpost and connective for a number of not necessarily contigu-ous scenes – or if one prefers, as opening bids in bridge against which the progress and risks in the play of narrative cards could be gauged. It became more or less conventional to show how expectations laid out in a first encapsulating letter were thwarted again and again by chance or by unexpected turn of events until, once despaired of and given up, they were unexpectedly realized at novel's end.

We begin with *Henrietta* (1758), one of two novels by Charlotte Lennox that Mrs. Barbauld said were "esteemed the best" and included in *The British Novelists* (1820) alongside exemplars of their literary progeny. Where Barbauld reprinted only one such exemplar for *The Female Quixote*, she reprinted a series of novels that were indebted to *Henrietta* (including *Cecilia*, *The Old Manor House*, and *Belinda*) to indicate – given *Henrietta*'s less than stellar publication history – that for novelists who esteemed it "the best," *Henrietta* was the more influential precedent. After considering how Burney and Maria Edgeworth rewrote Lennox's scenes and perfected encapsulating letters, we turn to Victorian narrative-epistolary fictions in which Wilkie Collins and Anthony Trollope repur-posed initial encapsulating letters and the concepts of expectations on which their stories depend. Collins and Trollope have been undervalued in comparison to Dickens. The expectations they tackled were not less "great;" neither was their popularity with nineteenth-century readers; but for modern tastes, embedded letters figured more unavoidably in their work.

Conventional Expectations and Unseen Letters: Charlotte Lennox's *Henrietta*

In the first volume of *Henrietta*, Lennox took up issues on which the third epistolary episode in *The Female Quixote* closed, but in serious rather than satiric mode: what happens when a calculating lover successfully manipu-lates a young girl's expectations, which she bases on cultural archetypes and conduct-book precepts inculcated by her elders? *Henrietta* reexamined the standard conduct-book strictures that "Nothing can be more unfortunate for youth and beauty than to be left to its own guidance and discretion" (251) and that, rather than rely her own prudence, a young woman should follow the guidance of an older woman or a male guardian. A composite of forethought, foresight, caution, and practical sense, prudence was the forward-looking virtue based on reasonable expectations *par excellence.* Deploying a rudimentary encapsulating letter to permit different prospective and retrospective readings of the same events, *Henrietta* problematized girls' conventional expectations of guardians and older female mentors.

The narrative-epistolary episodes discussed here are embedded in a retrospective first-person narrative, which is itself imbedded in a conversation that grows out of a correspondence between Henrietta and a lady she met in a coach on her way to London. Henrietta is telling her new friend her "unhappy story" chronologically, with the consciousness she had as it transpired, to obtain "her compassion and approbation for what she has been compelled to do."[10] By embedding Henrietta's first-person narrative in a later conversation about her past, Lennox intimates that the prudence of following conduct-book strictures and adult advice must be evaluated retrospectively by their outcome and empirical effects. Four letters in volume 1 are particularly relevant here. Significantly, three of them are, like those in *The Female Quixote*'s first courtship episode, unseen.

The first unseen letter figures in a scene that was often revisited by subsequent narrative-epistolary novelists. Its prefatory narrative describes her aunt's efforts to force Henrietta to marry a repulsive old baronet, and Henrietta's fear that if she continues to refuse, she will be banished to a convent in France. Henrietta writes a summarized letter to her guardian, the merchant Mr. Bale, expressing her contempt for the baronet, subjecting her aunt to some "satirical strokes," and asking his advice in this crisis. (1: 129). The reception narrative opens with Henrietta hastily hiding this letter in her pocket when her aunt enters her room. Lady Meadows assumes that she has caught Henrietta "writing to a favored lover with whom [she] correspond[s] privately" (1: 130) and demands to see the letter. Despite Henrietta's repeated denials that there is any such lover, her refusal to show Lady Meadows the letter only confirms her aunt's suspicions. But judging that it would be easier to prove that she had no lover than to overcome her aunt's resentment of her "satirical strokes," Henrietta destroys "the fatal letter" to prevent it from being read. In a second reception narrative, Mrs. White, her aunt's maid and Henrietta's friend, informs Henrietta that Lady Meadows's expectation that Henrietta has a clandestine lover has been planted in her head by her chaplain, a Catholic priest with "selfish dispositions and designs" who wants to "manage her conscience." The chaplain's influence is confirmed empirically later, in a third reception narrative, when her aunt again asks to see the letter in the chaplain's presence, and it appears that, were it not for the chaplain, her aunt would be "satisfied" with Henrietta's explanation that she tore up the letter to avoid offending her. In these scenes, then, Lady Meadows's understanding of everything that occurs is shaped by her expectation that Henrietta has a secret lover with whom she is secretly corresponding. Lady Meadows's expectation is proved to her satisfaction without sight of the letter, to demonstrate how her expectations determine her perception of reality and what she regards as proof. Here a familiar Romance archetype – girl corresponds clandestinely with lover – which had recently been promoted by *Clarissa*, trumps what actually occurs.

In the Bale Jr. episodes that follow, Lennox allows novel-readers to share Henrietta's conduct-book expectations and her perception of the encapsulating letter. This letter appears after Henrietta has run away to London to put herself under her benevolent guardian's protection, only to find that Bale Sr. is unexpectedly away in Holland on business. Gladly accepting his son's offers of protection and counsel meanwhile, Henrietta dutifully follows Bale Jr.'s advice to conceal herself under a false name in Mrs. Willis's lodging house and to obtain her clothes and effects from her aunt. The encapsulating letter arrives with her trunk. Lady Meadows writes to Bale Jr. that she is sending all Henrietta's things because this:

> ... unhappy girl, my niece ... has, by her scandalous running away from me, ruined her own character, and brought aspersions on mine; since even those who condemn her most, will likewise blame me, as if I had acted unkindly to her. May the loss of my affections be the least of her misfortunes; though the worst that can possibly happen are likely to be the punishment of her ingratitude and folly. (1: 224)

Highlighted by being the only fully transcribed letter in the Bale Jr. episodes, this letter encompasses Lady Meadows's present certainty that Henrietta has ruined herself by running off with the lover she had earlier expected her to have, and her expectation that Henrietta will be punished for it in the future by desertion, penury, and prostitution as fallen young ladies in conduct books and didactic fictions usually were. Like Henrietta, we know that Lady Meadows has her facts wrong: Henrietta has not run off with a lover; she has fled one guardian to take refuge with another. In the conversation with Bale Jr. that constitutes this letter's reception narrative, Henrietta therefore argues that those "unfavourable suspicions which Lady Meadows mentions so severely" would be removed if her aunt were supplied with the information she lacks: that Henrietta is living under a guardian's protection.

Bale Jr. prevents Henrietta from communicating with her aunt by promising to speak to her himself, and returns with the unwelcome tidings that "lady Meadows seems resolved never to forgive you for running away from her." (1: 227) This and Henrietta's observation that Mrs. Willis is suddenly treating her with unwonted coldness, (1: 22) prefaces the last two letters in this series, both of which are unseen by Henrietta and by readers alike. Bale Jr. reports that his father has written from Holland saying that he will be abroad for some time longer, recommending Henrietta to his son's care, and explaining that gout in his hand obliges him to employ an amanuensis. According to Bale Jr., his father's letters also instruct him to inform Henrietta that merchant acquaintances would soon be coming to lodge with Mrs. Willis, that his father "thought it would not be proper" for Henrietta to stay with Mrs. Willis in a house full of men, and that he wants her to move to a widow in Hampstead. (1: 230–231) In immediately agreeing to obey his wishes, Henrietta continues to behave as a dutiful young girl was expected to behave toward her guardian(s).

All this begins to unravel during the conversation with Mrs. Willis occasioned by these letters, when Mrs. Willis tells her that she is not expecting foreign lodgers and that Bale Jr.'s failure to show her his father's letters suggests that he has "not acted ingenuously" with her. By dint of judicious questioning, Mrs. Willis brings Henrietta to the realization that "Mr Bale has certainly deceived me, for what purpose I know not." (1: 250) Here, drawing Henrietta's attention to missing empirical information – things Henrietta either did not know or had not noticed before – is key to undeceiving her. After an unexpected visit from Bale Jr.'s wife, who accuses Henrietta of being her husband's whore, Mrs. Willis also explains Bale Jr.'s purpose, observing that "a very little reflection" on his "behavior might have informed you that he was in love with you, if that can be called love which seeks the ruin of its object." (1: 242) Though a servant of sorts, Mrs. Willis acts as Henrietta's friend and counselor, both by showing her that a deception has been practiced on her, and by advising her against going into the country with Bale.

Considered retrospectively in light of this conversation, Lady Meadows's encapsulating letter takes on a different aspect. This no longer appears wrong or misguided about the reality of Henrietta's situation, despite the false expectations that generated it. Lady Meadows's letter turns out to have been unexpectedly prophetic. Henrietta was wrong about the empirical facts with which she hoped to allay her aunt's suspicions: that she did not have a secret lover and was living safely under a guardian's protection as a proper young lady should. Indeed, her expectation that Bale Jr. *would* be acting as her guardian is precisely what blinded her to behavior that might otherwise have informed her that he was secretly her lover. The two unseen letters from his father in which Bale Sr. reportedly recommended Henrietta to his son's care, now testify to the fact that Bale Jr. has been reinforcing Henrietta's expectations of him as a guardian to deceive her into doing his will – that she conceal herself at Mrs. Willis's under an assumed name, obtain her effects from Lady Meadows, and go into the country with him – all acts that cut her ties to her "friends" and left her entirely dependent on him. Bale Jr.'s unseen letters again demonstrate the power of expectations over empirical facts. Like Arabella and Hervey or Lady Meadows in the first scene, Henrietta grounded her understanding of what was transpiring in reality on preconceived, conduct-book ideas and on letters she had not seen; and as novel-readers reading her narrative chronologically, we have done the same. Our discovery that Bale Jr. has been deceiving Henrietta therefore also raises questions about the expectations we developed on our first reading of these epistolary scenes. Was anything we were told based on unseen letters and Bayle Jr.'s words true?

The conduct-book precept that a girl should depend on an older woman's prudence and discretion rather than trust her own, is also subverted in the conversation with Mrs. Willis, which constitutes the unseen letters' reception narrative. When Henrietta asks why Mrs. Willis had not said anything to her before if she saw that Bale Jr. was in love with her and knew he was married, Mrs. Willis admits to split loyalties: since Bale Sr. was her long-time patron, she had done what prudence dictated – nothing. She had intervened – thanks to a reported letter's stupidly counterfactual statement about her prospective lodgers – only when Henrietta's imminent departure from her house put her in immediate danger of being ruined. There is unconscious irony in Henrietta's gratitude to Mrs. Willis for showing "so tender a regard to my honour" and in her conviction that she "may rely on [Mrs. Willis's] prudence." (1: 250) For in a retrospective view, Mrs. Willis's "prudence" was dilatory and self-regarding, aligning her with the chaplain, Bale Jr. and Mrs. White on a spectrum of counselors that runs from more to less self-interested. Mrs. Willis is certainly one of the best of these – as Henrietta observes, "How miserable might I have been had [Mrs. Willis] been less good" (1: 250). But the effects of Henrietta's dependence on Bayle Jr.'s advice, of Lady Meadows dependence on her chaplain, and of Mrs. Willis's "discretion" testify empirically to the danger for a girl of allowing her actions, or her understanding of a letter, to be directed by the expectation that she could depend on an older counselor's advice.

The imprudence of relying on counselors is compounded by demonstration that the advice of even older and supposedly wiser heads may be wholly or partly based on false expectations too. Having convinced her that she has been "imprudent" in "throwing herself into a situation which renders her liable" to "imputations, however unjust" – like that of Bale Jr.'s wife – which "sully, if they do not stain a character," (1: 252, 251) Mrs. Willis counsels Henrietta to return to her aunt as the only means of repairing the damage her flight has done to her reputation. Henrietta again asks the pertinent question: "But suppose that she will not receive me again; Mr. Bale found her inexorable." This brings the encapsulating letter back into play. Mrs. Willis's kindly response, that she is "sure that when your aunt knows in what manner he has acted, and the reasons you have to distrust him, she will think it necessary to take you out of his hands" (1: 153) shows up the selfishness and cruelty of Lady Meadows's encapsulating letter to Bale Jr. But that letter in turn indicates that Mrs. Willis's expectations are at odds with the reality of the situation. For Lady Meadows's letter suggests that she is likely to view the damage done by Bale Jr. as "punishment" for Henrietta's "ingratitude and folly" in running away from her and as welcome confirmation that Henrietta has "ruined her own character" – and saved Lady Meadows's character by doing so. Mrs. Willis has neither met Lady Meadows nor seen her encapsulating letter; she is filling these lacunae in her knowledge by projecting onto Lady Meadows, expectations of how a basically good and motherly woman like herself would act in the same situation. This makes Henrietta's expectation that the "good sense" of Mrs. Willis's argument will persuade Lady Meadows as likely to prove unrealistic as Mrs. Willis's advice.

Formally, *Henrietta*'s legacy included Lennox's memorable treatment of unseen letters especially in the first scene with Lady Meadows, her cleverly ambiguous deployment of an encapsulating letter, and her indication by beginning her novel at the end – with a frame story that shows Henrietta penniless and alone in London and a warning that hers will have been an "unhappy story" – that a chronological account of the progress of a character's false expectations must contain a retrospective view in which their empirical outcome shows them up for what they had been. Thematically *Henrietta*'s legacy included Lennox's demonstration of the imprudence of following conduct-book prescriptions that told girls to be dutiful, obedient, and deferential to their elders by depending unthinkingly on the "prudence" of others, and portrayals of guardians and female mentors as persons who were as self-interested and/or as easily blinded by their expectations as anyone else. But if prudence positively prohibited a girl from thinking and acting as she was told she ought, it remained a puzzle to know how else she might think and act, given the vicious epistemological circle that Lennox had created: everyone is "compelled" to act or advise others to act on the basis of their expectations of the conduct of others; but expectations blind people to facts; acting on expectations and testing them empirically against facts can reveal retrospectively whether expectations were true or false; but as Lady Meadows's encapsulating letter shows, false or unfounded expectations are sometimes validated by reality too. How then *avoid* an "unhappy" outcome by acting on expectations of others and prognostications for the future that are based on culturally sanctioned expectations derived from the past?

Expectations in Prospect and Retrospect: Frances Burney's *Cecilia*

Burney took up the problems raised in *Henrietta* by giving Cecilia three guardians, two older female mentors, and a married lover modeled on Bale Jr. who masquerades as her protector, all of whom are self-interested or blinkered in different ways, and create difficulties or impediments that almost destroy her. Burney not only "challenged her heroine to decipher who is and who is not to be befriended and trusted;"[11] she did so by addressing the questions of expectations that Lennox had raised. To this end, she gave some of the eighty-three fully transcribed letters embedded in *Cecilia* (1782) encapsulating functions.[12] Not strictly necessary in themselves in the sense that they tell us nothing that the narrative has not, will not or could not tell us in its own ways, Burney's encapsulating letters epitomize a relationship, lay out an argument, and/or highlight themes that are explored and tested in the narrative. They act like key notes in a piece of music, to prospectively foreshadow, shape, and connect a series of not necessarily contiguous scenes and to reconfigure and reinterpret them in retrospect. Burney also captured portions of narrative between two epistolary "book-ends" to segment the text thematically by marking the beginning and end of a narrative "movement" and mark the points at which difference between prospective and retrospective views of characters and narrated events obtain. This section will focus on two such encapsulating letters and on the different uses to which they are put.

The initial letter in *Cecilia* demonstrates Burney's complex use of an encapsulating letter to epitomize, activate, and foreshadow a group of narrative threads. It initiated the practice, popular among her narrative-epistolary successors, of presenting an encapsulating letter or correspondence at or near the beginning of a novel to present what Henry James would call its *donnée* and provide a concise but elliptical forecast and yardstick for what is to come.

The prefatory narrative to Mrs. Hill's letter consists of a scene in which Cecilia encounters an old woman whom she mistakes for a beggar outside her guardian, Mr. Harrel's, house, and discovers that this is the wife of a carpenter who has been injured working for Mr. Harrel. Desperate to feed her starving children, Mrs. Hill has come for the wages that Mr. Harrel owes her husband, but as she tells Cecilia: "I have been after his honor night and day to get it, and sent him letters and petitions with an account of our misfortunes, I have never received so much as a shilling." Harrel owes her £ 22 – a small sum for the prosperous – but "gentlefolk little think how much that is to poor people." (1: 116, 117) Cecilia requests this sum from Mr. Harrel, only to find him indifferent to Mrs. Hill's plight and unwilling to pay her. But when they see that Cecilia is upset, Mr. Harrell tells her that if Mrs. Hill will come back the next day, he will pay her then, and his brother-in-law lends him five guineas to give her now. The letter from Mrs. Hill is brought to Cecilia the next day while she is entertaining company:

> To
>   Miss,
> at his Honour Squire Harrel's,
>   These
>
> Honoured Madam,
> THIS with my humble duty. His Honour has given me nothing. But I would not be troublesome, having wherewithal to wait, so conclude
>   Honoured Madam,
>   Your dutiful servant to command,
>   Till death.
>   M. Hill (1:129)

The reception narrative opens with Cecilia's "vexation" at this letter and with her company's questions about its cause. Burney displaces to this male company Lady Meadows's suspicion about Henrietta's unseen letter, and Cecilia tells them the only thing that she, like Henrietta, is willing to disclose: that it "is not from any man." Like Lady Meadows, the company nevertheless concludes from Cecilia's concealment of a letter they have not seen that she is secretly corresponding with a lover. Cecilia's response to the letter is to rapidly settle the question of empirical verification – she checks the facts by sending her servant to "examine into the real situation of the carpenter and his family," (1:135) – and then to pursue three courses of action that initiate three threads of the plot: she tries again to obtain Mrs. Hill's money from Mr. Harrel; her "disgust" at Mr. Harrel's behavior makes her resolve (like Henrietta) to leave one guardian's house to live with another; and her discovery of the carpenter's "real situation" starts her on a course of charitable giving that will characterize her throughout the novel.

Cecilia checks her facts and obtains correct information; but she reads Mrs. Hill's letter only instrumentally, for the "intelligence" it contains. Considered instrumentally, Mrs. Hill's letter, with its memorable oddity, does not tell us anything we do not already know from the prefatory scene or that could not be summarized in half a sentence. Full transcription of the letter is required for its encapsulating functions, some of which become apparent only retrospectively, later in the narrative chain of events or on a second reading of the novel. Focused on the immediate and the local like most novel-readers on a first reading, Cecilia fails to look beyond these to the bigger picture and long-term consequences that the letter more elliptically presages.

One function of Mrs. Hill's letter is to encapsulate what will prove the core problem with Cecilia's first guardian and trustee. Cecilia unpacks Mrs. Hill's unconscious irony in "His Honour has given me nothing," by reflecting on the shocking "incongruity" here: "that a young man could appear so gay and happy, yet be guilty of such injustice and inhumanity . . . and live with undiminished splendor, when his credit began to fail." (I, 137) Honored while failing to pay his debts, living in splendor on borrowed money while sinking into bankruptcy, characterize Harrel and his wife's expensive, "heartless" and fashionable pleasure-loving way of life. Repetition with variations of the scene in which Harrel avoids paying what he owes and borrows what he immediately needs to pacify his creditors, ends only with Mr. Harrel's bankruptcy and suicide four books later – after Cecilia too has been inveigled into "lending" him most of her fortune. Letters posthumously discovered among Mr. Harrel's papers five books later, which reveal his villainously self-interested character and the deceptions he practiced upon Cecilia and her suitors to secure the money he needed, close the narrative "movement" that Mrs. Hill's letter began. While reminding readers that the powers given to the male guardians traditionally appointed for heiresses were all too often abused, Harrel's posthumously discovered letters close this narrative movement by revealing retrospectively that in its "injustice and inhumanity" to the innocent, Harrels conduct as Cecilia's guardian resembled his conduct toward the Hills.

Mrs. Hill's letter also encapsulates another of the novel's recurrent criticisms of high society through its contrast between the upper ranks' dishonorable abdication of their duty to those who serve them and the conduct of those like Mrs. Hill who act faithfully toward society's "Honorables" as "Your dutiful servant to command" – "till death" from poverty and sufferings ends their fruitless "wait" for wages, employment or succor. This not only highlights the novel's leitmotifs of poverty and miserable dependence, but allows readers to notice on a retrospective view the analogy between Mrs. Hill's situation at the beginning of the novel and Cecilia's at the end, when she too is a penniless suppliant fruitlessly seeking succor from selfish Egglestons and heartless Delvile Sr., and almost dies in penury and despair before her husband's return.

A third function of Mrs. Hill's letter is to demonstrate the possibility of unexpected incongruities between social forms and what they conceal, and to launch the novel's exploration of questions of sincerity and frankness. Mrs. Hill's awkward, incorrect, and absurdly elaborate use of the polite epistolary forms is incongruous with her letter's intrinsic frankness and factual truth. Indeed, her inept use of the polite formulae conceals the letter's true character by inviting us to suppose that this is just another satire on the epistolary shortcomings, faulty grammar, and unwarranted pretensions of the lower orders. Judging the letter by its awkward misuse of the conventional forms is a mistake that Cecilia does not make here. But part of her challenge throughout the novel will be to penetrate the masquerading occasional selves who surround her, when the incongruity in Mrs. Hill's letter is inverted – for instance, in characters like Mr. Harrel, Mrs. Harrel, Miss Lascelles, Sir Robert Floyd, or Mr. Monckton, whose deployment of good manners, conventional professions of love and friendship, and seeming frankness, are incongruous with the emptiness or dishonest machinations they conceal. Mrs. Hill's open honesty in her letter also contrasts with Cecilia's failure in the reception narrative to be frank with her company about the letter she has received. This foreshadows the difficulties that Cecilia will create for herself by her reluctance to speak frankly to anyone about Harrel's appropriation of her fortune; while her failure in the reception narrative to notice that her polite reticence has opened her to the unwarranted suspicion of her company foreshadows the problem that she will constantly face in society: false and damaging conjectures about her conduct based on common expectations, which she neither suspects nor foresees.

Mrs. Hill's letter encapsulates relationships grounded in the past and articulates expectation for the future. It makes sense only with knowledge given in the prefatory scene of the history of their relationship – Mrs. Hill's previous repeated efforts to obtain her husband's wages from Harrel and Harrel's repeated failure to pay. Mrs. Hill's letter also contains a plan of action and expectations of the future based on that history: "I would not be troublesome, having wherewithal to wait." She expects to have to continue to "wait" for her money as she had in the past. The contrast here is with Cecilia's failure to form any expectations at all on the basis of what the letter is telling her. Lacking forethought and foresight, she does not realize until it is too late even what her efforts to extract Hill's wages from Harrel most obviously portend: that a man who is constantly borrowing to hold off the most pressing of his creditors must end a bankrupt regardless of what sums she lends him; and that she might herself have occasion for the fortune she has lent at some future date. Responding generously and emotionally to the moment and seeking empirical verification only of facts about the letter's author prevents Cecilia from reading Mrs. Hill's letter and the circumstances that are by its agency revealed, as indicators of larger and more intractable problems. This is also the situation of novel-readers who, on a first reading, fail to recognize that this lowly character's letter is symptomatic of larger issues in its very ordinariness, and cautionary for the future course of the story in the very particularity of its concerns.

The second encapsulating letter to be considered here examines issues raised by expectations themselves. This letter appears at the beginning of volume 4 of all the first eighteenth-century editions, in a chapter entitled "A Letter." It is a very long, fully transcribed letter from Delvile to Cecilia, which conveniently summarizes the situation at the end of volume 3, where Delvile has proposed a clandestine marriage. Delvile explains what Cecilia has found incomprehensible in his conduct to date – the "unsubdued ... pride" in his ancient family name that made his father forbid him to marry Cecilia (whose husband will have to change his name to obtain her fortune) and Delvile's own struggles between "family pride" and the "bosom felicity" of making her his wife. The letter moves from this history of the present to Delvile's arguments for the clandestine marriage he has proposed. He argues that applying to his parents for their consent before marrying is certain to fail both because his parents have "long planned a splendid connection" for him and because no "conviction can be offered by reason, to notions that exist but by prejudice." (4: 10) Assuring Cecilia that "the time for secrecy would be short," (4:11) Delvile tries to persuade her that it will be better for them to marry clandestinely before consulting his parents because their "honor" will bring them around to accepting the marriage once they are enjoying her fortune and see how well she is gracing her new position. By laying out again, concisely in one place, Delvile's earlier, scattered arguments in favor of clandestine marriage together with the reasons for his parents' opposition to the match, this letter encapsulates assertions about the Delviles and expectations of clandestine marriage that the novel's last two volumes will develop and test. It also underlines the fact that, insofar as letters plan, require, suggest, or persuade to action, they posit a future, and involve expectations about the effects and outcomes of the actions they propose.

The first part of the reception narrative tells us that as Cecilia "read and reread this letter" of Delvile's "from paragraph to paragraph, her sentiments varied, and her determination was changed." (4: 12) Some paragraphs are confirmed by her reason, others are contradicted by her principles, others offend her delicacy. In some paragraphs "the earnestness of his supplication softens her into compliance;" in others, she is swayed by her feelings or hopes. The crucial point made here is that, even when designed to be rhetorically persuasive, letters are not like neoclassical histories and belletristic compositions, whose parts are all subordinated to a single action or "argument" and designed to make a single, unified impression on their readers. Letters make multiple points and point in different directions, some of which appeal to the mind, some to the heart or the imagination, some more persuasively than others. Letters are piecemeal compositions and may, as here – or like Darcy's letter to Elizabeth – have different piecemeal relations to reality and truth as well as different piecemeal effects. Letters must therefore not only be read and reread, but pondered and empirically weighed piecemeal, point by point and paragraph by paragraph.

The events that immediately follow in the narrative demonstrate the error in "the general tenor" of Delvile's letter: his expectation that he has only to gain Cecilia's consent and meticulously prepare every practical detail, to make their clandestine marriage happen in fact. In the event, he is defeated by a series of unforeseen occurrences – acquaintances unexpectedly encountered on the road to London, someone's unforeseen discovery of Cecilia's lodgings in London, the unanticipated interruption of the ceremony by an unknown objector – which send Cecilia back to Bury, unmarried and damaged in principle and reputation. Delvile's expectation that he can control what will happen by his single efforts is belied by these events, which demonstrate how much lies beyond an individual's control, and how interactions with others in society play their unpredictable part in the way things turn out.

Burney also complicated the predictive truth or untruth of other pieces of Delvile's letter – notably, his anticipation of the effects of a clandestine marriage on Cecilia and his expectation that his parents will come around – by complicating letters' shifting relations to time and to empirical fact in ways most clearly articulated by Dr. Lyster in a joke.

Dr. Lyster is visiting Mrs. Delvile (currently being nursed by Cecilia in Mrs. Charlton's house) when he receives a note from Delvile saying that he is "engaged with my friend Biddulph" and inquiring about his mother's health. Dr. Lyster decides to "punish" Delvile for "finding good entertainment" instead of visiting his sick mother by telling him that the ladies insist on keeping him at Mrs. Charlton's house for tea and that he is having a tête-à-tête with Cecilia there. Before dispatching an answer to this effect, he asks Cecilia: "May I treat myself to this puff?" and receives her reluctant assent. (4: 208) But after dispatching the note, he asks to be invited to tea because, as he jokingly remarks, "this young woman has connived at my writing a downright falsehood, and all the time took me in to believe it was the truth." (4: 209) One serious point here is that by treating what the letter-writer writes as truth, others validate the truth of what he writes, even if it is a downright falsehood. What is true in a letter is part of an ongoing social conversation in which others induce the writer to believe it true and/ or "connive" with him by their assent. A letter can therefore be true in the sense that it re-presents the shared reality thus interpersonally created, without being empirically true in fact. This is also how *Cecilia* shows that gossip and rumor work. People in the same social circle create truths intersubjectively in conversation by what they agree is true about people or situations, even when this is a downright falsehood; and such intersubjective truths have real effects. Delvile is repeatedly "deceived" by them throughout the first part of the novel.

The other important point that Dr. Lyster makes is that letters are often "puffs." A puff can range from the exaggeration of something actually observed to an empty and baseless boast, and from something consequential in its effects to something as ephemeral as "hot air." Puffs therefore have diverse possible relationships to reality, agency, and time. Dr. Lyster's puff that he has been invited to tea and is having a tête-à-tête with Cecilia is an empty boast when he writes it and when his letter is dispatched. But insisting on being left alone with Cecilia to tell her something privately makes this part of his letter factually true at a later point in time. Dr. Lyster has more limited agency when it comes to the other part of his puff – being invited to tea. For this, he must depend on the ladies to "connive" with him and make what he wrote true by really extending that invitation; they do so, but might equally not have done. The truth of this part of his letter depends on others, and on choices and actions that are beyond his control.

Delvile's encapsulating letter at the beginning of volume 4 is true in these same ways. It contains expectations that he believes to be true when he writes it. Its frankness and sincerity do not make all parts of the letter true; but neither do its immediate empirical effects make the letter untrue or show that Delvile is "deceived" (mistaken). The truth of the letter's "general tenor" – its expectation that Delvile by his single efforts could bring the marriage off – is, as we saw, immediately belied by the unexpected interventions of others who prevent the marriage by creating a series of unexpected turn of events that are entirely beyond Delvile's control. The parts containing arguments for the clandestine marriage and for his parents' eventual acceptance of Cecilia as his wife, require the "connivance" of Cecilia and of his parents to make them true. This too proves beyond Delvile's control: their connivance is dramatically withheld when, upon Cecilia's return from London, Mrs. Delvile persuades Cecilia never to see or communicate with Delvile again. But these empirical facts do not make Delvile's letter untrue, or show that he was mistaken, even though it initially seems so. For at a later date, Cecilia does go through a clandestine marriage ceremony with Delvile. At a later date, each of his parents does unexpectedly come around to accepting their union. Delvile's perception that no "conviction can be offered by reason, to notions that exist but by prejudice" is also validated later when Mrs. Delvile's unexpected encounter with death and Mr. Delvile unexpected horror at the sight of Cecilia's madness produce their respective changes of heart. Even Delvile's expectation that he can make things turn out as he wants is ultimately and unexpectedly validated by the novel's happy ending. Nevertheless, all Delvile's expectations are not realized: his expectations that a clandestine marriage will not be injurious to Cecilia and that the time of secrecy would be short are belied during his absence abroad after their clandestine marriage, by the numerous disasters that befall Cecilia both because their clandestine marriage does not remain secret and because it does.

Here, then, Burney showed that whether we judge any part of a letter's expectations to be empirically valid or not, may depend entirely on where on the subsequent temporal sequence of real events we look. Expectations in parts of a letter that are empirically untrue at one time may become empirically true at another, because people intervene to change circumstances in unforeseen ways. And when circumstances change, people change the way they think and act. As Cecilia points out, we are deceived (mistaken) if we expect the sequence of events in life to follow one smooth, steadily developing course: "My affairs have long been in in strange perplexity: I have not known myself what to *expect*; one day has perpetually reversed the *prospect* of another, and my mind has been in a state of uncertainty and disorder ... " (5: 118, my emphasis) Life is not a neoclassical drama; like the paragraphs in a letter, things happen piecemeal, day by day, with frequent changes of direction and reversals of course. This has implications for letters and their agency inasmuch as these implicitly or explicitly posit expectations of the future. Characters base their letters as well as their judgments, plans, and actions on the "*prospect*" they have of characters and events in their present situation. Here "prospect" means the "range of sight" or "view afforded by a particular position and location" (OED)– what they can see or know from where they stand in time and space. This prospect is in part based on their perception of past interactions and events and in part on how they imagine that others can be expected to think and act. Their prospect in these senses also affects their "prospect" in the sense of their "forethought," their "expectation or reason[s] to look forward to something," and the "mental picture or vista" they have of "something future or expected."(OED, 6, 7a, 7b) As their prospect changes with changes in their situation or information, so do their expectations and the ways they choose to act. And *prospects* change for many of the characters in *Cecilia* all the time.

This also why Burney rejects, as a false expectation, the idea that a young woman will do better with "a friend ... to tell her how to act" than she would by asserting her independence and thinking for herself. Burney is as hard on mentors and guardians in *Cecilia* as Lennox was in *Henrietta*, and for not dissimilar reasons. Because their advice depends in large part on their expectations in a world where prospects are forever changing and things turn out unexpectedly all the time, mentors and guardians are as liable to be "deceived" (mistaken) as anyone else. Burney agreed with Lennox that a girl can easily be deceived by a villainous mentor when she expects to be able to trust him because she has been "long accustomed to regard him as a safe and disinterested friend" and is grateful for his "readiness in advising and tutoring her." Mr. Monckton in *Cecilia* is Bales Jr.'s double in this regard, as well as in his hypocrisy, in his "frank and easy friendliness of behavior," (5: 155) in his marital status, and in his secret machinations to separate Cecilia from other suitors in order to marry her himself. Burney also agreed with Lennox that it is a mistake for a young woman to blindly trust the advice of even frank, sincere, and well-disposed female counselors. Mrs. Charlton changes her initial advice to Cecilia to give Delvile up and break all ties with his family after Cecilia shows her the above-mentioned letter in which he proposes a clandestine marriage because: "The frankness with which he had stated his difficulties, assured her of his probity, and by explaining his former conduct, satisfied her with the rectitude of his intentions." (4: 15) Mrs. Charleton changes her advice to Cecilia as her "prospect" changes, forgetting which road is paved with good intentions. Mrs. Delvile also changes her advice with her changed prospect – the last, long, fully transcribed letter in the novel is the letter she writes to Cecilia giving her "separate permission" for Cecilia's marriage to Delvile and acknowledging "that violence with which I so lately opposed what now I am content to advance." (5: 132). Cecilia recognizes that Mrs. Charlton's advice (which echoes Mrs. Willis) that Delvile "should apply openly to his friends" because she "know[s] not any family to which [Cecilia} would not be an honour," is unrealistic. But she places herself entirely under Mrs. Delvile's tutelage. As she tells her in a letter: "as my own agent I regard myself no longer." (4: 140) Cecilia dutifully follows all the instructions that Mrs. Delvile gives her in letters that address her "with openness and truth." (4: 123) And she wonders, when disaster has struck while Delvile and Mrs. Delvile are abroad and she is penniless, homeless, and disgraced in England, how in that last long transcribed letter, Mrs. Delvile could have advised her to marry Delvile clandestinely, in the expectation that such a marriage would prevent "wealth, ambition, interest, grandeur and pride" from "destroying" their happiness. (5: 131)

Burney is careful to demonstrate that no one and no situation is exempt from the unforeseen. Delvile's efforts to ensure that Cecilia will be safely provided for before leaving England with his mother do not save her from negative consequences of their clandestine marriage – her disinheritance upon Mr. Eggleston's discovery that she was secretly married to a man who had not changed his name was one of several eventualities that Delvile had not "foreseen." Cecilia apologizes to Henrietta and Mrs. Harrel for "the abrupt separation which must take place" when Mr. Eggleston turns her out of her house, by telling them that "she had been unable to prepare them, as the circumstances which led to it had been wholly unforeseen by herself." (5: 201) Only hindsight has access to the empirical evidence capable of testing the prospects envisioned by expectations. In retrospect – after she has read the letter from Delvile describing the bitter quarrel between Mr. and Mrs. Delvile over Mrs. Delvile's permission of their marriage and the letter in which Mr. Delvile Sr. rejects his wife's conciliating letter and willingly separates from her – Cecilia can tell Delvile that they should have "spared themselves" and Mrs. Delvile "those vain and fruitless conflicts which we ought better to have foreseen were liable to such a conclusion." (V, 129) Only when "she knew it was all over," does Cecilia's young protegee, Henrietta, realize "the folly she had committed" in "indulging her passion for Delvile" and feeding it with "visionary schemes" without foreseeing its "end." (5:151) Even villains like Mr. Monckton realize in retrospect that his plans were foiled by eventualities he had not foreseen: the death of Monckton's wife when it was too late for it to benefit him, and his disgrace upon Delvile Sr.'s discovery of his "perfidy," are "the unforeseen and melancholy catastrophe of his long arts." (5: 321)

While representing expectations as a form of "foresight" (or as the OED has it, "forethought"), Burney showed that, when "one day ... perpetually reverse[s] the prospect of another," anyone may lack sufficient foresight to judge, advise, or act correctly; and that the rightness of foresight can only be empirically determined by hindsight. But there is hindsight and hindsight. The contingency of particular cases in *Cecilia* reverses the moralizing conclusions that Dr. Lyster draws in hindsight from past events at the "Termination" of the novel, where he warns against clandestine marriages, criticizes the Delviles for their "Pride and Prejudice" and explains that all would be well if the governing ranks were more charitable to their dependents. In this particular case, as the narrative shows, Mr. and Mrs. Delvile's pride and prejudice unexpectedly dissipate with unforeseen changes in their "prospects." Cecilia's clandestine marriage, unexpectedly, turns out alright in the end. Excessive charity, which has proved irresponsible and self-destructive throughout the novel, turns out well when Cecilia herself unexpectedly becomes the beneficiary of an excessively large bequest. This produces the requisite happy ending. But as part of the unexpected contingency of life where one day can reverse the prospect of another, it also re-marks the inutility of general moral pronouncements like those of Dr. Lyster. Hindsight like Lyster's that distills past experience into simplified, moralizing general propositions as guides to future action only produce expectations that are liable to be belied by particular cases and by the unexpected contingencies of life.

Because prospects are so subject to error and change, hindsight becomes the subject-position of the novel's narrator-historian, who opens with an encapsulating letter encompassing the future and the past and who describes what occurs in between: the successive transitory webs of realized and unrealized expectations and temporary prospects that underpin characters' actions, produce outcomes, and repeatedly reshape social life. This is a hindsight rooted in the knowledge that contingency and chance (the unexpected and unforeseen, *par excellence*) ultimately determine outcomes in particular cases – not the prudent foresight on which we pride ourselves; and not Lyster-like a priori expectations based on past experience and expressed in general rules that prejudice our views.

Reasonable Expectations: Maria Edgeworth's *Belinda*

Belinda (1801) incorporated issues and devices from the kind of "Novel" that Maria Edgeworth was "not wishing to acknowledge" – among them, *Henrietta* and *Cecilia* – in order to counter and correct their views.[13] Edgeworth used irony and satire to "degrade ... the very performances to the number of which [*Belinda*] was added,"[14] while deploying what she called a "Moral Tale" to argue the efficacy of an idealized "prudence undeceiving, undeceived/That not too little, nor too much believed" and to reaffirm the validity of expectations produced by conventional conduct-book prescriptions for female conduct. (Epigraph, Advertisement). Inasmuch as it countered departures from these, as well as the "levelling" propensities of British radicals, *Belinda* can be read as part of the conservative backlash to the French Revolution.

Belinda opens abruptly with a vulgar encapsulating letter. This initial fully transcribed letter from Belinda's aunt Stanhope conveys the situation to date and lays out the latter's expectations of Belinda's visit to Lady Delacour: that she will use the education and "*name* of being perfectly accomplished" that Mrs. Stanhope has procured her, to catch a wealthy husband like Clarence Hervey whom Mrs. Stanhope has arranged for her to meet. Her aunt expects Belinda to use more "good sense" than other girls without fortunes, who "expose themselves before the very men they would attract" by "vying with one another in the most *obvious*, and consequently the most ridiculous manner" for masculine admiration because their heads are so "full of the present moment," that they "never reflect upon the future." Such girls "fail in [their] matrimonial expectations ... merely from not beginning to speculate in time." (8) Mrs. Stanhope's expectations of Belinda are, of course, thwarted for several hundred pages – by suspicions that Belinda is only another of Mrs. Stanhope's "catch-match nieces" (24, 15) and by damaging gossip maliciously spread by Sir Philip Baddeley – until the narrative has demonstrated that what *The Monthly Review* called "a perfect model of the female character" could successfully employ less obvious and ridiculous means to fulfill Mrs. Stanhope's expectations and catch-match Clarence Hervey in the end.[15]

In *Belinda*, the evils of occasional selves and of their fluid and deceitful manners are demonstrated and reformed. But here occasional selves like Lady Delacour, who "supported a fictitious character" in society (10–11) or Clarence Hervey who "could be all things to all men and all women" and whose Chesterfieldian "chameleon character seemed to vary in different lights according to the different situations in which he happened to be placed," (14) are produced by lives of fashionable dissipation, rather than by the conventions and system of hierarchical dependencies in *ancien regime* society.[16] Occasional selves could consequently be reformed without "overturning" English society – they had only to be removed from the fashionable world, returned to the family (the fundamental building block of the English state) and taught to perform their relative duties in exemplary, useful and moral ways. Edgeworth built on Clarence Hervey's care of Virginia and pleasure in teaching the Percival children to make him a domestic man, as she built on Lady Delacour's unhappiness and natural feeling to make her a domestic woman; and she gave Belinda conduct-book conduct designed to attract "men of sense" who sought a virtuous, prudent and dutiful wife.

There is a commensurate shift in polite manners. In *Belinda*, these are no longer dangerous instruments of hypocrisy and deception that entrap the innocent and unsuspecting. Polite manners are now only "the decent drapery of life." As Mr. Percival observes, nothing was therefore to be gained from "overturning society" to "tear away" this drapery: for drapery could be voluntarily lifted for a friend (as when Lady Delacour tells Belinda parts of her history that she usually conceals); and people could always discern the "mysteries" or "secrets" over which polite manners had draped their decent veil. Characters do not fail to notice when there is "some mystery" (19) about someone's conduct, some "secret" that occasional selves are concealing, or some inexplicable incongruity between the character attributed to them and the character they display – mystery is as obvious to the observant as the lock on the door of Lady Delacour's "Mysterious Boudoir" (114) and is as immediately penetrated by those with a key. Though fashionable society has its secrets and intrigues, these are now eminently detectable – Clarence Hervey's friends have only to follow him to discover that he is keeping a mistress at Windsor; Clarence easily "penetrates" Lady Delacour's machinations against Mrs. Luttridge. And while there is scarcely a scene in fashionable society in which the chief protagonists are not "surprised," "astonished," "confused," or "disappointed" by other characters' failure to speak, act or react as they expected, false expectations present no insuperable difficulty either. Rational characters treat their surprise, confusion, or disappointment as evidence that their expectations of others have been mistaken, and correct their mistake by further observation and reflection.

The essential condition for forming accurate expectations from empirical observations, and for drawing correct inferences and acting on them appropriately, is laid out in Edgeworth's two, contradictory, reworkings of the Lady Meadows scene from *Henrietta*. In the first of these scenes, Belinda is answering another vulgar letter of advice from her aunt Stanhope when Lady Delacour bursts into her room and demands to see the letter she is writing. Aunt Stanhope's letter is conveyed in free indirect discourse to reflect its "very guarded style" and its rebuke to Belinda "for her imprudence in mentioning names . . . in a letter sent by the common post." Like Henrietta, Belinda denies that she is writing "love letters" and tries to hide her aunt's missive, thinking it "not fit to be seen" by Lady Delacour: Aunt Stanhope's cynical, worldly advice about how Belinda should behave to that Lady is based on damaging information about Lady Delacour, which Belinda had conveyed to her in a previous letter. Fearing that she had been "treasonous" to Lady Delacour in criticizing her to her aunt, Belinda was writing to Mrs. Stanhope to ask her to burn her original letter, to forget its contents, and to "consider all this as an error in my judgement, and not of my heart" (16) when she was interrupted by Lady Delacour. Half in jest, to tease her for "shuffling [them] away" so "awkwardly," Lady Delacour "snatches" Mrs. Stanhope's letter despite Belinda's struggles and reads it; whereupon Belinda asks her to read the answer she was writing too.

In the first reception narrative to these letters, Lady Delacour folds up Mrs. Stanhope's missive "coolly" when she has read it "from beginning to end" and coolly ridicules the blanks and innuendoes that constitute its "guarded style." She pronounces Belinda's letter "worth a hundred of your aunt's," and "patting Belinda's cheek," tells her it is "a treasure to meet with any thing like a *new* heart—all hearts nowadays are secondhand at best." (17). In the second reception narrative, Lady Delacour is no longer "cool" thanks to Sir Philip Baddeley, who (aping Lady Meadows's chaplain) has planted the idea in her head that Belinda is cleverly positioning herself to become the second Lady Delacour after her death. Remembering that Belinda is "niece to Mrs. Stanhope," Lady Delacour now thinks it "not impossible" that Belinda "may have all her aunt's art and the still greater art to conceal it under the mask of openness and simplicity." (164) Reviewing Belinda's past behavior in light of this new idea and "now see[ing] a thousand things that escaped [her] before," (165) Lady Delacour returns to the above letters:

> Worthy niece of Mrs. Stanhope. I know you now! And now I recollect that extraordinary letter of Mrs. Stanhope's which I snatched out of miss Portman's hands some months ago, full of blanks, and innuendoes, and references to some letter which Belinda had written about my disputes with my husband. From that moment to this, miss Portman has never let me see another of her aunt's letters. So I may conclude they are all in the same style; and I make no doubt that she has instructed her niece, all this time, how to proceed. Now I know why she always puts Mrs. Stanhope's letters into her pocket the moment she receives them, and never opens them in my presence." (164–165)

Like Delamere in Smith's *Emmeline*, Lady Delacour's "ingenuity rapidly supplied her with circumstances and arguments to confirm and justify her doubts," (164) until she was "exhausted by the emotions to which she had worked herself up by the force of her powerful imagination." (166) The letter's two reception narratives thus demonstrate that when Lady Delacour is cool and impartial, she has no difficulty in reading letters and penetrating characters correctly; but when her passions have been aroused, she reinterprets seen and unseen letters as well as the characters of their authors, and twists selected facts to create a spurious imaginary narrative which misconstrues characters and events. Based on expectations of Belinda as "niece to Mrs. Stanhope," her retrospectively constructed narrative contradicts her earlier view of the letters. It also shows in hindsight, that a retrospective view is liable to be wrong.

In a chapter significantly entitled "Jealousy," Edgeworth provides a second version of the Lady Meadows scene to emphasize that passion inevitably derails reason. Here Belinda receives yet another of Mrs. Stanhope's fully transcribed letters of advice, this time to inform her of the rumor that she is pursuing Lady Delacour's husband and to advise her to save her reputation by marrying Sir Philip Baddeley without loss of time. After "glancing over the first page," Belinda "folded [the letter] up again . . . and put it into her pocket, colouring deeply." (179) Rendered suspicious by this furtiveness, Lady Delacour insists she read the letter in her presence and tell her what it says. Belinda hesitates because she cannot see "what was passing in her mind;" but remembering that Clarence Hervey told her that "half the miseries of the world arise from foolish mysteries—from the want of the courage to speak the truth," (176) Belinda tells Lady Delacour the truth about the "strange report" (185) that she is positioning herself to become the second Lady Delacour about which she has just learned. Though Belinda assures her that the rumor is absurd and untrue, Lady Delacour is so jealous, so angry that the rumor has become "public" and so indignant that Belinda has "duped" her, that she fails to recognize the truth when she hears it. She believes instead that Belinda has calculated that "speaking to me with this audacious plainness will convince me of her innocence" when it remained "the only thing [she] could do," and praises her with heavy irony for her "prudence" and unfailing "presence of mind." (186) Faced with Lady Delacour's furious ravings – her "rapid, unconnected" speech, her "unintelligible words," and her increasingly "disordered appearance" – Belinda concludes that "her intellects were suddenly disordered." (186) That "the possibility of her being actuated by the passion of jealousy" (186) does not occur to Belinda is easily explained, emphasizing again that one person cannot see into another's mind: "it is difficult to get at facts" about "causes" even in "trivial things" because "actions we see, but their causes we seldom see." (185, 156) Belinda does not know what has caused Lady Delacour's ravings; but that is not something she needs to know. Once she realizes that Lady Delacour now suspects her of deceit, "preserving her own composure" (203) enables Belinda to know how it is proper for her to act: reasoning that it is wrong to remain the guest of a lady who no longer likes or trusts her, Belinda decides that proper thing to do is to leave her house. When Belinda leaves, she does not run away on impulse, blind to the effect such an action can have on her reputation, as Henrietta did. Belinda acts on considered principle, calmly accepts an invitation she earlier refused, and removes herself –*with* all her trunks and without fuss, scandal or delay – to the safety of Lady Percival's house.

Belinda demonstrates that a girl armed with the proper conduct-book precepts, who applies them by observing others and thinking about her situation for herself in a rational, prudent, and honest way, will never be misled by an older woman's foolish expectations and erroneous guidance. Belinda discovers in short order what the heroines of earlier novels failed to realize about *their* older female counselors and mentors until it was too late: that Lady Delacour's worldly advice is as unworthy of being followed as Mrs. Stanhope's, and that Mrs. Stanhope's advice to marry Sir Philip Baddeley is as wrong-headed as Lady Percival's advice to marry Mr. Vincent. Reasoning empirically by "comparing characters" and the experiences of others that she has observed, shows Belinda the unhappy consequences of marriages of convenience: the marriages that aunt

Stanhope arranged for her other nieces demonstrate that "the very means which Mrs. Stanhope had taken to make a fine lady of her nieces, tended to produce an effect diametrically opposite of what might have been expected;" while Lady Delacour's household demonstrates that "if lady Delacour" with all her advantages "has not been able to make herself happy" by making a marriage of convenience and living "a life of fashionable dissipation," Belinda could not "expect to be more fortunate . . . should [she] follow the same course."(64)

There was thus no difficulty in deriving correct expectations from empirical evidence if one approached it in the proper, dispassionate and impartial, empiricist frame of mind. Being cold and dispassionate – or what would later be called "objective" – enables Belinda to guard herself against the misguided advice of female mentors such as Mrs. Stanhope and Mrs. Percival as well as against the confusing fluidity of occasional selves such as Lady Delacour and Clarence, just as it permits Lady Delacour to judge letters and characters correctly in the first of these epistolary scenes. Remaining cold and in command of her emotions, enables Belinda to reflect correctly on whatever empirical evidence presents itself, and to act consistently in prudent and principled ways, where failing to command her emotions makes Lady Delacour mistake truth for falsehood and lose command of the situations in which she finds herself. For a girl in command of her emotions who reflects rationally on situations as they present themselves in order to know which conduct-book rules apply, there was no difference between prospective and retrospective views. The girl who thinks and acts like Belinda need never look back.

However, Edgeworth's two reworkings of Lennox's Lady Meadows scene also complicate by subverting what they purport to demonstrate. Mrs. Stanhope warned Belinda in her opening letter not to compete with Lady Delacour, and Belinda has not done so. Clarence Hervey told her that "miseries arise from concealing 'mysteries' and want of the courage to speak the truth," and Belinda speaks the truth to Lady Delacour. She behaves exactly as she ought in both respects. But Sir Philip Baddeley's false report that Belinda is planning to become the second Lady Delacour places her unknowingly in direct competition with Lady Delacour; and telling Lady Delacour the truth about this report creates an open breach between them that makes it necessary for Belinda to leave her house. Belinda's misadventure on this occasion suggests that it may be *not* be prudent to throw the truth about when one cannot see "what was passing in [another person's] mind." The juxtaposition of Lady Delacour's contradictory reactions also indicates that there is no predicting how letters, words, and actions will be taken by occasional selves – whether they will be received "coolly" and rationally or met with extravagant and unexpected passion; whether they will be examined dispassionately or unexpectedly woven into imaginary narratives; or even whether the same letter and actions will be understood differently by the same person at different times.

Yet if emotion and imagination are incompatible with correct empirical reasoning – if Belinda had to be consistently "cold" and dispassionate to form correct expectations from empirical evidence and to judge correctly how prudence based on conduct-book rules required her to act – she was only a convenient moral fiction. As Edgeworth recognized, she belonged in a factitious "Moral Tale" rather than in a novel's messy history of mixed characters in ordinary life. Edgeworth saw Belinda's unnatural and inhuman "coldness" as *Belinda*'s central flaw. But once what Mary Brunton called "Self Control" (1811) and Wilkie Collins, "the cruel necessity of self-suppression,"[17] had become the indispensable foundation of the nineteenth century's "perfect model of the female character," Belinda's coldness and command over her emotions unexpectedly proved *Belinda*'s great strength. By 1820, Mrs. Barbauld considered it "superfluous" to preface this novel by "dwell[ing] on the excellencies of an author so fully in possession of the esteem and admiration of the public" as Maria Edgeworth was.[18]

Wilkie Collins's Dead Letters and Anthony Trollope's Bet

In an early novella, *The Dead Secret* (1857), Wilkie Collins displayed in embryo, and partially explained, the inherited structure to which his narrative-epistolary novellas would repeatedly return. Collins's Preface to this novella described the benefits of beginning with an encapsulating letter: "I thought it most desirable to let the effect of the story depend on expectation rather than surprise, believing the reader would be all the more interested in the progress of Rosamond and her husband towards discovery of the Secret, if he previously held some clue to the mystery in his own hand." Collins's innovation consisted of making his initial encapsulating letter an unseen letter, and using the narrative framing it to repeatedly attach an unknown "Secret" to it. Knowing the letter to be the clue to the mystery, readers must wait in the expectation of reading it and discovering its secret until Rosamund finds and reads it at the end.[19]

Collins devoted the whole of Book I to attaching the unknown Secret to the unseen letter: its prefatory narrative describes Mrs. Treverton's reluctance on her deathbed to tell her husband "the Secret [that] must be told" and her insistence that "it must be written;"[20] her anxiety that her maid and amanuensis, Sarah Leeson, deliver the letter to him after her death; and the promises she extracts from Leeson about its transmission. Upon completion of her letter, which is closely followed by her death, the anti-reception narrative describes Leeson's reluctance to give the letter to Captain Treverton; Leeson's "Hiding of the Secret" by hiding the letter where she believed it would never be found; her clandestine departure to avoid being questioned about Mrs. Treverton's last words; the note Leeson leaves informing Captain Treverton that "she had kept a secret from his knowledge;" (36) and the Captain's failure to solve the double mystery of the Secret and of her departure by finding her again. Thus while the Preface articulated the advantages of beginning a narrative-epistolary story with an encapsulating letter that draws readers in by engaging their expectations, Collins's innovation revealed how minimal were the conditions for the effectiveness of this device.

What was shocking was not that something had to be withheld from readers to create the secret or enigma about a character's true identity and history that the narrative would ultimately resolve, but that *everything* could be withheld – except the fact that the encapsulating letter harbored a terrible secret – without diminishing its capacity to perform its encapsulating functions. Indeed, the encapsulating letter's power to arouse expectations and engage readers' interest, anxiety, or curiosity were only heightened by using it to ensure that readers know that there is a sword of Damocles hanging over the characters and constantly expect it to fall, without knowing for sure what it is, when it may fall, or how it may impact its victims.[21] Like the unseen posthumous letter that appears unexpectedly one day at breakfast in *No Name* (1862) or the "blank" in the dying father's unfinished letter in *Armadale* (1866), the dead letter's blank silence is deadly – it transforms the letter from a living communication into an inert thing, whose ominous effects are deferred until the letter-as-object can be discovered, delivered, or repossessed, and until the characters destined to read it can, by reading it, imbibe and reactivate the deadly poison it secretes.

The initial encapsulating letters in these stories are dead letters not only in the sense that, like those in the Post Office's Dead Letter Office, they cannot immediately be delivered and lie for a long time unclaimed, but also in the sense that they are letters from the dead – confessions of a history that the dead, while living, sought at all costs to suppress. They tell a story of past, passion-driven, criminal or psychologically paranormal acts that broke through the restraint and "self-suppression" incumbent upon civilized Victorian characters and contravened the officially sanctioned moral and social norms of Victorian domestic life. These letters enter the present as bombshells that disrupt the expected course of characters' lives: they embody the Unexpected itself. As modern critics have observed, Collins used the impact of these extra-ordinary intrusions of the past on the present to address such problematic contemporary social issues as illegitimacy and "non-normative" family arrangements, and to demonstrate that "a legitimate family is merely an appearance created through a performance of the familial roles ... "[22]

But what is important structurally is what Lacan might call "the insistence of the letter" through repeated "returns of the repressed." Driven as much by the demands of serialization as by narrative-epistolary novelists' longstanding recognition that "fatal letters" do not enter story and history only once, at the moment of their initial writing and transmission, Collins devised an increasingly creative range of substitutions to permit the letter-object from the past with its dark, destabilizing secret to erupt repeatedly into the ordinarily peaceful, "sunny" and harmonious routines of present-day life. The fatal letter returns repeatedly not only as the object of obsessive-compulsive burglaries or quests, but in alternative generic forms. In *Armadale*, it returns as oral history, then as dream, then as a series of imaginary and real repetitions of the original criminal act; in *The Dead Secret*, its place is supplied by Leeson's substitute note and preternaturally white hair and by her uncle's music box. In *No Name*, it recurs as a dead father's faulty will and substitute letter, as handcrafted necklace and as talisman. Explaining that he liked to experiment with different ways of telling a story, Collins also tried other substitutions.[23] In *The Moonstone*, the encapsulating letter-object's principal properties are transferred to the stolen gem: the stone too arrives at its destination, silently trailing its dark history and terrible curse, to disrupt the ordinary sociability of English country life; it too produces the return of the repressed, this time by causing some characters to repeatedly attempt, and others to mysteriously succeed, in repeating the original imperial act of theft.

Encapsulating letters, as we saw, generally included plans or expectations for the future that they often evaluated, or invited readers to evaluate in a retrospective view. Collins took advantage of this practice to raise explicit questions about how the future could be expected to relate to the past. Would Leeson prove correct in the expectation expressed in her note, that "no harm would come" (36) to Captain Treverton and his daughter from hiding Mrs. Treverton's letter and Secret from him? Was it possible for a character to change the future course of events – could the Armadale boys burn a dead father's letter, and with it "the last link that holds [them] to the horrible past" and see "the promise of the future shining over the ashes of the past," or was there "a fatality that follows men in the dark?"[24] Was character capable of overcoming circumstances inherited from past parental actions or would Magdalen and her sister show that circumstances only fatefully bring out some innate disposition already latent in their characters? Collins adapted the practice of using a retrospective view to evaluate the truth of prospective expectations, by centering many of his narratives on an investigation. While linking the present to the past through characters' efforts to discover "the Truth" about what had transpired, this made the story's progress forward in time toward its narrative future also its progress backward in time toward the prequel in its past. And while suggesting that "Discovery of the Truth" about the past links past, present and future in ways that give terrifying and inexorable meaning to the dictum that "we can judge of the future only by the past," it produced the carefully crafted, elaborate, and closely knit teleological plots that elicited both the suspicion and the unwilling admiration of nineteenth-century critics and led modern scholars to view Collins as the precursor of classical detective fiction. But Collins's narrative-epistolary method of narration also counters the apparent teleology of his plots to address other epistemological concerns.

In *The Dead Secret*, the narrator provides separate and alternating accounts of what Rosamund and her people observe, discuss, think, and do at each point in their quest for the fatal letter, and of what Sarah Leeson and her uncle observe, discuss, think, and do at each point to prevent the fatal letter from being found. This not only echoes Lennox and Charlotte Smith by revealing that though engaged with the same letter and the same secret, the two camps are operating in realities shaped by different knowledge and different imperatives; it also enables Collins to show how the different lacunae in their knowledge lead Rosamond and Leeson to act in ways that inadvertently impede their achievement of their goals. This is more obvious in subsequent works where Collins gave letters the function of delineating the separate realities in which some characters act. In *No Name*, for instance, disconnected letters or brief letter-exchanges in the "Interludes" between narrative-epistolary "scenes" convey what was happening elsewhere, outside the "scenes" and outside the knowledge of the characters participating in them. These letters and letter-exchanges contain acts, plans, or machinations that disturb, refract, or render inadequate whatever action is taken by a principal character in the "scenes." In one interlude, for instance, Magdalen's old governess (Miss Galt) writes a well-intentioned letter to Noel Varistone's housekeeper in her attempt to discover Magdalen's whereabouts and save her from herself. But her letter unwittingly betrays the identity that Magdalen has painstakingly disguised from Noel and his housekeeper to a woman who, unbeknownst to Miss Galt, is Magdalen's enemy. The knowledge that Miss Galt has given her enables the housekeeper to surreptitiously collect evidence of Magdalen's disguise in the following "scene" and to regain her power over her master by unmasking Magdalen to Noel in a later "scene." But knowing nothing either of Miss Galt's letter or of the housekeeper's knowledge and designs, Magdalen continues to act in her assumed character in pursuit of the revenge she seeks, unaware that she is now exposed and vulnerable to the housekeeper's revenge. In *Armadale*, Miss Gilt's stratagems and separate reality are conveyed in her correspondence with her co-conspirator, as well as in her diary.

Modern scholars have pointed out that in novels that "perversely withhold a single source of truth," and where characters only have "partial knowledge," "the possibility of objective knowledge and ... objective narration is called into question." Here, they say, the "partiality of knowledge as constitutive of social relations" reveals the limits of empiricist pretensions to universal truth, and seems to call for "a model of sociability in which subjects depend on one another for knowledge."[25] But it is not clear that dependence on one another for knowledge would help. For butting against each other, characters acting on different knowledge produce partly or wholly unanticipated outcomes and unintended consequences that unexpectedly impact, derail, or temporarily rout their own, or someone else's, ability to actualize their plans. While characters continue to intrigue, deceive, and keep secrets from one another as they did in eighteenth-century novels, it is no longer just a matter of discovering who the bad actors are. For even more radically than in *Cecilia*, the outcome of encounters between good and bad actors is in no one's hands. The result of each set of partly blocked moves toward competing goals conforms only in part to what any actor foresaw or intended – indeed, what actually happens often happens by chance, coincidence, or accident rather than by anyone's design. This produces a plot that constantly surprises by constantly belying both the characters' and the readers' expectations about what is likely to happen next. But it also raises precisely those questions that Collins used his dead letters to articulate: is it chance or a dark fatality that kills Mr. Vanstone in a railway accident just before he can change his will, that carries Allan Armadale and Midwinter off-course to the wreck called *La Grace de Dieu*, that makes the doctor's opium jest in *The Moonstone* go so horribly wrong? Even when forewarned by a message from the past, can characters change or influence the circumstances that nevertheless come together to form the chain of events that constitutes their destiny? Does the message from the past embodied in the encapsulating letter inexorably foreshadow the future, or does it serve instead as an insistent reminder that those who look only to the present or future, in the happy illusion that the past has nothing to do with them, are almost inevitably doomed?

The sociality that Collins portrays by means of disparate, partial accounts is not one where characters can depend on one another for anything, including knowledge, either. An inquiry has to be launched and outside experts or helpers have to be brought in precisely because it is no longer possible to assume, as Charlotte Smith did in *Emmeline* or Burney did in *Cecilia*, that in a small society of related people the secret would eventually come out – whispered in confidence, to make those most immediately concerned secret sharers of the secret. *The Dead Secret* begins with Mrs. Treverton's refusal to tell her husband her secret, and continues with Sarah Leeson's; *No Name* begins with parents' refusal to share their secret with their own daughters; *The Moonstone* begins with Franklin's failure to be frank with Rachel about the curse on the gem she has inherited from her uncle. Characters stand alone even in their most intimate relations. And the composition of families is now transient and unreliable: brothers are estranged, a wife is not permitted to "know" her poor relation, sisters and servants disappear from the family circle, family relations are fraught with jealousy and murderous rage, interpersonal relations with vengefulness, self-interest, and frightful resentments.

And as circumstances shift, so do identities. In *The Dead Secret*, the Rosamond who is not Captain Treverton's daughter is no longer a prosperous young lady of good family – a servant's illegitimate daughter is poor, working class, and has no "name." In *No Name*, a prosperous upper middle-class young lady suddenly without means who has to find work as a governess, is a domestic servant in someone else's house; a governess who happens to be part owner of a school can unexpectedly assume the role of a respectable middle-class lady in her own domicile; and a fortunate marriage makes the governess a prosperous upper-class young lady again. Social identities such as these also make people interchangeable since such occasional selves can be assumed by anyone who looks and acts the part: Miss Galt and her erstwhile pupil trade places; at the end of *The Dead Secret*, Sarah Leeson is what Mrs. Treverton was at the beginning, Rosamond's honored and beloved mother on her deathbed. The circumstances of the theft in *The Moonstone* decide whether Franklin "is" an honorable detective or a shifty thief, Rachel's lover or Rachel's foe, just as the circumstances of her inheritance decide who Godfrey Ablewhite is, admired lover and philanthropist or fortune-hunter and cheat; either could have filled either role and almost did. Highlighting the persistence of occasional selves, Magdalen's impersonations, disguises, and changes of name, like those of Captain Wragge, Sarah Leeson, Miss Gwilt, or Midwinter, dramatize this artificial and temporary character of socially constructed identities and this interchangeability in the persons who enact them. Depending on circumstances, everyone is still, in fact or *in potentia*, an occasional self. The difference, dramatized by Franklin's unconscious acts under the influence of opium and by Midwinter's madness, is that now no one can be sure what they are capable of or what character and identity, given the right circumstances, they might assume. What a person's "inner disposition" truly is, who they are at their core, is a mystery even to them. A composite of multiple named identities, a person is at bottom like the blank in the dead letter – a dark, secret, and ominous silence from which, if circumstances warrant, we can expect something suppressed to emerge, without knowing what to expect before the accident happens that brings it suddenly and unexpectedly to light.

Collins's dead letters trailing their complement of dark secrets, unexpected discoveries, and occasional selves that burst into the Victorian present like a bombshell from the past to disrupt the expected course of characters' lives and raise unwanted questions, can also be regarded as a figure for what Collins and Braddon were using embedded letters trailing "dead" narrative-epistolary devices and occasional characters from the past to do to the expected, reassuringly omniscient narratives and teleological course of Victorian realism. Trollope, who disliked Collins's closed and tightly knit plots, went about it differently. He too used his initial encapsulating letters in *Phineas Finn* (1869) to raise issues of expectations; but he did so to initiate an open plot that drew readers in by engaging their expectations in order to repeatedly illustrate and infinitely defer revelation of how expectations play into the course of human lives.

Trollope used the first encapsulating letter in chapter 1 to present expectations as a bet on the future, and the future as a risk that can be assessed by opposite expectations in opposite ways.[26] The prefatory narrative consists of a series of short, future-oriented scenes, including one built around a letter from Phineas's father in Ireland "asking minutely as to his professional intentions:"

> His father recommended him to settle in Dublin, and promised the one
> hundred and fifty pounds [with which he had supported his son] for three

more years, on condition that this advice was followed. He did not absolutely say that the allowance would be stopped if the advice were not
followed, but that was plainly to be implied.[27]

This letter is cited and focalized through its recipient, Phineas, and
presented as it figures as a problem in his mind. Its outer prefatory
frame, which is also the beginning of the novel, positions this letter in
Phineas's life to date: Dr. Finn has supported his son through university at
Trinity in Dublin, and through three years of law study at London's
Middle Temple, and Phineas has just been called to the Bar. But disliking
the law, Phineas has joined the London Reform Club, where he "goes into
very good society," and has made some useful political friends. The
narrator also describes the immediate circumstances into which this pater-
nal demand for a decision on Phineas's professional future fell: "That letter
came at the moment of a dissolution of Parliament" (17), and "when
Phineas received his father's letter, it had just been suggested to him at
the Reform Club, that he should stand for the Irish borough of
Loughshane." (18) The problem raised in Phineas's mind by his father's
letter is how to support himself financially if, instead of beginning to earn
his living as a lawyer as his father expects, he chooses to stand for
Parliament. Members of Parliament were expected to be men of independent fortune, and were not paid.

Receipt of his father's letter is separated from Phineas's answer by
narrative describing Phineas's conversations with his political friends at
the Reform Club about the Loughshane election and detailing the "ambition" that "moved him" to "become a member of the British Parliament."
(19) Phineas's answer to his father, which is fully transcribed and set off on
the page, is then prefaced by an inner frame containing a narrative of his
reflections on his father's letter. Central to these reflections is the fact that
abandonment of the law in favor of unpaid parliamentary work meant
dependence on his father's continued financial support and his certainty
that he had nothing to expect from that quarter: "His father would of
course oppose the plan. And if he opposed his father, his father would of
course stop his income … .If he did this the probability was that he
might … go entirely to the dogs before he was thirty. He had heard of
penniless men who had got into Parliament, and to whom had come such
a fate." (20). The reason Phineas wants to take the risk nevertheless is
conveyed by reference to letters, and significantly, by reference to their
most external feature: "He almost thought that he could die happy if he
had once taken his seat in Parliament—if he had received one letter with

those grand initials written after his name on the address." (21) Phineas's choice of career is motivated by his desire for upward social mobility and social standing; it is about joining the elite and figuring publicly, demonstrably, on the outer face of the very letters addressed to him, as a privileged member of "very good society" indeed. This prefatory narrative also contains the narrator's warning of the risk in the attempt: "Young men in battle are called upon to lead forlorn hopes. Three fall, perhaps to one who gets through." (21)

When Phineas's encapsulating letter to his father is finally transcribed toward the end of chapter 1, it does not tell us anything that we do not already know. Rather, it pulls together information and ideas scattered here and there throughout the conversations and reflections in the prefatory scenes to re-present them in a single, coherent and well-structured, situationally grounded, argument that is inflected by Phineas's desires:

> "My dear Father ... .You are no doubt aware that the dissolution of Parliament will take place at once, and that we shall be in all the turmoil of a general election by the middle of March. I have been invited to stand for Loughshane and have consented. The proposition has been made to me by my friend Barrington Erle, Mr. Mildmay's [the Prime Minister's] private secretary, and has been made on behalf of the Political Committee of the Reform Club ... [I have] been assured that none of the expense of the election would fall upon me. Of course I could not have asked you to pay for it. But to such a proposition, so made, I have felt that it would be cowardly to give a refusal. I cannot but regard such a selection as a great honour." (21)

Issues of money and of "very good society" are again prominent in Phineas's justification of his choice to his father. The fact that practical reason has taken a back seat to his social ambition is demonstrated by his treatment in the letter, of information previously supplied by the narrative. For instance, Dr. Finn's "old Friendship" with Lord Tulla, who owns the pocket borough of Loughsbane, appears in his letter to his father only as Phineas's "doubt" about the impact on that friendship of his decision to replace Lord Tulla's brother, George Morris, in the seat. Phineas overlooks the practical considerations of the Reform Committee following Lord Tulla's quarrel with Morris: his father's longstanding friendship with Lord Tulla made it probable that Phineas would be the most immediately acceptable replacement for Tulla's brother. Instead of recognizing that the Reform Committee has a politique eye to the main chance, Phineas presents its support of his candidacy at Loughsbane as a great honor done to himself, and argues that, since "it seems that George Morris must go . . . if I do not stand, someone else will. . . . why should I not have it as well as another?" (21–22) The answer should, by now, be obvious: Phineas has no money.

In a brilliant innovation, Trollope inserted into the very texture of Phineas's transcribed and inset encapsulating letter Dr. Finn's mental comments on it as he reads:

> I own that I am fond of politics, and have taken great delight in their study ["Stupid young fool!" his father said to himself as he read this] and it has been my dream for years past to have a seat in Parliament at some future time. ['Dream! Yes; I wonder whether he has ever dreamed what he is to live upon.'] The chance has now come to me much earlier than I have looked for it, but I do not think that it should on that account be thrown away. Looking to my profession, I find that many things are open to a barrister with a seat in Parliament, and that the House need not interfere much with a man's practice. ['Not if he has got to the top of is tree,' said the doctor.] (21)

Dr. Finn's interpolated commentary mitigates the dulling effect of repeating what has already been conveyed at different points in the narrative. It also underlines by immediate juxtaposition the disjunction between what Phineas "feels" or imagines to be rational and realistic grounds for his choice of a parliamentary career – "I have weighed the matter all round" (21) – and the practical, worldly realism of an older and more experienced head. This disjunction between Phineas's rationalizations and his father's reasoning is further developed in the reception narrative, through Dr. Finn's conversation about the letter with his wife and daughters, who take Phineas's part. Mrs. Finn is filled with "motherly pride," certain that "parliament would be the making of her son" since "everybody would be sure to employ so distinguished a barrister." Phineas's sisters think it would be "brutal" not to let him have his chance. But Dr. Finn explains that "going into Parliament could not help a young barrister, whatever it might do for one thoroughly established in his profession" and that, since becoming an MP meant "abandon[ing] all idea of earning any income, . . . the proposition, coming from so poor a man, was a monstrosity." (21, 22) Their diametrically opposite expectations of Phineas's prospects intimate that "the chance that has now come" to Phineas is precisely that: pure chance, a bet on the future with a fifty-fifty chance of success. That no dependence can be placed on expectations is immediately demonstrated in the usual way, when Dr. Finn belies Phineas's expectation that his father would oppose him and stop his income, by going to visit Lord Tulla to secure the borough of Loughsbane for his son, and by postponing his retirement to be able to continue to support Phineas in London.

Trollope showed in other Palliser novels that the Victorians were as capable of using letters, discourse, and polite manners to further their intrigues, and mask their enmity, ambitions, or greed as their eighteenth-century forbears.[28] But in *Phineas Finn*, the thirty fully transcribed notes and letters, the more than twenty cited or partly transcribed letters, and the many more merely summarized missives are frank and honest. They state what characters know and genuinely think at the time of writing. The issue is whether characters are deceiving themselves about the realism of their choices, the rationality of their arguments and the moral purity of their motives, rather than how they are deceiving others. Sincerity and frankness in their communications do not preclude characters like Phineas or Lady Laura from fooling themselves. Their frankness enables Trollope to show how characters can "act irrationally by acting on their best judgement," and how "their judgment may fail to motivate [them] when the chips are down"[29] precisely because their expectations shape their "best judgement" and determine their choices when the chips are down.

At the same time, using the encapsulating letter to repeatedly posit opposite expectations introduces the open questions that the novel will address. What were a poor young outsider's chances? Could a penniless, educated, and gentlemanly young man realistically support himself in a political career during the 1860s and 1870s, when MPs were not paid – even if, like Phineas, he was given exceptionally "good fortune," the occasional self's facility for suiting himself to different companies and making the right friends, and the eighteenth-century philanderer's pursuit of conveniently transient "love" for a succession of serviceable women? How far could such a man expect to gain the acceptance he needed from the wealthy and aristocratic political and social elite despite his provincial, Irish Catholic, and modestly middle-class origins? When such an ethnic and class outsider considered the "prize . . . so great" that he was "prepared to run any risk to obtain it" (22), what was he risking if the obstacles to "making his way" in the political realm proved too great? Would Phineas's bet on the future prove Dr. Finn's or Phineas's and his mother and sisters' expectations correct?

To support himself, a man like Phineas had two options once an MP: he could seek a salaried government post under the current ministry; or he could acquire a wealthy, socially acceptable wife. Of course, he could also lose his post, or fail to acquire such a wife, or succeed in making a parliamentary career at first, and then fail. And having gambled and lost all, including the future once within his reach as a barrister-at-law, he could be left with nothing. *Phineas Finn* keeps the plot open and the initial opposite expectations in play by carrying Finn successively through all these possible futures. This concretizes risk as a chance grasped at one moment that can slip through one's fingers the next, and makes the future impervious to prediction and prognostication. Literally *anything* and *every-thing* can happen. Trollope did not place Finn on a path that would – ultimately – enable him to realize his ambitions until he was recalled to Westminster at the beginning of *Phineas Redux*.

Phineas Finn ends, not coincidentally on another letter, without settling the question of expectations raised by its initial encapsulating letter. Back in Ireland and engaged to his childhood sweetheart whom he has "really" loved all along, Phineas discovers that it is too late to establish himself in the legal profession in Dublin as his father had wished, and consequently that his marriage must be indefinitely postponed. Having risked and lost, Phineas faces poverty and misery. He sees no way forward – until, like a *deus ex machina*, Lord Cantrip's letter from Downing Street arrives to save the day by offering Phineas "a permanent government appointment" as Inspector of the Poor Laws at Cork. (575) Cantrip's unexpected missive supplies an equivocal answer to the questions posed by the novel's initial encapsulating letter. Offering Phineas the post of "Inspector of the Poor Laws" in Cork is not without its ironies – having risked and abandoned all in London, and failed to gain traction as a lawyer in Dublin, Phineas has experienced at firsthand how the laws of poverty operate on those who ignore the warnings of their elders and fail to establish themselves in a paying profession early in life. On the other hand, the patronage of the right friends in London was essential to obtaining a provincial government appointment such as this, which would permanently support him and permit him to marry – even if it did so by restoring Phineas to the class, life, wife, and provincial social milieu from which he had made his bid to rise. Consequently, at the end of *Phineas Finn*, it is impossible to say with certainty, even from a retrospective view, whether the expectations of the yay-sayers or nay-sayers about taking "the chance that came to [him]" to stand for Parliament had been proved more right.

Retrospective: On the Contingent, Unexpected, and Unforeseen

Narrative-epistolary novelists who tested the general rules, customary truths, or received ideas embodied in expectations empirically against events were attacking another bastion of empiricist knowledge-claims in the human sciences by demonstrating the inadequacy of their predictive power in particular cases. They were also confronting empiricism with its own unseen.

As we saw, Lennox and Burney demonstrated the incapacity of cultural archetypes, preconceived ideas and conduct-book rules to predict and control outcomes in particular cases, by confronting expectations with the unexpected in all its forms – accident, chance, the surprising, the unforeseen, the unintended, the unnoticed, and the un-designed.[30] Unexpected accidents, chance discoveries, an unforeseen rumor, unintended consequences, or the unpredictable effects of competing expectations showed the incapacity even of the most probable expectations to do what calculations of probability and received ideas were supposed to do – order the "chaos" of empirical phenomena, offset and control the contingency of life. One might call this the return of what Dalston argues empiricism's reliance on a priori rules and calculations of probability was designed to repress. But where Lennox remained traditional in the *Henrietta* episodes by attributing the unexpected to a calculated deception and the unforeseen to incomplete knowledge of all the relevant circumstances, Burney, like Charlotte Smith after her, put reality in motion to make chance and accident, the surprising, unexpected and unforeseen, intrinsic to the contingent, piecemeal, multi-directional, self-reversing fluidity of social life. Without denying the role of occasional selves, conscious deceivers, polite manners, and incomplete knowledge in belying expectations, Burney used Delvile's encapsulating letter to show that acting on expectations assumed a degree of control over the conduct and beliefs of others and over the outcome of interactions in society that no individual possessed, as well as the false expectation that reality would follow a regular, linear course predictably regulated by cause and effect. This meant that, like mistaken conjectures in *Emmeline*, the problem was not just some people's villainy; both the good and the bad act on partly or wholly false expectations all the time, and usually miscarried as a result.

Lennox and Burney confronted empiricism with its own unseen by addressing two other central empiricist principles. Lennox falsified the principle that "sensory experience constitutes our paramount source of knowledge"[31] by showing that, in the everyday form of expectations, received ideas take precedence over sensory experience, sometimes to the point of blinding us to the presence, never mind the significance, of empirical facts. We might be born *tabula rasa*; but once our minds are stocked with general ideas derived from books, from custom, from a mentor's precepts, from familiar stories, or from interpersonally held convictions, we deduce experience from them whether they are true or not. We use the expectations they generate to anticipate the conduct of others and the course of future events, and ground our conduct on suppositions about its outcome that conform to what they predict. Locke's cultural "archetypes" were thus more powerful than he had foreseen; for rather than being attached to ideas by the understanding *after* it had processed sense perceptions into more and more complex ideas, cultural archetypes quite absurdly controlled which sense perceptions the understanding selected from all those passing before it, and how they were turned into complex ideas. Burney also subverted the empiricist principle that "general propositions must be inductively inferred from particular facts"[32] by showing that the inferences usually made from particular facts are particular and local. They bear in utilitarian ways on the immediate situation in which particular facts occur, and do not rise to the level of general propositions or universal truths that apply to a multitude of analogical situations. Like Cecilia in her reading of Mrs. Hill's letter and of Mr. Harrel's actions, we tend to overlook or ignore any broader and more general inferences that could be made from particular facts, and thus fail to see where they are symptomatic of larger issues, or to foresee how what could, and perhaps should, have been inferred from a particular letter or situation, will play out.

Maria Edgeworth and John-Stuart Mill addressed these critiques defensively in curiously analogical, and essentially conservative, ways. Understanding the stakes for society and morality of discrediting customary expectations, Edgeworth tried to rescue general moral maxims and conduct-book rules by distinguishing between reasonable and unreasonable expectations and showing that, once coupled with self-control and dispassionate reasoning, implementation of received ideas gave her heroine almost complete control even over the most adverse and unexpected circumstances. Granting that our inferences are usually local and focused on what is immediately useful in the current situation, she treated the unexpected as the not-yet known – something discoverable empirically in the same particular and immediate way when expectations are belied in particular cases. But Edgeworth also answered Burney by showing that when this was useful to Belinda (for instance, in deciding whether to make a marriage of convenience), Belinda was perfectly capable of constructing general propositions by comparing the facts in several particular cases. Edgeworth's conservative solution to the unpredictability of people's conduct and of the outcome of interactions in society was to promote uniformity through conformity: if individuals were reformed so that everyone followed the same moral maxims and conduct-book strictures by commanding their passions and obeying the rules binding on polite and virtuous domestic men and women, there would be no earth-shattering surprises – only enlivening variations on the predictable and routine.

Later in the nineteenth century, Mill affirmed the importance of a priori rules and received ideas to positivism in a similar way: by making them as primary to reasoning as inferences from empirical facts. Indeed, he argued that "it is impossible to frame any scientific method of induction or to test the correctness of inductions, unless upon the hypothesis that some inductions of unquestionable certainty have been made." Downplaying the unknown by representing it as the not-yet known, Mill sought to give his combination of inferences from "positive facts" and inferences from "hypotheses" of "unquestionable certainty," the assured, utilitarian, predictive, and controlling power that the sciences were supposed to have by insisting that all investigation be directed to "uniformities in the course of nature" and to cause and effect. Emphasis on what was uniform and conformed to rule made received ideas and already established laws, strictures on scientific work that had to be respected to keep everyone on the same utilitarian page. Mill also made two other observations in this connection that narrative-epistolary novels had made in their own ways before him: that "it is not from the past to the future *as* past and future, that we infer, but from the known to the unknown, . . . from what we have perceived or been directly conscious of, to what has not yet come within our experience;" and that "what has not yet come within our experience" concerns not only the future, "but also the vastly greater portion of the present and the past."[33]

One might say that in their different ways, Collins and Trollope responded to positivism's claims to predictive power in the human or "moral" sciences and to the utilitarian control over contingency and chance that its methods and findings were supposed to guarantee, by using initial encapsulating letters to double down on the empirical impact of the unknown and uncontrollable and place them unexpectedly center stage. Lennox had used unseen letters to foreground lacunae in a character's knowledge of reality, in order to profile against the letter's now visible invisibility, operations of the mind that proceed as if blanks, lacunae, and omissions were not there. But Collins focused on the terrifyingly unpredictable power of the unseen and unknown by turning encapsulating letters into epistolary blanks carrying toxic secrets from the past that erupt explosively into the orderly and predictable course of Victorian conformity. This highlighted the cataclysmically destructive potential of the unexpected and unseen, as well as the frailty of lives built on known "positive facts." Showing that every character's plans and every action they took to implement them were wholly or partly foiled by the plans and actions of some other character, not only reiterated Burney's point about the unpredictable outcomes of human interactions in society; it also made the future precisely what no one could control. Trollope also denied expectations' predictive power, but by using his initial encapsulating letters in *Phineas Finn* to show that the same situation(s) could generate diametrically opposite expectations in different people, and by taking Finn successively through all the configurations that might be expected of a political career. This indicated, as Burney had, that expectations that proved manifestly false at one point might be unexpectedly realized later; but by allowing expectations to encompass all possible configurations of a parliamentary life and career, it also suggested that expectations could predict anything, and therefore nothing, about the future. All that expectations controlled were the present choices that characters made.

Lennox, Burney, and Edgeworth had used encapsulating letters at the beginning of a novel or narrative movement to articulate expectations that linked the past to the future, the known to the unknown, the seen to the unseen, and the unseen to the unforeseen, leaving the subsequent course of the story to make visible retrospectively what character-reader(s) and novel-readers reading "locally" for the immediate situation had not seen in the letter at the time. But in their different ways, Trollope and Collins robbed expectations and their initial encapsulating letters, of all substance. Though using them to perform their usual functions, they left encapsulating letters to run on empty. Collins, as we saw, made them signifiers of an unknown secret to create in novel-readers the expectation of being surprised at any moment by the terrible but indeterminate and unforeseeable something hanging over letter and story. This turned the present and future both of characters' lives and of novella-readers' reading into time in which unexpected, unpredictable, and unforeseen things are liable to occur at any moment. It also gave renewed importance to the retrospective view needed to fill in the threatening blanks in characters' knowledge of the past, and turned the forward progress of many of Collins's stories into piecemeal, retrospective investigative reconstructions of what had been unseen, unknown, and unforeseen before.

Trollope, by contrast, made his initial encapsulating letter in *Phineas Finn* the signifier of a bet on the future whose outcome could not be predicted, and emptied the retrospective view of knowledge and substance too. Taking Finn successively through all the possibilities suggested by contrary expectations of his parliamentary career permitted Trollope to introduce retrospective views each time a courtship, goal, or career-move failed, and thus to indicate, as Burney had, that what one saw or concluded from a retrospective view depended on where in the course of events one paused to look back. But Trollope also made it impossible to say, even from the retrospective vantage point at novel's end, what *Phineas Finn* had demonstrated empirically about the expectations that shaped characters' choices. What he had presented was only a shifting panorama of unforeseen twists and turns created by characters' interlocking and often incompatible, expectation-related choices, and the fluid, complex, unexpected, interminable, and always fascinating contingency of life.

CHAPTER 4

Epistolary Peripeteiae

Introduction: Pivotal Letters and Dilatory Lovers

Narrative-epistolary fiction often centered reversals in knowledge and revolutions in the course of events on letters. We have already encountered several such letters in passing: in Behn's *Love Letters*, Silvia's transformation from manipulated victim into manipulating siren turned on Philander's "Blame the Victim" letter; in Haywood's *The City Jilt*, a correspondence with her "ungrateful" lover marked the revolution in Glicera's treatment of men and of letters; in *Pride and Prejudice*, Darcy's letter-narrative occasioned a reversal of Elizabeth's previously ignorant judgments and later, of her previous action in refusing him. We have also encountered in passing, cases involving empirical tests where epistolary *peripeteiae* were complicated by the coupling of false and true *anagnorises* (discoveries or revelations) as well as by exploration of the associated *hamartia* – a term encompassing character flaws (such as excesses of passion, drunkenness, or madness) and errors in reasoning or judgment. In *Betsy Thoughtless*, Miss Flora's anonymous letter instigated a false discovery due to Trueworth's false reasoning, which created a reversal on the level of the plot; both were later corrected by Trueworth's accidental discovery of the truth about the letter and, once they were both free to marry, by another reversal in the plot. In *Emmeline*, James Croft's anonymous letter generated a false discovery on Delamere's part, caused both by his erroneous reasoning and by his excess of passion, which produced a reversal on the level of the plot; but here only the former was corrected by his discovery of the true facts. By contrast, the letters in the casket (itself a *locus classicus* for *anagnorisis* by signs or tokens), ultimately generated both a reversal in the course of events and a reversal of Emmeline's ignorance about her true identity and the Mowbrays' past.

These practices were heavily indebted to the Aristotelian Romance tradition. Authors and commentators had built for centuries on Aristotle's *Poetics* and on his preferred examples, *Oedipus Rex* and *The Odyssey*, to extend key plot features – *peripeteia, anagnorisis, hamartia*, and the secret of identity that drives the action – from Tragedy to Epic and from Epic to prose Romance.[1] Working in this inherited tradition, eighteenth-century British commentators argued that the most "beautiful" because the most "surprising" form of *peripeteia*, consisted of "a sudden reversal in the fortunes of the persons acting ... arising from the incidents" that is accompanied by the discovery or revelation of knowledge (*anagnorisis*) of which characters had previously been ignorant.[2] In other words, they made *peripeteia* and *anagnorisis* analogical and virtually simultaneous: *peripeteia* was a surprising reversal on the level of the action, *anagnorisis*, a surprising reversal on the level of characters' and/or readers' understanding of the action. *Peripeteia* and *anagnorisis* also cooperated as cause and effect: a new circumstance might cause knowledge to come to light, or constitute a new cause for reversing the blindness or ignorance under which a character had labored (*hamartia*); conversely, new knowledge might cause a character to change their course of action, and thus the direction of the plot. As modern scholars have shown, these terms were subject to diverse interpretations and reinterpretations during the *Poetics'* long reception history; but there was a tradition going back to Castelvetro, embraced by key seventeenth-century French and eighteenth-century British critics, which privileged discoveries based on inference and reasoning over recognitions through tokens and signs, and which held that an author might skillfully withhold knowledge from readers, while peppering his/her text with hints or foreshadowings, to ensure that readers experienced an *anagnorisis* as well as protagonists.[3] There was also widespread agreement that the unexpectedness inherent in *peripeteia* and *anagnorisis* produced surprise, which in turn heightened other possible emotions generated by the plot, such as pity, wonder, admiration, or terror.[4]

This chapter takes a closer look at epistolary *peripeteiae* and their accompanying *anagnorises* by examining some narrative-epistolary fictions where reversals in plot and knowledge are not only made conspicuous, even focal, elements of the story by centering them on a letter or correspondence, but where this is done in innovative and thought-provoking ways. The texts below all used their innovations to comment on some or all of the underlying Romance conventions, as well as on issues that we have encountered before. For brevity and convenience, I will use the term "pivot" for combined or simultaneous *peripeteia* and *anagnorisis*; however, in some texts, as we will see, the two were cleverly disjoined.

Thematically, the exemplars here address what I am calling "the dilatory lover" – the problem posed for a woman by the loved man who shows interest but delays or somehow fails to propose, and instead loves, courts, or marries another woman while she waits and suffers. This is a neglected theme in scholarship on women's writing, though it recurs quite frequently in eighteenth- and nineteenth-century fictions. Demographic shifts, due in part to men's deaths in the perpetual wars, and in part to economic changes, which impoverished the old families, left increasing numbers of genteel women to spinsterhood during this period. Women writers also addressed their difficulties in other ways, for instance, by portraying the evils faced by single ladies – evils of poverty and sexual vulnerability, of humiliation and unrewarding jobs as companions or governesses. In sharp contrast to this and to misogynistic caricatures of spinsters, stories about dilatory lovers portrayed the woman doomed (or almost doomed) to remain single as a woman who has truly loved and even, perhaps, been loved in return. Criticizing conventions that made choice and pursuit in courtship male prerogatives and that required women to remain passive and seemingly indifferent until chosen, they showed "what tortur'd *Female Hearts* endure/Compell'd to stifle what they feign would tell."

Jane Barker's Double Pivot: *Love Intrigues*

Current criticism favors allegorical, Catholic and Jacobite interpretations of Barker's romance; but the formal and thematic legacy of *Love Intrigues* (1713), which saw its last printing in 1743, stemmed from its complex analysis of a young woman's relationship to a disappointingly dilatory lover and from its conspicuous use of letters to signal, perform, and surprisingly double the narrative's *peripeteia* and *anagnorisis*.

There are only two letters in *Love Intrigues*. But brief and anodyne as they seem, Galecia's story turns upon them. These letters are embedded in a retrospective "history" of Galecia's interactions with her dilatory lover, Bosvil, during her "early Years," which is framed and interrupted by conversation in the present with her friend, Lucasia, as they sit in a garden at St. Germains. Galecia's narrative describes her lover and kinsman as blowing hot and cold – each time he showed his love or declared his passion, she expected him to speak to her parents about marrying her, only to be bitterly disappointed by his coldness and indifference the next time they met, or hurt by hearing that he meant to marry a Mrs. Lowland, or that he had suggested another husband for her. Galecia kept her love for Bosvil secret both from him and from her parents until his "open declaration to her parents" and their agreement to the marriage should "set [her Words] at liberty." She pretended an indifference she did not feel, thinking she "planted [her] actions in a good Soil on the Ground of Vertue and water'd them in the Stream of Discretion."⁵ But the marriage proposal she longed for never came. Her first-person narrative describes her growing resentment at Bosvil's repeated delays, her painful conviction that he was merely "a false Pretender" to love, and her agonized struggles to keep up her "mask" of "pretended Indifference." (13) The prefatory narrative to the two embedded letters informs us that she wrote to Bosvil when she could no longer bear the torment:

Cousin,

I thought you had been so well acquainted with my Humour touching a marry'd Life, as to know it is my Aversion; therefore wonder you should make such a Proposal to my Father on your Friend's Behalf. Perhaps you will say it was but in Jest, and I believe it to be no more . . . for I have done nothing dishonourable to myself, nor disobliging to you; therefore ought rather to be the Subject of Civility than Banter, which, perhaps Distance and Absence may accomplish; therefore, I beg you to see me no more, 'till Fortune commission you, by the Change of your Condition. In the mean Time, I remain, your Kinswoman and humble Servant,

Galecia (33)

Galecia explains to Lucasia that "in the Simplicity of these Words lay much Cunning, and under the Shadow of Frowardness much Kindness; which I knew he must discern, if he had any real Affection for me in his Heart." (33) She thought that her letter had testified her affection "in a covert manner" because "nothing but a fond Mistress" would use the words "See me no more" or show displeasure at the offer of an advantageous marriage with his friend. But she also recognized that she had brought matters to a crisis: he must now either come to her as an "open Lover" (34) or stay away. Bosvil's answer arrived the next day:

Madam,

I am extreamly astonish'd to find you so displeas'd at what pass'd the other Day, which was no Way meant to your Prejudice, but, on the contrary, much to your Advantage. However, Madam, I shall not justify what you are pleas'd to condemn; but add also to the Testimony of my Obedience, in submitting to our Prohibition, and not presume to see you more, tho' in it I sequester myself from those Charms I have so long ador'd, and only at a Distance admire what your Rigour forbids me to approach, and so rest,

Madam, Your Kinsman and humble Servant, Bosvil.

Introduction of these letters highlights the turning point in her narrative: Bosvil now withdraws, avoids her, and eventually marries someone else; Galecia buries herself in work and studies and wishes for a convent where she could "under a holy Veil bury all thoughts of Bosvil" (36). Looking back many years later from singleness and exile in France, Galecia is still bitter and bewildered. She has explained these "Adventures of her early Years" in contradictory ways. But she concludes her narrative by reiterating the *leitmotif* of her first-person perspective: Bosvil's conduct had been all "Falshood" (41) and "Treachery" (42) whilst hers had been all it should be – "I do remember nothing in which I can accuse myself, even now that I am free from Passion, and capable to make a serious Reflection." (46)

These letters that mark the *peripeteia* and *anagnorisis* in Galecia's narrative also have a second, conjoined function: to indicate the pivotal point in interpretation of it. Bosvil's letter provides Lucasia and novel-readers with an incommensurable *anagnorisis* or discovery by inviting an entirely different reading of the same characters and events. This turns Bosvil from a deceiving philanderer into a despairing Romance hero. For – surprisingly after all we have heard about him in Galecia's narrative – Bosvil's letter is not the letter of an inconstant male coquet or of a calculating "false Pretender" to love, deploying the usual panoply of flowery conceits and rhetorical clichés. It is the letter of a man without "Cunning" who has read Galecia's letter in its "Simplicity" to mean what it says: that she is not interested in marriage or in him. His are the words of an honest man who has, as he says, "long ador'd" her, and of a well-bred man, who knows how to conduct himself when given his conge': he obeys his mistress by withdrawing his suit as the only possible remaining "testimony" of his love. Later in the narrative, his confidant explains this conduct to Galecia, who characteristically dismisses his narrative of events from Bosvil's perspective as a mere "Screen for his Falshood." According to this confidant, love had "taken such deep Root in his Soul" that Bosvil could not "eradicate" it; but Galecia had "treated him always with such an Air of Indifference, as seem'd rather the Effect of Prudence than Affection." Bosvil invented the story of Mrs. Lowland to "try if Jealousy would work" on her; but meeting only with "Caution and Circumspection," and having failed to elicit any sign of "Passion or Tenderness" from her, he had concluded that "all her Amourous Inclinations" were buried with her first lover, Brafort. (45) Loving her truly and honorably, he scorned to force her into a marriage she did not want by addressing her parents. During the severe illness her letter of dismissal produced, he expressed his continuing love for her by willing her his wealth; but recognizing on his recovery that as an only child and heir to a prosperous estate, he had to marry, he did his duty, despite that love. Bosvil's conduct was thus capable of a construction quite different from that which Galecia had given it: he had repeatedly sought confirmation from her that she loved him, and had repeatedly retreated when failing to find it.

Viewed retrospectively in light of this information, juxtaposition of Galecia's and Bosvil's transcribed letters dramatizes how completely they had misunderstood one another. This is why Lucasia expresses her judgment that Bosvil was a true lover and that this had been a tragedy of errors by blaming Galecia for not consulting her mother, who could have "found out a Way to accommodate Things to your Satisfaction." (46) In Lucasia's view, then, the problem had lain, not in Bosvil's character or intentions, but in Galecia's mismanagement of the courtship by her dissimulating propriety and – as Galecia demonstrates again by insisting she was right not to consult her mother – by her stubborn adherence to her own perspective. Galecia had been as wrong in her judgment of Bosvil's conduct and character as in thinking "he *must* discern" the affection she imagined she had conveyed in a "covert manner" in her letter. Critique is directed through Galecia at a girl's obligation to "squar[e her] Actions by the exact Rules of Vertue and Modesty," which demanded that she "restrain [her] Tongue from telling the Fondness of [her] Heart." (29, 24) That Galesia had nothing to accuse herself of with regard to the rules of propriety and female modesty that society imposed on young ladies, was precisely the problem. Had she been able to tell Bosvil that he was her "idol, and rival'd Heaven in [her] Affections," the outcome would have been entirely different. This is also the reading of the novella indicated in George Sewell's prefatory poem: "How vain are all Disguises when we love; . . . what the tortur'd *Female Hearts* endure:/Compell'd to stifle what they feign would tell/While Truth commands, but Honour must rebel."

The pivotal correspondence in *Love Intrigues* thus enables Galecia's narrative to simultaneously tell two different stories, the first more safely conventional than the second, where she, not Bosvil, is the guilty party. Their pivotal letter-exchange produces a false *anagnorisis* in both characters' stories – each discovers from the other's letter that they are not loved. But thanks to Lucasia's questions and comments, the same letters are capable of pivoting novella-readers to *anagnorisis* of a different order in which uncomfortable truths come to light about the miscommunication and suffering promoted by extant courtship conventions and about women's disempowerment by cultural expectations of female silence, modesty, and virtue.

Getting It Backward: *Sense and Sensibility* and *Persuasion*

The problem of the dilatory lover recurs, in major or minor key, in all Jane Austen's novels. In *Sense and Sensibility*, Austen's first published novel, both sisters face dilatory lovers. In *Pride and Prejudice*, Jane, like Galecia, fails to adequately communicate her feelings to Bingley and has to watch him depart for London without having proposed. In *Mansfield Park*, Fanny has to silently watch Edmund courting Miss Crawford and resist his efforts to marry her off to someone else. After being banished from Northanger Abbey, Catherine supposes that Henry Tilney will now never propose. Believing like Elizabeth Bennett that there would be no second chance, Anne in *Persuasion* has to watch Wentworth courting and preparing to marry another woman. Frank Churchill courts Emma only to mask his engagement to Jane Fairfax, and Knightly is so dilatory that he gives no sign that he even thinks of proposing. Austen deployed pivotal letters in five of these six novels, *Emma* being the exception. Austen experimented in each with different ways of doubling and disjoining the pivotal letter's peripatetic and epistemological functions, and of destabilizing the retrospective narrative that *anagnorisis* entailed. Two of these will be addressed here.

In *Sense and Sensibility*, Austen highlighted the pivotal letter in the Marianne-Willoughby plot by extending the *peripeteia* and *anagnorisis* it entailed over several chapters in a narrative that otherwise contains few letters. This enabled her to defamiliarize *peripeteia* and *anagnorisis* by portraying them as a process, by presenting them backward, and by giving them to different characters to uncouple them from their traditional conjunction. Austen also marked the conventionality of the peripatetic convention by hastily repeating the identical pivot *pro forma* in the Elinor-Edward plot.

The turning point in Marianne's relationship to Willoughby is marked by his brutal letter of dismissal. Austen defamiliarized the pivot it entailed by nestling his letter in a surprising double reversal of the customary order of narrative exposition. First, she mimed the retrospective view of the investigator by reversing the embedded letter's usual tripartite sequence, and filling the outer prefatory narrative with what the reception narrative would normally contain – discussion of a letter's effects and consequences for its addressee. Focalizing through Elinor as she meditates at length on the unseen letters that she sees Marianne writing to Willoughby presents their correspondence as the signifier of a mystery, and as the agent of potentially opposite consequences for Marianne's life and reputation, depending on whether it signifies that they have secretly agreed to marry or that they were defying social norms by corresponding without any such agreement. Elinor's reflections thus make visible how the *peripeteia* in Marianne's story hangs on a single circumstance and differs in each case. The inner prefatory narrative contains the scene at the ball in which Marianne faints at her sudden suspicion – when Willoughby ignores her to devote himself to his fiancée, Miss Gray – that she has been deceived in the expectations he had raised. Willoughby's distraught reaction to her faint, which leaves his position ambiguous, motivates the decisive letter of dismissal that Marianne shows Elinor, along with three notes she wrote him, which he has returned with it.

These four missives, which are fully transcribed, echo the pivotal correspondence in Haywood's *City Jilt*; but Austen performs a second reversal by displaying them in reverse order. Willoughby's letter of dismissal, which is as "shocking," as "impudently cruel" and as much of an "insult" as Melladore's, appears first. It is followed a few pages later by Marianne's three earlier notes, which like Glicera's, become increasingly urgent to "ease . . . what I now suffer" by obtaining "certainty" from her lover about where they now stand.[6] Austen also revisited issues that Haywood's epistolary *peripeteia* had raised: Willoughby, like Melladore, has abandoned the penurious heroine for a woman of fortune, and like him, has tried to rid himself of Marianne's importunities by responding to her notes with silence; and Marianne, like Glicera, becomes so feverish and delirious after receiving his letter of dismissal that her life is in danger. Read first and by itself, as Elinor and we initially read it, Willoughby's letter creates more shock, surprise, and bewilderment than it would if we were prepared for it, as we were prepared for Melladore's letter, by the heroine's increasingly anxious missives. Read first and by itself, Willoughby's letter also raises obvious questions – which Elinor proceeds to ask – about what could possibly have transpired between them to terminate in a terrible letter of dismissal such as this. This uncouples *peripeteia* and *anagnorisis* by giving each to different characters – it is Marianne's *peripeteia*, Elinor's *anagnorisis* – and by deferring the latter while Elinor's gropes toward enlightenment by asking questions and evaluating information new to her.[7] Uncoupling *peripeteia* and *anagnorisis* and deferring the latter for several chapters impugned the credibility, and indeed the probability, of a Romance convention in which the requisite fateful turn of events is yoked to the requisite revelation.

Reversal of the embedded letter's usual tripartite structure concludes several chapters later, with what a letter's prefatory framing narrative usually contained: information about the motives and circumstances in which Willoughby's letter was written. This finally solves the mystery and answers the questions that his letter of dismissal posed. The information is transmitted in a conversation between Elinor and Willoughby when he unexpectedly turns up at their country house after hearing that Marianne is dangerously ill. Willoughby explains that his "infamous letter" (197) was dictated by Miss Gray, now his wife, from jealousy and "malice;" and that he had to submit, though realizing it made him a "scoundrel," because "in honest words, her money was necessary to me." (199) As one might expect of an author for whom money is invariably important, Willoughby's marriage for money is not condemned as Melladore's was.[8] Willoughby expresses his "penitence" for his "inconstancy" to Marianne and describes the "misery" (200) of loving her while condemned to live with a woman whose meanness and nastiness were evident to him from that infamous letter – "What do you think of my wife's style of letter-writing? – delicate – tender – truly feminine – was it not?" (199) And though telling him severely that he has freely chosen his lot, Elinor "betrays her compassionate emotion" by reversing her previous judgment of him as a man "deep in hardened villainy:" (111) "You have proved yourself on the whole, less faulty than I had believed you. You have proved your heart less wicked, much less wicked." (200)

Ending where the prefatory narrative conventionally began enabled Austen to juxtapose Elinor's illuminating conversation with Willoughby with the analogical conversation she has with Edward three chapters later, when he too shows up unexpectedly to express his penitence for his "inconstancy" in almost marrying another woman (224). The short scene describing Elinor and Edward's *peripeteia* and *anagnorisis*, depends for its meaning on its analogies with the more dramatic and extensively elaborated epistolary *peripeteia* in the Willoughby-Marianne plot. Edward shows Elinor the letter Lucy Ferrars wrote him to inform him of her marriage to his wealthier brother and uses it to indicate his awareness of his lucky escape: "How I have blushed over the pages of her writing . . . this is the only letter I ever received from her, of which the substance made me any amends for the defect of the style." (222) Edward rapidly supplies the missing pieces of that story; and he and Elinor are even more rapidly reconciled. Elinor's judgment of Edward's behavior is analogical to her "compassionate" judgment of Willoughby's: it was "certainly very wrong," but his "fancy" had led him to imagine that Lucy was something she was not. This leaves the only "question . . . undecided between them," the only "difficulty to be overcome," the fact that they "wanted something to live upon" (224). The problem of money is immediately resolved by Colonel Brandon's generosity; but that "something to live upon" is the *sine qua non* of their happy ending supports Willoughby's assessment of the "necessity" for money. Willoughby is living the marriage with a mean and malicious wife that Edward has narrowly escaped; and the analogy in Elinor's reaction to both men's "penitence" suggests that though, unlike her sister, she finally got the man she wants, Edward is less than the perfect romantic hero. Like Miss Gray and Colonel Brandon, Elinor is getting a slightly tarnished, secondhand spouse. The scene's rapid, perfunctory repetition of the pivot in the Willoughby-Marianne plot suggests likewise that we are getting a slightly tarnished, secondhand version of the obligatory reversal in such plots.

In *Sense and Sensibility*, then, Austen defamiliarized and uncoupled *peripeteia* and *anagnorisis* by presenting her epistolary pivot backward. In her posthumously published novel, *Persuasion*, she experimented with using backward constructions occasioned by her pivotal letter to reexamine another theory promoted by Aristotle's commentators: that *peripeteia* and *anagnorisis* were particularly satisfying when reversals occasioned by chance occurrences that elicit surprise are seen in retrospect to indicate the meaningful workings of some higher purpose or design.[9] Austen replaced her original ending, where a scene of quiet conversation accomplished the pivot as in the Elinor-Edward plot, with an ending more closely resembling her elaboration and magnification of the transgressive characters' pivot in *Sense and Sensibility*. But this time, the pivot is accomplished by a tissue of surprising, chance occurrences and produces two different retrospective narratives, to raise questions about the truth of backward-looking narratives that reshape the past teleologically in light of a present outcome and re-present it as testimony to some nobler design.

As critics have often noticed, the prefatory narrative to Wentworth's pivotal letter presents the events leading up to it as a concatenation of chance occurrences. Rain almost prevents Anne from keeping her appointment to meet the Musgroves at the White Hart Inn. When she does get there, she is surprised to find Mrs. Crofts and Captain Harville with the Musgroves, and Wentworth at a writing desk – their separate parties happen to be holed up together against the rain. Conversation happens to turn to the sudden engagements of Henrietta Musgrove to Charles Hayter, and of Louisa Musgrove to Captain Benwick. Easy-going Mrs. Musgrove justifies permitting Henrietta to marry Hayter despite his "small income;" kindly Captain Harville is pained by Benwick's engagement to Louisa so soon after the death of his Fanny: "Poor Fanny! She would not have forgotten him so soon." And as Linda Bree observes in her fine introduction, Anne becomes "so preoccupied with the analogy to herself and Wentworth" that her verbal responses speak to her own experience and reflections, rather than to Benwick's or Henrietta's.[10] Anne's words to Harville convey, in the most intense, economical, and understated manner, all that the narrative has shown her suffering since Wentworth's departure, as a once loved single woman who has continued to love in painful silence and been obliged to watch him courting the Musgrove girls on his return. Anne's words are marked by her years of private suffering "in the role of companion, amanuensis, nurse and listener." For she not only characterizes all women's lives in these terms – "we live at home, quiet and confined, and our feelings prey upon us." The very form of her words captures what this single life has made her – a "nobody with either father or sister," a maiden aunt whose "convenience was always to give way," (48) a woman isolated from others by their inability or unwillingness to enter into her thoughts and feelings. For she speaks in the third person rather than as an "I" – "[To forget] would not be in the nature of any woman who truly loved" – and as a member of the female sex rather than as an individuated self – "all the privilege I claim for my own sex . . . is that of loving longest, when existence or when hope is gone." (241, 244). It is unlikely that Wentworth, busy writing a letter at the other end of the room, would overhear this; but surprisingly, he does.

When all hope is gone, the letter comes. While describing how Wentworth writes and secretly conveys his unexpected letter to Anne, the prefatory frame signals its pivotal function: "On the contents of that letter depended all which this world could do for her! Anything was possible . . . " (245) The fully transcribed letter contains Wentworth's *anagnorisis* and *peripeteia*: he has realized from Anne's words to Harville that she may love him still, and offers himself to her again. The first reception narrative contains Anne's: "Such a letter was not soon to be recovered from" – in an instant, it had overturned her entire reality, and this was "an overpowering happiness." (246) But though Wentworth's *peripeteia* is unexpected and surprising, his characterization of himself in his letter is more unexpected and surprising still. For he presents himself at once as a male Galecia who imagines that Anne *must* have seen what he concealed, and as a Bosvil, the true lover who has never been inconstant despite his courtship of another woman: "For you alone I think and plan. – Have you not seen this? Can you fail to have understood my wishes? – I had not waited even these ten days, could I have read your feelings, as I think you must have penetrated mine." (245)

Wentworth reiterates this view of himself during the second reception narrative, when he and Anne "returned to the past" to exchange "explanations of what had directly preceded the present moment." (248) Their retrospective narratives unmask and gently ridicule what it means for a *peripeteia* to show, in retrospect, that a series of chance occurrences were in reality the meaningful working of some higher purpose or design, for Wentworth and Anne each give their common past a different and far nobler design than was evident in the course of the novel. Wentworth insists that: "He had persisted in loving none but her. She had never been supplanted." Constructed from the point of view of their happy ending, his counter-narrative of what led up to his letter gives the events and conversations that novel-readers have encountered primarily through Anne's experience a different construction, as he attempts to show that those same conversations and events led, almost inevitably, through a chain of cause and effect and a series of discoveries on Willoughby's part, to the letter in which he renewed his marriage proposal now, so that "Of what he had written, nothing was to be retracted or qualified." His narrative "proved" that there was nothing surprising about the pivotal letter; in reality or at least in retrospect, there had been no *peripeteia*, and no change of heart. Wentworth's "worth" as a true lover even after he "went" depends on this self-justifying narrative in which he argues that, all evidence to the contrary, he had *in reality* been as constant to Anne as she to him.

Anne concludes her retrospective narrative, which likewise revises the narrator's earlier version of events, like Galecia, by insisting she had done right: having thought about the past and judged its rights and wrongs "impartially," she has "nothing to reproach myself with; and if I mistake not, a strong sense of duty is no bad part of a woman's portion." (249, 253) The problem of miscommunication between lovers that was raised by Galecia and Bosvil is raised again here, not only by Wentworth's insistence in his letter that Anne "must" have understood his wishes, when she clearly did not, but by his observation after hearing her retrospective narrative: "I did not understand you. I shut my eyes and would not understand you or do you justice." (254) The decorums had not changed much in the hundred years since *Love Intrigues*, or the impediments they presented to men and women understanding each other's feelings and doing each other justice. Where Galecia's certainty that she had been right in observing the proprieties is put in question by Lucasia, Anne's certainty that she had been right to do her "duty" is put in question by Mrs. Musgrove's support of Henrietta's marriage to Benwick in circumstances identical to those in which Lady Russell refused to support Anne's marriage to Wentworth. If a girl's filial "duty" in the same circumstances could take diametrically opposite forms depending on a parental authority's opinion about the risk of marrying a man who had his way to make in the world, there was indeed nothing to justify Anne in *not* having married Wentworth when he first proposed but a "strong sense of duty" for duty's sake. But if the duty so highly prized by conduct books could arbitrarily take opposite forms in the same circumstances, did it justify what Anne's words in the letter's prefatory narrative highlighted and her retrospective narrative erased – all the suffering, isolation, and marginalization she had experienced by remaining a single woman "whose convenience was always to give way"?

The fact that the history of Wentworth's and Anne's relationship is capable of two retrospective narrative constructions that differ from each other and from the narrator's prospective, chronological version of events indicates the inadequacy of retrospective perspectives as accurate histories of the present or the past. It also suggests that self-justification and desire for reassuring intelligibility underly retrospective narratives that convert chance occurrences into the meaningful workings of some noble purpose or design. This too was getting things backward, since it gave purpose or design a priority that they had not in reality had. In reality, an unexpected concatenation of chance occurrences enabled Wentworth and Anne to break through the misdirection and miscommunications created by conduct-book decorums and past mistakes to reverse the course of events. Chance had been less favorable to Bosvil and Galecia. But rereading the three contradictory retrospective narratives in *Love Intrigues* in light of *Persuasion* suggests, in retrospect, that there was no reason to assume that Lucasia's retrospective view of how matters must have unfolded had Galecia consulted her mother was any sounder than Galecia's or than the confidant's retrospective versions of events – or more immune to misunderstanding, contingency and chance.

Austen explained and ridiculed the mechanism that makes us readjust our sense of things retrospectively to incorporate the surprising or unexpected into some coherent and probable design in her other posthumously published novel, *Northanger Abbey*. This is a novel in which her heroine is constantly surprised by the unexpected turn taken by everyday events in a satirical *reductio ad absurdum* of Burney's, Edgeworth's, and Lennox's treatments of expectations. Austen portrayed the mechanism at work in retrospective revisions of a past filled with unexpected events in the comical scene at Bath in which Catherine is hoping the weather will be fine enough for her to walk with Henry and Eleanor Tilney.[11] This scene revisits the example of clouds and rain that Hobbes and Hume had used to epitomize contingency and illustrate the impossibility of predicting the future with any certainty in everyday life.[12] It also developed Austen's treatment of rain at the outset of the White Hart scenes in *Persuasion*.

When Catherine wakes up on the day of the projected walk, she "augurs" from the "sober" cloudy sky and the sun's occasional efforts to appear, "everything most favourable to her wishes" because she thinks it probable that the weather will improve as the day advances. Asked her opinion, Mrs. Allen "had no doubt in the world of its being a very fine day, if the clouds would only go off, and the sun keep out."[13](62) When it begins to rain, Catherine's expectations change: "I do believe it will be wet . . . no walk for me today." Mrs. Allen again agrees: "I thought how it would be." Catherine now hopes that "perhaps" the rain may stop before noon, when the Tilneys are due to pick her up. Mrs. Allen agrees: "Perhaps it may." When the rain grows heavier, Catherine relates her present disappointment to her earlier expectations: "It was such a nice-looking morning! I felt so convinced it would be dry." Again, Mrs. Allen agrees: "Anybody would have thought so indeed." (62) Only when Catherine determines to "give it up entirely," (63) does the unexpected occur:

> "At half past twelve, when Catherine's anxious attention to the weather was over, and she could no longer claim any merit from its amendment, the sky began voluntarily to clear. A gleam of sun took her quite by surprise . . . Ten minutes more made it certain that a bright afternoon would succeed, and justified the opinion of Mrs. Allen, who had 'always thought it would clear up.'" But whether Catherine might still expect her friends, whether there had not been too much rain for Miss Tilney to venture, must yet be a question. (63)

The unexpected is (as one might expect) precisely what occurs when least expected. Surprise at the unexpected is therefore inseparable from some-one's expectations, a point that Austen makes in the novel whenever the unexpected occurs by juxtaposing a statement of the character's expect-ation with the unexpected occurrence that belies it. But as this scene indicates, the fact that expectations are often belied by events is counter-balanced by the fact that expectations and events share a curious circular, mutually informing and transforming, relationship. Expectations are con-stantly shifting with changing signs, sights, events, or information – as "circumstances change, opinions alter" (112) – but "reality" is constantly shifting too, and in ways which may later realize expectations that proved false before. Expectations autocorrect from moment to moment to account for the advent of the unexpected event, and they do so in such a way as to reintegrate it into what is probable and to be expected in the course of common life.

The curious role played by retrospection here is exposed through Mrs. Allen's seemingly absurd reactions to the onset of rain – "I thought how it would be" – and then to the bright afternoon that suddenly appeared – she "had always thought it would clear up." In each case, the way she "returned to the past" to address "what had directly preceded the present moment" changes with changes in the present moment. As an indifferent observer who considers all the twists and turns in Catherine's expectations equally likely, Mrs. Allen treats expectations as possibilities rather than probabilities. Her initial observation that she "had no doubt in the world of its being a very fine day, if the clouds would only go off, and the sun keep out" (62) is a conditional assessment of possibility: the day may prove fine, *if* certain conditions pertain. It is therefore perfectly logical for Mrs. Allen to agree both that the rain may prevent Catherine's walk and that the day may "perhaps" turn out to be fine. Both were equally possible – it all depended on what conditions ultimately pertained. But once she knew that the sun *would* keep out, that it would be a fine day in *fact*, Mrs. Allen was sure she had "always thought it would clear up," for in a retrospective view, she had eliminated or forgotten the possibilities that no longer applied.[14] Her certainty at different times that she had known how it would be, rain or shine, shows that retrospective narratives auto-correct in light of new information and in light of the present outcome, as much as expectations do. But here this is not only, as Burney thought, because our "prospect" changes as circumstances change; it is also because, once something *has* happened, once it is a fact, we retrospectively rearrange everything that came before to accommodate it, and forget, eliminate, or reinterpret whatever does not accord with it.

It is not only that the mere fact that something has occurred is enough to initiate a retrospective rearrangement of the past which gives it a design it never had. What *Northanger Abbey* adds to *Persuasion* through this scene and the narrator's teasing conclusion is the insight that because reality is constantly shifting, there is nothing necessarily permanent or final about *peripeteia* and *anagnorisis*, about the narrative design(s) constructed in their wake or about the vantage point from which that retrospective narrative is constructed: "as circumstances change, opinions alter." (112) The fixed and conclusive *anagnorisis* that reveals the truth about a heretofore hidden story to bring about the denouement is unmasked as one of fiction's marvelous fictions. Very much in this spirit, despite her denigration of Austen, Charlotte Bronte will therefore show in *Villette* not only that meaningful design and opinions about a thing's meaning shift and rearrange themselves each time present circumstances change; but also that, since present circumstances continue to change even after a narrator has paused the unceasing flow of life to present her retrospective rearrangements of the past, the writerly challenge extends to portraying in equally shifting and transitory terms the vantage point at the end from which that narrator narrates her retrospective narrative and the *peripeteiae* and *anagnorises* within it.

The Pivotal Letter as Shifter: Charlotte Bronte's *Villette*

In *Villette* (1853), Lucy Snowe's long, drawn-out epistolary *peripeteia* occupies ten chapters in the middle of the novel, centered on a chapter entitled "The Letter." There is no "evasion of plottedness" here.[15] On the contrary, these chapters describe simultaneous *peripeteiae* in Lucy's relationships to Dr. Graham-John, the man she has long loved in painful silence, and M. Paul, the man she begins to love. Her double *peripeteia* is accompanied and partly motivated by parallel *peripeteiae* in Graham-John's relationships to Genivra, who fails him, and to Paulina who (as Lucy discovers half way through these chapters) becomes the object of his love and determined pursuit. These ten narrative-epistolary chapters also contain and answer the questions posed by Ginevra Fanshawe – "Who are you Miss Snowe?" – and Lucy's response: "Who am I, indeed? Perhaps a personage in disguise."[16] This has been the focus of much recent critical work. Seeking to pin down a character they agree is "elusive" and presented in "contradictory" ways in a narrative full of "lacunae," critics have themselves characterized Lucy Snowe in contradictory ways. There is widespread agreement at present only on the fact that Lucy is an "unreliable narrator" who at once "exhibits" herself and willfully withholds, retards, unnarrates, disnarrates, or circumnarrates the kind of information that would give her character unity and coherence and that a nineteenth-century realist novel might be expected to supply.[17]

Genevra's question and Lucy's answer are carefully positioned in these narrative-epistolary chapters to link them to issues of identity, deception, and discovery raised by occasional selves that we have encountered in narrative-epistolary fiction before. Conceptions of the self and expectations of it had, of course, changed since the eighteenth century: characters now have problematical insides as well as outsides; and "the in-door view" of what Bronte calls "the natural character" and the "out-door view" often demonstrate "a seeming contradiction." (229) But like occasional selves, out-door views are social and performative: they are the conventionally "regulated," "equable" selves that characters "display" to others, disguises presented to the world – the "surface only [on which] the common gaze will fall."(207) Like occasional selves too, outdoor views are plural because dependent on a person's different relationships and on ascriptions of identity; but now the "contrary attributes of character we sometimes find ascribed to us" are attributed primarily to "the eye with which we are viewed," (348) and are more or less true depending on whether others see past what is immediately displayed. Most of the characters do not have eyes for anything beyond the surface turned to them. Nineteen-year old Paulina de Bassompierre is "child-like" in her interactions with her father, "docile and reliant but not expansive" with Mrs. Britton, "shy" and at moments "cold" with Graham, dignified and wary with Ginevra. Consequently, her father still views her as a child; Ginevra thinks her proud and selfish; and neither Mrs. Britton nor Graham suspects her of concealing her long-standing love for a character who is variously known as Graham and Dr. John. Lucy herself is the paradigmatic case of the character who differs according to "the eye with which [she is] viewed," as indeed she points out:

> Madame Beck esteemed me learned and blue; Miss Fanshawe, caustic, ironic and cynical; Mr. Home a model teacher, the essence of the sedate and discrete ... the pink and pattern of governess-correctness; whilst another person, Professor Paul Emanuel, to wit, never lost an opportunity of intimating his opinion that mine was a rather fiery and rash nature— adventurous, indocile and audacious. (348–349)

More painfully, "Graham" deemed her "inoffensive as a shadow." (387) Few characters other than Lucy and M. Paul look much beyond the surfaces that others display to them. But it is now supposed to be possible to "penetrate" beyond surfaces to a "view" of "the natural character," namely, the desirous, unregulated, and unsocialized being concealed within. (207)

Like this occasional self, "The Letter" in these ten narrative-epistolary chapters is a shifter, both by itself and in a packet with other letters from Dr. John.[18] For all its importance, "The Letter" is not transcribed. Bronte redeployed the unseen letter as an empty signifier of shifting significations to mark successive phases in Lucy's reading and reception of it, and with them, successive phases in her pivot away from Dr. John toward M. Paul. Despite her derogatory comments about Austen, Bronte's use of the letter as a signifier of its shifting significations illustrates and develops Austen's insight that "as circumstances change, opinions alter." "The Letter" is also a shifter inasmuch as "contrary attributes" are ascribed to it by other characters, again characterizing "the eye with which [it is] viewed." The focus in these pivotal chapters is always on The Letter's reception because – as Lucy indicates in her interpolated treatment of the portrait of Cleopatra and performance of Vashti – the meaning and value of written or artistic communications lie not in themselves, but in the different reactions they provoke in different people. The Letters' actual words are not at issue because, in practice, their meaning and importance lay in the reactions they elicited from Lucy and others, such as M. Paul and Madame Beck whose views of Lucy and whose relationships to her are forever changed by their own diverse perceptions of its significance.

"The Letter" is written by Dr. John Bretton after Lucy has spent several happy weeks with him and his mother at La Terrasse. When returning her to Madame Beck's school in chapter 21, he promises to "write—just any cheerful nonsense that comes into my head" to help Lucy "keep up [her] courage" by showing her that "my mother and myself" are "true friends" who will "not forget you." (264) The Letter figures here as a signifier of remembrance and token of a promise, testimony to the continuance of relationships that, during her time at La Terrasse, "cured" Lucy of her ailments by supplying her with social being and the opportunity to develop a closer relationship to Dr. John. Entitled "Reaction," this chapter describes Lucy's reactions to Dr. John's promise of a letter – "struggles with the natural character, the strong nature of the bent of the heart . . . to give [one's] actions and conduct that turn which Reason approves and which Feeling, perhaps, too often opposes." (207) Lucy's Reason tells her that it would be "folly" to build on the promise of a letter; that even if "Graham" wrote once, he might not write again; that if he should write and she should reply, she must not, must "*never,*" "express" what she "feels." But refusing to be "crushed, cowed and broken" by her Reason, Lucy breaks free of its bonds to "give a truant hour to Imagination," to "divine Hope," and to the feelings of her heart. (206) Her opposite reactions to the promise of The Letter thus reveal the daily deception she practices: the calm and restrained face that she invariably shows others, the "constitutional reserve of manner" that characterizes her public self, are a disguise, a mask, a shutter she drops between her in-door and outdoor selves to keep expressions of feeling in and the gaze of others out. As her name, struggles and lyrical imagery attest, at this point in time, she is both "Miss Snowe" and "Lucy," both that rational, icily repellent, wintry out-door self that she shows the world and that bright, warm, yearning, heartfelt being "in-doors, " both "the pink and pattern of governess-correctness" and "the natural character" within. We are assured that "both portraits are correct." (208)

Chapter 21, also describes The Letter's arrival, two weeks after the promise that has "haunted [her] brain." The Letter is now a precious, symbolic material object. Lucy details how The Letter was delivered to her desk in class after the arrival of the post. She lingers on the letter's white cover, its vermilion red seal, the impress of John-Graham's initials, the address to "Miss Lucy Snowe" in his "clean, clear, equal, decided hand;" the firm, substantial feel of the letter in her hand. She describes the care she took to lock the letter up from prying eyes until she had time to read it. This was "the letter of [her] hope, the fruition of [her] wish . . . the ransom from [her] terror;" she held in her hands "a morsel of joy" and its meanest and most mundane features were precious to her. (276–277) Lucy's response is contrasted with M. Paul's contrary but equally extravagant reaction to The Letter. M. Paul responds to what was to her a "life-sustaining . . . Godsend" by casting her "vicious glances" and finding cause to rage and storm. And while she seeks to secrete it and her reactions to it in her most secret physical and mental places, he seeks to insert himself between the Letter and her – "interfering" by intercepting The Letter from the portress when it arrives and delivering it to Lucy himself; interfering by forcing her to turn her attention from it to him; interfering by telling her he knows that she is saving it, like a special treat, to be enjoyed when she is alone.

Chapter 22, "The Letter," turns to Lucy's reading of it and of its author. Lucy describes her quest for a candle, her desperate yet comical efforts to find somewhere in the school where she can be alone to read it, her first impressions of its contents, and The Letter's disappearance in the course of the interruption produced by her sighting of the "spectral" nun, when Dr. John and others burst into her garret in response to her cries. This chapter works with contrasts between different reactions to The Letter as signifier of "overpowering happiness." Lucy's reaction to it at the time, when she read it as a poor English teacher in a frosty garret, and it seemed "juice of a divine vintage," and "vital comfort," is contrasted with her reaction to it when she reads it again it "in after years" in the knowledge that Dr. John would pain her and that they would lose touch, when it appears "simply good-natured" and "by feeling touched but not subdued." (293) A covert, unstated *peripeteia* and *anagnorisis* have intervened to make her aware of "the shallow origin" of her happiness in the garret and of its fleeting character. (284) But though separated by time, and held together by memory, "both portraits are correct."

One reason for the intervening *anagnorisis* is hinted by the implicit contrast that follows between Dr. John's reaction in the attic to Lucy's "frantic" search for The Letter, which he had hidden in his waistcoat, and M. Paul's reaction to her concealed emotion about the letter at the end of the last chapter. Both men intrude themselves between Lucy and her Letter. But rather than withholding the Letter he had intercepted, M. Paul delivered it. Though infuriated by it, he demonstrated with rough kindness, by word and deed, that he understood both what the letter meant to her and the pain it might cause her, by lending her his handkerchief and assuring her that she would not be alone: "I shall read the billet's tenor in your eyes." (281). But Dr. John "teasingly torments" her in order to satisfy his "vanity" by extracting from her a confession of how much The Letter meant to her as his price for returning it. He treats her emotion, her visible anguish, and despair, merely as medical symptoms of "a nervous state," which he recommends she counteract by "cultivating happiness." In contrast with M. Paul's penetration, Dr. John's blind insensibility makes The Letter what M. Paul thought it – a signifier of the pain and torment that Graham-John has long occasioned her. In these analogical scenes, Bronte shifted the issue of miscommunication between lovers to the difference between lovers themselves: here incomprehension, insensibility, and dilatoriness mark the shallowness of the false lover, concern, penetration, and urgency, the affection of the true lover.

Not surprisingly, therefore, when Lucy comes to answer The Letter in chapter 23, she writes two answers: one for herself, which gives expression to "the full liberal impulse of Feeling" in "the language of strongly adherent affection;" and one in her public persona "under the dry unstinting check of Reason," which she sends Dr. John. And then, after Lucy's visit to the theatre to see Vashti with Dr. John, and their meeting there with Paulina Maria de Bassompierre and her father, the letters unaccountably cease. Chapter 24 is devoted to the agonies Lucy suffered during seven long weeks of "inward winter" when she seemed to have "dropped out of the memory of her friends." Emphasizing how differently time passes for "those who live in retirement . . . in the seclusion of schools" and for "the denizens of a freer world" whose days are filled with "events and hurry" in an echo of Anne's observation in *Persuasion* (308), she portrays her bad dreams and interrupted sleep, her desperate efforts to "lock up" her emotions and "bear up," and her repeated reading and rereading of the five letters she had by now received from Dr. John. As signifiers of Dr. John's amnesia and of her own "oblivion," as tokens of a broken promise and of wanting friendship, the letters made her feel that she was "going mad from solitary confinement."

Eventually, Lucy gets news of Dr. John's visits to the Bassompierres from Ginevra who is Paulina's cousin, and eventually a letter comes. Lucy is bitterly disappointed and thinks her "fate too cruel to bear" when she sees "a pale female scrawl instead of a firm masculine hand" on its cover. And she has good cause. For Mrs. Bretton's letter of invitation – which stands out as the only fully transcribed letter in these chapters – indicates Lucy's real position with regard to the Brettons and foreshadows her cruel fate. Mrs. Bretton demonstrates her complete unconsciousness of the pain that her long silence, and that of her son, have caused Lucy: "I daresay you have been just as busy and happy as ourselves at La Terasse." (315) Living in a different reality, filled with "events and hurry," Mrs. Bretton cannot begin to understand Lucy's reality; indeed, in contrast with Lucy's obsession with The Letter, she has not given her any thought. The joke she recounts playing on Graham by putting a woman's sky blue turban on his head while he slept explains why. The turban is associated with Paulina; she was teasing her son about Paulina's sway over his mind. Lucy does not grasp what the letter is telling her about Graham-John and Paulina, or connect his turn to Paulina to the seven-week epistolary silence she has endured – until her visit to the Brettons in the next chapter. This shows her that she is treated with the same kindness as always by the Brettons and Bassompierres and reduced, as in their childhood, to a mere looker-on monitoring and recording the dynamics of a relationship between Graham and Paulina in which she can participate only as comforter and confidante.

Chapter 26, "A Burial," opens with two further physical disappearances of the letters. They disappear temporarily from Lucy's bureau when Madame Beck removes them to read them as part of her usual surveillance of everyone in her school. Madame Beck's reaction to them changes her relationship to Lucy: impressed by their testimony to Lucy's familiarity with the Brettons, Madame Beck's "respect" for Lucy is "improved into distinction." Her thinking here is echoed by Genevra who bases her question, "Who are you, Miss Snowe?" on the same assumption as Madame Beck: that social position is what gives Lucy, and everyone else in this hierarchical society, their identity. Genevra asks who "Miss Snowe" is because, seeing that someone she once dismissed as "a nobody" has risen from old lady's companion, to nursery governess, to school teacher, to friend of "that proud chit, my cousin," she is no longer sure how to place her. Genevra, who is herself striving to rise from poverty to social distinction, suspects Lucy of using the same calculatingly "cool hand" to advance herself in society that she employs herself.

When the letters disappear from Lucy's bureau for a second time and are returned in an untidy manner uncharacteristic of Madame Beck, Lucy suspects that M. Paul has removed and read them. The letters' exposure to

M. Paul is presented as one reason for Lucy's decision to bury them. The other reason for burying them derives from their disappearance in another sense: Lucy's realization that now that Dr. John was courting Paulina, there would be no further letters from him. Comparing the stream of letters to a river on whose banks she had sojourned, Lucy observes that the river's life-giving waters were leaving her field and "bending to another course." Though "the change was right, just, natural," she had "loved" her river, and wept and grieved for its loss. (340) She emphasizes that "I was not only going to hide a treasure—I meant also to bury a grief." (343). Once "the Hope" had died, The Letters became mere "mementos," signifiers of a past, of feelings and of hopes that had to be buried, made to disappear for a fourth and final time, to prevent sight of them from "stabbing the heart each moment by the sharp revival of regret."

The passage of The Letter from its promise to its burial leaves multiple lacunae. For instance, we are not told explicitly what hope or grief Lucy was burying with the letters; why M. Paul was so infuriated with its arrival, why Lucy suspects him of poking about in her bureau, or indeed why he is suddenly introduced as a figure who looms so large in Lucy's consciousness that his every action and reaction must be reported. These lacunae are addressed only now, as she prepares to put The Letters in the ground, to invite a different, retrospective view of these pivotal chapters. They read quite differently in light of the new knowledge that now appears.

There have been scattered hints throughout these chapters of what hope The Letter signified – for instance in "the language of strongly adherent affection" that Lucy expressed and suppressed in her answer to The Letter, or in relating her grief to a "destiny" that condemned her to living life "single-handed." Lucy now clarifies the issue by explaining why she has only been willing to hint: women were not supposed to entertain "warmer feelings" where "they have a conviction this would be an absurdity" (294); and a person is not obliged to "state facts" that would make them "contemptible in [their] own eyes" and in those of others. (358) For a woman, loving a man who does not love her with so much persistence and intensity that she almost wastes away, is an absurdity. And rejection so complete that her affection and devotion are not even noticed, makes her seem contemptible, unworthy of a man's love. Lucy was therefore careful to "keep [such] fatal facts out of sight" or to surround them with "an accumulation of small defences." (359) Women were still "Compell'd to stifle what they feign would tell/While Truth commands, but Honour must rebel." But viewed in retrospect, this means that what Lucy had been recounting was her humiliation, shame, and self-contempt.

M. Paul's presence in these chapters is also explained now, after the burial of the Letters, when her narrative turns fully to M. Paul's "affection" and "true friendship," which henceforth become the dominant thread in her story. Lucy describes how M. Paul courted her by provoking her into showing her passionate and unregulated, "indocile and audacious," "natural character." Refusing to let Lucy be "a poor self-swindler who lies to [her]self" (387) and judging that her "judgment is warped," M. Paul assumes the familiar role of tutor-lover. He forces honesty from Lucy, and in the battles between them, "stamps with his deep brand of approval" only what was "struggling into life" from "the furtherest recesses of existence" in her heart. His "vicious glances" at the arrival of The Letter and expectation that it would give her pain, had been part of the same rough courtship. Equally important, M. Paul teaches Lucy to express her thoughts and feelings honestly in writing by setting her essays on abstract themes. Lucy learns to activate her Imagination and seek illumination from "The Creative Impulse" to write "impromptu" essays for him. She learns to "breathe life" into abstract arguments about Human Justice or The Creative Impulse (413) by personifying abstract ideas and dramatizing their actions and interactions in settings borrowed from the real world; and she learns to express her feelings in lyrical metaphors. Lucy's narrative account of her successive reactions to The Letter used these same devices to communicate her struggles between Reason and Feeling, Fear and Hope. In a retrospective view, it now becomes apparent that the chapters devoted to The Letter already contained Lucy's grateful testimony to the teaching and influence of M. Paul's "true friendship" in her very style of writing, as well as in her openness about her feelings, her lack of self-deception, and her acknowledgment of the "natural character" that, thanks to him, had struggled into life.

This pivotal sequence of chapters closes with The Letter's final appearance in chapter 31 as a mere reminder of buried feeling and of a "curious one-sided friendship." (420) With her foot resting victoriously on the stone sealing the letters' sepulcher and M. Paul literally as well as figuratively standing behind her, Lucy is able to say wholeheartedly: "Good night, Dr. John; you are good, you are beautiful; but you are not mine." But Lucy is not done with Dr. John's letters yet. She has yet to confront his clandestine correspondence with Paulina in analogical epistolary scenes. Paulina's narrative to Lucy in chapter 32, "The First Letter," repeats in brief all the phases of reception that Lucy's narrative covered at length before.

Giving Lucy sight of Graham-John's correspondence with Paulina, shows her and us the difference between the letters he wrote as a casual act of kindness, and the letters he wrote the woman he loved and sought to marry despite the obstacles presented by her father. In chapter 37, in a conversation between them composing the reception narrative to one of Graham-John's letters, Paulina also raises Genevra's question about Lucy's identity again – "Lucy, I wonder if anybody will ever comprehend you altogether."

Their talk turns to the role played by wealth and social position in forging characters and destinies. Paulina and Lucy address assumptions about identity that are common to Ginevra, Madame Beck, and M. Bassompierre, all of whom equate who a person is with their position in society and thus with their public self, and agree that while social position might determine a person's destiny, it did not "comprehend [people] altogether" since it made them interchangeable. Graham-John required wealth and beauty in his "victrix;" so had their social positions been reversed, had Lucy had wealth and social standing and Paulina been the poor grisette, he might have written to Lucy before as he wrote to Paulina now. But as M. Paul observes, affinities in the "natural character" counted for something too. M. Paul and Lucy are united, despite differences of nationality, class, and wealth, by the fact that they are "alike— there is affinity between us," which extends even to their looks. Paulina and Graham-John too are united across social differences by their affinities, as are Ginevra and Hamal. Affinities duel with social position in the last part of the novel to determine each couple's fate. While Paulina and Graham-John rapidly overcome M. Bassompierre's objections to the disparities in their wealth and social status, these demonstrate their force by condemning Ginevra and Hamal to aristocratic poverty and by ruthlessly tearing M. Paul and Lucy apart. The question of how far social position determines fate is therefore never definitively settled.

What has been demonstrated in the pivotal chapters is that Ginevra's question, "Who are you Miss Snowe?" was misguided not only because it equated identity exclusively with social standing and the public self, but also because it assumed that identity is something fixed that Miss Snowe "is." Benchmarked by The Letter, Lucy's perceptions, emotions, and reactions shifted with each change in circumstances, as did the relation between her in-door and out-door selves, and her very sense of self. And as circumstances continued to alter, they also altered her retrospective views. As Lucy explains, each retrospective "revival is imperfect" because subject to "conditions" in the present that bring some "circumstances, persons, even words and looks" back to mind and make others "slip the memory." (366) One might say that Bronte was extending plural and discontinuous occasional selves from "out-door" views of the self-disguising character to "in-door views" of "the natural character," and from performance and perceptions to recollections, to show that personal identity on all levels was occasional, fluid, and contingent, and that "in-door" views and retrospective views were the most occasional, fluid, and contingent views of all.

This is also why Bronte gives Lucy Snowe's first-person memoir the form of an open letter. Open letters, which became popular in print culture at the turn of the nineteenth century, eliminated superscriptions, subscriptions, and the usual intra-diegetic character-recipient, to address novel-readers directly and exploit the familiar letter's character as an informal address. *Villette* begins and ends *in medias res* as letters, not memoirs and realist novels, do. Memoirs or autobiographies are generally composed at the end of a life or career, once things have run their course and outcomes are known; and like the classical works of literary realism that are written from "the vantage point of the end," they foster the kind of retrospective narrative that selects and reshapes the past teleologically according to whether things turned out well or badly in the end. But Bronte was invoking a narrative-epistolary tradition that had recognized, at least since Aphra Behn, that a letter is always situated: it issues from a particular place at a particular date, to convey the consciousness of its writer, and what is of concernment to her, at a particular halting point in the flowing streams of life, when the future is still uncertain and final outcomes are unknown. This was a tradition that had also acknowledged, at least since Lennox, Burney, and Smith, that we pause at intervals to look back all the time; and at least since Austen, that retrospective narratives do not correspond to the way things actually unfolded in the past but, instead, supply what were in reality contingent events with meaningful design.

Lucy invokes the force of these insights by emphasizing at the end that she is writing her retrospective letter-narrative from the cusp of a particularly contingent place, at a time when her "mind is tortured by the pangs of uncertainty (the events then hidden in the womb of fate)." She is writing after three years of Paul's absence in Guadaloupe, which had been "the happiest in her life" because she at last had all she needed to be happy as a single woman: "my sort of life apart" and "one friend of my own." (494). She had her "sort of life apart" in the independence, intellectual engagement and meaningful, other-oriented work of successfully running her own school. She had the emotional sustenance she craved and a soul-mate's companionship in the letters with which Paul's "true friendship" unceasingly supplied her. But as Lucy also tells us, she is recording her perceptions in and of the past at a moment when circumstances are about to change in unforeseeable ways, depending on the outcome of a storm at sea that will either end her happy life as a single woman or leave her single still, but unhappily without "one friend of my own." As her circumstances change one way or the other, her retrospective narrative will change. She will never be able to remember or write her story in precisely the same way again.

The Pivotal Letter as Nonevent: Trollope's *Phineas Finn*

Recurrence of epistolary *peripeteiae* in narrative-epistolary fiction made its subversion possible and perhaps desirable. Once they had become sufficiently familiar, novelists could play against readerly expectations by marking the place where a *peripeteia* and *anagnorisis* should occur – and withholding them. This section offers one such example. It is not the first by any means. But Trollope's treatment of Lady Laura's last encounter with her now dilatory lover in *Phineas Finn* (1869), which can be viewed as a rewrite of the *peripeteia* in Lucy's relations to Dr. John when he is courting Paulina, pursues the idea that opinions change with circumstances to denaturalize assumptions about *peripeteia* that even critical narrative-epistolary novelists continued to share. These assumptions include the idea that *peripeteiae* are preceded by an error due to some form of ignorance or miscommunication rather than by a conscious choice; that *anagnorises* in everyday life involve questions of truth rather than of belief; and that the pivotal moment changes the whole situation for everyone at once. Like the epistolary *peripeteia* in *Villette*, the counter-pivotal scene discussed in this section contributes unobtrusively to what Nicholas Dames calls the narrative's "forward propulsion (suspense, surprise and denouement)."[19] As part of a series of analogical scenes, it also revisits issues raised by Lucy's suffering and terrible aloneness when abandoned by her false and dilatory lover.

Lady Laura had refused Phineas Finn's proposal of marriage in favor of marriage to Mr. Kennedy, a wealthy member of parliament of her own class, three years before. But unhappy in her marriage and realizing that she has "really" loved Phineas all along, she now decides to leave her husband. Like Lucy, Lady Laura is turning from one man to another. She had cleverly engineered the *peripeteia* in her relationship with her husband by using a telegram and a letter, whose contents she ensured were unseen by him,

to nudge him into believing that Phineas was her lover. And in what the
illustrator of 1873 recognized as a key scene, she now forces a reluctant
Phineas to read the letter she wrote her husband explaining why she is
leaving him. The putative *peripeteia* that follows occurs at Lady Glencora's
garden party at the very cusp of this change in her marital situation. As she
tells Phineas in the letter's prefatory narrative, she "has come alone," having
left her husband this letter that he will have read by now, and she will leave
the garden party with her father to return to her ancestral home.[20]
"Compell'd to stifle what [she] feign would tell," she tries to convey the
peripeteia this permits in her relationship with Phineas by making him read
her parting letter to her husband, which uses Kennedy's accusation that
Phineas is her lover as her justification for leaving him, and by insisting that
Kennedy's accusation concerns Phineas too:

> After what you have said to me it is impossible that I should return to your
> house. I shall meet my father at the Duke of Omnium's and have already
> asked him to give me an asylum. It is my wish to remain wherever he may be,
> whether in town or in the country . . . .You have accused me of having
> a lover. You cannot have expected that I should continue to live with you
> after such an accusation. For myself I cannot understand how any man can
> have brought himself to bring such a charge against his wife . . . That it is
> untrue I believe you must be as well aware as I am myself. How intimate
> I was with Mr. Finn, and what were the limits of my intimacy with him you
> knew before I married you. After our marriage I encouraged his friendship
> till I found that there was something in it that displeased you—and, after
> learning that, I discouraged it. You have said that he is my lover, but you
> have probably not defined for yourself that word very clearly. You have felt
> yourself slighted because his name has been mentioned with praise, and
> your jealousy has been wounded because you have thought that I have
> regarded him as in some way superior to yourself. You have never really
> thought he was my lover—that he spoke words to me which others might
> not hear, that he claimed from me aught that a wife may not give, that he
> received aught which a friend should not receive. The accusation has been
> a coward's accusation. (546–547)

But Phineas fails to make the discovery that her hints and this letter herald
and invite: that the way is now open to him to renew their former
"intimacy" and be her lover in deed. He shows his incomprehension in
the prefatory narrative by wondering: "Why did she come to him with this
story—to him whom she had been accused of entertaining as a lover: to
him who of all her friends was the last whom she should have chosen as the
recipient for such a tale?" (545) His reference to himself as one of Lady
Laura's many friends, reminds us that Phineas has moved on since his

proposal of marriage to her three years earlier. He has transferred his affections to Violet Effingham, and his head is now full of the possibility that Violet's termination of her engagement to Lord Chiltern would reopen the way for him with *her*. Phineas is so far from considering himself Lady Laura's lover now, that his only response to the letter is to interpret its charge that Kennedy is "jealous" of his "superiority" as a reference to his professional success in Parliament, rather than to Lady Laura love. Here the miscommunication between Lady Laura and Phineas derives from the fact that Phineas has "gone as circumstances have directed me" (543) and that these have led him and Lady Laura in opposite directions to incompatible present realities. Taken to its logical conclusion, then, the idea that "as circumstances change, opinions alter" means that lovers' circumstances can change over time in incommensurable ways and that their opinions of what is desirable and/or feasible change accordingly.

The resulting a-synchronicity in Lady Laura's and Phineas's sentiments and the lack of concurrence in their present desires abort the *peripeteia* in their present relationship, which Lady Laura invites. This is indicated, after Phineas's unsatisfactory response to the letter, by their tacit agreement to displace the pivotal moment retrospectively from the present to three years earlier, when Lady Laura "had chosen to be Lady Laura Kennedy" rather than "Lady Laura Finn." (465) She may wish now that she had "believed" Phineas then when he told her that Kennedy was "weak and poor and unworthy." (547) And Phineas may wonder now "How would it have been with both of them if Lady Laura had accepted him three years ago, when she had consented to join her lot with that of Mr. Kennedy, and had rejected him?" (547) But she had weighed her options then and made her choice; there was no going back now to reverse her decision and recreate the moment that had passed. Lady Laura had tried to do so. She had used her letter to her husband to create an opportunity for "that young man who would have been her lover, if she would have let him" then (465) to become her lover now; but he does not even notice. Lady Laura realizes that she has made "a shipwreck of myself" only after Phineas's reaction to the letter makes his present indifference plain. But this is no *anagnorisis*: she already knows the truth about Phineas – that he is an "adventurer" and a "fickle" lover, in whose "heart . . . love can have no durable hold." She told him so during their previous encounter (474). All she discovers now is a fact – that she has no future with Phineas. She therefore chooses to leave Phineas as she left Kennedy, "alone." (547)

This is *peripeteia* anticipated and undelivered, *peripeteia* as a nonevent. Trollope uses it to revisit questions about the truth of retrospective views.

Lady Laura opens the reception narrative by describing the retrospective narrative in her letter as "at any rate true." (547) And unlike her husband – who, having caught her in a lie of omission, "does not believe a word I say" (547) – both Phineas and Violet Effingham are willing to believe that her letter is true. But comparison to earlier narrative events shows that Lady Laura has justified leaving Kennedy by again committing lies of omission. She "forgets" that she has told her brother that she needs a reason to leave Kennedy, which the world will understand and accept – "To be simply miserable as I am, is nothing to the world." (464–465). She omits to mention that she has provided herself with the reason she needs by using that unseen telegram and unseen letter to falsely suggest to her husband that Phineas is her lover. Phineas also rewrites the past: erasing months of sorrow and despair after Lady Laura's rejection of his proposal, he only remembers now that he "soon got over" her "and as far as he himself was concerned, had never regretted Lady Laura's marriage." (548) Indeed, Phineas so "absolutely ignored his old passion for Lady Laura" that, like a Bosvil or Wentworth, he "regarded himself as a model of constancy" to Violet Effingham (443). Retrospective versions of the past do not coincide with the truth of what happened. It is foolish to believe that they represent greater truth about the past than perceptions contemporary with events. But here that is not because they select among prior possibilities in light of the outcome as in Austen's rainy-day scene; it is because – like the choices people make, and their judgments of other people's versions of events – retrospective narratives only represent states of belief. Lady Laura tells Kennedy in her letter what she now believes, including that she does not believe that he ever really thought that Phineas was her lover. She tells Phineas that she wishes she had "believed" what he said about Kennedy when she made her choice on the basis of her beliefs then – she had "accepted the owner of Loughlinter" in preference to Phineas whom she "could have loved" because as she told herself then: "I verily believe that I shall thus do my duty in that sphere of life to which it has pleased God to call me" and that "I will love him" once his wife. (122, 123)

Beliefs are opinions about what is true. They govern everyday transactions. Trollope indicated that beliefs have no epistemological or predictive value by using analogical scenes to show that different choices based on different beliefs in slightly different circumstances can all lead to the same unfortunate outcome. In the analogical conversation that follows the non-*peripeteia* in Lady Laura's relationship to Phineas, Violet tells Phineas that though she has broken her engagement with Chiltern, she has told Chiltern she loves him and "cannot now give [herself] to another man." (550)

Believing that it is wrong to love again, Violet has made the choice that Lady Laura had considered making three years earlier: to remain single living with her father rather than risk the "dangerous" marriage to the suitor she could love, or put this marriage out of her power by marrying the suitor she does not, or does not yet, love. Violet's constancy to Chiltern leaves Phineas in the same position as his inconstancy leaves Lady Laura: he views Violet's rejection of him as the shipwreck of his fortunes and it leaves him, like Lady Laura, "alone—quite alone." (550) Before his encounter with Lady Laura's letter, Phineas conversed with Madame Goesler, who, as she now reminds us, resembles a Lucy who has returned to England as a rich widow – her wealth derives from her marriage to a wealthy foreigner, and she must periodically go abroad to attend to her business interests there. Like Lucy, she is accustomed to be much alone. Madame Goesler who has just rejected a proposal from the Duke of Omnium, whom she does not love, on the grounds that it is folly to marry outside one's social sphere, explains that she considers it equally foolish to marry a man like Phineas whom she could love merely as a "friend." This leaves her, like Lady Laura, coming to Lady Glencora's garden party and leaving it, "alone." (540)

By the time they leave Lady Glencora's garden party, then, despite their different choices, all the principal characters – Mr. Kennedy, Lady Laura, Chiltern, Violet, Madame Goesler, and Phineas – are alone. But as there are different possible choices and different possible beliefs, there are different possible ways of being alone. No generalization – such as Lady Laura's, that while "no man is capable of suffering … a woman, if she is thrown aside, does suffer" (474) – is therefore universally true. Madame Goesler tells Phineas that she is "much accustomed to be alone," and is "in truth an animal that feeds alone and lives alone." (540) She chooses to have "no particular friend," because she has no opinion of friends in high society: "What are such friends worth? What would they do for me?" According to Lady Laura, Mr. Kennedy is likewise "an animal that feeds alone:" his preference for solitude and prayer to sociality make him fitter to live without a wife. After Violet breaks their engagement to Chiltern, he writes her: "I live much alone; but you are always with me;" but when Phineas finds himself "alone—quite alone" after Violet's rejection, he wants to throw himself in a river to drown; while Violet, who leaves Lady Glencora's party with Laura and her father, has friends to mitigate her solitary state. These are not the only possibilities, as Trollope indicates by placing all these pivotal and non-pivotal moments at Lady Glencora's garden party. For having been forced to abandon the unsuitable man she loved, rebellious and unconventional Lady Glencora had married cold, undemonstrative

Plantagenet Pallister without loving him, and had made the marriage work, as Lady Laura thought to make her marriage to Mr. Kennedy work. We have yet to see what Lady Laura will make of being "alone." But it should be clear that this chapter's title, "The Horns," refers not to the horns of cuckoldry that Lady Laura's letter addresses, but to the horns of dilemmas that force characters to make choices that impact the course of their lives. The choices characters make generate *peripeteiae* in the circumstances they have to live with; but whatever these circumstances turn out be, they will have to live with them as best they can– and without any *anagnorisis* or epiphany to give them meaning much less a place in some larger design.

In the garden scene, Trollope used his representation of *peripeteia* as nonevent to screen another kind peripatetic absence. For Lady Laura and Phineas are ignoring or stupidly underestimating the *bouleversement* launched by her letter-narrative. While the two of them think and talk about their relationship and part in the belief that Lady Laura can return to her father's house and live there as she had before her marriage, reverberations of her letter and her fall are rumbling behind their back. Leaving Mr. Kennedy is the really consequential *peripeteia* in Lady Laura's life, as Victorians familiar with upper-middle class societal norms would have known. This is something Phineas will discover only two years later in *Phineas Redux* when he and we next meet father and daughter in Dresden. It is to such unstated and unperceived epistolary pivots that we now turn.

Covert Epistolary Pivots and Letter-Narratives in Smith, Austen, and Trollope

Love Intrigues also presented one pivot as a screen for another, as we saw, but it relied on simultaneous competing narrative constructions to do so. In what I am calling covert epistolary pivots, an embedded letter-narrative was used to portray a situation in which a *peripeteia* that is unperceived by the characters and sometimes also by novel-readers on a first reading, is hidden in full view. Charlotte Smith introduced this form of epistolary pivot in *The Old Manor House*, her second most popular novel, while conjoining to it two important characteristics of her previous letter-narratives and verbalizing or even theorizing the three elements together: the spatial distance and the temporal distance of the letter-narrative from its reader together with the cognitive distance of imperception. These three elements continued to be linked in Austen's and Trollope's adaptations of the covert pivot, as we will see in what follows.

Embedded letter-narratives were a signature feature of Charlotte Smith's narrative-epistolary fiction – she experimented with them throughout her career. A literary outgrowth of sociable letters of news, letter-narratives were primarily associated with epistolary novels, travel letters, and letters from a gentleman in town to his friend in the country before Smith began to incorporate them into her narrative-epistolary fictions in her first novel, *Emmeline* (1788). This substantially changed their character. For once embedded in a narrative, letter-narratives inserted a partial, usually fragmentary, first-person narrative into the principal omniscient third-person narration that was boxed off from the latter by the letter form's characteristic opening salutations and closing subscriptions as well as by its prefatory and reception materials. This enabled Smith to confront two different and/ or conflicting realities – that inhabited by the letter-writer and described in the letter-narrative with that inhabited by the character-reader and described in the third-person narrative – to invite comparison between the two. In *The Old Manor House*, it also enabled her to use a letter-narrative to portray a reality in which a *peripeteia* was occurring that neither of the correspondents perceived.

Smith had also consistently deprived her embedded letter-narratives of agency and instrumentality – she portrayed them as something people only read. Before Smith, narrative-epistolary novelists emphasized the proximity created by letters' ability to "make the absent present" and intervene in ongoing events, even when they came from afar. In *Betsy Thoughtless*, for instance, Betsy is placed at the center of a network of correspondents – friends, brothers, and advisors –whose letters bear directly on the heroine's plot. Most are also integrated into Betsy's domestic circle by being discussed and acted upon or by being woven back into her history through their empirical aftereffects. By contrast, when placing her heroine at the center of a web of correspondents in *Emmeline* – which Austen and Scott both admired – Smith used the two, still sketchy, letter-narratives sent to her heroine at Clapham to mark Emmeline's physical, moral, and experiential distance both from her uncle's family and from her closest friends, while indicating their merely cognitive character by denying them agency. Where instrumental letters summoned their interlocutors to action and intervened in the course of the plot, Smith's letter-narratives converted their addressees into mere readers–observers of events and recipients of epistolary information that they could not, or would not, act upon.

The letter-narrative containing the covert pivot in *The Old Manor House* works with all these features. The only letter to reach Orlando in America, it erupts into the narrative of his experiences as a British soldier in General

Burgoyne's army with troubling news from afar: Monimia's account of what has happened since his departure from England both to his own family and at Rayland Hall, where she has been subject to repeated sexual attack by Sir John Belgrave. By collecting in one place all that its recipient did not and could not be expected to know, Monimia's letter both revisits the issue of lacking or inadequate knowledge which, as we saw, preoccupied narrative-epistolary novelists from Behn's *Love Letters* on, and confronts Orlando's reality in America with reality back home. But Smith gives this an additional twist by dividing Monimia's letter-narrative stylistically into two parts.

Monimia details as a novelist might what she has directly seen and experienced herself – notably Sir John's terrifying efforts to seduce or rape her – recounting this in a series of visualizable scenes, complete with dialogue and descriptions of her sensations and reflections at the time. But she uses general terms to tell Orlando about changes at the Manor and in his family, which she knows only by observation or hearsay: "All your friends have suffered greatly by Isabella's going from them, and by their not knowing what is become of her." Already present in this part of the letter, in Monimia's report of Mrs. Rayland's failing health and of the crooked new estate manager that Mrs. Leonard has introduced into the Hall, are the elements of the *peripeteia* which, unbeknownst to Monimia as well as to Orlando, will make Orlando Mrs. Rayland's heir and oblige him to claim his inheritance at law. These changes have already begun to change Orlando's destiny behind his back, so to speak, while he is occupied elsewhere. But their significance is overlooked due to Monimia's obliviousness to their import, to Orlando's Philander-like failure to take any notice of this part of her letter and to his Philander-like emotional reaction to what is vividly shown:

> ... Mrs Rayland ordered Patterson to lead the chaise round thither, and stopped some moments there, while she talked to the carpenter and plasterer, who were just going from their work. She kindly said to me 'If you are tired, Mary, sit down at my feet and rest yourself.' – I assured her I was not; but she bade me get her a glass of water out of the house, and give her a few drops, lest she should find the ride too much before she got home. There was not a glass in the house; so I ran across the way to James Carter's cottage, which is, you know, about fifty yards beyond the lodge, on the opposite side. His wife went out with the water, and I followed her; when a gentleman attended by two servants rode up so very fast, that his horse almost trampled on me before I could cross the road. He checked it, however, when he saw me, and exclaiming with a great oath –'My lovely little-wood-nymph! By all that's sacred, she shall not now escape me!' He then alighted from his horse

and (as I conclude, not seeing Mrs. Rayland and her servants, who were concealed partly by the projection of the lodge on that side, and partly by the slight turning in the road) rudely seized me. – I shrieked aloud . . . ."[21]

As the reception narrative indicates, Smith was deploying the power of narrative in this part of the letter together with the vaunted ability of words to summon up vivid images in the mind, to transport character-reader and novel-readers back from America to the Manor: "Orlando, during the perusal of this letter . . . forgot where he was. The Hall and all its inhabitants were present to him." The physical and experiential distance separating Monimia, the letter-writer in England, from Orlando, the letter-reader in America, is marked by the sudden brutal contrast between what the letter made "present to him" and what was present around him: Orlando "started up to demand instant satisfaction of Sir John Belgrave . . . when he found himself, by the distance of many thousand miles, deprived of all power of protecting his Monimia, under marching orders to remove he knew not whither, and cut off from all communications with her." (363–364) The miraculous power of letters to "make the absent present" and to bring the distant close, which had been touted since the Renaissance, was only a fleeting illusion. Inherent in the act of reading, it did not outlast it. The associated idea, that the force and immediacy of their "silent speech" enabled letters to intervene in their recipients' present as easily and directly as the oral speech of a person in the same room, was equally fallacious. Orlando is "deprived of all power" to intervene in events at the Hall; Monimia's letter is deprived of all power to recall him to England. Awakening from imagined proximity and the illusion of presence when he looks up from the letter, Orlando can only turn back to *his* real present and go wherever the army sends him.

Transitory though it is, the illusion of presence created by Monimia's letter-narrative opens a "prospect" that serves important perspectival functions. Using a letter-narrative to summon up before our eyes events as they transpired in England while we, like Orlando, are immersed in the narrative of what is transpiring in America, confronts one vivid narrative with another, one experienced reality with another, to dramatize the distance between them. In England, Mrs. Rayland has been driving about her estate in a comfortable carriage surrounded by her servants; in America, Orlando has just held his "respectable friend" in his arms as Fleming died from a bullet to the lungs worrying about his "poor wife" at home. In England, Sir John Belgrave has been demonstrating his manhood by forcing himself on a servant girl and bribing male servants to carry clandestine letters of assignation, while Orlando has been plunging into the thickest of the battle and serving his country by leading a "perilous" clandestine expedition to New York. The two worlds, the two realities, and the two forms of manliness could not be more different. Each provides perspective on the other; and comparison of the two makes the vicious irony visible: poor men like Fleming and Orlando are heroically risking their lives in the American war to defend the self-indulgent, timorous life-style of wealthy landed gentry like Sir John and Mrs. Rayland. The prospect of England opened by Monimia's letter-narrative provides a perspective on the American war from outside it, as the brutal American war does on what is occurring at home.

Smith also attached characters' perception or lack of perception to their standpoints at different distances from the events described. The stylistic distinction between Monimia's narrative summaries and her detailed narrative re-presentation of Sir John's sexual assaults distinguishes things she has not thought much about (the future of Mrs. Rayland's estate) from what has preoccupied all her waking hours (preventing Sir John from raping her). Monimia's perspective on reality and understanding of what is really going on is shaped by what is closer or more distant from her personally, and limited both by her direct experience of events and by her pressing personal "concernments" at the time of writing. In writing about Sir John in the re-presented scenes as a narrator-actor describing her own experience, Monimia delineates a personal perspective on events that are not even noticed by Mrs. Rayland and Mrs. Leonard, whose concernments lie elsewhere. That our perspective is limited too is brought home to novel-readers by ensuring that the covert *peripeteia* in Monimia's letter-narrative becomes apparent to us only on a second reading.

Monimia's letter also invokes various forms of temporal distance to indicate that letters have limited value even as narratives of events: "28th June, 1777. Though I know it is yet impossible for me to hear from you, every moment now seems to me an age. –Alas, Orlando, how little satisfactory was the short letter I received from Portsmouth … .You have now been gone six long – long weeks, and that is only a very small portion of the time you are to be absent … " (353–354) Monimia's subjective experience of time compounds the length of her correspondent's absence measured objectively in calendar time, while the time passing between letters conspires with distance to make experienced absence and loss of contact predominate over the momentary satisfaction of epistolary communication. Further implications of loss of contact and temporal lag are brought to the fore when Orlando "recollects" Monimia's letter again eighteen months later on his shipboard journey home and wonders "how many [more] events might in that time have occurred, anyone of which would embitter, with eternal regret, his return to his native country." (378) Like Orlando's Portsmouth letter, Monimia's letter-narrative is past history in relation to any present in which it is read, recollected, or made present to the mind. The history its narrative conveys is "little satisfactory" because a letter necessarily stops short long before any of these presents, leaving its reader(s) in ignorance of what might have occurred between the time its narrative was written and dispatched and the time it was received and read. For a letter's readers, temporal distance translates into narrative lack, historical lag, and crucial information gaps – one cause of the covertness of any *peripeteiae* it may contain. For letter-writers, temporal distance translates into de-realization. Like Monimia's allusion to his Portsmouth letter that reaches Orlando months later near New York, Monimia's letter-narrative has become detached from the reality it once represented by the time it is read; she is no longer "there" where and as she was when her letter was written – a point underlined by Orlando's discovery, on his return to England, that Monimia had left the Manor and disappeared – and neither are circumstances at the Hall.

Austen adopted and corrected Smith's device both in *Pride and Prejudice* and in *Mansfield Park* (1814). When Fanny Price has been banished to Portsmouth by her uncle as Orlando had been banished to America by his aunt, she receives letter-narratives from present and past inhabitants of Mansfield Park. They inform her of what she could not otherwise know about what is happening in her uncle's family to highlight her "present exile from good society and distance from everything that had been wont to interest her."[22] Like Monimia's letter-narrative, their letter-narratives enable Fanny to follow, from afar and as a reader who is unable to intervene, the changes unfolding at a distance in her uncle Bertram's family that will permit and necessitate her return. Austen's use of letter-narratives to convey these changes indicates that Fanny's fate was being determined by what was happening far away, behind her back, and wholly beyond her control. She can only participate in the events recounted in the letters imaginatively as a reader. Austen foregrounded what Smith had left more implicit – that Orlando took from Monimia's letter only what was of immediate concernment to him when he read it, namely, what had happened to Monimia – to insist that it was Fanny's attachment to Edmund and to Mansfield rather than any illusion of presence created by the act of reading, that made everything connected to them so vividly present to her imagination. Fanny's constant preoccupation with these letter-narratives, and anxiety about the outcome of the events unfolding at

Mansfield, outlast the act of reading to demonstrate that while her body was in Portsmouth, her mind was constantly off "where her heart lived" (395). These letter-narratives thus illustrate and concretize Fanny's assertion that "Portsmouth was Portsmouth, Mansfield was home" (430) while demonstrating not merely that a person's mind and body can be in different places even when they are going about the business of everyday life, but more importantly, that inhabiting another time and place in imagination was precisely how a woman coped in a physical location and living situation that was highly disagreeable to her.

Injection into narrative describing Fanny's sojourn with her birth-family at Portsmouth of vivid letter-narratives about her adoptive family at Mansfield juxtaposes the different realities of families at different ranks with different values and ways of life. But where Smith had left her contrast between England and America in *The Old Manor House* implicit, Austen made her contrast explicit by focalizing through Fanny as she "uses her powers of comparing and judging" the conduct of life in these different locations. This tactfully converted a contrast unflattering to the working poor from objective social analysis into an expression of Fanny's private, self-regarding, personal views. In this respect, Fanny's reflections resemble the letter-narratives she receives from Mary Crawford, Edmund, and Lady Bertram, since each has written from their own partial and limited perspective about their own concernments at the time of writing. Though diverse and sometimes mutually contradictory in content, their letter-narratives allow Fanny and novel-readers to watch a new reality – Mansfield after Tom's war-wound, after Julia's disgrace and after betrayals by both Crawfords – emerging unexpectedly and piecemeal over time, as reader-observers contemplating the changing situation from a distance. But they are as "little satisfactory" to Fanny as Monimia's letter-narrative was to Orlando, not only due to physical distance or temporal delay, but more importantly, due to their individual omissions and collective failure to cohere into a seamless whole. When pieced together by Fanny, these narrative fragments leave crucial gaps. The correlative of writing from one's own limited personal perspective is not including everything one's addressee might need or wish to know, especially when, like Fanny, the recipient is considering events from a different perspective of her own.

Fanny discovers from trying to piece together a story from letter-narratives written from other people's diverse perspectives, each of which provides only those fragments of the story that its writer knows or cares about, that key parts of the story are missing. Her questions remain unanswered until her return to Mansfield, where she is able to infer answers to some of them by observation and to fill some gaps from Edmund's confidential and unrecorded oral narrative. But other questions, such as her uncle's thoughts and feelings, remain unanswered and presumably always will; and she remains oblivious to how the letter-narratives explain the covert *peripeteia* that has occurred. Not only did she not realize in Portsmouth while her mind was filled with the narratives conveyed by the letters that the changes they described would encompass her return; but Fanny is so overjoyed at the prospect of finally marrying her dilatory lover that she never wonders at Edmund's shabbily perfunctory proposal or notices what, taken together, those letter-narratives reveal about this *peripeteia* in her fortunes. Like Wentworth, Edmund has turned to the woman who has always loved him only after all other available marital options have fallen through. Edmund marries the only eligible woman left in his circle, knowing he can do so at his pleasure. Worse, he marries Fanny because, as he and his family agree, she is so "suitable." This is hardly the ideal way for a woman to finally get her dilatory man.

Comparison of *Mansfield Park* with the earlier *Pride and Prejudice* is most interesting for the elements that Austen thought important enough to repeat and rework. As we saw in Chapter 1, devoting a whole chapter to her reading of it, emphasizes the fact that Darcy's letter-narrative reduces Elizabeth to a mere reader. As we saw too, Darcy's letter-narrative confronts Elizabeth and novel-readers with a reality quite different from that which she and we have inhabited in the third-person narrative, this time not insignificantly by recounting histories of Wickham and Bingley that are long past. Elizabeth, like Fanny, "uses her powers of comparing and judging" between these different realities; but here the comparison is folded into Elizabeth's (false) *anagnorisis* and indicates, quite wickedly, that neither testing narratives against empirical evidence nor discovering what "really" happened guarantees that the right conclusions must be drawn from the facts. Elizabeth is as helpless to act on the letter-narrative she reads as Fanny or Orlando – but where Fanny compensates by living in her imagination, Elizabeth turns on herself in a violent emotional outburst of bitter self-reproach. Austen was quite insistent on this point: knowing that one is "deprived of all power" to intervene in events does not necessarily entail stepping back, forgetting and like Orlando, going about one's business as before – at least if one is a woman. Precluded from outward action, women turn inward; and women like Elizabeth, Anne, and Marianne turn painfully, even destructively, upon themselves. As in *Mansfield Park*, Austen again deploys an almost invisible covert *peripeteia*. For while Elizabeth's changes of mind and heart are evident to her and to us, those that will induce Darcy to engineer the *peripeteiae* in Jane's and Lydia's stories and ultimately to propose again are screened by his self-justifying epistolary histories, intimated only by the fact that he cares enough to write to correct her preconceptions. Darcy will confess after their reconciliation that the devastating blow that Elizabeth's rejection dealt his pride was already changing his prejudices when he wrote. But in reading Darcy's doubly pivotal missive, novel-readers who know that imbedded letter-narratives are necessarily fragmentary, incomplete, and overtaken by events, may suspect, contrary to Elizabeth, that all may not be over between them yet.

Trollope made the covert *peripeteia* in Lady Laura's letter-narrative a little more obvious than this, since what awaited Laura would be discernible to any novel-reader who knew how upper-middle class Victorian society punished divorcees. He innovated by overlaying this with a projected pivot in Lady Laura's relationship with Phineas that turns into a nonevent and by separating the covert *peripeteia* in the letter-narrative temporally from the *anagnorisis* in Dresden even more radically than Smith and Austen had done by placing them in different novels. Though following *Pride and Prejudice* by making the comparison of two different realities – Lady Laura's life before and after leaving Kennedy – part of the *anagnorisis*, he focalized the shock of discovery through Phineas rather than through her.

Phineas does not see Lady Laura for two years after the garden party in *Phineas Finn*. When he encounters her and her father, Lord Brentford, again in *Phineas Redux*, they are in Dresden. Phineas finds them living "disagreeably" in "exile" and "without society" in a couple of rented rooms, and exhibiting the effects of Laura's marital *peripeteia* shockingly in their very bodies – she "had become old and worn, angular and hard-visaged," positively "middle-aged," while her father had "passed from manhood to senility" and "cared nothing for the outward things of the world around him."[23] Despite the new divorce law and perhaps from fear of contagion, society punished any woman who dared leave or divorce her husband viciously, by ostracism and disgrace. As Lady Laura says: "Who would care to have me at their houses or to come to mine? . . .. I am as much lost to the people who did know me in London as though I had been buried for a century." (85) Her father too has lost all political influence and his place in society as a result of her act. Phineas's pity and horror dramatize the extent of her fall by reflecting on the magnitude of the contrast between Lady Laura as he had seen her before, amongst her friends in the privileged and propertied environment of an elite English garden party, and Lady

Laura as he saw her now, pathetic, pinched, outlawed, and confined to narrow foreign rooms. Lady Laura herself gives the familiar story of the once beloved woman watching her dilatory lover court another, a new twist by confessing that she loves and will always love Phineas and participate vicariously in all his successes and by promising that she will "never be jealous again ... never stand between you and your wife." (87) Though complaining that society is not fair to women, Lady Laura accepts that her own choices and her own acts have made her that suffering silent watcher of her beloved's marriage to another, and that she can expect nothing better. Here Trollope seems as hard on those whose *hamartiae* produced catastrophes as Aristotle: intended or not, Lady Laura could not hope to escape the consequences of her act.

Trollope's formal innovation here was to make the same pivotal letter-narrative *both* instrumental and not, depending on character-readers' personal distance from the event. Considered as the missive that Lady Laura leaves behind for Kennedy to read after she has departed for the garden party and thence for her father's house, Lady Laura's letter-narrative is the very instrument of her separation. It both increases and finalizes the distance between husband and wife that it describes. It thus inexorably sets in motion the *peripetia* that leads to Dresden. This *peripeteia* is covert both in the sense of being unnoticed and of being unrecounted – Lady Laura's social fall and departure from England transpire offstage, behind Phineas's and the novel-reader's back. However, this instrument of Lady Laura's separation is not an instrumental letter for those like Phineas and Lady Laura's friends who read it at the garden party and believe, rightly or wrongly, that it does not concern them. Lack of "concernment" is what converts letters into something people merely read and lay aside. Lack of concern(ment) is what makes friends like Violet Effingham and Phineas believe what they read about the marriage in Lady Laura's letter-narrative and then turn back to their own realities and their own concerns. Lady Laura's friends are certainly not "deprived of all power to intervene," if only by reminding her of how harshly society treats women who leave their husbands. Their failure to even think about what she is risking reveals their lack of real concern for their supposed friend, and the distance they place between the contents of the letter-narrative and themselves. That this too is a choice is made clear by Phineas, who is invited to act upon the letter-narrative during the garden party, and could have done so if he chose. But Phineas is also fooling himself in thinking that the matter is of no concern to him; for when later in *Phineas Redux*, Kennedy acts on Lady Laura's letter-narrative to attack Phineas and publicly undermine his credit, he finds that it had in reality involved him and that he was now obliged to act. Like Smith, then, Trollope worked with standpoints at different distances from the events described and showed that this distance can change over time with changes in circumstances; but he characteristically attributed distance, and assumption of the standpoint of a mere reader, to that reader's choice and beliefs.

Conversation between Phineas and Lady Laura in the Dresden scenes picks up where their conversation left off in the garden scene to allow Lord Brentford to repeatedly ask the question that connects *anagnorisis* to *peripeteia*: why won't Lady Laura return to her husband, why don't she and Phineas "think how much she loses" by not doing so? (2:88) Brentford's phrasing intimates how little Lady Laura had actually *thought* about what she was really doing when she imagined that leaving Kennedy would give her a future with Phineas and how little in that earlier scene, Phineas had thought about anyone but himself. Reflecting now upon how much she loses by leaving Kennedy reveals the illusions upon which her imagination had earlier dwelt: about turning the clock back with Phineas, about living with her father as she had before her marriage, about the dependability of societal friendships, even about the loyalty of her particular friends. Brentford questions whether leaving her husband is worth this terrible, and now fully revealed, personal and social cost. Only Lady Laura's erstwhile letter-narrative, here invoked retrospectively, complicates Lord Brentford's simple binary – live with your husband or suffer all this – to explain why she refuses to return to Kennedy even now. For as Violet and Phineas agreed during the garden party, it convincingly shows how insufferable Mr. Kennedy was and how intolerable the marriage had been. In reality, then, whether or not Lady Laura had been thinking straight at the time, this had been a Hobson's choice – not the *peripeteia* from good to ill-fortune consecrated by Aristotelian theory, but a *peripeteia* from one form of ill-fortune to another. In practice, to "think how much [one] loses" was to think about which of two miserable options one believed the lesser evil. It said a lot that for Lady Laura, even Dresden was better than Kennedy.

Retrospective: On Chimeras in Literary Realism

Earlier, when it was believed that the-thing-itself could not be known, narrative-epistolary novelists worked quite happily with true and false *anagnorises*. The product of faulty observation or reasoning, of excessive emotion or of inadequate knowledge, a false *anagnorisis* could be corrected by a true one, permitting a causal, consequential retrospective narrative to be constructed that satisfactorily explained what had really occurred. It seems that when fiction intervened in all representations so that even immediate perception was only "*founded* on facts," arriving at total, correct comprehension of what had in reality occurred was a wish-fulfilling fantasy, like the inevitable happy ending and other desiderata of Romance. But it also seems that the status and meaning of retrospective narratives began to shift after empiricists began to present themselves as the subjects-supposed-to know. Once positivism, with its insistence that reality could be known and all its underlying laws discovered, became the dominant regime of truth, it became increasingly important for narrative-epistolary novelists both to reaffirm earlier forms of knowledge and to show that it was romantic and chimerical for realism to pretend that reality and truth were faithfully reflected in a single unified or unifying omniscient narrative from the vantage point of the end.[24] Epistolary pivots went to the heart of this issue because the *anagnorisis* produced by the *peripeteia* was traditionally supposed to reveal true knowledge of "what really happened," and because this traditionally took the form of a retrospective narrative that correctly rewrote and re-emplotted the past.[25] As Philip Kennedy and Marilyn Lawrence observe, *anagnorisis* was "invested with the idea of knowledge" with the knowledge it revealed "oscillat[ing] . . . between the relative simplicity of unveiled kinship ties, on the one hand, and psychological – even broadly philosophical – facts pertaining to the human condition, on the other."[26]

In the wake of Roland Barthes and poststructuralism, most critics would agree with Robert Louis Stevenson that the "question of realism . . . regards not in the least degree the fundamental truth, but only the technical method, of a work of art," and with Carlyle that "reality escapes us." As at least some nineteenth-century literati recognized, realism was a set of "fashionable" conventions, not the faithful reflection of reality it pretended to be.[27] Our comparable recognition made it incumbent upon us, as Elizabeth Ermarth put it, "to locate the premises that are implied in realistic conventions," and we have gone about that in two principal ways.[28] Some modern critics tried to restore to literary realism its boasted unity and insight into what Dickens called reality's "subterranean forces" by displacing its truth-claims – for instance, by arguing that realist conventions demonstrated that "the [moral] ideal was achievable through the real."[29] Others went about it more in the spirit of Trollope, who argued (like Wilkie Collins) that "the realistic . . . [is] just so far removed from truth as to suit the erroneous idea of truth which the reader may be

supposed to entertain."[30] Here the underlying premises are demytholo-
gized as merely conventional too. But because some critics now credit
realist novelists with questioning their own representations of reality and
casting doubt upon their own truth,[31] it is important to notice that
Braddon, Trollope, and the other nineteenth-century narrative-epistolary
novelists considered in this chapter denaturalized supposedly "realistic"
narrative conventions precisely because they did not share this view. They
took issue with narratives written from the vantage point of the end, which
retrospectively select and reshape the story as the teleological prehistory of
that end and challenged closure of that iron chain of cause and effect which
"completes a pattern ... creates a sense of necessity" and effaces chance.
Perhaps above all, they contested the idea that a single continuous, unified
or unifying omniscient narrative can constitute a faithful reflection of
reality.[32]

   The epistolary pivots considered here made realism considered as "a
form of understanding and explanation" appear thoroughly unrealistic by
showing that in reality, things happened quite differently from what its
conventions led readers to expect. As we saw, Austen's epistolary pivot in
Persuasion showed that retrospective narratives where "the end writes the
beginning and shapes the middle" to create meaningful design do not
correspond to what happened as things were transpiring: such narratives
controvert the real contingency of events, and belie their own truth inasmuch as the same events support different narratives with different perspectives on what had "really" happened.[33] Bronte and Trollope
demonstrated in different ways that since our retrospective narratives
change as circumstances change, there is in reality no one, final, all-
encompassing true narrative of events. There are only pauses in the fluid
and constantly changing stream of life when someone looks back – so many
serial presents in which shifting *anagnorises* produce shifting constructions
of the past that will almost certainly be overtaken or corrected by events.
Here, as *Villette* points out, each "revival is imperfect" because subject to
"conditions" in the present that bring some "circumstances, persons, even
words and looks" back to mind and make others "slip the memory." (366).
This means that even the same person produces different narrative emplotments of the same events at different junctures, each of which is fragmentary, incomplete, and "to be continued." Moreover, as Trollope, Braddon,
and Collins all liked to show, the past itself is unstable: people and events
one thought safely past have a disconcerting knack of rearing their inconvenient heads in the present at some later date. Time and life are not an
evolving line ending in a full stop.

The narrative-epistolary pivots here also built on Smith's insistence in *Emmeline* and in *The Old Manor House*, that characters live in different realities due not only to their different experiences in different localities but also to the different information at their disposal, while exploiting her fondness for showing how this promoted characters' failure to notice or understand that a *peripeteia* was occurring in someone else's reality that was of concernment to them. Both in *Sense and Sensibility* and *Pride and Prejudice*, Austen highlighted the role of information in characters' perception and discovery of what had "really" happened in someone else's reality by separating *peripeteia* from *anagnorisis* to make *anagnorisis* the fruit of a drawn-out process of investigation and reflection. In *Pride and Prejudice* and *Mansfield Park*, she also explored the possibility that true discoveries might conceal the fact that the real import of events had been overlooked. Bronte in *Villette* and Trollope in the Lady Laura episodes likewise separated *anagnorisis* from *peripeteia* to portray *anagnorisis* as a long, discontinuous and drawn-out process. But where Bronte showed that *peripeteia* and *anagnorisis* could not be achieved without psychological change, painful learning, and new material prospects, Trollope played with different ways of overlooking *peripeteiae* and of misunderstanding the meaning and consequences of reversals. In their different ways, these writers all used their epistolary pivots to show that characters with different realities and different "concernments" at different distances from events produce different narratives, each of which, though containing some truth, was in its own way limited and incomplete.

In reality, then, for these nineteenth-century writers there is no single "vantage point" at the end from which an iron chain of cause and effect can be constructed, no single unbroken narrative that yields omniscient knowledge of reality and total, unchanging, all-penetrating truth. In reality, *peripeteiae* often sneak up on people unobserved; and even obviously radical changes are unlikely to produce instant *anagnorises*. Understanding comes later, after investigation, observation, struggle, and reflection, if at all. And everyone is not bound to make the same discovery. In reality, there are only multiple, shifting, incomplete and discontinuous narrative perspectives, each of which contains some truth.

CHAPTER 5

Hermeneutics of Perspective

Introduction: Personal and Generic Perspectives

Nineteenth-century novels such as *Redgauntlet* (1824), *Confessions of a Justified Sinner* (1824), *No Name* (1863), or *The Moonstone* (1868) eliminated any permanent omniscient narrator and gave the perspectives of different characters, or of the same characters at different times, different generic forms – including letter-narratives, narrative-epistolary writing, and letter-narratives containing narrative-epistolary narration – to tell the story entirely through the perspectives afforded by a discontinuous patchwork of genres. Telling a story through characters' partial and conflicting perspectives was not new – it had been done by eighteenth-century epistolary novels, and other nineteenth-century novels fragmented their story into personal narratives that recounted the story from different narrative perspectives (for instance, *Wuthering Heights*) or used genre-switching to mark different phases or views of the same story (for instance, *The Tenant of Wildfell Hall* and *Lady Audley's Secret*) without, for all that, eliminating the connecting and guiding narratorial voice. Superimposing generic and personal perspectival boundaries in the absence of an omniscient narrator was different. It not only left novel-readers, Fanny-like, to "use [their] powers of comparing and judging" subjective perspectives at different removes from events for themselves; it also de-composed narrative-epistolary fiction into its components. While enabling writers to experiment with *mixta genera*, it thus foregrounded for examination uses, limitations, and conjunctions of genres and allowed novels such as *Redgauntlet* and *The Moonstone* to self-reflexively address the perspectival issues thus raised.

Both classical structuralist narratology and the new German or cognitive school of narratology supply the place of traditional understandings both of perspective and of genre with terms and structures of their own making that are intended to apply to all genres of writing, and to all written and visual media.[1] Fresh theorization of perspective that is more responsive to historical difference is offered in the first section of this chapter and illustrated primarily by *The Moonstone*. Historically, genres – each with their own typical, trad-itionally defined characteristics – were distinct as well as familiar and funda-mental parts of writers' and readers' toolkits. Perspective was conceived in ways we are only beginning to recover. And writers of nineteenth-century fragmentary *mixta genera* texts were marrying a tradition of genre-mixing that reached back at least to the Renaissance to an even older tradition of discontinuous, miscellaneous writing.[2] As Jane Barker explained in 1723, "reducing" a "History" into a "Patch-work Screen" of different genres – composed in her case of narrative-epistolary "Pieces of Romances" as well as of "Poems, Love-Letters and the like" – juxtaposed and included the views of people whose "Sentiments are as differently mix'd as the Patches in [Ladies] Work."[3] Patchworks re-presented and re-marked the diversity of people's views and modes of expression. Barker's metaphor is better suited to what Henry James dismissively called "hybrid and paradoxical compositions" than Barthes' now prevalent image of texts as "tissues" of intertwining threads or Henry-James-inspired understandings of perspective as a dominant, uniting "point of view." For patchworks were literally pieced together from leftover bits of cloth with different, often ill-matched shapes, sizes, textures, and colors. Viewed side by side, each patch remained distinct and self-contained while visibly attached to others and contributing to the overall effect.

Patchwork continued to figure as a simile for artistic perception in the nineteenth century, for instance, in Ruskin's impressionistic observation of 1859 that "Everything that you can see in the world around you presents itself to your eyes only as an arrangement of patches of different colors variously shaded."[4] And as we will see in the second section, which focuses on *Redgauntlet*'s self-referential reflections, a not negligible function of screens that was here performed by those very reflections, was to cover, protect, or conceal. As a Jacobite Roman Catholic writing in Protestant, Whig, Hanoverian Britain, Barker understood as well as Sir Walter Scott would a century later, that a narrative that "reduc'd" a "history" to fragments, refracted it through different generic perspectives, and dele-gated its telling to characters with different "Sentiments," also acted as a protective "Screen" for any dangerous, politically incorrect positions its author might wish to suggest.

The last section concludes the chapter and the book by suggesting that nineteenth-century *mixta genera* patchwork texts exploited and brought to the fore features characteristic of the narrative-epistolary fictions earlier examined in this study. This section uses Sir Walter Scott's account of perspective in *Redgauntlet* as a springboard for a different retrospective perspective on this narrative-epistolary fiction, which addresses what was perhaps also a function of *mixta genera* compositions more generally: that of bringing alternative perspectives to bear on characters, genres, and "reality" in order to make us more fully aware of their multifaceted complexity, of the inadequacy of each mode of mediation taken by itself, and of how little we ever really know.

Overall, this chapter works backward from the twentieth century, to remind readers of this book of what narrative-epistolary writers so often trenchantly showed: that a retrospective narrative written from the vantage point of the end only patches together a *terminus ad quem*. Since in reality this finalizes nothing, it invites further experience, further knowledge, and novel work instead.

Generic Perspectives and Patchwork Screens: Wilkie Collins's *The Moonstone*

In their uses of perspective, nineteenth-century novels and novellae such as *Redgauntlet, The Moonstone, No Name,* or *Confessions of a Justified Sinner* belie the modern scholarly argument that perspective became nothing more than an abstract "metaphor" for perception after the Renaissance, when it had been conceived as a set of practical, technical methods for drawing objects in space. Such novels gave perspectives an aggressively visible, technical foundation by fragmenting the story into discontinuous segments of text, by separating segments typographically through gaps and new beginnings on the page, and by marking each paratextually with a different character-author, place of origin, and/or title. Above all, this subset of nineteenth-century novels distinguished subjective character-perspectives formally by genre-switching, and included letter-narratives and narrative-epistolary segments in their generic mix. In *No Name*, for instance, discontinuous third-person narrative-epistolary "Scenes" alternate with "Interludes" containing disconnected first-person letter-narratives or bits of correspondence among characters in other locations who have not appeared in the scenes. The Interludes show novel-readers what is happening at a distance, behind the heroine's back and beyond her ken, to wittingly or unwittingly disrupt her Machiavellian plans to regain the fortune that she and her sister had lost. *Redgauntlet* is composed of an exchange of first-person letter-narratives, followed by a "Narrative" and a "Journal" both of which include letters, followed by two differently focalized narrative-epistolary "divisions," each neatly labeled by author, title, and location, and separated by empty space on the page.

Multiplication of subjective character-perspectives in these novels "creates distance between human beings and things" and provides a "distancing and objectifying sense of the real" that differs, often radically, from character to character; but it does so without producing the "relativism" associated with Nietzschean "perspectivism" where no perspective is more true or reliable than any other.[5] In these nineteenth-century novels, reality exists solidly, objectively, and independently of any character's perspective. Indeed, since each perspective contains some truth, and details some aspect(s) of reality with the precision of an empiricist observer, what actually happened or is happening in the storyworld can be pieced together by any reader who compares, contrasts, and combines perspectival accounts. But some part or parts of reality ultimately elude novel-readers. Once characters' diverse perspectives are pieced together, our knowledge of what really happened remains incomplete – there is always still some mystery, some uncanny paranormal psychological factor, something about a key character or event, that remains inexplicable and unexplained at the end. Reducing a story to a patchwork of generic fragments that did not quite cover the ground distinguished these prose fictions from realist novels whose unity and continuity were guaranteed by the third-person narration of an omniscient Cyclops, who enacted and substantiated positivism's claim to total, accurate, all-encompassing empirical knowledge of reality and truth.

In *The Moonstone*, for instance, diverse characters recount what they knew about the Verinders' acquisition and "loss" of the moonstone "as far as [their] personal experience extends, and no farther" in a series of discontinuous segments that take different generic forms – letter-narratives, diurnal entries in diaries, official statements, first-person narra-tive-epistolary reports.[6] The stated goal is to place "the whole story . . . on record in writing" in "the interests of truth" by creating "a record of the facts" consisting of "genuine documents . . . endorsed by witnesses who can speak to the facts." (19, 166) Each character's narrative describes things that really and objectively occurred in the storyworld at a series of determinate points in time and space. Except for letter-narratives in the prologue and epilogue addressed to Mr. Bruff, the Verinder family solicitor, which describe events in India fifty years before and a year after theft of the moonstone in Yorkshire occurred, these "documents" cover a period of two years and contain the direct experiences of character-witnesses who were present at Lady Verinder's country house when the moonstone was removed from Rachel Verinder's room. But while overlapping on several points that show that they are addressing aspects and variously overlapping temporal segments of the same story, their narratives present the different perspectives of characters in different subject-positions. Their different social classes and different customary habitations (town or country, the family's or the servants' quarters), give narrator-characters different social realities and diversely limited knowledge of events, and place them at different distances from the events and characters concerned in the theft. Their narratives therefore contain lacunae, some of which are pointed out – for instance, when Mr. Bruff intervenes to shed "necessary light on certain points of interest" that Gabriel Betteridge's and Miss Clack's narratives "left in the dark." (223) The characters' narratives are also often partial and subjective in the sense that they are "disfigured" by "peculiarities in the treatment" of facts, which make their narratives "exhibitions" of the writer's "character" rather than impartial records of characters and events.(166) To understand the theft, novel-readers have to piece together "the whole story" from these discontinuous narratives with their hybrid forms and variously limited perspectives in order to reconstruct the reality existing "objectively" beyond partial perspectives, which encompasses, transcends, and escapes them.

However, this does not return us to any single omniscient point of view. For there is more than one way of piecing the story together, depending on what we, as novel-readers, think the story is about and on our corresponding generic attributions.[7] Critics now often assume that the characters' discourses are addressed to Franklin Blake, who is trying to solve the mystery of how the moonstone was filched from Rachel's room. They read *The Moonstone* as a proto-detective story, centered on an amateur detective and resolved by Franklin's discovery from a local doctor of a little known, but supposedly scientifically "proven," quirk of the human psyche. But Betteridge – who begins his second narrative by explaining with pride that he has not only "opened" the story but is "the person who is left behind, as it were, to close the story up" – describes this as "the history of the family" that he has so long served, and insists that the "strange" part of the Verinder "family story" closes with Rachel Verinder's marriage to Franklin Blake. (379, 392, 19) Here, the story is a domestic saga and proto mystery-romance, where the love story is both promoted and impeded by the mystery with which the lovers have to contend. A third possibility is indicated near the beginning of the first narrative when Franklin Blake tells Betteridge that it was Mr. Bruff's idea to create a documentary record of the "whole story" so that the innocent could appeal to it "hereafter" should they need to prove their innocence – a very lawyerly suggestion indeed. Bruff reads the "documents" concerning the theft of the moonstone as well as Franklin. But the letter-narratives addressed to him in the prologue and epilogue – which do in fact open the story and close it up – show that "the whole story" begins for him with Murthwaite's account of John Herncastle's theft of the moonstone from Hindus in India and closes for him with Murthwaite's account of the moonstone's restoration to India by Hindus. For Bruff, then, this is a story about the Moonstone – a stone with a mysterious, legendary, Oriental curse that is supposedly capable of punishing the depredations of greedy British colonials and of redressing imperial injustice. Generically, this makes this an imperial or rather an anti-imperialist novel, whose political incorrectness is screened by the possibility of other generic readings. Piecing "the whole story" together thus yields diverse generic understandings of it depending on different characters' concernments and which novel-readers give the preference to; but lacunae remain in all cases. We never discover, for instance, how the moonstone got from Franklin Blake's room in Yorkshire to the three Hindus in London who ultimately return it to India, or if the Moonstone's legendary curse has really been at work in this "strange" history. Most significantly, perhaps, the identity of Rachel's thief is not uncovered by detectives or on the basis of the "facts" recorded by the "witnesses." The mystery of the theft is solved by a local doctor's discovery of a paranormal misfunction in Franklin Blake's psyche which, though possibly induced by a drug, is as strange and mysterious in its way as the Moonstone's curse. Thus while the obvious questions can be answered by piecing together the empirical facts supplied by the characters' discontinuous narratives – who stole the Moonstone and how? What happened to it after its disappearance? Who would Rachel marry? – patches of mystery continue to haunt the reconstructed empirical reality of past events, which evade rational empirical reasoning and puzzle common sense.[8]

"Hybrid and paradoxical compositions" such as this defy twentieth-century criticism's treatment of perspective as "point of view." Point of view was a term coined by Henry James and popularized by Percy Lubbock in 1922 to describe Henry James's technique of giving his stories a "center" or "focus" by "framing the action inside the consciousness of one of the characters within the plot itself."[9] Expounders of perspectival drawing described point of view in similar terms – as the point of the virtual pyramid that was calculated geometrically by the artist to make all visual lines issuing from the objects in the painting converge on the beholder's eye. To stand in the correct place and behold a painting from this point of view was to see all the objects and characters in it (regardless of the directions of their own bodies and gazes), disposed in harmonious relation to each other at various distances from the beholder's eye, without any illusion-breaking irregularities. It was to see the work composing itself into a united whole, to admire works composed in this way, and to denigrate or ignore "hybrid and paradoxical compositions" that contained plural foci and repeatedly breached the aesthetic illusion that twentieth-century critics considered essential to art. Point of view proved an apt metaphor not only for the task that the New Critics set themselves in elucidating the organic unity of great works, but also for forms of twentieth-century ideological criticism that made the author's *Weltanschauung*, politics, class, race, gender, or historico-phenomenological vantage point, the work's characteristic, orchestrating point of view. This metaphor also aptly characterized the work of classical narratologists whose taxonomies and stratifications reduced all stories to variants on the same coordinated set of elements, to make narrative "itself" the point from which all extant narratives could be viewed.

Fortunately – since this metaphor precluded description and appreciation of patchwork screens – art historians have begun to show that perspective as a single, static, organizing spatial point of view was a modern misinterpretation of Renaissance conceptions and uses of perspective. The painting by Abraham Bosse included in Desargues' landmark seventeenth-century text about perspective as an artistic technique, showed several people occupying different positions on the same terrain, each freely directing their visual pyramid at different places on the ground (see frontispiece).[10] It showed, in other words, that perspectives were individual, plural, mobile, and therefore mutable. It seems that perspectival Renaissance paintings likewise often included a plurality of putative visual pyramids all pointing in different directions. Hubert Damish has therefore argued that historically, "perspective … has that in common with language that, in and by itself, under the auspices of a point, a factor analogous to 'subject' or 'person' in language is always posited in relation to 'here' and 'there'."[11] In other words, like the "I" in language, perspective was a shifter. As such, it was characterized – as scholars from Carlo Ginzburg to Wolf Schmid now agree – by "tension" between "subjective points of view" and "objective and verifiable truths guaranteed by reality … or by God."[12] These characterizations of perspective accord better with the generically marked perspectivism of patchwork screens.

"Hybrid and paradoxical" fictions such as these also defied classical realism's claim to "reflect" reality if, as we have assumed, this means that novels can faithfully mirror the real because reflections proceed directly from real objects to the physical or mental eye, as light proceeds in straight

lines in geometrical versions of the visual pyramid. John Wood's popular
1797 schoolbook on perspective said otherwise. Wood explained that rays
or particles of light proceed in straight lines only until turned *out* of their
path by "reflection," "inflection" or "refraction." Since "reflection" meant
that rays of light were *stopped* by substances they could not penetrate, it
became relevant to perspective only when light bounces obliquely off
a surface to create a measurable "angle of reflection." To study perspective
was primarily to study "dioptrics" that "treats of *refracted* light." Dioptrics
addressed whatever relates to "seeing through different mediums," and to
"the pictures of objects formed by refraction through them."[13] This shares
the modern perception articulated by Clifford Siskin and William Warner,
that we need to think in terms of different forms of "mediation;"[14] but it
offered a richer range of formal possibilities than narratology's rearranged
stratifications and narrative "levels." For dioptrics admitted "parallel rays"
and "diverging rays" as well as rays converging on a single point; it
admitted "blind spots" and diverse material compounds that stopped or
redirected the light in diverse ways; and there was the intriguing possibility
of introducing "a virtual focus" separate from the "principal focus," where
rays only *seem* to converge or diverge at a particular point. One might
describe two of *The* Moonstone's three generic cruxes as virtual foci in this
sense. Virtual foci such as these provide false *anagnorises* to partially or
wholly screen the true one.

Pursuing Wood's model, one might also say that genres – each with their
characteristic subject-matter, style, scope, perspective, and modus oper-
andi – corresponded to diverse materials or media through which objects
were refracted in a painter's dioptrics. To superimpose perspectival and
generic perspectives in characters' diverse accounts of events was thus also
to explore the refractions produced by the medium of genres and to
consider how a narrator-character's choice(s) of genre shaped and controlled what they could and could not convey about characters and events.
In Kant's formulation and Jonathan Crary's explanation of it: "our representations of things as they are given does not conform to these things as
they are in themselves, but . . . to our mode of representation." And modes
of representation (such as genres) are "opaque" rather than transparent
media, in which the observer's activity, perceptions, and misperceptions
are "inextricably mixed with whatever objects they behold."[15] Combining
generic forms with character perspectives, especially when their narratives
also exhibited "disfiguring" "peculiarities in the treatment" deriving from
the peculiarities of the character-narrator's mental, moral, or emotional
subworld, doubled the "opaqueness" of the medium, and multiplied the

ways in which characters' perceptions of reality were stopped or redirected by it. Making characters' perspectives central to the telling as well as to the action of a story doubly satisfied nineteenth-century readers' delight in, and preoccupation with, character. Giving characters divergent perspectives, and these perspectives different generic forms, also reminded nineteenth-century reviewers, who judged novelists principally by their ability to "paint human characters . . . naturally" and to "delineate human nature as it really is," that "storytellers" displayed their "artistry" by refracting characters and events through genre, while inviting them to consider what each genre could and could not adequately do.

Self-referentiality and Dioptrics: Scott's *Redgauntlet*

Sir Walter Scott addressed this issue explicitly in *Redgauntlet* (1824), which contains a sustained meditation on its component genres in the voice of a self-proclaimed writer-persona who increasingly intervenes in the narration. *Redgauntlet* is a "Tale of the Eighteenth Century" about Jacobitism in post-Union, Hanoverian Scotland, which takes up familiar eighteenth-century themes. Set in the 1760s and rife with allusions to eighteenth-century writers and texts, this is a story about an orphan in search of his identity, discovery of which depends on penetrating the mystery of his birth in a world peopled by occasional selves – characters who reappear at different times and places as seemingly different people with different names. Here those who resort to occasional selves are Highlanders who have participated in the failed Jacobite Rebellion of 1745 and continue to be in danger of British government reprisals as long as there are still "warrants and witnesses to names—and those names – Christian and Surname – belong to an attainted person . . . "[16]

   The first "division" of the novel takes the form of a correspondence between orphaned Darsie Latimer and his friend, Alan Fairford, which ends with the end of the first volume of the 1824 Edinburgh edition.[17] Phatic elements and summary background histories apart, it consists of two series of letter-narratives that follow parallel tracks as each correspondent describes his experiences in his present location from his own characteristic perspective. Darsie writes long, leisurely travel letters from the Highlands describing its breathtaking natural scenery and his "adventures" with mysterious and magical characters such as the Laird of the Lake who saves his life or the blind bard and strolling fiddler, Wandering Willie, who tells marvelous tales of the '45, like that of Redgauntlet. Alan's letter-narratives, by contrast, describe his life in the mercantile Lowlands under a puritanical father who keeps his nose to the grindstone, determined that his son shall rise to eminence by tireless labor in the law. Alan's dull everyday routine is rarely enlivened by anything as curious as the unwelcome visit of a Mr. Heresies of Birrenwork, a participant in the '45 who is trying to locate Darsie, or the appearance of the mysterious veiled woman he dubs "Green Mantle" who warns him that Darkie will be in danger if he sets foot in England. But Alan's unruffled letters narrate these "adventures" as he narrates everything else – in a plain style characterized by observed empirical detail, rational analysis, and calm expressions of the social and filial affections. There are points of convergence between these two, parallel series of letter-narratives – Darsie, who has been raised and educated alongside his friend Alan, is equally capable of empirical description and narration; and "adventures" attached to mysterious Highland characters "find" Alan too. But both letter-writers emphasize the divergence in their characters and perspectives, the impact of this divergence upon the content and style of the narratives in their letters, and its effect on the course of their lives. Alan is becoming a lawyer; Darsie has rejected this career. Alan tells Darsie that he, Alan, "views things as they are, not as they may be magnified through thy teeming fancy" and criticizes Darsie for "conceiv-[ing] thyself to be the hero of some romantic history" (1: 35, 32) and giving "all that happens to thee . . . a touch of the wonderful and the sublime from thy own rich imagination." (1: 95) In defending his practice of what Alan calls "making histories out of nothing" (I 35) (and Wandering Willie's practice of doing the same), Darsie makes a generic distinction between histories deriving from empirical observation, and those at some remove from reality that derive from imagination: "We fools of fancy, who suffer ourselves, like Malvolio, to be cheated with our own visions, have nevertheless, this advantage, that we have our whole stock of enjoyments under our own command, and can dish for ourselves an intellectual banquet with most moderate assistance from external objects." (1:270)

The writer-persona who introduces himself at the beginning of the second "division," which is entitled "Narrative," and who is about to take over part of the narration, draws attention to the angles of refraction of the letter-narratives in the previous division. He is echoing Scott's earlier assessment of Samuel Richardson's angles of refraction in his Preface to the 1821 Ballantyne edition of Richardson's works. Scott had argued there that Richardson's letter-narratives had the advantage of "plac[ing personages before us bare-faced, in all the actual changes of feature and complexion, and all the light and shade of human passion" while permitting the author to "screen [himself] behind" them in the character of an editor. But Scott had complained that letter-narratives written to the moment "painted [all] in the foreground, and nothing in the distance;" and this, together with "detail[ing] the incidents again and again by the different actors to their different correspondents" had the disadvantage that it "arrested the progress of the story."[18] The writer-persona in *Redgauntlet* likewise explains at the beginning of "Narrative" that he had used letter-narratives "as practiced by various great Authors" in the first division because these had "the advantage of laying before the reader, in the words of the actors themselves, the adventures which we must otherwise have narrated on our own" and thus of enabling readers to form "something approaching a distinct idea of the principal characters." (2:3, 4) But he had ensured that Darsie and Alan's letter-narratives did not arrest the story both by having them recount complete and continuable episodes of their adventures retrospectively, and by giving them different adventures to recount. This had enabled him to place the story unfolding in the Highlands at various distances from the correspondents: in Darsie's letter-narratives, encounters with vivid Highland characters are very much in the foreground, both because he is traveling among them and because he is in his element in Highland society. Highland characters and scenes are more removed from Alan, engrossed in his Lowland law studies; they interest him primarily for their relevance to his friend. Distance is greatest in the single letter written to Darsie by Alan's father, for whom the Highlands represent enchantments to be strenuously resisted, and dangerous social connections from the '45, which he wants kept as far away from his family as possible.

In the first division as the writer-narrator explains, he had alternated his foregrounds and backgrounds and successfully eliminated the "various prolixities [which] occur in the course of an interchange of letters, which must hang as a dead weight on the progress of the narrative."(2: 3) But he had discovered in the process that a correspondence consisting of letter-narratives between two friends could not adequately "instruct the reader for his full comprehension of the story."(2: 3) Parallel letter-narratives could not tell us, for instance, that Darsie and Alan were meeting the same personages under different names and assumed identities. Moreover, the principal protagonists had to remain separated to write; and this gave him no way of connecting their stories which, with Alan's involvement in the Peter Pebbles law case, had begun to veer from parallel into entirely divergent paths. There were also "circumstances" (such as Darkie's approaching capture and imprisonment) that naturally prevented letters from reaching their destination and correspondence from taking place. These limitations militated against conveying "full comprehension of the story" through the medium of letter-narratives in a correspondence, and made it advisable for the writer-narrator to turn to a change of genre and a change of pace.

The writer-persona in *Redgauntlet* proposes to "avoid" the difficulties presented by letter-narratives in epistolary correspondence by turning to a practice borrowed from narrative-epistolary writers, which "resembles the original discipline of the dragoons who were trained to serve either on foot or on horseback, as the emergencies of the service required." (2:4) Using both letters *and* narrative as needed offered better angles of refraction by giving writers the best of both worlds. This enabled the writer to "use the letters of the personages concerned or liberal extracts from them, to describe particular incidents, or express the sentiments which they entertained, while connect[ing] them occasionally with such portions of narrative, as may serve to carry on the thread of the story." (2:4) Narrative-epistolary writers could *both* use letters to give readers "something approaching a distinct idea of the principal characters" *and* deploy narrative to connect letters, say what letters could not say for readers' fuller comprehension of the story, and control the pace of the story by moving the action along. In the division called "Narrative," the writer-persona accordingly uses what he calls "direct narrative" (2: 56) to connect three fully transcribed letters: a letter from Dumfries about Darsie's mysterious disappearance from the Highlands, which his father mistakenly hands Alan in the midst of the Peter Pebbles trial; a letter Alan leaves behind him for his father, announcing his departure in quest of his friend; and a letter from Dumfries to Mr. Fairford confirming Alan's arrival there. This avoids prolixity by compressing events that are required by the story only to get Alan to the Highlands, and instructs readers more fully than these letters can by describing things that Alan could not have known (such as what happened after his sudden departure in the midst of the trial) and things that he would not have mentioned (such as the cost to his career of abandoning the trial in midcourse).

But since this particular compound of narrative and letters distances readers from the experiences of the principal protagonists and the writer-persona wants to return us to direct experience of at least one of the chief characters, the "next division assumes . . . a form somewhat different from direct narrative and epistolary correspondence, though partaking of the character of both." (2: 56) What follows is a different variant of narrative-epistolary writing. The "Journal of Darsie Latimer" is a journal in the sense that eighteenth-century correspondents used the term for long letters that were written at intervals on different days as "continues" and sent off as

a "packet." Enclosed as a packet in an envelope with an "Address" on its
inner face, Darsie's journal consists of a long letter-narrative addressed
primarily to Alan, which is divided into chapters and contains narrative-
epistolary writing – fully transcribed letters each framed, following narrative-epistolary convention, with all necessary information about their
occasion and reception. The journal is turned into what I have called an
"open letter" by insistence – both in the "Address" within the envelope and
in the narrative frame at the outset of Darsie's letter – that he is addressing
his journal-letter-narrative simultaneously to Alan and to anyone whatever
into whose "hands . . . these leaves may fall." (2: 51) Darsie's journal-letter-
narrative with its embedded letters will simultaneously "instruct" both
a particular addressee and unknown readers "during a certain time at least,
in the history of the life of an unfortunate young man who, in the heart of
a free country, . . . has been, and is, subjected to a course of unlawful and
violent restraint." (2:51) Novel-readers are thus invited to view themselves,
not as voyeurs peering over the intended recipient's shoulder, but as in
open letters, as addressees who are directly implicated by the fictional
personage who intends his letter to fall into "different hands" than
Alan's. (2:52) Darsie addresses his call for liberation from captivity and
death to us as a consciously rhetorical act – a call designed to "prepossess
even a stranger in my favor" by the "open simplicity and frankness" with
which it relates "the history of the events that have befallen [him] since
[his] last letter to Alan Fairford dated 5th August." (2: 53, 54) This is all the
more necessary because un-prepossessed strangers might easily blame
Darsie for bringing his captivity upon himself by ignoring Alan's warning
about the danger of remaining where he was, and dismiss as absurd Darsie's
claim that he was "blinded by a fatality" and "swept along" by "a train of
events" that no one could "resist." (2: 55)

Darsie's experience is refracted by elements of the diary-genre, as well as
by its generic characteristics as a letter-narrative and journal. Like a diary,
his narrative is private or secret inasmuch as Darsie takes care to keep it
from "the hazard of detection" by his captors. Like a diary too, it is filled
with "what may appear trivial" and "exerts [Darsie's] faculties" on the past,
in order not to "waste them in vain and anxious anticipations of the
future." (2: 53, 61) But questions about the future haunt this journal and
this past nevertheless. A fugitive from the '45 who believes he is under
attainder, his captor, Mr. Heresies, insists that ""the liberty of which the
Englishman boasts" is a sham, because "the privilege of free action belongs
to no mortal—we are tied down by the fetters of duty—our mortal path is
limited by regulations of honour—our most indifferent actions are but

meshes in the web of destiny by which we are all surrounded." (2: 185)
Without going so far as to deny Englishmen freedom, this is also how Alan
Fairford has characterized his own situation: tied to the law by fetters of
duty to his father, enmeshed by the destiny created by his birth to this
lawyer-father and lawyer-grandfather, Alan is not free to do as he wishes
and go where he will. There are chains other than iron ones that can hold
a man captive. Catching sight of himself in a mirror and noticing "a
remarkable resemblance" between himself and Mr. Heresies, Darsie wonders if "his fate is somehow interwoven" with that of his captor, to raise the
question of whether a person's destiny must necessarily resemble his
family's. (2: 154) Alan has partly invalidated Mr. Heresies assertion that
"nothing is the consequence of free will" at the end of the previous division
by abandoning his father and his duty to set off to find his friend. A central
question is whether Darsie will too.

The journal-diary-letter-narrative in this division also falls short of ensuring the reader's "full comprehension of the story," but this time not only
because Darsie's first-person perspective is necessarily limited, but because –
like Monimia in the first part of her letter to Orlando – he does not fully
understand the experiences he describes or the characters and letters he
reports. Darsie can narrate what has happened to him, but he cannot explain
why things are happening and what they mean. Scott, who considered
Charlotte Smith the most "eminent" of all eighteenth- and early nineteenth-
century women novelists, and *The Old Manor House*, her "chef d'oeuvre,"
praised the first narrative-epistolary part of that novel, particularly as it
centered on Mrs. Rayland's letter.[19] He argued that *The Old Manor House*
belonged to "the best specimens of that class of composition" which did not
offer evolving, "well-arranged stories," but, like *Gil Blas* or *Roderick Random*,
presented "adventures'like Orient pearls at random strung,'" which are not
connected to one another otherwise than having occurred to one person in
the course of their life.[20] Giving this tradition of composing novels from
"Orient pearls at random strung" a multi-generic twist enabled the writer-
pesona in *Redgauntlet* to "drop the journal" and "carry the story" forward by
means of two complementary pieces of narrative-epistolary writing produced
by himself as writer-narrator: a "Narrative of the proceedings of Alan
Fairford in pursuit of his friend, which forms another series in this history;"
and a "Narrative of Darsie Latimer," which "shifts to Darkie's adventures in
the Precarious custody of the Laird of the Locks." (2: 209; 3: 97)

Both series are narrative-epistolary in character like the division called
"Narrative" before, but here the proportions and functions of these genres
are reversed. Where narrative was used in "Narrative" principally to

connect a series of letters that contained the bones of the plot, and secondarily to mention things that Alan could not know, here the writer-narrator's narrative dominates. The angle of refraction is wider because he includes only letters that usefully connect the characters and events in the immediate "forefront" of the story to mysterious characters elsewhere who are about to come to the fore. The conventional omniscient narrator partly returns in these narratives "of" as opposed to "by" Alan or Darsie, to define characters and their motives for us; to articulate and explain what Alan and Darsie each discover about the shifting names, occasional identities, secret networks, and carefully concealed pasts of clandestine Jacobites in the Highlands; and to guide readers through the muddle of mysteries and identities, which it is the task of the story to resolve.

Though each narrative-epistolary series focuses on the adventures of Alan and Darsie separately as the letter-narratives in the first division did, they pursue convergent paths. Alan's quest for his friend takes him to the Highlands, and involves him in a process of detection in which he questions Jacobite characters like Mr. Heresies, Mr. Maxwell, Natty Ewart, and Father Bonaventure, who bring him ever closer to his friend. Though still in captivity, Darsie too is engaged in a process of detection inasmuch as he is gradually initiated into the mystery of his family and its past. The novel concludes with a brief, wholly narrative, third-person "Narrative of Alan Fairford," which picks up where the previous "Narrative of Alan Fairford" left off. Its business is to unite England and Scotland, as well as Alan and Darsie again. General Campbell arrives at the head of a battalion from Carlisle to the meeting of secret Jacobites that Redgauntlet has arranged in the hope that Darsie would lead a new uprising in support of the Pretender, Charles Edward. Campbell quashes this, not by violence, but by granting the elderly Jacobites present a general pardon from the King in London if they will disperse and keep the peace. Meanwhile Darsie demonstrates his likeness to Alan, as well as the benefits of his Lowland upbringing in Alan's family, both by declining to lead another Jacobite uprising and by recognizing that the future for him and for Scotland lies with England now.

The writer-narrator's increasing narrative intervention in the novel's final divisions where detection occurs and mysteries are unraveled creates the impression that Scott was supporting Scotland's Union with Britain; but the resolution centered on Campbell might be described as a "virtual focus." One does not celebrate Scotland's Union with England by vividly evoking Highland legends of "romantic" Jacobite heroes, the independence of powerful Highland warrior-lairds, the enchantment of bewitching Scottish musician-bards, and the mystery of sublime and magical events – or by contrasting all this with the stolid empiricism, the dull, work-a-day routine, and the grinding, law-bound labor of colorless characters in the Anglicized Lowlands. Alan and the Lowlands were, like Britain, subject to "the government of laws, not men," as Hume had put it; but the Highlands are still being governed more colorfully by men despite Britain's laws. The novel's generic patchwork and the writer-persona's formal reflections screen the writer-narrator, and Scott himself, from being directly implicated either in celebrating the Highlands and Scotland's gallant past or in lamenting Scotland's bleak Lowland present, by attributing these perceptions to Darsie and Alan in segments in which they speak for themselves. Darsie and Alan's angles of reflection are expressed in letter-narratives and journal, generic forms that present the "sublime and wonderful" Scottish Highlands and the wonder-less Anglified Lowlands as their merely personal perspectives. The virtual focus supporting England's union with Scotland adds its mite by screening the principal focus, which Darsie indicates precisely when he declines to lead another Jacobite uprising against England. Like Alan and the elderly defeated Jacobites, Darsie now "views things as they are, not as they may be magnified by ... fancy." To propose another uprising is "romantic" in the contemporary sense of mad and unrealistic. The reality was that all previous Jacobite uprisings had been defeated and that England ruled Scotland now. But this does not change the fact that resemblances to Redgauntlet are imprinted on Darsie's features, that his affinity to Highland bards and musicians is ingrained in his soul, that he has himself been "the hero of [a] romantic history" and that, having finally discovered his true identity, he is forever linked by family, friends, and inheritance to Scotland's cultural past. Darsie's education in Alan's Lowland family and long exposure to English practices and English law have not erased his Highland legacies. Even Alan's father – who is firmly anchored in the Lowlands and the law, and desperately wants to distance himself and his family from all that Darsie re-presents – finds that he can no more disavow his erstwhile Jacobite friends or erase his memories of Highland "enchantment," than Alan can break his attachment to Darsie. Darsie remains a Redgauntlet and his Highland father's heir even as "a subject of George II." Despite Union with England, then, all was not lost.

Retrospective: *Mixta Genera* and the Hermeneutics of Perspective

Scott's comparison of narrative-epistolary novelists to "dragoons who were trained to serve either on foot or on horseback as the emergencies of service required," and insistence that both were required to "instruct the reader for his full comprehension of the story" provide the springboard here for a different, retrospective perspective on practices explored in previous chapters. The dragoon is a toolbox image: it represents narrative and letters as two separate and distinct genres, each with its own characteristic and divergent perspectives, which well-trained novelists combined tactically in different ways as required at different junctures by the story being told. Like letters and narratives, foot soldiers and cavalry officers differ not only in the speed of their locomotion and in their status or authority, but also in their angle of vision on the landscape through which both must pass. Like the man on foot, letters are slower and closer to the ground. They "place personages [immediately] before us," but in doing so, they "paint [every-thing] in the foreground and nothing in the distance;" and because they move quite slowly, they tend to "arrest the progress of the story." Letters allow us to hear "the words of the actors themselves," but those words only describe the prospects and personal perspectives available to them in the successive locations in which they temporarily find themselves. The man on horseback can move faster and see more. He is more flexible and has the wider and longer view. Perched above the infantry at a strategic distance from the ground, the horseman, like the third-person narrator, can observe the motions of men at some remove, and perceive what lies behind, around and ahead. Poised to trot, canter and gallop, jump fences, circle around, scout ahead, skirt difficult terrain, and travel back and forth between infantry units, the horseman, like the narrator, has a more mobile, various and comprehensive perspective than the man on foot. Both perspectives were needed to "instruct" readers in what they need to know for "full comprehension of the story," because combining the two genres enabled narrative-epistolary writers not only to control the pace of the story and vary its dioptrics, but also to tell it from generic perspectives that inscribe their difference while supplying each other's lacks.

Scott's dragoon image broadly describes the work of narrative-epistolary writers who alternated between narrative and letters, at once connecting them by means of their scaffolding devices and re-marking them as separate genres by transcribing whole letters complete with superscription and subscription and setting them off on the page. But it is important to bear in mind that Scott selected for remark only features of narrative-epistolary writing that he was using, and that he was interested in the narrative-epistolary form favored by the many women writers who preceded him only as a story-teller seeking to "instruct" readers for "full comprehension of a story." This made his representations both of perspective and of narrative-epistolary writing one-sided and reductive. Scott not only coopted the work of his female predecessors to belittle their achievement as was his wont; he also ignored women writers' more complex narrative-epistolary practices and different writerly goals, in order to justify returning to the omniscient authorly narratives he preferred.[21]

As we saw, women writers before and after Scott favored narrative-epistolary writing because this gave them the means of promoting reflection in the unreflecting, of warning the unwary of the perils confronting them in their domestic and social situations, of instructing women and the unlearned in a variety of contemporary literary and philosophical issues, and of instilling in them some salutary skepticism about texts, stories, and the occasional selves they were shown. Women writers had therefore sensibly mixed the two genres, letters and narratives, with which women and the unlearned were most familiar and to which they were most frequently exposed in their everyday lives, both in written and oral modes. Scott's dragoon image cleverly highlighted the complementary functions of epistolary and narrative perspectives narrowly conceived, while his practice kept narrative in *Redgauntlet* in the realm of "positive facts," confined imagination to Highland song, scenery, and romance, and treated the unknown as the yet-to-be-discovered. But as we saw, narrative-epistolary novelists before and after him also allowed narrative and epistolary perspectives to conflict or to confute one another, or they composed each of mixtures of congruent and incongruent parts. And they often showed how imagination participates in our perception even of the most ordinary empirical realities, and used the unknown, the surprising or the unexpected to discredit narratives built on positive facts. Some narrative-epistolary novelists did directly "instruct the reader" as Scott liked to do; but many also played ironically on readerly incomprehension, left readers to instruct themselves on significant points, or used embedded letters to indicate that full, reliable, and permanent comprehension of a situation or story was unattainable. All used transcriptions of whole letters to "place personages before us" and allow us to "hear the words of actors themselves" as Scott recognized; but many also exploited the fact that this could also free letters from helpless subjection to the narrative's authority and enable them to act as a measure of characters' and/or the narrator's "labor to attain truth." And where Scott alternated between placing Alan and Darkie in the foreground and used the letters embedded in his narrative divisions instrumentally as additional positive facts, they moved letters back and forth between foreground and background, and used their elaborations and adaptations of narrative-epistolary fiction's characteristic devices to multiply and complicate perspectives. Scott stripped narrative-epistolary writing of content as well as of social and intellectual purpose in

Redgauntlet, and reduced it to a few complementary formal-aesthetic func-tions before tossing it away as unwieldy and turning in the last division – and indeed in his subsequent novels – to a third-person narrative form. In short, Scott was certainly right in thinking that mixing generic perspectives goes to the heart of narrative-epistolary writing. But Scott's insight has to be released from Scott's limitations to offer a helpful means of understanding and describing women novelists' narrative-epistolary work.

Both scaffolding conventions that female narrative-epistolary novelists favored relied on narrative to supply what letters, taken by themselves, could not say, and thus to provide perspectives on them that went beyond what was evident even to the most accomplished reader from epistolary texts alone. By supplying the motives and circumstances of its writing, transmission, and reading; by putting the letter back into "the dense and complex web of [its] contemporary relations;" by conveying what might be known to a character-writer that a letter's contents distorted or failed to represent; and by indicating to novel-readers what a character-reader failed to notice; framing narratives from Behn on provided complicating con-textual perspectives on epistolary texts, on their roles in interpersonal communications, and on the culturally and psychologically informed transactions involved. After Mary Davys and Delivier Manley, expanded framing narratives also addressed and connected the successive transac-tional meaning(s) a letter obtained in the course of its circulation, and showed how the agency of a letter might impact and change perceptions, relationships, and the course of events. Narrative framing thus situated letters within the wider field of practices, ideas, social relations, and temporalities that they inhabited empirically. This not only provided a broader perspective on letters by situating them as an occasional genre in the already complex history of their initial production, reception, and instrumentality, but extended that historical perspective down a corridor of discontinuous scenes by recording subsequent occasions on which the same letters recurred in conversation or memory to produce rippling, long-term effects. Narrative-epistolary framing demonstrated that a letter's meaning was never completely contained in a sheet of writing or solely determined by what its words most obviously said, but that its empirical significance and actual effects were perilously intricated with whatever supplementary perspectives, external to the sheet of writing, were brought to bear.[22]

Disjunctions between prefatory narratives and reception narratives describing one or more characters' understandings of it at the same or different times, multiplied perspectives on a letter's meaning and significance by showing how each character-writer's and character-reader's "angle of refraction" was subjectively shaped by their ambitions, credulity, passions, biases, or preconceptions; by deception or self-deception; by errors in their reasoning or lacunae in their knowledge, and/or by the different realities they inhabited at different times. This made a letter more like the ground in Abraham Bosse's painting, where different characters moving singly over the same terrain each direct their visual pyramid at a different spot, than like a missile where everything hits a single mathematically targeted point (see frontispiece). Letters figure as the ground over which characters move singly, each reflecting some piece(s) of it at an angle and blocking other pieces of it in their own way. One might say that Burney applied Bosse's picture of plural and fragmented perspectives to the composition and reading of Delvile's letter by portraying it as a piecemeal composition, in which each piece points in a different direction and converges with or diverges from empirical facts at past, present, and future times in diverse and shifting ways. But elsewhere too, as we saw, each fully transcribed letter could function as a baseline and measure both of the refractions of each of its character-readers and of the narrator's partial or unreliable "inflections." As in Philander's reading of Octavio's letter, Amoranda and her maid's different readings of the two anonymous letters, Betsy's reading of Hyssom's letter, the Bennet family's readings of Mr. Collins' letter, Audley's reading of the telegram, or Phineas's reading of Lady Laura's letter, the transcribed missive's presence on the page enabled novel-readers to see from their own reading of it what character-readers had ignored or overlooked, and what the narrator mischaracterized or passed over in silence. Setting a complete letter before us and keeping it distinct from the narrative exposed characters' different readings of it and of the characters and circumstances to which it referred, as well as whatever spin the letter-writer had given these, as so many limited perspectives on both. The presence of complete letters on the page could also expose omissions, distortions, deceptions, and dissimulation in the narration by narrators who assumed the role of "master of lies" and only hinted at what was "really" going on. Here letters provided a trenchant perspective that made visible the artificial, factitious, and inflected character of narratives themselves. Freed from subjection to the principal narrative, as in *The Reform'd Coquet, Love Intrigues,* Darcy's letter-narrative in *Pride and Prejudice,* or Talboys's letters in *Lady Audley's Secret,* transcribed letters and letter-narratives could, in their different ways, tell a separate story that contradicted or partially discredited the narrator's master-narrative by supplying an entirely different perspective on what has occurred. Here letters profiled the limits of the narrative's "labor to attain truth."

As letters permitted different readings, so they permitted different plausible, fact-based narratives about characters and their past actions to be built in, by, and around them. As we saw, the skewed narrative perspectives here were often shown to be an effect of blind spots – of perspectives blocked or distorted by blindness to or ignorance of relevant information and key empirical facts. Inasmuch as characters constructed narratives on their partial understandings of letters and circumstances and acted upon them, this led – through Smith and Burney who still assumed a right reading – to the position taken in novels such as *Villette* and *Lady Audley's Secret* where what mattered most about a letter (or a work) empirically, was how a character-reader reacted to it from their own subjective psychological perspective, to give it meanings that it did not objectively possess and weave it into a story of their own devising.

Like the hermeneutics of suspicion directed at credulous readers who took letters at face value, comparison of letters to the narrative's empirical facts, which demonstrated that letters did not invariably yield their secrets to empirical investigation or showed that culturally sanctioned expectations had little or no predictive power given the fluidity of life, depended on provision of an alternative perspective on the same letters, facts, or events. It was not enough to demonstrate a letter's distortions of reality, the fallibility of a character's empirical reasoning, the incompleteness of the available evidence, or the surprising contingency of everyday life. It was also necessary to show that, seen from a different angle, refracted through a different medium, or given a different context, the same letter, facts, or course of events could be explained or narrated in another, truer or more plausible way. One might say that true narratives put false or faulty ones in perspective, as the principal focus in a painting did virtual ones. Mary Davys, Eliza Haywood, Austen in Darcy's letter-narrative, and Braddon in *Lady Audley*, introduced confessions, letters or letter-narratives to supply this second narrative perspective that repositioned and replaced the factitious and partly fictional narrative which other protagonists had constructed on the basis of incomplete facts, false epistolary documents, and preconceived ideas. Early narrative-epistolary writers were apt to confront characters' false conjectural narratives with the narrator's account of what had actually occurred. But Lennox, Burney, Smith, Edgeworth, Austen, Bronte, Trollope, and Braddon also worked in various ways with temporal perspectives, to contrast mutable prospective and retrospective views of the same letters, characters, and events; and Collins's novellas showed how eruption into the status quo of a shocking perspective on a family contained in a letter from the past, might disrupt and forever alter characters' present and future prospects.

In this narrative-epistolary fiction, the letters embedded in narratives might "place personages before us," as Scott said; but contrary to what he argued, they did not always "paint [themselves] in the foreground." Some letters – most obviously, summarized letters, partly cited letters, letters focalized through characters' minds, and form-letters – meld into the narrative along with description of all the other details of everyday life, such as locales, dress, conversations, or movements from place to place. Here narrative elbows letters into the background to paint itself in the foreground. Alternation between narrative and fully transcribed letters as suggested by the dragoon image did not necessarily give each its turn in the foreground either. Fully transcribed instrumental letters could be over-shadowed by narrative, especially when the narrator's account of characters' actions, conversations, and interactions seem to sufficiently "instruct the reader for his comprehension of the story" without reference to, or close reading of, the letter(s) that occasioned and generated them. This could be an advantage, for instance, when it was used to control the pace of the story, to temporarily conceal something about the letter's writing or to screen writers from prosecution for dangerous or unacceptable views. But narrative could also overshadow letters in such a way as to render them superfluous, as happened in the successive, increasingly narrative divisions of *Redgauntlet*. Here Scott demonstrated as the writer-narrator wrote that comparatively straightforward letters whose principal or only function was to contain or to complement the narrative were less useful to the storyteller than might be expected. Having strictly limited their use, he showed that they were easily and more efficiently replaced by a writer-narrator on horseback who, whenever necessary, replicated the foot soldier's perspective by such narrative means as focalization through characters' minds and detailed expository characterization. Not surprisingly, Scott's stuck to third-person narratives in his subsequent novels.

Narrative-epistolary novelists, by contrast, often used narrative means to "magnify" letters they wished to emphasize in order to push them into the foreground. These included framing them with double prefatory and/or double reception narratives or puffing them fore and aft with conversations, debates and reflections that bear directly on them, to extend the amount of story-time they occupy, expand the attention they demand, and make them focal points for multiple narrated scenes. Narrative means of magnifying letters also included multiplying letters in the text or, on the contrary, reserving them for a key point in the narrative; making recursion to them useful or necessary to the reader during the forward march of the plot, or simultaneously exploiting and subverting their customary modes of operation. Narrative-epistolary novelists also used notable kinds of letters – encapsulating letters, pivotal letters, unseen letters, and letter-narratives – as a means of painting select letters in the foreground, para-doxically perhaps by giving them major functions in the narrative beyond their immediate instrumentality.

When placed at or near the beginning of a novel or narrative movement, as we saw, encapsulating letters drew attention to the story's *donnée* and principal threads by collecting these together economically and memorably in one place. By elliptically articulating the narrative's thematics and fore-shadowing the narrative course of events, encapsulating letters foregrounded a perspective on the story that the narrative would both belie and play out. By contrast, epistolary *peripeteiae* broke into the narrative and overturned it, radically altering, with the course of events, what the characters thought and/ or what the narrative had led us to believe, was going on. Using a letter or correspondence to occasion a major turn in the narrative or to introduce a new and unexpected perspective on what the narrative had presented as the story before, not only made visible earlier narrative lacunae; it also fore-grounded pivotal letters by deploying them to highlight a key part of the narrative structure, by putting them in the driving seat and by using them to invoke a different perspective on the earlier narrative.

Unseen letters and letter-narratives operated more insidiously from behind to unseat narrator-horsemen by showing how cavalier their com-manding perspective could be. As we saw, letter-narratives coopted narra-tive itself to allow characters to tell a subjective and fragmentary story about something occurring elsewhere at another time, which could be inserted into the narrator's narrative and bracketed off from it, to confront two different narrated realities and enable them to supply perspectives on each other that changed the reading of both. Attached to the narrator's narrative through their character-reader(s) and detached from the narra-tor's omniscience, letter-narratives thematized narrative's distance both from the events they recounted and from their character-readers' experi-ence, to expose the inadequacy, incompleteness, or inapplicability of narrative's seemingly all-encompassing but in reality inevitably fragmen-tary, "slices" of life.

Unseen letters brought to the fore the problem of the unseen, unknown, and unexpected which, in one way or another, figured into narrative-epistolary deployment of all its formal devices, even when narrators pro-vide novel-readers with information that characters lack. One might say that the nineteenth-century novelists considered in this chapter who used gaps and discontinuities between letter-narratives and juxtaposed genres to foreground the limited subjective perspectives from which narratives were narrated, were only formalizing the gappiness that narrative-epistolary novelists since Aphra Behn had shown plagued letters, empirical facts, and explanatory narratives. Unseen letters mark spots in the narrative where documentary evidence is lacking or where it has been visibly suppressed. They make visible blind spots in characters' and/or novel-readers' perceptions and knowledge, and the ludicrousness of using conjecture, probabilistic narratives, generalizations, expectations, culturally sanctioned ideas, or familiar story lines to cover them over, as each eye does its own blind spot, in order to proceed as if gaps, omissions, and ignorance were not there. This is also, as we saw, how narrative-epistolary novelists often took issue with empiricist methods, narratives, and knowledge-claims in history, law, and the human sciences – by re-presenting them from the perspective of what they did not see, failed to foresee, or could not discover.

Unseen letters also served perspectival functions by demonstrating why narratives, generalizations, preconceived ideas, and familiar story lines cannot be eliminated or dismissed even when unmasked as mere illusions of cultural competence, knowledge, and control. Faulty though they may be, they are – like literary conventions and formal devices – precisely what make visible what is unseen in social interactions, empirical reality, and literary texts. The preconceived idea in Darsie's society that people need to know who their parents are, makes the invisibility of his own parental filiation visible and remarkable enough to motivate his Highland quest for his "true" identity. Knowledge that the contents of letters have to be seen to know what they say likewise makes visible the ludicrousness of thinking, like Arabella or Lady Meadows, that one knows what letters say without seeing them. Similarly, familiarity with the practice of including certain stock information in framing narratives makes omissions from them visible and worthy of note; and the practice of making letters visible by transcription, summary, or citation makes unseen letters visible *as* invisible letters, and remarkable for being so.

This was also the advantage of recycling old, discredited romance plots centered on secrets of identity and seventeenth- and early eighteenth-century narrative-epistolary conventions well into the Victorian era. Iteration made visible what must otherwise pass unseen; namely, what particular authors were adding or abandoning on the way, and how this reflected back as comments on their predecessors' premises and perspectives. Burney and Smith's reuse of the second scaffolding device made visible their introduction of fluidity and contingency into the real and their abandonment of the practice still current in the 1750s, of confronting letter and narrative reality in a succession of static presents, in order to explore letters' now dynamic and interactive relations to mutable empirical facts and to constantly shifting past, present, and future times. Or to take another example: reuse of an analogical letter in analogical circumstances makes visible Lennox's transposition of the heroine's discovery that her guardian is really her lover from the end of *The Reform'd Coquet* to the middle of *Henrietta*, to indicate that having a guardian who wants to be her lover is a girl's misfortune, not the happy ending to her difficulties that Davys supposed. Narrative-epistolary novelists answered and commented upon one another by rewriting each other's characters and scenes, by recycling narrative-epistolary conventions and *topoi* denuded of some or all of their previous literary, epistemological, and/or empirical baggage, and by introducing variants of their own. Trollope and Collins epitomized this practice – Trollope when he used a letter to occasion a reversal in Lady Laura's life that was, for once, barren of *anagnorisis* and totally unnoticed by the other characters directly involved or when he inserted fragments of a reception narrative into letters themselves; and Collins when he used dead letters to eerily perform all the requisite functions of encapsulating letters and of pivotal letters, both – despite being emptied of content and eviscerated of substance. This practice of simultaneously reusing and re-visioning formal narrative-epistolary conventions not only made them "open sets;" it added to the perspectives narrative-epistolary fiction offered that of their authors' successive retrospective perspectives on previous uses of the generic conventions themselves.

Scott's practice and meta-critical observations in *Redgauntlet* was just such another personal and limited retrospective perspective on narrative-epistolary conventions and practices. But his dragoon image did make a key point that all the chapters in this book have illustrated: for "full comprehension of the story" in narrative-epistolary fictions, letters, and narratives must be read together – not as narrative or as letters alone. *Mixta genera* compositions work with the dynamics between and among genres. Bringing different generic media to bear in different combinations multiplied perspectives for "fuller comprehension" of a story, of its methods of narration and of the genres involved. Multiplying perspectives also complicated understandings of texts, genres, characters, and events, and indicated that no perspective or combination of perspectives necessarily supplies the whole story. These seem small things for eighteenth- and nineteenth-century narrative-epistolary novels to go to so much trouble to do. At least, they seem small things until we consider the consequences for individuals and society of what this hermeneutics of perspective set its many facets against: unfounded credulity; conjectural or biased narrative constructions based on false, distorted or mis-contextualized facts; alternative realities; selective, superficial, and headlong reading practices; easy theoretical generalities; surface judgments; the persuasiveness of plausible narratives that belie or distort the truth; unquestioning certainty; and unthinking reliance on familiar narratives and preconceived ideas.

Notes

Preface: "To the Reader"

1. Linda S. Kauffman, *Discourses of Desire* (Ithaca: Cornell University Press, 1986); Simon Sunka, *Mail-Orders: The Fiction of Letters in Postmodern Fiction* (Albany: SUNY Press, 2002); Ann Bower, *Epistolary Responses: The Letter in Twentieth-Century American Fiction and Criticism* (Tuscaloosa: University of Alabama Press, 1997); Shari Benstock, "The Printed Letters in *Ulysses*," *James Joyce Quarterly* 50:1 (2012): 167–179.
2. Stephen J. Hicks, "Eliza Haywood's Letter Technique in Three Early Novels (1721–1727)," *Papers on Language and Literature* 34:4 (Fall 1998): 420–437 (432).
3. Laura Rotunno, *Postal Plots in British Fiction 1840–1898* (Houndsmills: Palgrave-Macmillan, 2013); Kate Thomas, *Postal Pleasures: Sex, Scandal and Victorian Letters* (Oxford University Press, 2012); Karin Koheler, *Thomas Hardy and Victorian Communications: Letters, Telegraphs and Postal Systems* (London: Palgrave-Macmillan, 2016).
4. Catherine J. Golden, *Posting It: The Victorian Revolution in Letter Writing* (Gainsville: University Press of Florida, 2009); William B. Warner, "Resistance on the Circuit: The Novel in the Age of the Post," *Novel* 43:1 (Spring 2010): 169–175; Thomas Karshan, "Notes on the Image of the Undelivered Letter," *Critical Quarterly* 53:2 (2011): 12–29 (14).
5. Nicola Watson, *Revolution and the Form of the British Novel, 1790–1825* (Oxford: Clarendon, 1994): 21.
6. Robert Adams Day, *Told in Letters: Epistolary Fiction before Richardson* (Ann Arbor: University of Michigan Press, 1966): esp. chaps. 1 and 3; Janet Gurkin Altman, *Epistolarity: Approach to a Form* (Columbus: Ohio University Press, 1982): note 17, p. 46.
7. Julia Epstein, "Jane Austen's Juvenilia and the Female Epistolary Tradition," *Papers on Language and Literature* 21:4 (Fall 1985): 399–414 (403); Elizabeth Campbell, "Re-Visions, Re-Flections, Re-Creations: Epistolarity in the Novels of Contemporary Women," *Twentieth-Century Literature* 41:3 (Autumn, 1995): 332–348 (333).

8. Diane Cousineau, *Letters and Labyrinths* (Newark: University of Delaware Press, 1997): 16, 13. Thomas, *Postal Pleasures*; Cheryl L. Nixon and Louise Penner, "Writing by the Book: Jane Austen's Heroines and the Art of the Letter," *Persuasions OnLine* 26: 1 (Winter 2005) n. p.; Liz Stanley, "The Death of the Letter? Epistolary Intent, Letterness, and the many Ends of Letter Writing," *Cultural Sociology* 9:2 (2015): 240–255; Fay Bound, "Writing the Self? Love and the Letter in England, c. 1660–1760," *Literature and History*, 3rd ser., 11:1 (March 2002): 1–19. For a useful survey of scholarship on the letter genre, Claudine Van Hensbergen, "Towards an Epistolary Discourse: Receiving the Eighteenth-Century Letter," *Literature Compass* (2 July 2010): n.p.

9. In *Graphs, Maps, Trees* (London: Verso, 2007), Moretti's introduction of a long list of modern critics from whom he has taken the names and dates of different genres of novel (Courtship Novel, Gothic Novel, Evangelical Novel etc.) belies his claim that "Quantitative data are useful because they are independent of interpretation" (30) – the list demonstrates that his initial data are modern interpretative acts. This is why, as he says, "continuity between the two, the real object and the object of knowledge, disappears." (76) Making our critical categories "the object of knowledge," instead of "the real object," which are novels themselves, makes his finding from quantification that two-thirds of novel genres "arise and disappear" every 23–35 years (27) a finding about the upshot of our critical acts rather than about eighteenth-century novels. Similarly, Moretti's choice of the single indicator "clues" to "define the genre [of detective fiction] as a whole" (76) determines the exclusions which produce the "growing apart" (70) of genres that his quantitative method "discovers." Critics who choose other generic indicators – say, "use of contemporary forensic science" – find that "detective fiction" includes texts that "clues" excludes. Similarly, because graphs, maps, and trees only present patterns of successive linear movement, they preclude a priori the possibility of tracing resurgences of older genres – for instance, eighteenth-century recognition of Gothic fiction as a resurgence of romance.

10. "Introduction," in Liisa Steinby and Aino Makikalli (ed.), *Narrative Concepts in the Study of Eighteenth-Century Literature* (University of Amsterdam Press, 2017): 20.

11. For "open sets," Wai Chee Dimock, "Genres as a Field of Knowledge," *PMLA* 122:5 (October 2007): 1377–1388 (1379).

12. Rachel Carnell, *Partisan Politics, Narrative Realism and the Rise of the British Novel* (New York: Palgrave-Macmillan, 2006): 3.

13. For survival of earlier fiction, see William St. Clair, *The Reading Nation in the Romantic Period* (Cambridge University Press, 2004), esp. chaps 2, 3, and 7.

14. "Absorptive" is William Warner's term in *Licensing Entertainment* (Berkeley: University of California Press, 1998).

15. For transatlantic debates about it among eighteenth-century historians, see Eve Tavor Bannet, "Letters on the Use of Letters in Narratives: Catharine Macaulay, Susannah Rowson, and the Warren-Adams Correspondence," in Theresa Strouth Gaul and Sharon Harris (eds.), *Letters and Cultural Transformations in the United States, 1760–1860* (Farnham: Ashgate, 2009): 35–56.

Introduction: The Letters in the Story

1. William Jones, *Letter from a Tutor to His Pupils* (1780), 2nd ed. (London, 1784): 132, 130.
2. I am using "frame" here in the relatively straightforward sense of Marie-Laure Ryan's : "A narrative territory frames another territory when its verbal representation both precedes and follows the verbal representation of the framed territory." In "Stacks, Frames and Boundaries," in Brian Richardson (ed) Narrative Dynamics: *Essays on Time, Plot, Closure and Frame* (Columbus: Ohio State University press, 2002): 359. For other treatments of narrative framing, see Monika Fludernik, *Towards a Natural Narratology* (London: Routledge, 1996); Manfred Jahn, "Frames, Preferences and Reading of Third-Person Narratives," *Poetics Today* 18:4 (1997): 441–468; Stan Palmer, *Fictional Minds* (Lincoln: University of Nebraska Press, 2004); and John Frow, *Genre* (London: Routledge, 2006).
3. Roman Jakobson, "Closing Statement" in Thomas Sebeok, *Style in Language* (New York: MIT Press, 1960).
4. For the importance of "interpersonal" meanings and of the context of writing, see respectively Susan Fitzmaurice, *The Familiar Letter in Early Modern England* (Amsterdam: John Benjamins, 2002) and Rebecca Earle, "Introduction" in her *Epistolary Selves: Letters and Letter-Writers, 1600–1945* (Aldershot: Ashgate, 1999).
5. Jonathan Goldberg, *Writing Matters: From the Hands of the English Renaissance* (Stanford University Press, 1990).
6. Eve Tavor Bannet, *Empire of Letters: Letter Manuals and Transatlantic Correspondence, 1680–1820* (Cambridge University Press, 2005): chap. 2.
7. John Locke, *Thoughts on Education*, 5th ed. (London, 1705): 342–343.
8. Aphra Behn, *Love Letters to a Gentleman* in *Histories and Novels of the Late Ingenious Mrs. Behn* (London, 1698): Letter 4.
9. Samuel Johnson, "Life of Pope," in *Prefaces Biographical and Critical to the Works of the English Poets*, 10 vols. (London, 1779): 7: 238.
10. Hugh Blair, *Lectures on Rhetoric and Belles Lettres* (1783) (rpt: 2 vols. Carbondale: Southern Illinois Press, 1965): 2: 62–64.
11. John Locke, "Of the Conduct of the Understanding," in *Posthumous Works of Mr. John Locke* (London, 1706); Isaac Watts, *The Improvement of the Mind: or*

a Supplement to the Art of Logick (London, 1741); also Eve Tavor Bannet, *Eighteenth-Century Manners of Reading* (Cambridge University Press, 2017): chap.3.

12. Janet Gurkin Altman, *Epistolarity; Approaches to a Form* (Columbus: Ohio University Press, 1982): 207.

13. Barbara Shapiro, *A Culture of Fact: England 1550–1720* (Ithaca: Cornell University Press, 2000); Ian Watt, *The Rise of the Novel* (London: Chatto & Windus, 1957); Michael McKeon, *The Origins of the English Novel, 1680–1740* (Baltimore: Johns Hopkins, 1987).

14. Roger Maioli, *Empiricism and the Early Theory of the Novel* (Houndsmills: Palgrave-Macmillan, 2016): 57.

15. Quoted in Lorraine Dalston, *Classical Probability in the Enlightenment* (Princeton University Press, 1988): 242.

16. For Newton, Locke and Hume, see Zvi Biener and Eric Schliesser (ed), *Newton and Empiricism* (Oxford University Press, 2014) and Graciella De Pierris, *Ideas, Evidence, Method: Hume's Skepticism and Naturalism Concerning Knowledge and Causation* (Oxford University Press, 2015): chap. 3. For the difficulty separating narrative and the imagination from empirical operations of the mind, Jonathan Lamb, "Locke's Wild Fancies: Empiricism, Personhood and Fictionality," *The Eighteenth Century* 48:3 (Fall 2007): 187–204; Mary Poovey, *A History of the Modern Fact* (University of Chicago Press, 1998); and Tita Chico, *The Experimental Imagination* (Stanford University Press, 2018). For "the representational theory of mind," Jonathan Kramnick, "Empiricism, Cognitive Science and the Novel," *The Eighteenth Century* 48:3 (2007): 263–285.

17. Geoffrey Baker, *Realism's Empire: Empiricism and Enchantment in the Nineteenth-Century Novel* (Columbus: Ohio State University Press, 2009): 10.

18. These are Ros Ballaster's adjectives in "The Economics of Ethical Conversation," *Eighteenth-Century Life* 35 (Winter 2011): 119–132 (120).

19. Eve Tavor Bannet, "Letters" in Alasdair Pettinger and Tim Youngs (ed), *The Routledge Research Companion to Travel Writing* (New York: Routledge, 2020): 115–127.

20. Walter Scott, *Redgauntlet* 3 vols (Edinburgh, 1724): 2: 4.

21. Scott Black, "Romance Redivivius," in Robert L. Caserio and Clement Hawes (ed) *The Cambridge History of the English Novel* (Cambridge University Press, 2012).

22. April London, *The Cambridge Introduction to the Eighteenth-Century Novel* (Cambridge University Press, 2012); Terence Cave, *Recognitions* (Oxford: Clarendon, 1988).

23. Cave, *Recognitions*: 132.

24. Roland Barthes, *S/Z* (New York: Hill and Wang, 1974); Tzvetan Todorov, *The Poetics of Prose* (Ithaca: Cornell University Press, 1977) and Peter Huhn's useful "The Detective as Reader," *Modern Fiction Studies*, 33:3 (Autumn 1987): 451–466.

25. Delarivier Manley, *The Secret History of Queen Zarah and the Zaranians* (London, 1705): To the Reader, n.p. Also J. A. Downie, "Mary Davys's 'Probable Feign'd Stories' and Critical Shibboleths about the Rise of the Novel," *Eighteenth-Century Fiction* 12:2–3 (2000): 309–327.

26. Wilkie Collins, *The Moonstone and The Woman in White* (New York: Modern Library, 2015): 42.

27. See Introduction, note 9.

28. Udo Thiel, *The Early Modern Subject: Self-Consciousness and Personal Identity from Descartes to Hume* (Oxford University Press, 2011); Gideon Yaffe, "Locke on Ideas of Identity and Diversity," in Lex Newman (ed) *The Cambridge Companion to Locke's Essay Concerning Human Understanding* (Cambridge University Press, 2007); Galen Strawson, *Locke on Personal Identity: Consciousness and Concernment* (Princeton University Press, 2011).) For eighteenth-century debates about Locke, Christopher Fox, *Locke and the Scriblerians: Identity and Consciousness in Early Eighteenth-Century Britain* (Berkeley: University of California Press, 1988). See also note 35 below.

29. Strawson, *Personal Identity*, 8.

30. Though Locke's political and philosophical writings were interpreted and appropriated differently by opposite political and religious camps, conservatives and skeptics agreed that Locke's empirically observed self lacks a stable core or soul – hence the need for Hutchinson and others to at least give it a stable innate moral sense. Modern philosopher-historians have tended to assume that the now familiar unified self must appear somewhere in Locke's *Essay*, and attribute absence thereof to Hume. But Hume's description of consciousness as an ever-changing bundle of perceptions is faithful to Locke.

31. To Anne Wortley, c. 25 Aug., 1708, in *The Complete Letters of Lady Mary Wortley Montagu*, 3 vols, ed. Robert Halsband (Oxford: Clarendon, 1965): 1:3.

32. For other examples, see Peter Linebaugh, *The London Hanged* (Cambridge University Press, 1992).

33. Mary Jo Kietzman, *The Self-Fashioning of an Early Modern Englishwoman: Mary Carleton's Lives* (Aldershot: Ashgate, 2004): 9, 8.

34. Cynthia Lowenthal, *Lady Mary Wortley Montagu and the Eighteenth-Century Familiar Letter* (Athens: University of Georgia Press, 1994): 8, 11.

35. For conflicts between metaphysical concepts of the soul and the Lockean self, Raymond Martin and John Barresi, *Naturalization of the Soul: Self and Personal Identity in the Eighteenth Century* (London: Routledge, 2000) and Roger Smith, "Self-Reflection and the Self," in Roy Porter (ed), *Rewriting the Self* (London:

Routledge, 1997). For the passive, "sensible" self, Scott Paul Gordon, *The Power of the Passive Self in English Literature, 1640–1770* (Cambridge University Press, 2002); Stephen D. Cox, *"The Stranger within thee:" Concepts of the Self in Late Eighteenth Century Literature* (University of Pittsburgh Press, 1980); and Stephen Ahern, *Affected Sensibilities* (New York: AMS Press, 2007).

36. Sir William Blackstone, *An Analysis of the Laws of England*, 3rd ed. (Oxford, 1758): 25.

37. Jonathan Kramnick, "Empiricism, Cognitive Science and the Novel," *The Eighteenth Century* 48:3 (2007): 263–285 (271); Kramnick, "Locke, Haywood and Consent," *English Literary History* 72:2 (July 2005):453–470 (454). There is slippage in the latter essay to Haywood's description of her heroines' internal states, which obscures this point. Like Locke turning his understanding on the processes in his own mind, Haywood's heroines can know what they think and feel, but cannot know what is going on in the heads and hearts of their deceptive lovers, and can judge them only by what they say and do. This inability to see into others heads and hearts is also why Locke seeks clear, external manifestations of tacit consent.

38. Shaftesbury, *Sensus Communis* (London, 1709): 39, 40; Jenny Davidson, *Hypocrisy and the Politics of Politeness* (Cambridge University Press, 2004).

39. Deidre Lynch, *The Economy of Character: Novels, Market Culture and the Business of Inner Meaning* (University of Chicago Press, 1998).

40. Jane Barker, Preface to *Exilius* (1715) in *The Entertaining Novels of Mrs. Barker*, 2 vols. (London, 1736): 1:2.

41. Elaine McGirr, *Eighteenth-Century Characters* (Houndsmills: Palgrave-Macmillan, 2007): 4. Also Paul Korshin, *Typologies in England 1650–1720* (Princeton University Press, 1982, 2014) and Susan Manning, *The Poetics of Character* (Cambridge University Press, 2013), esp. chaps 3 and 7.

42. Chesterfield, *Letters to his Son* (2 vols, Dublin, 1774):2: 108, 180; *Town and Country Magazine* 8 (June 1776): 283–284; Sidney Lewis Gulick, "The Publication and Reception of Lord Chesterfield's *Letters to His Son*," Ph.D dissertation, Yale University, 1931; Rosemary Whiteway Nelson, "The Reputation of Lord Chesterfield in Britain and America," Ph.D dissertation, Northwestern University, 1938; Eve Tavor Bannet, *Transatlantic Stories and the History of Reading: Migrant Fictions* (Cambridge University Press, 2011): 193ff.

43. Alexander Welsh, *George Eliot and Blackmail* (Cambridge, MA: Harvard University Press, 1985): 75–76.

44. Mary Elizabeth Braddon, *Lady Audley's Secret*, 2 vols, (Leipzig, 1862): 1:202; Thomas Carlyle, *Sartor Resartus*, 2nd ed. (London, 1841): 77.

45. John Kucich, *The Power of Lies: Transgression in Victorian Fiction* (Ithaca: Cornell University Press, 1994); Martin Kayman, *From Bow Street to Baker*

Street: Mystery, Detection and Narrative (New York: St. Martin's Press, 1992); Anne-Lise Francois, *Open Secrets* (Stanford University Press, 2008).

46. Jon Snyder, *Dissimulation and the Culture of Secrecy in Early Modern Europe* (Berkeley: University of California Press, 2009): 99.

47. *The Complete Works and Letters of Charles Lamb* (New York: The Modern Library, 1935): 126.

48. Jane Spencer, "Narrative Technique: Austen and her Contemporaries" and Linda Bree, "*Emma*: Word Games and Secret Histories," both in Claudia Johnson and Clare Tuite (ed), *A Companion to Jane Austen* (Oxford: Blackwell, 2009).

49. Anthony Trollope, *An Autobiography* (Project Gutenberg ebook #5978, 2013): chap.10.

50. Anthony Trollope, *Phineas Redux* (London, 1858): 18.

51. Naomi Tadmor, *Family and Friends in Eighteenth-Century England* (Cambridge University Press, 2001).

52. Clare Brant, *Eighteenth-Century Letters and British Culture* (Basingstoke: Palgrave-Macmillan, 2006): 5.

53. This shift was placed with the Industrial Revolution at the end of the eighteenth century until Leonore Davidoff and Catherine Hall's *Family Fortunes: Men and Women of the English Middle Class, 1780–1850* (University of Chicago Press, 1987) argued that in practice, both began to have real impact only in the middle of the nineteenth century.

54. The extensive scholarship on history's relationship to fiction as narrative genres includes: Mark Phillips, *Society and Sentiment: Genres of Historical Writing in Britain, 1740–1820* (Princeton University Press, 2000); Philip Hicks, *Neoclassical History and English Culture: From Clarendon to Hume* (New York: St. Martin's Press, 1996); Hayden White, *The Content of the Form: Narrative Discourse and Historical Representation* (Baltimore: Johns Hopkins, 1987); Joseph M. Levine, *Humanism and History: Origins of Modern English Historiography* (Cornell University Press, 1987); Leo Braudy, *Narrative Form in History: Hume, Fielding, Gibbon* (Princeton University Press, 1970); and Devoney Looser, *British Women Writers and the Writing of History, 1670–1820* (Baltimore: Johns Hopkins Press, 2000).

55. Henry St. John Bolingbroke, "Letters on the Study and Use of History," (London, 1752): 34, 32.

56. See Phillips, *Society and Sentiment.*

57. Eve Tavor Bannet, "The Narrator as Invisible Spy," *Early Modern Cultural Studies* 14:4 (Fall 2014): 143–162.

58. Rebecca Bullard and Rachel Carnell (ed), *The Secret History in Literature, 1660– 1820* (Cambridge University Press, 2017); Tony Bowers, *Force or Fraud: British Seduction Stories and the Problem of Resistance, 1660–1760* (Oxford University

Press, 2011); Rebecca Bullard, *The Politics of Disclosure 1674–1725: Secret History Narratives* (London: Pickering & Chatto, 2009); Eve Tavor Bannet, "Secret History," *Huntington Library Quarterly* 68:1 (2005): 375–396.

59. Isaac Watts, *Logick: or the Right Use of Reason in the Enquiry after Truth*, 2nd ed. (London, 1725); David Hume, *A Treatise of Human Nature* (London, 1739).

60. *The Spectator, Tuesday, June 24, 1712 in The* Papers of Joseph Addison (Edinburgh, 1790): 3: 252.

61. Thomas Babington Macaulay, "Hallam" (1828) in *Critical and Historical Essays*, 2 vols (London: J: M. Dent, 1907): 1:1.

62. Barry Waller, "How We Live Now: Edgeworth, Austen, Dickens and Trollope," in Robert Caserio and Clement Hawes (eds), *The Cambridge History of the English Novel* (Cambridge University Press, 2012): 292, 295, 297. See also Murray Pittock, "Sir Walter Scott: Historiography Contested by Fiction" in the same volume; Jurgen Straub (ed), *Narration, Identity and Historical Consciousness* (New York: Berghen Books, 2005); and Ruth Mack, *Literary Historicity: Literature and Historical Experience in Eighteenth-Century Britain* (Stanford University Press, 2009).

63. "Essays of Elia" in *Complete Works:* 94, 95.

64. Quoted in Barbara Shapiro, *A Culture of Fact* (Ithaca: Cornell University Press, 2000): 51.

65. Anthony Grafton, *The Footnote* (Cambridge, MA: Harvard University Press, 1997).

66. Catherine Macaulay, *The History of England from the Accession of James I to the Elevation of the House of Hanover*, 5 vols, 3rd ed. (London, 1769):1: xv.

67. Franco Moretti, "History of the Novel, Theory of the Novel," *Novel* 43:1 (Spring 2010):1–10 (8, 9).

68. Wai Chee Dimock, "Genres as a Field of Knowledge," *PMLA* 122:5 (October 2007): 1377–1388 (1379).

1 Framing Narratives and the Hermeneutics of Suspicion

1. For Haywood's sales, see Introduction, in Paula Backscheider (ed), *Select Fiction and Drama of Eliza Haywood* (Oxford University Press, 1999): xx; *Love Letters* were reprinted in London for the ninth time in 1736 and again in Dublin in 1739.

2. Henry Fielding, *Joseph Andrews and Shamela*, ed. Martin Battestin (London, 1965): 23. Subsequent references will be in the text.

3. Michael McKeon, "The Eighteenth-Century Challenge to Narrative Theory," in Lisa Steinby and Aino Makikalli (eds), *Narrative Concepts in the Study of Eighteenth-Century Literature* (University of Amsterdam Press, 2017): 53

4. Part 1 is not in ECCO; The whole story is accessible in William H. McBurney, *Four Before Richardson: Selected English Novels, 1720–1727* (Lincoln: U of Nebraska Press, 1963): 153–231.

5. For instance, Rita Felski, "Suspicious Minds," *Poetics Today* 30:2 (2011): 215–234; Felski, "Critique and the Hermeneutics of Suspicion," *M/C* 15:1 (2012); and Hans-Georg Gadamer, "The Hermeneutics of Suspicion," *Man and World* 17 (1984): 313–323.

6. Rebecca Tierney-Hynes, *Novel Minds, 1680–1740* (Houndsmills: Palgrave-Macmillan, 2012), chapter 1; for a correction of her overall argument, see Tita Chico, *The Experimental Imagination* (Stanford University Press, 2018) and Cathy Caruth, *Empirical Truths and Critical Fictions* (Baltimore: Johns Hopkins University Press, 1991).

7. James Howell, *Epistolae Ho-Elianae*, 6th ed. (London 1688): "To the Knowing Reader"

8. Ellen Pollak, *Incest and the English Novel, 1684–1814* (Baltimore: The Johns Hopkins Press, 2003).

9. Janet Todd, "Fatal Fluency: Behn's Fiction and the Restoration Letter," *Eighteenth-Century Fiction* 12: 2–3 (Jan-April, 2000): 417–434 (423).

10. Aphra Behn, *Love Letters between a Nobleman and His Sister* (London, 1684): *Argument*, last page.

11. Janet Todd (ed) *The Works of Aphra Behn*, 2 vols (Columbus: Ohio State University Press, 1992) 2: vii.

12. Warren Chernaik, "Unguarded Hearts: Transgression and Epistolary form in Aphra Behn's *Love Letters* and *The Portuguese Letters*," *Journal of English and Germanic Philology*, 97:1 (Jan, 1998): 13–33 (25).

13. *The Trial of Ford Lord Grey of Werk* (London, 1716): 17, 17, 20, 22. The trial was also reprinted in *A Compleat Collection of State Tryals* (London, 1719, 1730, and 1742). Extended narrative summaries of this trial also appeared in Thomas Salmon's *Tryals for high Treason and other crimes* (London, 1720–1731); in *Critical Review of State Trials* (London, 1735); and in *A New Abridgement and Critical Review of State Trials* (Dublin, 1737).

14. Todd, "Fatal Fluency," 428.

15. [Aphra Behn] *Love Letters between a Nobleman and his Sister*, Part 2 (London, 1708): 138. Subsequent references will be in the text.

16. For "friend," Naomi Tadmor, *Family and Friends in eighteenth Century England* (Cambridge University Press, 2001); for servants, William Fleetwood, *The Relative Duties of Parents and Children, Husbands and Wives, Masters and Servants* (London, 1705) and Daniel Defoe, *The Family Instructor*, 2 vols. (London, 1715).

17. OED. Also Deidre Lynch, *The Economy of Character* (University of Chicago Press, 1998): chaps 2 and 3.

18. Ros Ballaster, "'The Story of the Heart:' *Love Letters between a Noble-Man and His Sister*," in *The Cambridge Companion to Aphra Behn*, ed. Derek Hughes and Janet Todd (Cambridge University Press, 2004): 144.

19. Anthony Grafton, "The Footnote from De Thou to Ranke," *History and Theory* 33:4 (Dec. 1994): 53–76 (62).

20. Chernaik, "Unguarded Hearts," 28; Janet Todd, "The Hot Brute Drudges on: Ambiguity and Desire in Aphra Behn's Love Letters," *Women's Writing* 1:3 (1994): 278

21. *The New Academy of Complements, erected for Ladies, Gentlewomen, Courtiers, Gentlemen, Scholars, Soldiers, Citizens, Countrymen; and all Persons of what Degree soever, of both Sexes* (London, 1698). This was in its 14th edition by 1754.

22. Isaac Watts, *The Improvement of the Mind* (London, 1741): 309. Also John Locke, "Of the Conduct of the Understanding" in *Posthumous Works of Mr. John Locke* (London, 1706): and Ambrose Philips, *The Free Thinker*, 3rd ed. (London, 1722–1723).

23. Janet Todd, "*Love Letters* and Critical History" in *Aphra Behn (1640–1689): Identity, Alterity, Ambiguity*, ed. Bernard Dhuicq, et al (Paris: Sorbonne, 1999): 198.

24. Backscheider, *Select Fiction*, xx.

25. Kathryn R. King, "Henry and Eliza: Feudlings or Friends," in J. A. Downie (ed) *Henry Fielding in our Time* (Newcastle-upon-Tyne: Cambridge Scholars, 2008): 219ff.

26. *The Works of Mrs. Eliza Haywood*, 4 vols. (London, 1724): 3: 29, 8.

27. Haywood, *Works*, 3:7.

28. Eliza Haywood, *Fantomina and Other Works*, ed. Alexander Pettit et al (Peterborough: Broadview, 2004): 58. Subsequent references are in the text.

29. Backscheider, *Select Fiction*, 90. Subsequent references are in the text.

30. Kirsten T. Saxton, "Telling Tales: Eliza Haywood and the Crimes of Seduction in *the City Jilt*," in Kirsten Saxon and Rebecca Bocchicchio (eds), *The Passionate Fictions of Eliza Haywood* (Lexington: University Press of Kentucky, 2000): 126.

31. Haywood, *Works*, 3: 25, 21. For Austen's reuse of this *topos*, Cheryl Nixon and Louise Penner, "Writing by the Book: Jane Austen's Heroines and the Art of the Letter," *Persuasions OnLine* 26:1 (Winter 2005) n. p.

32. Haywood, *Works*, 3:9.

33. Margaret Case Croskery, "Novel Romanticism in 1751: Eliza Haywood's *Betsy Thoughtless*," in Miriam L. Wallace, *Enlightening Romanticism, Romancing the Enlightenment* (Farnham: Ashgate, 2009): 25, 36.

34. Samuel Richardson, "Preface by the Editor" to the first edition, in John Bullitt (ed), *Pamela and Shamela*, (New York: Meridian Classic, 1980): 21.

35. Haywood, *Anti-Pamela* (London: 1741).
36. For other contemporary attacks, Tom Keymer and Peter Sabor, *Pamela in the Marketplace* (Cambridge University Press, 2005).
37. Other allusions to Romances in this novel include Fielding's attack on voluminous seventeenth-century French Romances in his Author's Preface, and embedded narrative-epistolary romances modeled on Haywood's ("The Unfortunate Jilt," the Wilson story) For useful but condescending discussion of these: Jeffrey Williams, "The Narrative Circle: The Interpolated Tales in *Joseph Andrews*," *Studies in the Novel* 30:4 (1998):473–488; and Homer Goldberg, "The Interpolated Stories in *Joseph Andrews*" *Modern Philology* 63:4 (May 1996): 295–310.
38. Tom Keymer, *Richardson's 'Clarissa' and the Eighteenth-Century Reader* (Cambridge University Press, 1992); Eve Tavor Bannet, "Readers and Reading" in *Samuel Richardson in Context*, ed. Peter Sabor and Betty Schellenberg (Cambridge University Press, 2017).
39. Scholars who recognize that "*Joseph Andrews* was participating in a debate that was as much about the current state of historiography as it was about the development of the novel," disagree on whether Fielding was writing as an empiricist or as a universalizing neoclassical historian, entirely overlooking his allusions to secret history. See Noelle Gallagher, "Historiography, the Novel and Fielding's *Joseph Andrews*," *SEL* 52:3 (2012): 631–650 (632); Roger Maioli, "Empiricism and Fielding's Theory of Fiction," *ECF* 27:2 (Winter 2014–2015): 201–228 and Rudiger Campe, "Improbable Probability: On Evidence in the Eighteenth Century," *The Germanic Review* 76:2 (Mar. 2010): 143–161.
40. Haywood, *The Female Spectator*, 4 vols. (London, 1774–1746) 1: 4; Eve Tavor Bannet, "The Narrator as Invisible Spy: Eliza Haywood, Secret History and the Novel," *Early Modern Cultural Studies* 14:4 (Fall 2014): 143–162.
41. April London, *The Cambridge Introduction to the Eighteenth-Century Novel* (Cambridge University Press, 2012): chap 2; Mark Philips, *Society and Sentiment: Genres of Historical Writing in Britain, 1740–1820* (Princeton University Press, 2000); Ted Underwood, "Historiography" in *A Handbook of Romanticism*, ed. Joel Faflek and Julia Wright (Hoboken, NJ: Wiley-Blackwell, 2012).
42. William Warner, *Licensing Entertainment* (Berkeley: University of California Press, 1998): 257, 235, 261.
43. Eliza Haywood, *The History of Miss Betsy Thoughtless*, ed. Christine Blouch (Peterborough: Broadview, 1998): 66. Subsequent references are in the text.
44. On the puppet-show chapters, Eve Tavor Bannet, *Eighteenth-Century Manners of Reading* (Cambridge University Press, 2017): Afterword.
45. The relationship between Fielding and Haywood has been in dispute, most recently among John Richetti, Kathryn King, and Margaret Case Croskery,

all correcting the view propounded by John Elwood ("Henry Fielding and Eliza Haywood: a Twenty Year War," *Albion* 4 (Fall 1973): 184–192), that Fielding and Haywood were feuding. Haywood and Fielding clearly knew each other: Haywood joined Fielding's theatre company in its last year; Fielding cast Haywood as Mrs. Novel and the Muse in plays. Assuming perhaps that Fielding was the great writer that everyone wished to emulate, Richetti and Croskery describe Haywood as an imitator of Fielding. I am arguing the contrary: Fielding drew on Haywood.

46. Henry Fielding, *Amelia* 2 vols. (London: Everyman, 1962): 2, 78. Subsequent references are in the text.

47. Alison Conway observed in 1995 that, having dismissed Amelia as Fielding's failed attempt to emulate Richardson's portrayals of the virtuous woman and virtuous wife, "critics today tend to ignore *Amelia*." Robert Hume shows that this is still the case. Alison Conway, "Fielding's Amelia and the Aesthetics of Virtue," *Eighteenth-Century Fiction* 8:1 (Oct. 1995): 35–50 (36) and Robert D. Hume's very useful "Fielding at 300: Elusive, Confusing, Misappropriatd, or (Perhaps) Obvious?," *Modern Philology* 108: 2 (Nov. 2010): 224–262.

48. Felicia Bonaparte, "Conjecturing Possibilities: Reading and Misreading Texts in Jane Austen's *Pride and Prejudice*" *Studies in the Novel* 37: 2 (July 2005): 141–161 (152); Claudia Brodsky, "Austen's *Pride and Prejudice* and Hegel's 'Truth in Art': Concept, Reference, History," *ELH* 59:3 (Fall 1992): 597–623 (607); Rosanne Cavallero, "*Pride and Prejudice* as Proof: Quotidian Fact-Finding and Rules of Evidence," *Hastings Law Journal* 53: 3 (February 2004): 697–785 (699); Janet Todd, *An Introduction to Jane Austen*, 2nd ed. (Cambridge University Press, 2015): 15;. Peter Knox-Shaw, *Jane Austen and the Enlightenment* (Cambridge University Press, 2004); Mark Canvel, "Jane Austen and the Importance of Being Wrong," *Studies in Romanticism* 44:2 (July 2005): 123–150; Gary Kelly, "The Art of Reading in *Pride and Prejudice*," *English Studies in Canada* 10:2 (1984): 156–171.

49. Thomas Keymer, "Narrative," in Janet Todd (ed) *The Cambridge Companion to Pride and Prejudice* (Cambridge University Press, 2013): 10.

50. Jenny Davidson, *Reading Jane Austen* (Cambridge University Press, 2017): 51.

51. Bonaparte, "Conjecturing possibilities;" also Zelda Boyd, "The Language of Supposing: Modal Auxiliaries in *Sense and Sensibility*" *Women and Literature* 3 (1983): 142–154.

52. Knox-Shaw, *Austen and the Enlightenment,* 12; John Wiltshire, *The Hidden Jane Austen* (Cambridge University Press, 2014): 55.

53. Martha Satz, "An Epistemological Approach to *Pride and Prejudice: Humility and Objectivity,"* in Janet Todd (ed) *Jane Austen: New Perspectives* (London: Holmes and Meir, 1983): (171–186); 171, 173, 177, 179.

54. Cavallero, "*Pride and Prejudice* as Proof," 704–705, 717–718, 722.

55. For other approaches to "Austen's resistance to Romance" and equivocal writing see essays by E. J. Clery, Tom Keymer and Margaret Ann Doody in Edward Copeland and Juliet McMaster (ed), *The Cambridge Companion to Jane Austen*, rev. ed. (Cambridge University Press, 2011).

56. *Universal Magazine*, 11:66 (May 1809): 394–397 (394).

57. See Introduction, "Mystery Plots and Romance Conventions" section.

58. See Introduction, "Mystery Plots and Romance Conventions" section.

59. For Cave, see Introduction. For an approach to Fielding's "gaps" and "omissions" inspired by Wolfgang Iser's *The Implied Reader* (Baltimore: Johns Hopkins University Press, 1974), see Wilhelm Fuger, "Limits of the Narrator's Knowledge in Fielding's *Joseph Andrews*: A Contribution to a Theory of Negated Knowledge in Fiction," *Style* 38:3 (Fall 2004): 278–291 and Stephen Dobranski, "What Fielding Doesn't Say in *Tom Jones*," *Modern Philology* 107:4 (May 2010): 632–653.

60. For other women writers' methods of discrediting their happy endings, see Laurie Langbauer, *Women and Romance* (Ithaca: Cornell University Press, 1990).

2 Letters and Empirical Evidence

1. Anon [Delarivier Manley], *Bath Intrigues in Four Letters to a Friend in London* (London, 1725): 7–8.

2. As a topos, this can be traced back to Brilliard's forged letter in Behn's *Love Letters*, part 2.

3. Jane Spencer, *The Rise of the Woman Novelist* (Oxford: Clarendon, 1986): 146.

4. Jan Stahl, "Violence, Friendship and the Education of the Heroine in Mary Davys's *The Reform'd Coquet*," *Studies in the Literary Imagination*, 47:20 (2014): 23–38 (23); Andrew Dicus, "Everything Is Lost in Amoranda's Garden: Epistemology and Legitimacy in Mary Davys's *The Reform'd Coquet*," *Eighteenth-Century Fiction* 28:2 (Winter 2015–2016): 263–285 (266); Michael Genovese, "Middlemen and Marriage in Mary Davys's *The Reform'd Coquet*," *Studies in English Literature* 54:3 (Summer 2014): 555–584 (555).

5. Mary Davys, *The Reform'd Coquet* (London, 1724): 12. Subsequent page numbers are in the text.

6. For the importance of female friendship in this novella, see Stahl, "Violence."

7. Eliza Haywood, *The History of Miss Betsy Thoughtless*, ed. Christine Blouch (Peterborough: Broadview, 1998): 250. Subsequent page numbers are in the text.

8. David Hume, *Philosophical Essays Concerning Human Understanding* (London, 1748): 36.

9. David Hume, *The History of England from the Invasion of Julius Caesar to the Revolution in 1688*, 8 vols (London, 1767): See for instance, 1: 128–130; 2: 34–35; 3: 82.

10. Catharine Macaulay, *The History of England from the Accession of James I to the Elevation of the House of Stuart*, 5 vols; 3rd ed. (London: 1869): I: xii.

11. Oliver Goldsmith, *The Life of Richard Nash Esq.* (London, 1762): 68, 69, 70, 101, 104.

12. Goldsmith, *Life*, 22, 3, 4, v.

13. Goldsmith, *Life*, 76.

14. Macaulay, *History of England*, I: xv

15. For the wider argument among historians, Eve Tavor Bannet, "Letters on the Use of Letters in Narratives: Catharine Macaulay, Susannah Rowson, and the Warren-Adams Correspondence," in Theresa Strouth Gaul and Sharon Harris (eds), *Letters and Cultural Transformations in the United States, 1760–1860* (Farnham: Ashgate, 2009): 35–56.

16. Oliver Goldsmith made the same points about letters in *The Vicar of Wakefield*. Burchell's authorship of an unsigned letter that Primrose's son finds lying on the green is immediately "detected" and Primrose's misreading of it as evidence of his "villainy" is soon corrected when his daughter contextualizes it. When Primrose's son George writes a letter about his success in the army, the family has no sooner finished rejoicing at his good fortune, than they look up to see George being dragged to prison, bloodied and in chains. Empirical evidence of the truth or falsity of a letter is always readily available. And none of the letters embedded in this novel have any impact on reality: letters of recommendation meet rejections, letters warning those concerned of Thornhill's villainy cannot even be delivered.

17. *The Moral and Political Writings of Thomas Hobbes of Malmsbury* (London, 1753): chap 4, # 10; Hume, *Philosophical Essays* (1748): 590, see esp. Essays 3, 4, 6; For a history of conjecture, James Franklin, *The Science of Conjecture: Evidence and Probability before Pascal* (Baltimore: The Johns Hopkins Press, 2001) and Douglas Lane Paley, *Probability and Literary Form* (Cambridge University Press, 1984).

18. H. M Hopfl, "From Savage to Scotsman: Conjectural History in the Scottish Enlightenment," *Journal of British Studies* 17:2 (1978): 19–40 (19, 20).

19. Thomas Reid, *An Inquiry into the Human Mind*, 3rd ed. revised (London 1769): 281.

20. William Stukeley, *Stonehenge a Temple restor'd to the British Druids* (London, 1740): 48; W. Salmon, *A New Survey of England*, 2 vols (London, 1731): I: 233; Locke, *Essay Concerning Human Understanding* (London, 1753): chap 10, 125.

21. Alexander Welsh, *Strong Representations: Narrative and Circumstantial Evidence in England* (Baltimore: Johns Hopkins University Press, 1991); Barbara Shapiro, *Probability and Certainty in Seventeenth-Century England* (Princeton University Press, 1983); Lorraine Dalston, *Classical Probability in the Enlightenment* (Princeton University Press, 1988).

22. Cited in Dugald Stewart, *Elements of the Philosophy of the Human Mind*, 3 vols (London, 1792): 351, 408.
23. This omits the forty letters in the casket and twenty to thirty awaited letters.
24. Samuel Johnson, *A Dictionary of the English Language* (London, 1756, 1777): "Conjecture." Also Kevin Goodman, "Conjectures on Beach Head: Charlotte Smith's Geological Poetics and the Ground of the Present," *ELH* 81:3 (2014): 983–1006.
25. Charlotte Smith, *Emmeline: The Orphan of the Castle*, ed. Loraine Fletcher (Peterborough: Broadview, 2003): 254. References are subsequently in the text.
26. Hopfl, "Savage to Scotsman," 32.
27. Eve Tavor Bannet, "Adulterous Sentiments in Transatlantic Domestic Fiction, c 1770–1805," in Toni Bowers and Tita Chico (ed), *Atlantic Worlds in the Long Eighteenth Century* (New York: Palgrave-Macmillan, 2012).
28. Mary Elizabeth Braddon, *Lady Audley's Secret*, 2 vols. (Leipzig, 1862): 1: 242. Subsequent references are n the text.
29. Sir James Graham, "Criminal Returns. Metropolitan Police," *Edinburgh Review*, July 1852: 6. Also Ronald R. Thomas, *Detective Fiction and the rise of Forensic Science* (Cambridge University Press, 1999).
30. William Paley, *The Principles of Moral and Political Philosophy*, 2 vols. (London, 1788): 2: 300. Paley was much reprinted during the nineteenth century; these passages were still being quoted as authoritative in the 1860s.
31. Alexander Annesley, *Strictures on the True Cause of the Present Alarming Scarcity of Grain and other Provisions* (London, 1800): 9; S; Hahnemann, "Speculative Systems of Medicine" in William Radde, *The Lesser Works of S. Hahnemann* (1852): 489.
32. For the pigeonhole as *topos* of "archival anxieties," Anne Jacob, "The Pocket-Book and the Pigeon Hole: *Lady Audley's Secret* and the Files of Victorian Fiction," *Victorian Studies* 61:3 (2019): 371–394.
33. William Willis, *An Essay on the Principles of Circumstantial Evidence* (London, 1860): 17, 18, 30, 35, 42, 43. For the larger context, Katherine Anders, "Detecting Arguments: The Rhetoric of Evidence in Nineteenth-Century British Fiction," (Proquest Dissertation, 2014).
34. John Charles Bucknell and Daniel H. Tuke, *A Manual of Psychological Medicine* (Philadelphia 1858): 130, 132, 192, 193. Also Vicki Pallo, "From Do-Nothing to Detective: the Transformation of Robert Audley," *Journal of Popular Culture* 39:3 (June 2006): 466–476.
35. Sir John Hill, *Hypochondriasis* (London, 1775): 10, 18; Thomas King Chambers, "Lecture on Hypochondriasis," *The British Medical Journal* (July 5, 1873): 6–8 (6). Recent scholarly arguments for Audley's homosociality or homosexuality and for the two men as doubles or doppelgangers, attach here.

36. Lady Audley's confession uses arguments that working and lower-middle class defendants regularly made in bigamy trials, in which judges handed out merely token sentences. See Ginger Frost, "Bigamy and Cohabitation in Victorian England," *Journal of Family History* 22:3 (July 1997): 286–306 and Rebecca Probart, *Double Trouble: The Rise and Fall of the Crime of Bigamy* (London: Selden Society, 2015): 8–9. For bigamous plots elsewhere in Victorian fiction, Maia Macleavey, "The Plot of Bigamous Return," *Representations* 123 (2013): 87–117. Bigamy plots were not unknown earlier; see, for instance, Frances Sheridan's *Memoirs of Miss Sidney Biddulph* (1761).

37. For women's fear of wrongful confinement, and other treatments of testimony, mental competence and lunacy in nineteenth-century fiction, see Christine Krueger, *Reading for the Law: British Literary History and Gender Advocacy* (Charlottesville: University of Virginia Press, 2010).

38. Ann-Marie Dunbar, "Making the Case: Detection and Confession in *Lady Audley's Secret* and *The Woman in White*," *Victorian Review* 40:1 (Spring 2014): 97–116 (101).

39. The classic work here is John Gillis, *For Better or Worse* (Oxford University Press, 1985) Divorce became possible in England in 1857, but remained very expensive, ensuring that traditional practices of self-divorce and remarriage continued to the end of the nineteenth century. Problems in English marriage law, and discrepancies between marriage laws in England, Scotland, and Ireland, which facilitated voluntary and involuntary bigamy led in 1865 to establishment of a Royal Commission on the Laws of Marriage. See Jeanne Fahnestock, "Bigamy: the Rise of A Convention," *Nineteenth-Century Fiction* 35:1 (June 1987): 47–71.

40. Gail Turley Houston, "Mary Braddon's Commentaries on the Trials and Legal Secrets of Audley Court," in Marlene Tromp et al (ed) *Beyond Sensation: Mary Elizabeth Braddon in Context* (Albany: State University of New York Press, 2000): 18, 20.

41. Jill Matus, "Disclosure as 'Cover-Up:' the Discourse of Madness in *Lady Audley's Secret*," *University of Toronto Quarterly* 62:3 (1993): 334–355; John Kucich, *The Power of Lies: Transgression in Victorian Fiction* (Ithaca: Cornell University Press, 1995).

42. "Multiple Personality," rpt in *New Library of Medicine*, vol. 7 (April 30, 1876): 397; for arguments against the medical establishment, John King, *Man an Organic Community, being an Exposition of the Law that the Human Personality . . . is a Multiple of many Subpersonalities* (New York: 1893); and "Multiple Personality as a normal Condition of Human Existence," *Current Opinion* 57:2 (August 1914): 115–116. For Victorian psychological schemata, Rick Rylance, *Victorian Psychology and British Culture 1850–1880* (Oxford University Press, 2000).

43. "On Insanity Considered in a Pathological, Philosophical, Historical and Judicial point of View," *The Medico-Chirurgical Review* 4:7 (July 1846) 49–68 (50).

44. Edward Hocken, "Amaurosis from Hysteria, Acute and Chronic, Its Diagnosis, Pathology and Treatment," *Edinburgh Medical-Surgical Journal*, 57:150 (January 1, 1842): 49–62 (51–52). For the importance of "the strong personality or character," Henry Maudsley, *The Physiology and Pathology of Mind* (London 1867): 158–160.

45. Murder and attempted murder are not the same. This novel should also be related to the many afterlives of medieval tales about supposedly murdered people who turn up alive. During the eighteenth century, JPs were instructed to void the sentence for murder when this occurred.

46. Adam Smith, *Lectures on Rhetoric and Belles Lettres delivered at the University of Glasgow, reported by a student in 1762–1763*, ed. John M. Lothian (London: T. Nelson, 1963): 47.

47. See also Tita Chico, *The Experimental Imagination* (Stanford University Press, 2018).

48. The phases of empiricist developments here are distilled from the work of Barbara Shapiro, Lorraine Dalston, Douglas Lane Patey, Alexander Welsh, James Franklin, Tita Chico, Ronald Thomas, and Katherine Anders.

49. Bolingbroke, quoted in Shapiro, *Culture of Fact*, 114.

50. Alexander Welsh, *Strong Representations: Narrative and Circumstantial Evidence in England* (Baltimore: Johns Hopkins Press, 1992).

51. "Fact," OED, 8a.

52. Giles Jacob, *A Law Grammar or Rudiments of the Law* (London, 1749): 131, 132.

53. This is more fully explored in Lorraine Daston, "Marvelous Facts and Miraculous Evidence in early Modern Europe," in James Chandler et al (ed), *Questions of Evidence: Proof, Practice and Persuasion across the Disciplines* (University of Chicago Press, 1994).

54. John Stuart Mill, *A System of Logic*, (New York, 1846): 3. Subsequent references are in the text.

55. Richard Simpson, "Positivism," *The Rambler* 9 (May 1858): 316–352 (317, 352).

3 Cultural Expectations and Encapsulating Letters

1. Douglas Lane Patey, *Probability and Literary Form: Philosophic theory and Literary Practice in the Augustan Age* (Cambridge University Press, 1984): 35.

2. James Franklin, *The Science of Conjecture: Evidence and Probability before Pascal* (Baltimore: The Johns Hopkins Press, 2001; Barbara Shapiro, *Probability and Certainty in Seventeenth-Century England* (Princeton University Press, 1983)

and ibid., *A Culture of Fact: England 1550–1720* (Ithaca: Cornell University Press, 2000).

3. Amy Witherbee, "The Temporality of the Public in *The Tatler* and *The Spectator*," The Eighteenth Century 51:1–2 (Apr. 2010): 173–192 and her dissertation, "New Conceptions of Time and the Making of a Political-Economic Public in Eighteenth-Century Britain" (Boston College, 2009).

4. Useful studies of these include: Michael Whitmore, *Culture of Accidents: Unexpected Knowledges in Early Modern England* (Stanford University Press, 2001); Christopher R. Miller, *Surprise: The Poetic of the Unexpected from Milton to Austen* (Ithaca: Cornell University Press, 2015); Jesse Molesworth, *Chance and the Eighteenth-Century Novel: Realism, Probability, Magic* (Cambridge University Press, 2010).

5. Lorraine Dalston, *Classical Probability in the Enlightenment* (Princeton University Press, 1988): 213. The quote is from Condorcet.

6. Dalston, *Classical Probability*: 66, 67, 65, 159, 155.

7. Charlotte Lennox, *The Female Quixote*, ed. Margaret Dalziel (Oxford University Press, 1989): 10. Subsequent references are in the text.

8. Elizabeth Inchbald is still using this cultural archetype for Hannah in *Nature and Art* (1796).

9. Mrs. Barbauld, *The British Novelists* (London, 1820): vol. 24: iii.

10. Charlotte Lennox, *Henrietta*. (London, 1758) 1: 8, 9. Subsequent references are in the text.

11. Christine Davidson, "Conversation as Signifiers: Characters at the Margins of Morality in the First Three Novels of Frances Burney," *Partial Answers* 8:2 (2010): 277–304 (282).

12. Thirty letters are fully transcribed; ten rendered in free indirect discourse; one is presented through a mix of transcription and free indirect discourse; two are treated at length as letter-objects; and the contents of the rest are summarized with varying amounts of detail.

13. Maria Edgeworth, *Belinda*, ed. Linda Bree (Oxford University Press, 2020): Advertisement. Subsequent references in the text.

14. Jane Austen, *Northanger Abbey* (London: J. M. Dent, 1994): 23; for Edgeworth's rewrite of *Cecilia*, see Linda Bree's Introduction to *Belinda*, xxix ff.

15. *The Monthly Review* 37 (1801): 369.

16. See Eve Tavor Bannet, "Letters, Expectations and the Ancient Regime in Charlotte Smith's *The Old Manor House*," *Journal of Epistolary Studies* 1:1 (Fall 2019) online.

17. Mary Brunton, *Self-Control* (London, 1811) was reprinted in 1838 and 1849. Wilkie Collins, *Armadale* (London, 1866).

18. Barbauld, *British Novelists*, vol. 49: i.

19. For the importance of waiting, Michael Tondre, "The Interval of Expectation: Delay, Delusion and the Psychology of Suspense in *Armadale*," ELH 78:3 (2011): 585–608.
20. Wilkie Collins, *The Dead Secret*, (Leipzig, 1857): 13, 14. Subsequent references are in the text.
21. See Christine Bolus-Reichert, "The Foreshadowed Life in Wilkie Collins's *No Name*," *Studies in the Novel* 41:1 (Spring 2009): 22–42.
22. See Vicky Simpson, "Selective Affinities; Non-Normative Families in Wilkie Collins' No Name," *Victorian Review* 39:2 (2013): 115–128 (117).
23. Preface to *No Name*.
24. Wilkie Collins, *Armadale*, 2 vols (London, 1866): 1: 99.
25. Tondre, "Interval," 587; Irene Tucker, "Paranoid Imaginings: Wilkie Collins, the Rugeley Prisoner and the Invisibility of Novelistic Ekphrasis," *Partial Answers* 1 (Jan 2010): 147–167 (147); L. Roberts, "The Shivering Sands of Reality: Narration and Knowledge in the Moonstone," *Victorian Review* 23:2 (1997): 168–183 (168); Sue Lonoff, "Multiple Narratives and Relative Truths," *Browning Institute Studies* 10 (1982): 143–161.
26. This is followed by a second encapsulating letter, written by Phineas to his lawyer-patron and employer, which is absolutely analogical to this, for emphasis.
27. Anthony Trollope, *Phineas Finn* (Hertfordshire: Wordsworth Classics, 1996): 17. Subsequent references in the text.
28. Surprisingly little has been done with Trollope's letters; but see Ellen Moody, "Partly Told In letters: Trollope's Story-telling Art," *Trollopiana* (February 2000); rpt. *The Victorian Web* (2007); and David Pearson, "The Letter Killeth: Epistolary Purposes and Techniques in *Sir Henry Humblethwaite*," *Nineteenth-Century Fiction* 37:3 (December 1982): 396–418.
29. Patrick Fessenberger, "Anthony Trollope on Akrasia, Self-Deception and Ethical Confusion," *Victorian Studies* 56:4 (Summer 2014): 649, 664.
30. In this they were not unique; see note 4.
31. Roger Maioli, *Empiricism and the Early Theory of the Novel* (Houndsmills: Palgrave-Macmillan, 2016): 62.
32. Ibid.
33. John Stuart Mill, *A System of Logic* (New York, 1846): 192, 184.

4 Epistolary *Peripeteiae*

1. See Introduction, sect. 3. For the numerous Prefaces claiming their novels would elicit "pity and terror," see Cheryl Nixon (ed) *An Anthology of Commentary on the Novel, 1688–1815* (Peterborough: Broadview, 2009).
2. *The Poetics of Aristotle,* translated with notes by Henry James Pye, (London, 1781): 61. There were only two eighteenth-century English translations with

notes: Pye's and Thomas Twining's *Aristotle Treatise on Poetry Translated with Notes on the Translation and on the Original and Two Dissertations on Poetical and Musical Imitation* (1789). But Aristotle's rules were also available in schoolbooks, such as Charles Gildon's "The Art of Poetry" attached to Brightland's best-selling *Grammar of the English Tongue* from 1714 on, or Hugh Blair's *Lectures on Rhetoric and Belles Lettres* (1783).

3. See the Retrospective to Chapter 1.

4. I am indebted here to Terence Cave, *Recognitions* (Oxford University Press, 1988); J. C. Eade *Aristotle Anatomised: The Poetics in England 1674–1781*, (Frankfurt: Peter Lang, 1988); John MacFarlane, "Aristotle's Definition of Anagnorisis," *American Journal of Philology* 121:3 (Autumn 2000): 367–383; Roger Herzel, "Anagnorisis and Peripetia in Comedy," *Educational Theatre Journal* 26:4 (Dec. 1974): 495–505; and Henry W. Johnstone, "Truth, Anagnorisis and Argument," *Philosophy and Rhetoric* 16:1 (Jan 1983): 1–15.

5. *Love's Intrigues* in Carol Shiner Wilson (ed) *The Galesia Trilogy and Selected Manuscript Poems* (Oxford University Press, 1997): 18, 26. Subsequent references in the text.

6. Jane Austen, *The Complete Novels* (Oxford University Press, 1994): 111, 113. Subsequent references are in the text.

7. Novel-readers who are puzzled by Marianne's unexplained and curiously rapid reaction to Willoughby's letter without reading it, have to do the same as Elinor: read backward from Marianne's third transcribed note (which reaches us last) and put the correspondence back into chronological order. Since this note concludes by asking Willoughby to return her lock of hair and previous notes if his "sentiments are no longer what they were;" Marianne knows what Willoughby's missive will contain the instant she opens his letter and her hair and notes fall out.

8. Robert Hume, "Money in Jane Austen," *Review of English Studies* 64: 264 (2013): 289–310.

9. Aristotle's much cited example is the story of the statue of Mitys that suddenly fell on Mitys's murderer while the latter happened to be watching a spectacle, and killed him.

10. Jane Austen, *Persuasion*, ed. Linda Bree (Peterborough: Broadview, 1998): 241, 30. Subsequent quotations in the text.

11. For analysis of this scene in terms of wish-fulfillment, see Christopher Miller, *Surprise: The Poetics of the Unexpected from Milton to Austen* (Ithaca: Cornell 2015), 152ff

12. See Chapter 3, p. 131 above.

13. Jane Austen, *Northanger Abbey*, ed. Elisabeth Mahoney (London: Everyman, 1994): 62. Subsequent references in the text.

14. For the novel's wider "dynamic of remembering-forgetting," Jilian Heydt-Stevenson, "*Northanger Abbey, Desmond* and History," *The Wordsworth Circle* 44:2–3 (Spring/Summer 2013): 140–148; for its treatment of conjecture, Jonathan Lamb, "Imagination, Conjecture and Disorder," *Eighteenth-Century Studies* 45:1 (Fall 2011).

15. Elisha Cohn, "Suspended Animation in Charlotte Bronte's *Villette, SEL* 52:4 (Autumn 2012): 847, 845.

16. Charlotte Bronte, *Villette* (New York: Modern Library, 2001): 356. Subsequent references in the text.

17. See for instance, Gretchen Braun, "A Great Break in the Common Course of Confession: Narrating Loss in Charlotte Bronte's *Villette*," *English Literary History* 78:1 (2011): 189–212; Heidi Helen Davis, "I Seem to Hold Two Lives: Disclosing Circumnarration in *Villette* and *The Picture of Dorian Grey*," *Narrative* 21:2 (2013): 198–220; Beverly Forsyth, "The Two Faces of Lucy Snowe: A Study in Deviant Behavior," *Studies in the Novel* 29:1 (Spring 1997): 17–25; Sally Chuttelworth, *Charles Bronte and Victorian Psychology* (Cambridge University Press 1996); Leila Sylvan May, "Lucy Snowe: A Material Girl?: Phrenology, Surveillance and the Sociology of Interiority," *Criticism* 551:1 (2013): 43–68.

18. For other views of letters in *Villette*, see Tamara S. Wagner, "Containing Emotional Distress: the Elusive Letter Novel in *Villette*," Bronte Studies 36:2 (July 2013): 131–140; Steven Earnshaw, "Charlotte Bronte's Fictional Epistles," *Bronte Studies* 40:3 August 2015): 201–214.

19. Nicholas Dames, "Trollope and the Career: Vocational Trajectories and the Management of Ambition," *Victorian Studies* 45:2 (Winter 2003): 247–278 (253).

20. Anthony Trollope, *Phineas Finn* (London, 1873): 542. Subsequent references in the text.

21. Charlotte Smith, *The Old Manor House* (London: Pandora, 1987): 358. Subsequent references are in the text.

22. Jane Austen, *Mansfield Park* (Peterborough: Broadview, 2003): 395. Subsequent references in the text.

23. Anthony Trollope, *Phineas Redux* (London, 1859): 78, 82. Subsequent references in the text.

24. Peter Brooks, *Reading for the Plot* (Cambridge, MA: Harvard University Press, 1992): 10. His book is based entirely on "the great nineteenth century narrative tradition ... that conceived certain kinds of knowledge and truth to be inherently narrative ... " (xi) For nineteenth-century *peripeteia* understood as "the idea of the moment as a turning point" (18) and a reading of different materials, see Sue Zemka, *Time and the Moment in Victorian Literature and Society* (Cambridge University Press, 2012).

25. Cave, *Recognitions*, 122.

26. Philip Kennedy and Marilyn Lawrence (ed), *The Poetics of Narrative: Interdisciplinary Studies in Anagnorisis* (New York: Peter Lang, 2009): 2. This makes the detective novel the ultimate Romance – as well as literary history's most complete incarnation and reaffirmation of realism's pretense.

27. Roland Barthes, *S/Z* (1970; tr. New York: Hill & Wang, 1974); Robert Louis Stevenson, "A Note on Realism" (1883) in *Essays in the Art of Writing* (London, 1919): 97–98, 95; Carlyle quoted in Henry Levin, "What is Realism?" *Comparative Literature* 3:3 (Summer 1951): 193–199 (193).

28. Elizabeth Deeds Ermarth, *Realism and Consensus in the English Novel* (Edinburgh University Press, 1998): ix.

29. Charles Dickens, *A Tale of Two Cities* (1859): John Reed, *Victorian Conventions* (Athens: Ohio University Press, 1975): 4.

30. *Reading for the Plot*; Anthony Trollope, *Thackeray* (London, 1887): 185.

31. Geoffrey Baker, *Realism's Empire: Empiricism and Enchantment in the Nineteenth-Century Novel* (Columbus: Ohio State University Press, 2009); Michael McKeon, "The Eighteenth-Century Challenge to Narrative Theory," in Lisa Steinby and Aino Makikalli (eds) *Narrative Concepts in the Study of Eighteenth-Century Literature* (University of Amsterdam Press, 2017).

32. Gary Morson, "Contingency and Poetics," *Philosophy and Literature* 22:2 (October 1998): 286–308 (291); Brooks, xi–xii; Peter Huhn, "The Detective as Reader: Narrativity and Reading Concepts in Detective Fiction," *Modern Fiction Studies* 33:3 (Autumn 1987): 451–466.

33. Brooks, 22.

5 Hermeneutics of Perspective

1. There are welcome departures in Tobias Scholter, "Pluralism and Perspectivism: Knowledge and the Condition of its Limits" in Michael Anacher and Nadia Moro (ed), *Limits of Knowledge: The Nineteenth-Century Epistemological Debate and Beyond* (Mimesis International, 2015) n. p.; Ruth Ronen, *Representing the Real* (Amsterdam: Rodopi, 2002): chap 5; Wilkie van Peter & Seymour Chatman (ed), *New Perspectives on Narrative Perspective* (Albany: State University of New York Press, 2001) and Peter Huhn, Wolf Schmid and Jorg Schonert (ed), *Point of View, Perspective and Focalization* (Berlin: De Gruyter, 2009). The latter argues that perspective is central to all verbal, visual, and multimodal "mediations" and demonstrates as many divergent perspectives on perspective as there are authors of its chapters.

2. Rosalie Colie, *The Resources of Kind: Genre Theory in the Renaissance* (University of California Press, 1973); Ralph Cohen, *Genre Theory and Historical Change*, ed. John Rowlett (Charlottesville: University of Virginia

Press, 2017); Eve Tavor Bannet, *Eighteenth-Century Manners of Reading* (Cambridge University Press, 2017): chap. 4.

3. Jane Barker, *A Patchwork Screen for the Ladies* (London, 1723): iii, v, 52. Also Ioanna Patuleanu, "Deep Readings and Thin Screens," *Journal of Narrative Theory* 44:2 (Summer 2014): 159–182; and Constance Lacroix, "A Patchwork Screen: La preuve par le manuscript," DOI, xvii-xvii, #70 (12/31/2013): 247–264.

4. Ruskin, *The Elements of Drawing*, (1859); quoted in Jonathan Crary, *Techniques of the Observer: on Vision and Modernity in the Nineteenth Century* (Cambridge, MA: The MIT Press, 1992): 95.

5. James Elkins, *The Poetics of Perspective* (Ithaca: Cornell University Press, 1994); Erwin Panofsky, *Perspective as Symbolic Form* (New York: Zone Books, 1997): 67; Kevin DeLapp, *Partial Values: A Comparative Study in the Limits of Objectivity* (London: Rowman & Littlefield, 2018).

6. Wilkie Collins, *The Moonstone and the Woman in White* (New York: Modern Library, 2005): 19. Other references in the text.

7. For another example of this phenomenon, Nils Clausson, "Dickens' Genera Mixta: What Kind of Novel is Hard Times?" *Texas Studies in Literature and Language* 52:2 (July 2010): 157–180.

8. For partial knowledge, see also Sue Lonoff, "*Multiple Narratives and Relative Truths: The Ring and the Book, The Woman in White and The Moonstone*," Browning Institute Studies, 10 (1982): 143–161; L. Roberts, "The Shivering Sands of Reality: Narration and Knowledge in *The Moonstone*," *Victorian Review* 23:2 (1997): 168–183; Irene Tucker, "Paranoid Imaginings," *Partial Answers* 8:1 (January 2010): 147–166; and for the stone, Stephanie Markovitz, "Formed Things: Looking at Genre through Victorian Diamonds," *Victorian Studies* 52:4 (Summer 2010): 659–619.

9. Norman Friedman, "Point of View in Fiction: The Development of a Critical Concept," *PMLA* 70:5 (1955): 1160–1184 (1163); Also Mario Ortiz-Robles, "Point of View's Point of View," *The Henry James Review* 39:3 (Fall 2018): 218–225.

10. Abraham Bosse, "Theory of Notion of Lines" from [Gerard Desargues] *Maniere Universelle de M. Desargues pour pratiquer la perspective* (Paris, 1648).

11. Hubert Damisch, *The Origin of Perspective*, (Cambridge, MA: the MIT Press, 1995): 53; also Elkins, *Poetics of Perspective*.

12. Carlo Ginsberg, *Wooden Eyes: Nine Reflections on Distance* (New York: Columbia University Press, 1998): 157; Wolf Schmid, *Narratology: an Introduction* (Berlin: De Gruyter, 2010): 99ff.

13. John Wood, *Elements of Perspective* (Edinburgh, 1797): chapter 1.

14. "Introduction" in Clifford Siskin and William Warner (ed), *This is Enlightenment* (University of Chicago Press, 2010).

15. Crary, *Techniques of the Observer.* 70, 73.
16. [Author of *Waverley*], *Redgauntlet, a Tale of the Eighteenth Century*, 3 vols. (Edinburgh, 1824): 2: 160. Other references are in the text.
17. For discussion of the divisions as "critiques of the idea that historical narratives are examples of simplistically mimetic or transparent representation," Rohan Maitzen, "'By no means an Improbable Fiction:' *Redgauntlet's* Novel Historicism," *Studies in the Novel* 25:2 (Summer 1993): 170–183; for the novel as "a compendium of the narrative methods of the eighteenth Century," Everett Zimmerman, "Personal Identity, Narrative and History: *The Female Quixote and Redgauntlet*, " *Eighteenth-Century Fiction* 12:2–3 (2000): 369–390.
18. Sir Walter Scott, *The Miscellaneous Prose Works*, vol. 3 (Edinburgh, 1834): 33, 69.
19. See Eve Tavor Bannet, "Letters, Expectations and the Ancient Regime in Charlotte Smith's *The Old Manor House*," *Journal of Epistolary Culture*, 1: 1 (Fall 2019): Online.
20. Scott, *The Miscellaneous Prose Works*, vol 4 (Edinburgh, 1849): 63, 66.
21. For Scott's denigration of female predecessors from whom he had heavily borrowed and self-aggrandizement at their expense, see, for instance, Michael Gamer, *Romanticism and the Gothic: Genre, Reception and Canon Formation* (Cambridge University Press, 2000) and Ina Ferris, *The Achievement of Literary Authority: Gender, History and the Waverley Novels* (Ithaca: Cornell University Press, 1991).
22. For an early postmodern version of this, see Stanley Fish, *Is there a Text in this Class* (Cambridge, MA: Harvard University Press, 1980).

Index

For EU product safety concerns, contact us at Calle de José Abascal, 56–1°,
28003 Madrid, Spain or eugpsr@cambridge.org.

www.ingramcontent.com/pod-product-compliance
Ingram Content Group UK Ltd.
Pitfield, Milton Keynes, MK11 3LW, UK
UKHW020357140625

459647UK00020B/2514